"The book is a milestone in this emerging discipline. It provides an eye-opener for all involved in education, from preschool to learning later in life. The contributions of the three parent disciplines of education, neuroscience and psychology—which are equally important for the subject—are described with their unique contributions to the integrated domain. Issues are described which are encountered by teachers every day. Some of them are not given enough consideration in everyday practice, and the book provides relevant background information and also 'tools' with which to participate in this area.

All in all, the book provides an important basis from which to bring mind, brain, and education insights into the classroom and educational practice in a broader sense. I expect that it will also be of interest and support for many parents who are now seeking to expand their insights into their developing child and his or her needs, learning strategies and interests. Scientists, researchers, policy makers, curriculum designers, publishers of school materials, school directors, teacher educators, and teachers have different levels of previous knowledge and look at MBE in different ways. Disagreement among researchers from different disciplines may cause lack of common focus. Yet, Dr. Tokuhama has done a great job in providing a book with a broad view and a both multidimensional and multidisciplinary approach. In this way, it is of relevance for many different professionals in the domain of teaching."

— Jelle Jolles, Director, Leonardo Institute for Research in Education,
    VU University Amsterdam, the Netherlands and director of the National
    Platform on Brain & Learning in the Netherlands

"Recent discoveries in cognitive neuroscience have major consequences for teachers and educators. In this accessible volume, Tracey Tokuhama-Espinosa provides the first in-depth survey of this exciting field of research. Anyone interested in how education works and how it can be attuned to the child's brain should read this important review."

— Stanislas Dehaene, PhD, Professor, Collège de France, Chairman of the Experimental
    Cognitive Psychology Department, Director of the Cognitive Neuroimaging Unit, and
    author of *Reading in the Brain: The Science and Evolution of a Human Invention* and *The
    Number Sense: How the Mind Creates Mathematics*

"This volume casts a wide net to define the interdisciplinary work needed to base new research on basic principles arising from education, neuroscience and psychology. It forms an excellent introduction to this vast and important field."

— Dr. Michael Posner, Professor Emeritus, University of Oregon, and author of over
    200 books and articles on attention and memory, including *Cognitive Neuroscience
    of Attention*

WITHDRAWN

"Tokuhama-Espinosa provides a whirlwind tour through the emerging interdisciplinary field of Mind, Brain, and Education. Along the way, she bursts many of the neuromyths that plague the field, and proposes in their place a list of tenets that range from the well-established to the controversial and provocative. The highlight for me was the history of recent (and not so recent) attempts to bridge between psychology, neuroscience, and education, which have coalesced and matured and are beginning to bear fruit."

> — Dr. Sashank Varma, Assistant Professor of Educational Psychology,
> University of Minnesota

"Tokuhama-Espinosa unravels the conceptual and practical confusions that inevitably arise with the self-formation of a new but composite field of academic endeavor, particularly one which seeks to integrate the natural and social sciences. Such a task, it has often been noted, has rarely if ever been successfully undertaken, but the shortcomings of our modern systems of education—so well-noted but so frustratingly opaque to effective change—cry out for such an evidence-based, neuroscience-based, and educator-inclusive reform agenda. I recommend this book to all educators who are interested in taking stock of current thinking about these matters in order to embark on pursuing the revolutionary agenda of basing their educational endeavors on what is known about the workings of their students' brains, to the mutual benefit of all involved."

> — Professor John Geake, Deputy Head of School (Research & Research Training),
> School of Education, University of New England, Australia

Mind, Brain, and Education Science

NORTON BOOKS IN EDUCATION

Mind, Brain, and Education Science
A Comprehensive Guide to the
New Brain-Based Teaching

Tracey Tokuhama-Espinosa, PhD

W. W. Norton & Company
New York • London

KH

All art, unless otherwise cited, was created by the author.

For information about permission to reproduce selections from this book, write to
Permissions, W. W. Norton & Company, Inc., 500 Fifth Avenue, New York, NY 10110

For information about special discounts for bulk purchases, please contact W. W. Norton
Special Sales at specialsales@wwnorton.com or 800-233-4830

Manufacturing by Hamilton Printing
Book design by Martha Meyer, Paradigm Graphics
Production manager: Leeann Graham

Library of Congress Cataloging-in-Publication Data

Tokuhama-Espinosa, Tracey, 1963-
Mind, brain, and education science : a comprehensive guide to the new brain-based teaching /
Tracey Tokuhama-Espinosa ; foreword by Judy Willis.
p. cm. -- (A Norton book in education)
Includes bibliographical references and index.
ISBN 978-0-393-70607-9 (hardcover)
1. Learning, Psychology of. 2. Cognitive learning. 3. Teaching--Psychological aspects. 4. Brain. I. Title.
LB1060.T644 2011
370.15'2--dc22   2010007355

ISBN: 978-0-393-70607-9

W. W. Norton & Company, Inc., 500 Fifth Avenue, New York, N.Y. 10110
www.wwnorton.com
W. W. Norton & Company Ltd., Castle House, 75/76 Wells Street, London W1T 3QT

2 3 4 5 6 7 8 9 0

3/6/12

I would like to dedicate this book to several inspirational leaders.

Stanislas Dehaene has been a model and leader in Mind, Brain, and Education (MBE) science, conducting powerful and transformative research in both Math and Reading.

David Daniel, the Managing Editor of the International Mind, Brain and Education Society Journal has perhaps the most extensive knowledge of leaders MBE and is an amazing "connector," bringing people and ideas together across disciplines.

Antonio Battro, the former president of the International Mind, Brain and Education Society, medical doctor, psychiatrist and educator, is the epitome of the interdisciplinary expertise that MBE stands for.

Hideaki Koizumi, leading researcher, inventor and founding board member of the International Mind, Brain, and Education Society, who generously mailed me boxes of books on the Japanese contribution towards MBE and who selflessly reviewed not only my doctoral thesis, but the draft for this book is deserving of my deepest gratitude.

These four leaders have selflessly displayed a level of intellectual generosity that only scholarly giants possess. Not only were they a part of the original research project that is the foundation of this book, but over the past years have responded to every query with not only meticulous detail but also with enthusiasm. As mentors they have guided with silk gloves, as friends they have shared a joy for new discoveries, and as scholars and research-practitioners, they have enlightened.

This book is also dedicated to Cristian, Natalie, Gabriel and Mateo, who not only share in the world of ideas, but who are also the pillars of "real life."

Contents

Acknowledgments

A single person cannot write a book that seeks to define a new academic discipline, there are hundreds of people who have established the foundations of Mind, Brain and Education (MBE).

I am thankful to Kurt Fischer, one of the main initiators of the MBE movement and the Society's first president, for his encouragement. Howard Gardner, Jelle Jolles, Hideaki Koizumi, Michael Posner, and John Bruer are all amazing, internationally renowned professionals who have generously guided my thinking over the years; my sincerest thanks. I am grateful to Sarah-Jayne Blakemore, Daniel Ansari, and Cristina Hinton whose own work has guided my developing viewpoints on MBE. My thanks to Mary Helen Immordino-Yang and Marc Schwartz who are my heroes for working tirelessly to ensure that educators, neuroscientists, and psychologists share visions, vocabulary and viable research projects. They are part of the new generation who will lead MBE into the 21st century with fanfare and strong foundations. Thanks to Judy Willis and once more to David Daniel, Stanislas Dehaene and Antonio Battro who have enthusiastically supported my work. Patricia Wolfe cannot be thanked enough for her inspiration, guidance and challenges to presumptions. Special thanks to all of the members of the Delphi panel who generously contributed to the invaluable bibliography for this text and to many core ideas: Donna Coch, Jane Bernstein, Michael Atherton, John Geake, Usha Goswami, Marian Diamond, Eric Jensen, Renata Caine, and Rita Smilkstein. A warm thanks to Sashank Varma for his careful reading, comments and the joint development of the Glossary found here.

I am indebted to the subtle, structured, consistent guidance of Deborah Malmud at W. W. Norton for her professionalism and thoughtful reflections (which were changes disguised as questions). I am also very thankful for Vani Kannan and Margaret Ryan, also of W. W. Norton, for their editorial guidance.

I am grateful to Daniela Bramwell who has never said no to a single request for support, the double-checking of a source, the redesigning of a graphic, the re-reading of manuscripts, or the bouncing around of new ideas. No one could ask for a better student-turned-assistant-turned-work companion-turned friend.

Finally, thanks to the Universidad San Francisco de Quito in Ecuador and specifically to Santiago Gangotena, Carlos Montúfar, Gonzalo Mendieta, and Diego Quiroga, who offered me the intellectual freedom, beautiful working facilities, and time to write this book.

While I am indebted to all, any errors are mine alone.

Tracey Tokuhama-Espinosa
Quito, Ecuador

Foreword
Judy Willis, MD, MEd

The need for an analysis of education-related mind and brain research has never been so critical. Educators are in need of ways to teach the most overwhelming quantity of information for which students have ever been accountable on standardized tests. There is no time or money that can be afforded to programs, curricula, or consultants who claim that their "brain-based" intervention is the solution to everything from differentiation and "behavior management" to expanding working memory and boosting test scores.

These concerns need to be met, but as most educators are not trained in the background knowledge needed to evaluate the research tagged onto these commercial products or gurus, it takes the collaboration of experts from the specialties of neuroscience, cognitive psychology, educational testing, and others to evaluate the methods used to conduct the research and the interpretations of the data.

Mind, Brain, and Education Science is the Rosetta Stone that educators and researchers need to translate the research data into their daily work—whether in the lab or the classroom. Tracey Tokuhama-Espinosa draws from her own neuroscience, classroom, and academic administrative background, as well as research from over 4,500 studies—a scale that clearly demonstrates the degree of support currently available for dozens of classroom strategies and practices. Tokuhama-Espinosa successfully tackles the complex and abundant research and meticulously achieves her goals with a book that is as highly readable as it is pertinent to all people dedicated to understanding how teaching can be best correlated to the brain's processing of information.

Because this book has useful and powerful information on every page, it is a challenge to select highlights. Readers will surely find chapters highly pertinent to their own interests and specialties.

Educators in the trenches will find this book profoundly useful for evaluating the best available tools and consultants, and the interventions best suited to their own teaching. Tokuhama-Espinosa's methodological evaluation of the research will help all of those dedicated to improving the quality and joy of education through the best teaching practices, effective curriculum, informative assessment, and planning techniques by which students can construct transferable concepts from the excess of often isolated facts they are pushed to memorize for standardized tests.

In the section "What Great Teachers Do and Why It Works," classroom teachers will be pleased to discover scientific evidence that supports and explains the neural foundations relevant to their best teaching successes. Admirers of the work of educational visionaries such as Piaget will be delighted by the section dedicated to how many of his, and other early theorists', keen observations correlate with the laboratory research available today.

Educators on the front lines will expand their toolboxes of practical applications of relevant research as Tokuhama-Espinosa consolidates and clarifies the theoretical, experimental, and practical findings as illuminated by the transdisciplinary field of mind, brain, and education. Because Tokuhama-Espinosa is such a careful analyst of the research, the applications she offers can be trusted to correlate with ample research, which she scrutinizes for validity.

As a neurologist who became a classroom teacher, one of my goals was to use my neuroscience background to bust the neuromyths and inaccurate applications of lab research being used to support faulty and costly commercial goods, programs, and self-proclaimed gurus. In this book and in the author's own words she addresses "tough questions in education that have not been answered by conventional means such as differentiated student needs, new types of learning problems, and educational challenges, which have not found satisfactory responses, and require a fresh look with new eyes as well as the need for remediations *and* celebrations."

One of the best characteristics of top scientists is their desire to continue to reevaluate what is believed to be true, in light of new evidence, often provided by new technology. Chapter 4 identifies 24 "neuromyths" that currently plague the educational process, such as a right and a left brain that compete for students' attention and use. Tokuhama-Espinosa identifies the negative consequences that are the results of the application of these myths. Scientists will find this chapter so well documented that they may reconsider some of their own assumptions through the descriptions provided about recent research in overlapping fields just outside their own specialties. Tokuhama-Espinosa's insights will give our best researchers in their specific fields relevant cross-disciplinary research findings to fortify, modify, or expand their budding hypotheses.

I am grateful, both for the knowledge this book has provided me, and for the wisdom, dedication, passion, and compassion that Tokuhama-Espinosa applied to create it. I am certain that *Mind, Brain, and Education Science: A Comprehensive Guide to the New Brain-Based Teaching* will excite as well as inform all those fortunate enough to read it, and expand the ripples of each reader's new insights to the benefit of the most important people we serve—our students—the future caretakers of one another and of the planet.

Preface

We live in a time in which we count on professionals in all fields to know certain basics and adhere to certain standards. Unlike other generations, in which parameters were laxer and training depended solely on a single mentor or tutor, this generation is accountable to far stricter guidelines because far more people contribute to the formation of professionals than ever before. In the 17th century one cobbler on the road could make a bad shoe and his neighbor might make a far better one, with most of the variation in quality due to the knowledge each cobbler gained as an apprentice. While we still go through apprenticeships of sorts today, there are far more collective measures of a professional's worth, and more regulation of the quality of individual members. Holding professionals accountable for having basic core knowledge, skills, and attitudes means better service, practice, and attention, and we all benefit. (Most shoes these days have basic minimum quality characteristics, and the overall industry quality has improved because of this.) This is true of all professions, whether it be a shoemaker, social scientist, physician, or otherwise. Minimum core knowledge benefits each professional individually, but also contributes to the overall advancement of society.

How does all this impact professional formation? Through key core knowledge requirements. For example, the study of modern psychology requires certain basics in terms of core knowledge. Professionals are assumed to be versed in at least a minimal level of understanding in topics as wide ranging as consciousness, perception, emotion, personality, behavior, cognition, and interpersonal relationships. This requirement has not changed in decades, if not centuries.

Over the decades psychologists have studied the course of the mental processes of perception and memory, of speech and thought, of the organization of movement and action. Hundreds of courses for university students have been prepared and thousands of books have been published during this period of intense activity to teach and describe the character of the human gnostic processes, speech, and behavior. The close study of these areas, in the context of behavioral science, has yielded information of inestimable value and has given important clues to the nature of the scientific laws that govern these processes.

Likewise, in cognitive neuroscience there are also certain basics required of professionals, despite being a "younger" field of study than psychology. General neuroscience formation focuses on the nervous system, the brain, and an understanding of neurons, synapses, and neurotransmitters (which can be specialties in and of themselves: neurophysiology, neuroanatomy, neuropharmacology, and molecular neuroscience). Studies for the neuroscientist in training also normally include classes in neural networks, sensory systems, and motor control (as in systems neuroscience). Beyond these basics, neuroscience studies learning and memory and cognition and arousal mechanisms, which relate directly to developmental neuroscience, behavioral neuroscience, and most especially, cognitive neuroscience.

In education we have certain basic core curriculum subjects as well, but they are suffering a change in modern teacher training programs. When I studied for my master's in education degree at Harvard over 20 years ago, I focused on international comparative curriculum studies (what is "smart" in different cultures based on what different countries choose to teach), but I was also expected to know something about teaching practices, planning, assessment, educational research, philosophy, and technology, as well as the application of this information to a variety of age groups. But the world is changing.

When I completed my doctorate in 2008 my focus was on Mind, Brain, and Education science, a creation I was allowed to devise from a basic education program by adding elements of psychology and neuroscience. This program was decidedly interdisciplinary in nature and celebrated the union of basic courses, concepts, knowledge, skills, and attitudes traditionally found in the once separate disciplines of neuroscience, psychology, and education (see Figure P.1).

FIGURE PREFACE.1
How Education, Cognitive Neuroscience, and Educational Psychology Equal
Mind, Brain, and Education Science

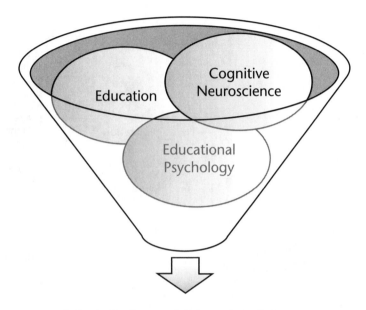

Mind, Brain, and Education Science

The new discipline of Mind, Brain, and Education science is indicative of new parameters that embrace the tough questions in education that have not been answered by conventional means. Differentiated student needs, new types of learning problems, and educational challenges, which have not found satisfactory responses, require a fresh look with new eyes. According to Palmer (1997), "[t]he way we diagnose our students' condition will determine the kind of remedy we offer" (p. 41). I believe that the exactness with which we can analyze learning problems has become more accurate with the new discipline of Mind, Brain, and Education science. Maximizing the potential of each student means clearly detecting individual strengths and weaknesses, problems, and gifts, as well as the need for remediations *and* celebrations. This is not a simple task by any means (see Figure P.2).

FIGURE PREFACE.2
Core Knowledge in Mind, Brain, and Education Science

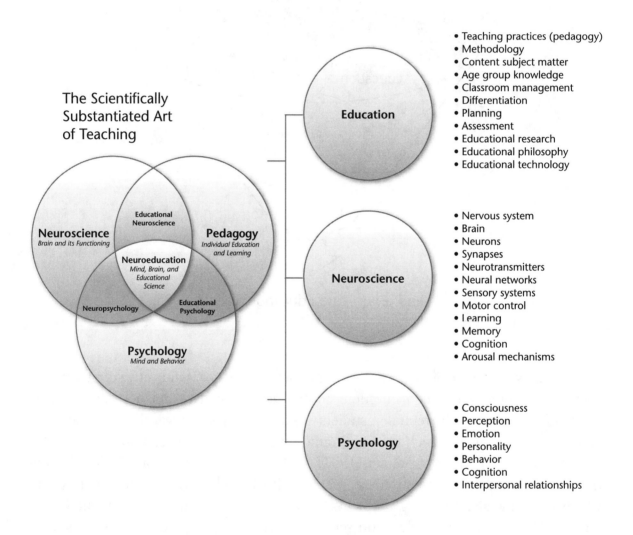

The Scientifically
Substantiated Art
of Teaching

Neuroscience
Brain and its Functioning

Educational
Neuroscience

Pedagogy
*Individual Education
and Learning*

Neuroeducation
*Mind, Brain, and
Educational
Science*

Neuropsychology

Educational
Psychology

Psychology
Mind and Behavior

Education

- Teaching practices (pedagogy)
- Methodology
- Content subject matter
- Age group knowledge
- Classroom management
- Differentiation
- Planning
- Assessment
- Educational research
- Educational philosophy
- Educational technology

Neuroscience

- Nervous system
- Brain
- Neurons
- Synapses
- Neurotransmitters
- Neural networks
- Sensory systems
- Motor control
- Learning
- Memory
- Cognition
- Arousal mechanisms

Psychology

- Consciousness
- Perception
- Emotion
- Personality
- Behavior
- Cognition
- Interpersonal relationships

Teaching was a simpler craft in generations past. Only the wealthy and well-prepared aspired to education past grade school a hundred years ago. Today the Universal Declaration of Human Rights (Article 26) suggests that all people (rich, poor, intelligent, and challenged) are equally entitled to a place in our classrooms. Not only do students come with a far greater spectrum of abilities, but there are also more children than ever before in our classrooms begging for the attention and guidance they need to help them reach their own potential. This wealth of differences provides us with dynamics never before seen in the history of education and offers the promise of richer learning experiences, if we know how to take advantage of the situation and not lament the challenge. The resources and cross-germination of many disciplines found in Mind, Brain, and Education science can offer such a perspective.

Mind, Brain, and Education Science

Introduction

This book is the culmination of several years of consensus building, debate, and discussion among professionals who came together from distinct disciplines around the world. As a teacher who has worked with children from pre-kindergarten through university levels, with over 20 years of experience in the classroom and in 17 different countries, in 2007 I ventured out of my comfort zone to complete my PhD studies in the new discipline of Mind, Brain, and Education (MBE) science. This stretched my research and reflection into areas of neuroscience and psychology in ways that I had never done previously. I found that I had to adapt to a new vocabulary and language, as well as a different protocol of interaction among peers studying the discipline. Although I had taught university courses on the basics of the brain and learning and was familiar with the general literature, at first I struggled with much of the medical terminology, brain anatomy, and biological and technological jargon that were commonly used by leaders in MBE. From the earliest moments of my studies, however, I was deeply impressed by the intellectual humility of the key players in this new discipline who never missed the chance to gently correct my presumptions or to congratulate me for insights. In fact, the more well-known the person, the higher the degree of his or her intellectual generosity when it came to suggesting an article or critiquing the exact wording chosen for this definition or that.

By the end of 2007 I had identified 39 of the most frequently cited experts. "Experts" in MBE science come from two main sources. They are either people well-known in two of the three parent fields of MBE science (neuroscience, psychology, or education), with working knowledge in the third, and/or they have published specifically in the area of

MBE and are known experts in one of the three areas. For example, Michael Posner is both an expert in psychology and neuroscience, and he also is well known for his work with teachers. Similarly, Kurt Fischer was trained as a psychologist, but has published countless papers and books specifically in the MBE discipline. Given its emerging status, there are a limited, though accessible, number of professionals who can claim expertise in the discipline. All 39 individuals were invited to participate on a Delphi panel, which is an anonymous exchange of opinions between experts that tries to reach consensus. Twenty experts actually did so, and six others commented on the final results. These experts came from 9 countries (Argentina, Australia, Canada, France, Germany, Japan, the Netherlands, the United Kingdom, and the United States), testifying not only to the interdisciplinary nature of the work being done, but also to the international reach that the new science of teaching and learning has in the world. The months of exchanges with these experts led to parameters for the new MBE discipline, which were used to evaluate the current state of "brain-based education"; the results are shared here.

Warmest thanks go to the expert Delphi panel members and commentators Daniel Ansari, Michael Atherton, Virginia Berninger, Jane Bernstein, Sarah-Jayne Blakemore, John T. Bruer, Renate Nummela-Caine, Donna Coch, David Daniel, Stanislas Dehaene, Marian Diamond, Kurt Fischer, Howard Gardner, John Geake, Usha Goswami, Christina Hinton, Paul Howard-Jones, Mary Helen Immordino-Yang, Eric Jensen, Jelle Jolles, Hideaki Koizumi, Michael Posner, Marc Schwartz, Rita Smilkstein, David Sousa, and Judy Willis. A special thanks to Robert Sylwester, who reviewed the pilot, and Patricia Wolfe, who gave important feedback on all aspects along the way. Only the highest quality of information came from these experts and I have done my best to reflect the group's conclusions; if there are any errors I alone am at fault. The profiles of the experts can be found in Appendix B.

This book is organized into nine chapters that move from the basic, but crucial definition of MBE science in Chapter 1 to the role of the individual in improving teaching in Chapter 9. In Chapter 2 we consider the five well-established "truths" of the new discipline as well as clarify the key conceptual debates in the discipline. In Chapter 3 we consider the way in which education has evolved over the past centuries to point to the current state of understanding about how the brain learns and what teaching methods should be employed to best take advantage of this knowledge. Chapter 4 provides an overview of the goals and standards of MBE science and identifies 24 "neuromyths" that currently plague the educational process, warning teachers of the negative consequences that are the results of their application. Chapter 5 explains the who, what, how, and why of the different dimensions of human learning that are studied in MBE science. Chapter 6 identifies eight core human survival and life skills relevant to MBE (affect–empathy–emotions and motivation; executive functions and decision-making; facial recognition and interpretation; memory; attention; social cognition; spatial sequential management; and temporal–sequential organization) and describes how they impact the teaching and learning process. Chapter 7 moves the laboratory information into the classroom and identifies the best sources available on the most studied academic fields of language and math, including the handful of well-established interventions and remediation programs supported by MBE science. Chapter 8 reviews the core universal principles of MBE science, the individual tenets that shape best-practice teaching, and the instructional guidelines that can be gleaned from the information. Finally, the book closes with a consideration of what all this means for the new teacher-practitioner in education, and how each of our roles in the act and the art of teaching is changed by the new MBE science. There were thousands of studies reviewed for this book, and space does not allow for a mention of them all. Where appropriate, there are example studies cited in the footnotes and in other instances there are direct quotes or passages cited in text.

The glossary and appendices include a discussion of the communication challenges facing professionals in neuroscience, psychology, and education if they profess to join forces in the new MBE discipline. Appendix A identifies several publications, societies, congresses, journals, and conferences that are shaping the new discipline. Finally, a list of some of the main leaders in MBE science thinking is offered in Appendix B.

This book is just a humble beginning. When Henry Ford launched the automobile industry he cautioned that "coming together is a beginning; keeping together is progress; working together is success." MBE should be as cautious. The future of MBE science is in the hands of all who embrace the challenges facing teachers in the classroom and who are able to view them with a new lens. A new approach to education—one that is nurtured by neuroscience and psychology—may be just the perspective needed to tackle education's modern, complicated, and challenging problems.

CHAPTER 1

A Celebration

This book celebrates, defines, promotes, and explains the birth of the new academic discipline of Mind, Brain, and Education (MBE) science. It is not a defense or an argument for the creation of this new discipline; others have already made this case very convincingly.[1] Nor is this book a new type of neuropsychology, biological neuroscience, or cognitive neuroscience textbook—far more experienced writers have done justice to those fields as well.[2] This book is a guide for conscientious teachers who are out to improve their practice through a paradigm shift in thinking about the way people learn and how we should teach as a consequence.

MBE science began as a cross-disciplinary venture between cognitive neuroscience and developmental psychology, but then it reached further beyond these parameters to integrate education via educational psychology and educational neuroscience (Figure 1.1). However, to actually become its own academic discipline, MBE science went through what Hideaki Koizumi (1999) calls a transdisciplinary developmental process, as noted in Figure 1.2.

Similar to other evolutionary processes, MBE science drew from the dominant "genes" of its parents to produce a better-adapted being. That is, rather than including anything and everything that falls under the labels of education, neuroscience, and psychology as a whole, MBE science is a careful selection of only the best information that can inform the new science of teaching and learning. The development of MBE science results in a new and innovative way to consider old problems in education and offers evidence-based solutions for the classroom.

---

1. Key works include Fischer, Daniel, Immordino-Yang, Stern, Battro, et al. (2007).
2. For excellent examples, see Gazzaniga, Ivry, & Mangun (2002); Baars & Gage (2007); Dehaene (2002); Gazzaniga (2005a).

FIGURE 1.1
MBE Science as a Multidisciplinary Field

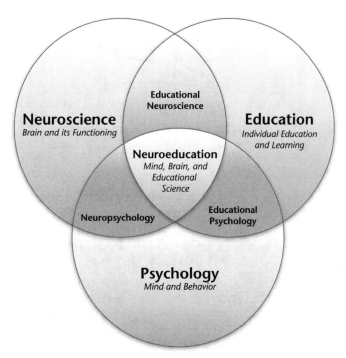

Bramwell for Tokuhama-Espinosa, 2010.

In Figure 1.2 we see how the three core academic disciplines intersect to change the lens with which problems in the teaching–learning process are approached. This new vision takes into account the different histories, philosophies, and especially the different epistemological lenses through which common problems in neuroscience, psychology, and education are approached. Given that the new science of teaching and learning was born of these three parent disciplines, it bears the "cultural baggage" of its parents. This means that the history as well as the philosophy—and subsequently the epistemologies— of these three disciplines influence the existence of MBE science. As Samuels (2009) put it in a recent Mind, Brain, and Education journal article, "Historically, science and education have demonstrated separate, but interwoven, influences on society; philosophically, the values by which they operate are often in opposition; and epistemologically, the disciplines have relied on different conceptualizations of knowledge" (p. 45). This means that MBE faces three important challenges.

FIGURE 1.2
MBE Science: Transdisciplinarity

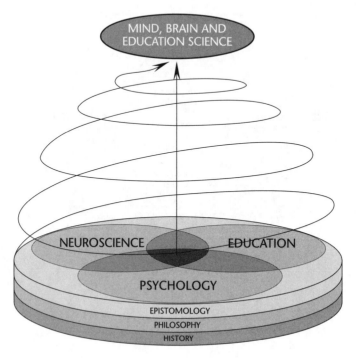

Bramwell for Tokuhama-Espinosa, 2010.

First, the greatest challenge to new professionals in MBE science is to accept the different historical roots of the three disciplines. This means that those working as teachers need to appreciate that some information from psychology and from neuroscience will have different foci, goals, methods, and procedures than those found in education, but they are equally useful to learning how to teach better. Similarly, psychologists practicing in the new discipline need to recognize that information from neuroscience and education is valuable, despite differences in histories. And neuroscientists, used to a different type of experimental rigor in their research, will have to learn to appreciate the importance of qualitative studies and the impact that studies from education and psychology can have on the new discipline.

Second, we have to recognize and accept that these multiple foundations have impacted the philosophies through which professionals in each of the three disciplines view the world. MBE scientists have a somewhat broader view, therefore, because they can apply multiple lenses through which to view the same problem. Classroom discipline, learning problems, instructional practices, and evaluation methods (among other teaching–learning issues) can now be approached in an innovative way using the multiple viewpoints provided by the new science of teaching and learning.

Finally and most importantly, we must understand that the respective histories and philosophies of the three parent disciplines explain why each embraces different episte-mologies. These epistemologies focus the lens through which problems are viewed. "A mode of knowing arises from the way we answer two questions at the heart of the educa-tional mission: How do we know what we know? And by what warrant can we call our knowledge true? Our answers may be largely tacit, even unconscious, but they are contin-ually communicated in the way we teach and learn" (Palmer, 1997, pp. 50–51).

The academic lens through which we see the world influences what is viewed as knowledge, how it is acquired, who among us knows, and why we know what we do.[3] MBE scientists, by their very nature, have a broader worldview than those rooted in just one discipline. Whether you are a teacher, neuroscientist, or psychologist—or someone working in a related field—you are invited to join this paradigm shift in thinking about the way we educate. Stephen Jay Gould once said, "Nothing is more dangerous than a dogmatic worldview—nothing more constraining, more blinding to innovation, more destructive of openness to novelty" (1995, p. 96). A new take on old problems needs open minds.

What MBE Science Is and Is Not

Although it is not hard to agree that MBE science exists, it is harder to agree what it actu-ally is. One way to consider this new discipline is to think of MBE as a "baby" born to adolescent parents. Many teen parents need to work hard to try to define their own place in the world while at the same time help nurture a new offspring and guide his or her growth: This basically results in children raising children. One of the parent disciplines, *cognitive neuroscience*, was "born" itself about 25 years ago.[4] *Education for the masses* is also a relative latecomer to the global stage, only becoming truly universalized in the late 1890s.[5] *Psychology* is a contemporary of the goal of universal education, being just slightly

3. Hay (2008).
4. Caramazza & Coltheart (2006); Gardner (1987); Posner (1989).
5. See Samuels (2009) for an excellent review.

older in foundation.[6] In 2010, this makes education and psychology about 125 years old each. Though 125 might seem old in human terms, these disciplines are mere adolescents in light of other academic disciplines, such as biology or philosophy, which are over a thousand years old. Now, while a three-way "marriage" between a 25-year-old and two 125-year-olds might sound odd, it is a good metaphor for understanding, more or less, what happened with MBE science: Three "young" disciplines intersected and their product was Mind, Brain, and Education science.

This union gets even more complicated. Aside from being a teen marriage, this is a *mixed* teen marriage. Mixed marriages between two disciplines (called *hybrid disciplines*) have become more common in recent years, but this is not to say that unions of this type are without their criticisms. Mixed marriages can be rejected and even accused of "diluting" once-pure entities. Mixed marriages require compromises from both sides as well as a new type of communication, sometimes at the sacrifice of elements of one or all involved. In the best cases these mixes are fruitful unions, but they demand continual maintenance, more so that homogeneous coalitions. Why? Because each of the parents comes with the weight of its history, philosophies, epistemologies and ways of viewing the world—which can coincide but may often collide.[7]

As well as being a transdisciplinary discipline, MBE science is a cross-cultural entity.[8] The discipline was conceptualized literally around the world at almost the same time in numerous countries.[9] Between 2002 and 2009, countries as varied as Japan, the United States, Canada, Australia, Germany, Holland, the United Kingdom, Italy, and France launched initiatives to promote the discipline. The international collaboration implies that the developing standards for MBE are based on cross-cultural acceptance of certain norms and shared values.

It is useful to view this phenomenon in light of another important world trend that was initially rejected by its parents: multilingualism. In an interesting parallel, it was once thought that multilingualism was "bad" because it purportedly reduced an individual's language potential by dividing it. That is, until the 1950s it was thought that children were born with a certain "language potential," and if they divided their brain space between several languages, they also divided their potential in each. It is now known that there are social, cognitive, economic, psychological, and educational benefits to speaking

---

6. See Wundt (1882) and James (1890/2007) in Butler-Bowden (2007).
7. It also bears remembering that mixed marriages have been limited to two partners; Mind, Brain, and Education science is an even more complex amalgamation because three "parents" are involved.
8. Samuels (2009).
9. Fischer (2009).

more than one language: More is better in this sense.[10] The benefits of MBE science's combined vision, thanks to the baggage of the three parent disciplines, are quickly replacing outdated beliefs that linking the social and hard sciences is "a bridge too far."[11] The many labor pains that culminated in the recent birth of MBE science as a transdisciplinary baby should not, however, be underestimated.

MBE's strength is also its greatest weakness. Viewpoints, knowledge schemas, and values that are usually complementary, but which can also sometimes be contradictory, contribute to this discipline. The contradictory aspect offers an explanation of (but not an excuse for) some problems MBE faced in the early years. Samuels (2009) recently wrote about the MBE challenge, saying, "Transdisciplinarity is a perspective on knowledge creation that integrates disciplines at the level of a particular issues. It is an approach ideally suited for finding complex solutions to complex problems" (p. 46). This book begins with the premise that solutions to problems in education today require the more sophisticated and complex approach offered by MBE science.

Who Should Read This Book

This book is for MBE scientists. In some instances this label will mean *teachers* who are integrating cognitive neuroscience and psychological foundations into their practice. In other cases it will mean *psychologists* who seek to bridge the hard and soft sciences. In yet others it will mean *neuroscientists* who dare to bring laboratory findings into the classroom. While many educators, psychologists, and neuroscientists remain pure practitioners within their single discipline, a growing number of others straddle the three academic fields of education, psychology, and cognitive neuroscience that wear the new MBE hat. This book does not claim that work as a "purist" is any less valuable than work in the transdisciplinary discipline of MBE science; it does, however, acknowledge the need for new professionals who speak the language, walk the talk, and can work seamlessly as MBE specialists as well.

To be an MBE scientist involves a particular set of professional responsibilities that differs from those of the "pure" fields of education, psychology, and the neurosciences. Aside from adhering to the combined standards of education, psychology, and cognitive neuroscience, MBE professionals adopt certain unique attitudes. Some of these attitudes were described in a review of the monumental work conducted by the Organisation for

10. Tokuhama-Espinosa (2008a).
11. Bruer (1997).

Economic Co-Operation and Development (2002, 2007) to define the new learning science. Bruno della Chiesa, Vanessa Christoph, and Christina Hinton (2009) delineate certain characteristics of the experts in the new discipline who were helpful in their research. I propose that these same characteristics are useful at the least, and absolutely required at an extreme, of all new MBE scientists. Three of the most important characteristics are described below.

First, MBE professionals are "willing to share knowledge with those outside their discipline rather than just their peers" in their original disciplines of formation.[12] This means (1) neuroscientists who are willing to share their findings with educators, for example, (2) psychologists who stimulate research questions in the neurosciences, and (3) educators who suggest research questions in psychology.

Second, MBE scientists recognize the need to "adapt their 'language' and context to the audience to make their knowledge comprehensible" to those outside of their original discipline of formation.[13] That is, MBE professionals understand the need to develop a common vocabulary to enhance interdisciplinary communication[14]—which can be seen in the teacher who writes for a psychology audience (or vice versa), or a neuroscientist who can explain his or her findings to educators (or vice versa). One of the greatest challenges in stimulating collaboration between professionals in neuroscience, education, and psychology is the absence of a shared language (see more on this point in the Glossary).

Third, MBE scientists generally accept, and perhaps are most compelled by, the belief that "connecting information across fields is advantageous for both others and themselves," and they accept the importance of nurturing their own practice with information from other fields.[15] For example, this belief can be seen in the neuroscientists who understand that the value of their lab work increases when it can actually be applied in the classroom, or the teachers who pose testable questions to cognitive scientists.

This last point also tacitly implies another key aspect of MBE science. All three fields (neuroscience, psychology, and education) are on equal footing and contribute in identical parts to the new discipline's research, practice, and policies. For this reason all three fields inform as well as learn from one another. This perspective differs from that of other disciplines, which are often unilaterally independent. For example, in educational neuroscience, neuroscience informs education (not usually vice versa). In educational

---

12. della Chiesa, Christoph, & Hinton (2009, p. 20).
13. della Chiesa, Christoph, & Hinton (2009, p. 20).
14. Heinze (2003).
15. della Chiesa, Christoph, & Hinton (2009, p. 20).

psychology, psychology informs education (not usually the other way around). The flow of information in MBE science is, by definition, three-way (see Figure 1.3):

FIGURE 1.3
The Flow of Information in MBE Science

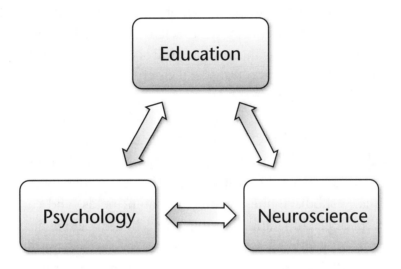

This three-way flow means that for a concept to be accepted in the new discipline, educators, psychologists, and neuroscientists must confirm their hypotheses not only in their own disciplines, but also within the other two. MBE science is the formal bridge linking the fields of neuroscience, psychology, and education that has been missing for decades.[16] We need teachers who know about the brain and how it learns best, and we need neuroscientists and psychologists who can envision the application of their work in school settings. Why? Because education is full of complex problems that have not been addressed successfully enough through pedagogical approaches alone.

Gardner writes about the need for the mind of the future to be able to synthesize and judge the quality of information that currently exists in the world.[17] There is so much information that bombards individuals on a daily basis (in MBE science and otherwise), that teacher training now needs to include explicitly taught skills on how to sort the wheat

16. For examples of this petition, see Fischer, Daniel, Immordino-Yang, Stern, Battro, et al. (2007); Goswami (2006); Hall (2005); Schall (2004).
17. Gardner (2007).

from the chaff; that is, determine what is "good" information and what is "bad."[18] This sorting can be achieved, in part, through a clear synthesis of the information.

Synthesizing information is a complex process that requires the ability to take in a variety of information sources, understand the main concepts within each, and then judge their applicability to the topic at hand. Teachers must be armed with excellent critical thinking skills in order to be able to pass such abilities on to their students. The process of synthesis plays an important role in MBE science, which is related to the ability to assess and judge information. This means that MBE science is vulnerable if teachers aren't able to think critically. The ability to transcend disciplines and synthesize data is crucial for professionals in the discipline.

Because of its complexity, MBE science is difficult to define and is multifaceted in execution. It is no wonder that several years have passed since the first call to put parameters around the discipline. The problems and challenges found in the parent disciplines of neuroscience, psychology, and education add to the complexity within MBE science itself. There are many subdisciplines within the parent fields, and each places different emphasis on aspects of teaching and learning, compiling the elements for consideration. Nevertheless, the complexity of MBE science is also part of its attractiveness as an academic discipline. MBE science is alluring in part because, after all, as Derrida claims, "if things were simple, word would have gotten around" (1988, p. 119). Once complexity is accepted as part and parcel of the new discipline, then its importance is confirmed. A hundred years ago, one of the greatest writers of our time, Thorndike (1874–1949), said: "The intellectual evolution of the race consists in an increase in the number, delicacy, complexity, permanence and speed of formation of such associations," (cited in Thorndike & Bruce, 2000, p. 294) affirming that the continually more complex problems in education today require solutions that are not simplistic. This fact calls attention to the idea that if a solution to educational woes seems too simple to be true, it probably is. The caution for "buyer beware"[19] should guide teacher consumption of brain-based fixes.

---

18. James S. McDonnell Foundation (2005b).
19. An intriguing article by K. Madigan in 2001 made the call for *Buyer beware: Too early to use brain-based strategies*, and called for caution in adapting quick fixes in education.

CHAPTER 2

Evidence-Based Solutions for the Classroom
MBE Science Defined

> *"What a thing is and what it means are not separate, the former being physical and the latter mental as we are accustomed to believe."*
> —James J. Gibson, *More on Affordances* (1982, p. 408)

How do we learn best? What is individual human potential? How do we ensure that children live up to their promise as learners? These questions and others have been posed by philosophers as well neuroscientists, psychologists, and educators for as long as humans have pondered their own existence. Because MBE science moves educators closer to the answers than at any other time in history, it benefits teachers in their efficacy and learners in their ultimate success.

Great teachers have always "sensed" why their methods worked; thanks to brain imaging technology, it is now possible to substantiate many of these hunches with empirical scientific research. For example, good teachers may suspect that if they give their students just a little more time to respond to questions than normal when called upon, they might get better-quality answers. Since 1972 there has been empirical evidence that if teachers give students several seconds to reply to questions posed in class, rather than the normal single second, the probability of a quality reply increases.[20] Information about student response time is shared in some teacher training schools, but not all. Standards in MBE science ensure that information about the brain's attention span and need for reflection time would be included in teacher training, for example.

---

20. Studies that offer evidence to this effect include Chun & Turk-Browne (2007); Pashler, Johnsyon, & Ruthruff (2001); Posner (2004); Sarter, Gehring, & Kozak (2006); Smallwood, Fishman, & Schooler (2007); Stahl (1990); Chiles (2006); Thomas (1972).

The basic premise behind the use of standards in MBE science is that fundamental skills, such as reading and math, are extremely complex and require a variety of neural pathways and mental systems to work correctly. MBE science helps teachers understand why there are so many ways that things can go wrong, and it identifies the many ways to maximize the potential of all learners. This type of knowledge keeps educators from flippantly generalizing, "He has a problem with *math*," and rather encourages them to decipher the true roots (e.g., number recognition, quantitative processing, formula structures, or some other sub-skill in math). MBE science standards make teaching methods and diagnoses more precise. Through MBE, teachers have better diagnostic tools to help them more accurately understand their students' strengths and weakness. These standards also prevent teachers from latching onto unsubstantiated claims and "neuromyths" and give them better tools for judging the quality of the information. Each individual has a different set of characteristics and is unique, though human patterns for the development of different skill sets, such as walking and talking, doing math or learning to read, do exist. One of the most satisfying elements of MBE science is having the tools to maximize the potential of each individual as he or she learns new skills.

Defining Our Terms

MBE science is concerned with studying how humans learn best in order to develop more effective teaching methods. Several experts define MBE science as the use of empirical scientific research to confirm best practices in pedagogy.[21] According to one of the discipline's founders, Kurt Fischer, "an important goal of the emerging field of mind, brain, and education (MBE) is the creation of a strong research base for educational practice—a groundwork of usable knowledge about what makes for effective learning and teaching" (2009, p. 1).

According to the Delphi panel of experts who considered what information was applicable to MBE science and to the resolution of problems in education, the emerging discipline brings together natural, life, neural, and social sciences from which the major guiding principles are derived, the most prominent of which are education, neuroscience, and psychology. Sub-disciplines of education (i.e., pedagogy, special education, gifted students), neuroscience (e.g., cognitive neuroscience, neuroethics, neuropsychiatry, developmental neuroscience, pediatrics), and psychology (e.g., developmental

---

21. Battro, Fischer, & Léna (2008); Fischer, Daniel, Immordino-Yang, Stern, Battro, et al. (2007); Sheridan, Zinchenko, & Gardner (2005).

psychology and neuropsychology) are the foundations of the new way to look at teaching. As a multidisciplinary science, it should also be noted that several sub-disciplines in biology (biopsychology, neurobiology, genetics) and chemistry (nutrition, psychopharmacology, toxicology) are also important contributors to the emerging discipline, as are many social sciences (sociology, anthropology, philosophy). Finally, mathematical theories and models of learning also add to the discipline. The history of MBE spans centuries; it is old as the combined histories of education, psychology and neuroscience. These many and varied areas intersect when it comes to education.

FIGURE 2.1
Sub-disciplines in Mind, Brain, and Education Science

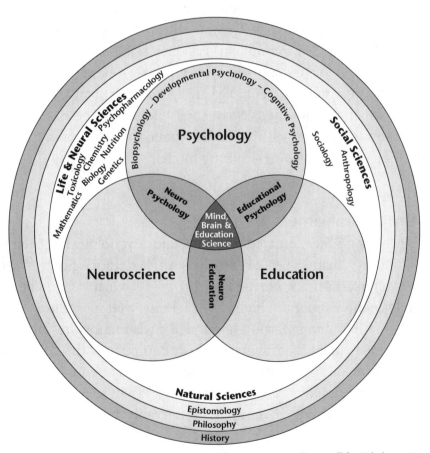

Bramwell for Tokuhama-Espinosa, 2010.

Education is now seen as the natural outgrowth of the human thirst to know oneself better combined with new technology that allows the confirmation of many hypotheses about good teaching practices. Past models of learning, many of which came from psychology and neuroscience, lay the path for current research problems being addressed today to devise better teaching tools. For example, early in the development of psychology, Freud theorized that part of successful behavior management techniques, including teaching, was the result of actual physical changes in the brain, not just intangible changes in the mind.[22] This theory has since been proven through evidence of *neural plasticity* and the fact that the brain changes daily, albeit on a microscopic level, and even before there are visible changes in behavior. These changes vary depending on the stimulus, past experiences of the learners, and the intensity of the intervention. What were once hypotheses in psychology are now being proven, thanks to this new interdisciplinary view and the invention of technology. On the other hand, other past beliefs about the brain have been debunked. For example, it was once fashionable to think of a right and a left brain that competed for students' attention and use. It has now been proven beyond a doubt that the brain works as a complex design of integrated systems, not through specialized and competing right- and left-brained functions. These examples show how past beliefs are now partnered with evidence about the functioning human brain to produce this powerful, new teaching–learning model.

A Rose By Any Other Name?

The intersection among education, neuroscience, and psychology has been referred to in many ways and through many labels over the past three decades. Some of the terms used to describe this intersection are *brain-based learning*[23] (which is a mainly commercial packaging of information about the brain for teachers); *educational neuroscience*[24] (which is primarily information about learning grounded in laboratory research but that uses more technical terms than teachers are typically comfortable with); *educational neuropsychology*[25] (whose origins in psychology are substantiated by neuroscience and then seen in light of learning situations); *educational psychology*[26] (whose origins in psychology are an attempt to explain learning in terms of observable behavior); *cognitive neuropsy-*

---

22. Doidge (2007).
23. Caine & Nummela-Caine (1997); Jensen (1998b).
24. Gardner (2006); Jacobson (2000a); Varma, McCandliss, & Schwartz (2008).
25. Geake (2005a); Kral & Maclean (1973); O'Keefe & Nadel (1978); Selye (1974).
26. Pressley & McCormick (1995); Schunk (1998); Zanker (2005).

chology[27] (whose origins in psychology are substantiated by neuroscience and then seen in light of thinking processes), and neuroscience[28] (which is the study of the nervous system and often includes studies on how nonhuman organisms learn). These disciplines all add to the knowledge about the learning process as conceptualized in MBE science, but they are not identical to it. The biggest distinction among these labels is in the way they emphasize learning, whereas MBE gives equal playtime to teaching.

Teaching versus Learning in MBE Science

> *"All animals learn; very few teach."*
> —Sara-Jayne Blakemore & Uta Frith, *The Learning Brain: Lessons for Education*
>   (2007, p. 119)

MBE science is the key to a paradigm shift in teaching techniques and a new model of learning from early childhood to adulthood for one basic reason. In MBE science there is an equal emphasis in research on how humans learn (which is the focus of brain-based learning, educational neuroscience, educational psychology, cognitive neuropsychology, and neuroscience) as well as how we teach (pedagogy). Usha Goswami, distinguished faculty of Psychology and Neuroscience in Education at the University of Cambridge, was one of the first to call attention to this imbalance by acknowledging that "neuroscience does not as yet study teaching," (Goswami, 2008b, p. 34) as illogical as it sounds. However, just as ironically, educator Eric Jensen called his popular first book *Teaching with the Brain in Mind*, calling attention to the fact that most educators spend very little time getting to know the primary organ of their life's purpose: the brain. MBE science addresses the imbalance that has existed in the research on learning versus teaching, and it establishes a new lens through which to address learning problems by identifying better teaching techniques. Sarah-Jayne Blakemore of the University College of London Institute of Cognitive Neuroscience, and Uta Frith of the Institute of Cognitive Neuroscience at University College London, note that "we know a little of what goes on in the brain when we learn, but hardly anything about what goes on in the brain when we teach" (Blakemore & Frith, 2008a, p. 118). They add, "The ability to learn is vastly more ancient and automatic than

27. Caramazza & Coltheart (2006); Coltheart (2004); Harley (2004a); Martin & Caramazza (2003); Roe (2005).
28. Ansari (2005); Ansari & Coch (2006); Atherton (2005); Berninger & Corina (1998); Byrnes & Fox (1998a); Friederici & Ungerleider (2005); Katzir & Paré-Blagoev (2006); Westermann, Sirois, Schultz, & Mareschal (2006).

the ability to teach. All animals learn; very few teach" (p. 119). Thousands of studies have established how and even why different species learn different types of information, but only a handful of studies has established how to teach human students to maximize learning.[29] The goal of the new science of teaching and learning, unlike the goals of neuroscience or neuropsychology, is not only to understand how humans best learn, but to also determine how they should best be taught to maximize their potential. Between 1977 and 2010, thousands of studies contributed to identifying several major themes in MBE science, including research on how to take advantage of humans' natural attention span to teach more effectively, studies about memory systems that have been applied to take advantage of both sense and meaning in lesson planning, and research on the role of emotions and learning to better equip teachers with strategies that engage the natural curiosity of their students. For a full bibliography of these studies, readers are invited to see the 4,500 references reviewed during the Delphi panel consultation.[30]

An additional reason why MBE science is different from other preexisting disciplines is that it places equal emphasis on research as on practice. Neuroscience lab research has often been criticized for being too far away from the classroom, whereas teaching has often been criticized for lacking foundations in evidence.[31] MBE science seeks to address these gaps by presuming that information produced in the discipline is grounded equally in research as in practice.

Academic Discipline or Professional Field?

MBE science is an academic discipline, not a professional field. It is important to make this distinction because an academic discipline implies research and study, whereas a professional field implies an association of individuals who work under the same professional code. I developed the distinguishing characteristics of academic disciplines, found below, in late 2008 based on recommendations from the Delphi panel. Academic disciplines:

- Tend to be governed, regulated, and/or guided by a society or membership
- Tend to recognize one or more peer reviewed journal(s), which embrace(s) and challenge(s) the established norms, epistemology, findings, and practices of the discipline

29. For some examples, see documentation in Blakemore & Frith (2008a, p. 119).
30. Tokuhama-Espinosa (2008b).
31. Economic and Social Research Council Teaching and Learning Research Programmes, (2005).

- Tend to meet regularly (e.g., annual conferences)
- Tend to have recognized opinion leaders who are seen to protect the best interests of the discipline.

What binds an academic discipline?

- Shared mission
- Shared trajectories of professional and academic development
- Standards
- Shared vocabulary (an outcome of shared academic preparation)
- Prominent paradigms used to interpret phenomena of interest (i.e., academicians can easily identify the major as well as controversial paradigms and the conflicts that emerge as they attempt to use them to solve problems of interest)
- Acknowledgment and value of different members' sub-segment goals (e.g., in *history* some subsegments concern themselves exclusively with *Greek* history).

Professional fields (e.g., medicine, law, education, psychology) license members in addition to all of the above criteria for academic disciplines. Licensing brings additional rights and responsibilities, which might include the right to treat clients, prescribe medication, and implement other interventions or resources.[32] Based on this licensing criterion, it is clear that MBE science is a new academic discipline; however, it is not a professional field.

How is information studied in MBE? It seems like there is no denying that the more sub-fields that offer support for different teaching methods, the more reason we have to believe that those methods will work. However, the sheer number of sub-fields make this science appear overwhelmingly complex. Actually, it is easier than it first appears.

Applying MBE Science
In practical terms, the best way to apply MBE science is by first determining how, when, where, and within which topics cognitive neuroscience, education, and psychology

---

32. Tokuhama-Espinosa & Schwartz (2008). It should be noted that both authors' opinions have evolved since this initial discussion, and these parameters should be seen as starting points for further clarification.

overlap. Second, MBE scientists use a transdisciplinary lens to consider the core questions of mutual interest to the three parent disciplines and what is known about each. This research uses the points of commonality within the work of the existing three disciplines in order to create a unique take on "old" problems. For example, improving reading skills is a common learning objective. Some neuroscientists study how the brain works as it approaches reading and document the changes that take place on a microscopic level, as in minute changes in brain structures that occur as the brain learns to read.[33] Some psychologists, on the other hand, consider the socioemotional and motivational questions around learning how to read.[34] Finally, some educators consider how certain teaching methods or activities impact student performance in reading.[35] An MBE scientist would consider all of these perspectives and unite the findings for a more comprehensive understanding of how one learns to read.

Another example relates to concepts in math. Neuroscientists have demonstrated that the brain understands *3*, *three*, *III*, and "● ● ●" in slightly differing and sometimes overlapping ways.[36] Pedagogues understand that different methods of teaching resonate with different levels of success, depending on the student; some students benefit more from manipulatives and other hands-on activities, others from repetitive exercises, yet others from small-group explanations, and so on. Psychologists have also learned that "mental number lines"[37] and general processes of categorization (e.g., what is near or far, what is large or small, what is a lot or a little) impact a student's ability to successfully maneuver the math classroom. If teaching math were viewed through an MBE science lens instead of solely from the perspective of a neuroscientist or a teacher, then teaching would be improved. If we applied the information above to the classroom, it would mean that teachers would use a variety of teaching methods and activities to try and reach the broadest range of learning preferences and styles. This combined approach leads to better teaching and better learning. Unfortunately, many people in each discipline have focused on their field alone in regard to learning, sometimes turning a blind eye to the valuable information in other disciplines that could nurture a better understanding of how to teach. This is changing with MBE science.

---

33. An excellent explanation can be found in Dehaene (2009) and in Cohen, Dehaene, Naccache, Lehericy, Dehaene-Lambertz, et al. (2000).
34. A good example of this can found in McCandliss & Noble (2003).
35. A good example of this can be seen in Reynolds, Nicolson, & Hambly (2003).
36. See Stanislas Dehaene's work for an exhaustive and ingenious treatment of this theme.
37. For a fascinating summary, see Coch et al. (2007) p. 42.

Conceptual Debates in the Discipline

One way to understand the conceptual debates in the discipline is to recognize that "neuroscience is focused on the neuron as the primary unit of study while psychology's unit of study is the mind and pedagogy's view is on society and the individual, as manifested through formal educational practice."[38] It is clear that a person who views learning through a microscope, one who concentrates on behavioral changes in animals (including humans), and one who views learning through classroom interaction all have different perspectives on learning. Mental schemas, including whom we view as key actors or mentors, and what we view as core loci for execution, are influenced by our academic formations. In one of the first searches on "brain and learning" in academic journals I conducted, I found a surprising array of perspectives. When the key words "brain" and "learning" were inserted in a search engine, there was a myriad of interpretations of these two words ranging from the "neuro views" (how cells learn) to the pop psychology perspective. In a great number of cases these peer-reviewed journals focused on nonhuman brains and the learning of cells and very few related to kids in classrooms. In other cases, as in peer-review psychology journals, the focus was on therapy and behavioral changes, but again, with no classroom application. Curiously enough, there were few journals in education that specifically considered the brain. Though it may seem ironic, *brains* and *classrooms* were not often found in the same articles. All of this is to say that each of these disciplinary perspectives views the brain and learning in very different ways, and each perspective impacts our understanding of how the brain learns to read, and subsequently, how we should teach to maximize that performance. Cross-germination of understandings about these different topics leads to a unique vision of how knowledge is learned and can be nurtured by specific teaching interventions. To unite these different and valuable perspectives, MBE scientists combine the knowledge from each of these disciplines and synthesize the findings to develop a new approach to learning substantiated by all three parent fields.

In terms of reading, the combined approach can be seem in research such as that of Juliana Paré-Blagoev (2006), Maryanne Wolf (2007), and Stanislas Dehaene (2009), who manage to balance information from neuroscience, psychology, and education to create more powerful teaching tools than those that come from just a single discipline. In terms of math, this is seen in work conducted by Stanislas Dehaene (1997) and colleagues, as well as analyses by Donna Coch, Kurt Fischer, and Geraldine Dawson (2007).[39] In Chapters 6 and 7 we review several more examples of the specific application of MBE science to

---

38. Tokuhama-Espinosa, 2010, p. 31.
39. Also see Wilson, Dehaene, Pinel, Revkin, Cohen, et al. (2006).

core topics in education with the purpose of demonstrating just how and why it is a more comprehensive approach to understanding learning and teaching.

Viewing old learning problems through the new MBE science lens will change the traditional perceptions in neuroscience, psychology, and education. For example, let's say a teacher observes that students' retention of new information is enhanced through cooperative learning activities. The teacher wonders if cooperative learning can be considered an instrument worthy of MBE science. The teacher begins with a clear definition of cooperative learning: Cooperative learning techniques are activities in which groups of students democratically share the responsibility for generating solutions to problems. In such situations, the stress level felt by students is drastically reduced as the competition level is lowered. The teacher finds that cooperative learning and peer teaching include feedback and modeling.[40] She researches the literature in psychology for evidence and finds that feedback and modeling have a great deal of evidence. Confirming the evidence in psychology, the teacher then turns to neuroscience.

For educators (see Figure 2.2):

FIGURE 2.2
Suggested Cycle of Information Generation for Educators

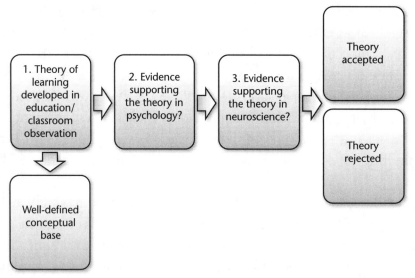

Neuroscience studies show that learning is enhanced when stress levels are lowered. The release of stress hormones inhibits natural pathways for learning.[41] The documentation of such evidence provides a physiological explanation for the psychological discom-

40. As in Henderson & Buising's work (2000); Kerka (1999); Rubin & Herbert (1998).
41. As demonstrated in the work conducted by Lupien, Maheu, Tu, Fiocco, & Schramek (2007).

fort that fear, stress, and anxiety cause in the brain. The teacher realizes that this information is evidence in favor of cooperative learning activities and determines that they classify as good MBE science activities.

Let's look at another example from a psychologist's perspective. Let's say a psychologist observes that rats seem to learn in enriched environments where there are toys and other rats. The psychologist wonders if enriched environments also have an impact on human brains. To look for evidence in pedagogy and neuroscience, the psychologist must first define *enriched environments* and then decipher the elements that comprise such an environment. He determines that enriched environments include different types of stimulation, varying materials, manageable challenges, predictable rewards, and company. The psychologist then looks to pedagogy for evidence and finds that students who are given similar stimulation also tend to do better in school.[42] The psychologist also discovers that there is evidence showing how a lack of stimulation affects the brain negatively, the most noteworthy in research done with Romanian orphans who were often left tied to their cribs with no human contact.[43] To confirm whether or not enriched environments are supported by all sub-disciplines in MBE science (which would elevate the likelihood of success), the psychologist turns to neuroscience for final confirmation. In neuroscience he finds that enriched environments change the brain, evidencing more synaptic activity, in rat, but not in human, studies.[44] The psychologist finds that this evidence, however, is generally related only to certain aspects of enriched environments, as in rehearsal of a skill in different environments,[45] or due to socialization, but not due to increased toys or plentiful and varied activities.[46] To top it off, "there is no evidence in humans linking synaptic densities and improved learning" (Hall, 2005, p. 17). There are also criticisms that the "enriched" environments in which the original rat studies upon which this theory is based were conducted were actually more like "normal" environments for rats (sewers), meaning that the studies proved that *impoverished environments* cause harm, but not necessarily that enriched environments are beneficial. The psychologist determines that there is compelling evidence for the inclusion of enriched environments in general, but that the evidence does not merit complete acceptance yet. This means that the consideration of good learning environments may be important, and the evidence shows it is "probably so" or "intelligent speculation," but not "well established"

42. As in examples offered by writers such as Jensen (2006a); Marzano, Pickering, & Pollock (2004).
43. See Eluvathingal, Chugani, Behen, Juhász, Muzik, & Maqbool (2005) for a review of this tragic case.
44. See Diamond, Krech, & Rosenzweig (1964, 1988) for a discussion of this key point.
45. A classic study in this area can be found in Maguire et al. (2000).
46. See Diamond (2001b).

at this point in time. The psychologist accepts that further compelling evidence should be offered before full acceptance.

For psychologists (see Figure 2.3):

FIGURE 2.3
Suggested Cycle of Information Generation for Psychologists

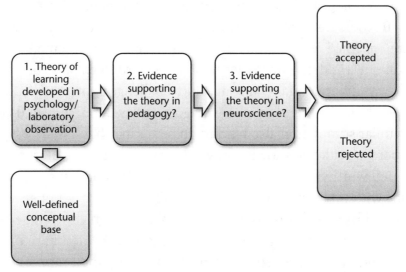

A final example from neuroscience helps us understand how information can and should be critiqued in the new discipline. Let's say a neuroscientist notes that a patient loses the ability to read (or interpret humorous remarks, or spell correctly) after suffering a stroke. Using this information, he makes some generalizations about how language works in the brain.[47] This neuroscientist might wonder if the particular neural pathways, which appear damaged after the stroke, can contribute to knowledge about how to teach better. First, the neuroscientist must identify exactly what stimulates this part of the brain and precisely how the neurophysiology changed after the stroke. Once the neuroscientist can determine how to measure such changes, he can look for research in education and psychology that supports evidence that reading is, indeed, triggered through such mechanisms. Have experiments investigated the effects of extra stimulation of this particular brain region, for example? Did such experiments result in improved reading abilities of children? Have others documented how damage to these brain areas caused skill loss? If and when the neuroscientist can identify such support from education and psychology, then he can be sure that his single case was not unique and begin to generalize a theory of reading and the brain.

47. For examples of this kind of study, see Booker, Invernizzi, & McCormick (2007); Holden (2004); Schlaggar & McCandliss (2007).

An illustrative case in neuropsychology was that of Phineas Gage, whose accident while working on a railroad caused the destruction of his right frontal and parietal lobes. This region was later identified to be related to metaphorical expressions and interpretation of humor via language.[48] This finding, though celebrated in psychology, is rarely shared with educators, which means that we teachers have missed out on valuable information. For example, Gage's case led to the understanding that although some students might excel at some aspects of language, they may not do so in all, as different parts of language are mediated by different systems of the brain. Specifically, spelling travels through one neural network, metaphors another, vocabulary another, and syntax and grammar yet another. It should come as no surprise to teachers, then, to find that children may not be globally "good" at language, but rather they might have strengths and weaknesses. This finding also has policy implications because it means that not only should teachers differentiate their methodology, they must also differentiate their assessment of students by dividing up overall skill areas (e.g., in language) into several sub-skills (e.g., metaphors, spelling, grammar, written, spoken).

For neuroscientists (see Figure 2.4):

FIGURE 2.4
Suggested Cycle of Information Generations for Neuroscientists

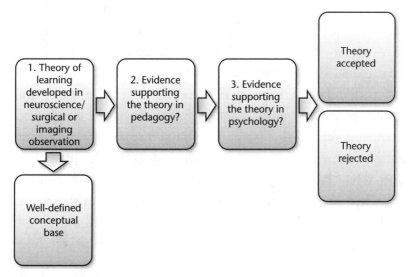

The disciplines of neuroscience, psychology, and education can inform each other in many ways, as demonstrated in the contents of this book. Some specific examples of each

48. Argyris, Stringaris, Medford, Giampietro, Brammer, & David (2007); Kacinik & Chiarello (2007).
49. For a good example, see Keri (2003).

of these exchanges are mentioned below as a way to summarize the findings and possible conclusions about the interdisciplinary nature of the discipline.

Neuroscience Can Inform Pedagogy

There are a myriad of ways in which neuroscience can inform pedagogy. Some of the most prominent studies can be found in math and reading. Other areas are less developed, but equally important. For example, the cognitive neuroscience of category learning[49] points to specific practices that help teachers instruct their pupils in a way that corresponds with the brain's natural categorization mechanisms. This is one of the first formal skills small children learn in school as they begin to sort out the concepts in their world. Other studies on the neuroimaging perspective of conceptual knowledge illustrate how different types of ideas are linked in different ways in the brain.[50] These neuroscience studies can help educators understand which concepts are best taught in tandem, and which create problems if taught together. For example, it has been found that it is harder if someone studies French and Spanish (which are very similar, as far as languages go) at the same time, than if they study French and Japanese (which are very different due to orthography and syntax). Other studies in neuroscience attempt to bridge the gap between our understanding of mind and brain through the study of neurobehavioral integration.[51] Such studies consider how the brain and mind work to manage all external as well as purely mental activity, which helps teachers understand the complexities of decision-making, for example. To what extent do external stimuli distract or guide thought patterns and how does this impact student behavior in the classroom? Other neuroscientific studies explain the relationship between sleep and learning, which has huge implications for teachers. For example, we now know that sleep is vital for memory consolidation, yet many students "pull all-nighters" to study for tests, then wonder why just a few days later, they cannot remember what they thought they had studied.[52] There are literally thousands of different ways in which neuroscience can inform pedagogy, but this is only one of several paths through which information can be generated. There should be a three-directional exchange of information—for example, pedagogy can inform psychology.

49. For a good example, see Keri (2003).
50. See Martin & Caramazza (2003).
51. For examples, see Meissner (2006); Saxe (2006).
52. Miller (2007).

Pedagogy Can Inform Psychology

There are several ways in which pedagogy can inform psychology. Teacher observations about student reactions to different methodologies as well as a measurement of their metacognitive development can inform psychology. Similarly, the study of differentiated teaching practices related to perceived learning styles can identify preferences for memory storage.[53] These studies profess to enhance memory and therefore learning. Teaching and assessing students based on their individual potential in a subject area is a basic tenet of MBE science. Students' different levels of intelligence and cognitive preferences, combined with their varying levels of knowledge and skills, justify differentiation in classroom practices. This does not mean that instruction is conducted in a one-on-one fashion, but rather that the teacher takes the time to diagnose student needs and plan learning experiences in a more personalized way. We now know that we should avoid rushing through topics to cover the material (even if in a logical order), and rather be sure those topics are anchored to the past knowledge or mental schemas (read "realities") of students.

If we can increase teachers' perceptive abilities about the different ways people learn, then they could become better in their practice. Likewise, research into how different methodologies and classroom activities impact the quality of student output within classroom settings is a valuable way of gaining insight into psychological thought processes.[54] Perhaps the most common studies are those of classroom activities that test the validity of psychological concepts, including those related to self-esteem and motivation[55] and their impact on learning. Just as pedagogy can inform psychology, psychology can also inform neuroscience.

Psychology Can Inform Neuroscience

Psychology has been perhaps the principal source of neuroscientific investigation. Indeed, what has been "known" for years in psychological contexts is now being "proven" in terms of brain activity through neuroscience. For example, psychologists have known for centuries that humans tend to imitate one another for social reasons; people act like their valued peers in order to "fit in" and be accepted. Such studies can be used to develop theories of brain activation during social cognition,[56] including that

---

53. An example of this can be found in Sprenger (2003).
54. For example, see Stahl (1990).
55. See Caprara, Fagnani, Alessandri, Steca, Gigantesco, & Sforza (2009).
56. Meltzoff & Decety (2003) offer an excellent explanation of this idea.

which occurs in classroom settings. In other instances, psychological hypotheses about certain behavior can be documented in neuroscience to determine patterns or systems of brain mechanisms during that specific behavior.[57] For example, Staumwasser (2003) demonstrated how the psychological development of the mind of a child can actually be measured within neuroscience. He sought to better define "what is truly 'unique' in the development of the [human] mind" by comparing humans and chimpanzees and the mental pathways used to make decisions. He was able to show that there are "four inherent behavioral differences" demonstrable through Event-Related Potential (ERP) brain activity measurement between the species (p. 22). This is, in effect, the true mind–brain confirmation. Not only has psychology had an impact on neuroscience, it can also inform pedagogy.

Psychology Can Inform Pedagogy

Psychology has been a rich source of information for pedagogy. For example, the basic conceptual beliefs about the thinking process were contemplated first in psychology with subsequent applications in formal learning environments.[58] In other studies, psychology has demonstrated how beliefs about intelligence influence learning success[59]—such research can greatly impact the way in which we teach and our relations with our students. Students tend to live up to the expectations of their teachers: High expectations yield better results.

Some of the links between psychology and pedagogy are overt. *Monitor on Psychology*, a journal of the American Psychological Association (APA), considered how brain scans can turn into lesson plans, for example.[60] Other psychological research is subtler in its consideration of the hypothetical role of working memory on education,[61] or of evidence for pedagogical practices that engage the learner. For example, Sherrie Reynolds's work (2000) reminds practitioners that "learning is a verb," or an active process, when considering the psychology of teaching and learning. All of these studies clearly demonstrate the major role psychology has played in designing current teaching methodologies in MBE science. In a similar fashion, pedagogy can inform neuroscience.

---

57. See Schall (2004) for an example.
58. For an example, see Markham & Gentner (2001).
59. This can be seen in work by Mangels, Butterfield, & Lamb (2006).
60. See Murray (2000a).
61. See Pickering & Phye (2006).

Pedagogy Can Inform Neuroscience

Pedagogy can inform neuroscience in a variety of ways. For example, educators have written about the need to have a better presentation of scientifically based research.[62] This evaluation informs neuroscience about education's level of understanding of scientifically based research, which can be corroborated in future neuroscientific study. In essence, neuroscientists are asking teachers to find utilitarian aspects to their research that have direct applications to the classroom. In other instances, educational settings can confirm or defy findings in neuroscience labs by offering environmentally valid settings—something often missing in lab research.[63] Other educational studies have provided specific methodology for scrutiny in neuroscience and have shown that how we teach impacts what can be learned.[64] Some educational research has demonstrated how classrooms are the ultimate proving ground for neuroscience related to MBE science—which literally means that without this final "passing grade," neuroscientific research remains purely an intellectual exercise without real-life applications.[65] Finally, evidence in pedagogy should be used as the bases of confirming hypotheses in psychology that have been confirmed in neuroscience.[66]

Perhaps the most important link between pedagogy and neuroscience occurs when neuroscientists take proposals in education and put them to the test in real classrooms. For example, neuroscientists can compare the basic premises in Alfie Kohn's work (1999) (called *The Schools Our Children Deserve: Moving beyond Traditional Classroom and Tougher Standards*) and Kathie Nunley's *layered curriculum design* (2002b) with information in the neurosciences. Educational claims are an under-used and rich source to access in identifying new neuroscientific questions for research. Far more research in neuroscience should begin with educational premises, rather than with neuroscientific findings that are molded to fit educational settings. In a similar way, neuroscience can inform psychology.

Neuroscience Can Inform Psychology

Neuroscience can inform psychology in several ways. Perhaps the most obvious way is through the confirmation of specific claims. For example, psychology has spent decades

62. See Eisenhart & DeHaan (2005).
63. For an example, see Harley (2004b).
64. See Fellows, Heberlein, Morales, Shivde, Waller, & Wu. (2005).
65. Found in Fischer (2007a).
66. See Johnson, Chang, & Lord (2006).

discussing consciousness. Neuroscientists such as Russell Poldrack and Anthony Wagner (2004) have ventured to ask "What Can Neuroimaging Tell Us about the Mind?" In a similar vein, others have queried "how the emerging neurosociety is changing how we live, work, and love."[67] Others have tackled the nature versus nurture query in psychology and reframed the question as one of the combination of "genes, brain, and cognition"[68] to consider the "making of the self."[69] Neuroscience is being used to establish psychological claims about social, cognitive, and affective learning.[70] While many are enthusiastic about what neuroscience can do for psychology, there are a good number of more conservative perspectives that put parameters around the debate of "what neuroimaging and brain localization can do, cannot do, and should not do for social psychology."[71] These types of studies point to the natural interaction of neuroscience and psychology as well as their many areas of overlap. Considering how the three parent disciplines can successfully inform one another is exciting and points to a potentially bright future for MBE science.

Using multiple lenses and a transdisciplinary perspective, MBE science can facilitate the advancement of teaching methods through the reinterpretation of findings in neuroscience, psychology, and pedagogy. There are dozens of ways this reinterpretation can take place. For example, best-practice pedagogy can guide the focus of studies in neuroscience, as leaders in the discipline have noted: "The identification and analysis of successful pedagogy is central to research in education, but is currently a foreign field to cognitive neuroscience" (Goswami, 2004, as cited in Hall [2005, p. 3]). Similarly, educational psychology can inform educational neuroscience, which in turn can inform pedagogy. Currently "it is rare to find an article written by a neuroscientist in the educational literature," (1998b, p. 9) according to John T. Bruer; educational journals should solicit articles from the neurosciences in order to inform their readership of relevant information. Likewise, neuroscientists can and should point out errors or overgeneralizations of information about the brain to the public at large and educators in particular. This type of gentle correction can elevate the quality of information used in classrooms.

67. Restak (2006).
68. Ramus (2006).
69. Reid & Baylis (2005).
70. Schmidt (2007).
71. Willingham & Dunn (2003).

MBE Science Is State-of-the-Art, Yet Nothing New

Contemporary theories of learning can also benefit from review by MBE science. The importance of findings in all areas will multiply if they can somehow be confirmed via an interdisciplinary effort. This is a paradigm shift in thinking about teaching and learning. A decade ago it was thought that cognitive neuroscience should inform educational psychology, and vice versa.[72] This has now expanded to a ménage a trois, in which education plays an equal role and all three fields must share responsibility for the advancement of teaching.

MBE scientists can either be trained in academic programs aimed at this balanced view, or they can come from any one of the three parent disciplines and learn the knowledge and skills, as well as adopt the attitudes of MBE science. Research practitioners in MBE science understand how and why interdisciplinary sharing is vital to the growth of the discipline and to reaching its goals, as mentioned in the introduction. The general research practice of an MBE professional is to identify problems common to neuroscience, psychology, and education, integrate findings, and propose new solutions. Perhaps the most difficult, yet also the most vital, quality of MBE scientists is the ability to not only understand how the epistemologies of neuroscience, psychology, and education differ, but also how a new understanding of knowing emerges through the application of MBE principles.

It is curious to note that in the history of epistemology we have come full circle from Grecian times. The Greeks greatly valued the global thinker, who is once again lauded in 21st-century education. Interdisciplinary thought was valued by the Greeks through the 16th century, in which the balance of science and art could make one a "Renaissance man." However, the importance of specialization increased and was prized over generalists starting in the 17th century and continuing until just recently. The "specialist" in a certain field was seen as more important than the "general practitioner," who is supposed to have sufficient knowledge about quite a lot of areas in his or her discipline. This view changed with the establishment of the cognitive sciences in the 1980s. The ability to think across academic disciplinary lines and to merge understandings from different fields is not only valued once again, but it is seen as the only true way of understanding the increasingly complex nature of human ideas. To illustrate this point, we now turn to the only five concepts that are well established in all three parent disciplines. These five well-established concepts are the cornerstone of MBE science practice.

---

72. See Byrnes & Fox (1998a) and Byrnes & Fox (1998b) for this classic seminal work.
73. Tokuhama-Espinosa (2010).

The Five Well-Established Concepts of MBE Science

The following summary of the well-established concepts in MBE science comes from *The New Science of Teaching and Learning: Using the Best of Mind, Brain, and Education Science in the Classroom*,[73] which I wrote:

1. *Human brains are as unique as faces.*[74] Although the basic structure is the same, no two are identical. While there are general patterns of organization in how different people learn and which brain areas are involved, each brain is unique and uniquely organized. The uniqueness of the human brain is perhaps the most fundamental belief in MBE science. Even identical twins leave the womb with physically distinct brains due to the slightly different experiences they had; one with his ear pressed closer to the uterus wall and bombarded with sounds and light, and the other snuggled down deep in the dark. There are clear patterns of brain development shared by all people, but the uniqueness of each brain partially explains why students learn in slightly different ways. Many popular books try to exploit this finding by using it as an "excuse" for the inability of teachers to reach all learners. This is simply irresponsible. The uniqueness of each brain is not to be overshadowed by the fact that humans as a species share clear developmental stages that set parameters for learning.

2. *All brains are not equal because context and ability influence learning.*[75] Context includes the learning environment, motivation for the topic of new learning, and prior knowledge. Different people are born with different abilities, which they can improve upon or lose, depending on the stimuli or lack thereof. How learners receive stimuli is impacted by what they bring to the learning context, including past experience and prior knowledge. This means that children do not enter the classroom on an even playing field. Some are simply more prepared for the world from birth. This is a harsh reality to face because it explicitly establishes a definitive framework for potential. The key, however, is to maximize this potential. There are thousands of people who are born with the potential or circumstances to be quite smart who do not live up to this possibility, while there are thousands who are born with modest potential, but who maximize this "limitation" well beyond expectations. Genes, previous experiences, and what the child does with his or her potential contribute to the child's success as a learner.

3. *The brain is changed by experience.*[76] The brain is a complex, dynamic, and integrated system that is constantly changed by experience, though most of this change is

---

73. Tokuhama-Espinosa (2010).
74. Tokuhama-Espinosa (2008b, p. 356).
75. Tokuhama-Espinosa (2008b, p. 356).
76. Tokuhama-Espinosa (2008b, p. 356).

evident only at a microscopic level. You will go to bed tonight with a different brain from the one you had when you awoke. Each smell, sight, taste, and touch you experience and each feeling or thought you have alters the physical form of your brain. Although these brain changes are often imperceptible unless viewed under a powerful microscope, they constantly change the physical makeup of the brain. With rehearsal, these changes become permanent—which can work in both positive and negative ways. Areas of the brain that are used together tend to be strengthened, whereas areas that are not stimulated atrophy. This truth gives rise to the Hebbian synapse concept (1949): Neurons that fire together, wire together. The "wire together" part is a physical manifestation of how life experiences change the brain. In short, it is nearly impossible for the brain not to learn as experience—broadly defined as "knowledge or practical wisdom gained from what one has observed, encountered, or undergone"[77]—changes the brain on a daily basis.

4. *The brain is highly plastic.*[78] Human brains have a high degree of plasticity and develop throughout the lifespan, though there are major limits on this plasticity, and these limits increase with age. People can, and do, learn throughout their lives. One of the most influential findings of the 20th century was the discovery of the brain's plasticity. This discovery challenges the earlier belief in localization (i.e., that each brain area had a highly specific function that only that area could fulfill), which lasted for hundreds of years. It has now been documented that neuroplasticity can explain why some people are able to recuperate skills thought to be lost due to injury. People born with only one hemisphere of the brain, who nevertheless manage to live their lives normally, are an extreme example of this plasticity. Antonio Battro and Mary Helen Immordino-Yang offer documentation of people with half a brain. Antonio Battro's work on *Half a Brain Is Enough: The Story of Nico* (2000) is a remarkable documentation of one child's life with just a half a brain and defies previous concepts about skill set location in the brain. Taking Battro's lead, Immordino-Yang offers the detailed story of two cases in her recent work, "A Tale of Two Cases: Lessons for Education from the Study of Two Boys Living with Half Their Brains" (2007b). She shows how the entire brain works as a single large system, and when parts are missing, as in the case of these two children who were born with only half a brain each, then other parts of the brain can "take over" and learn functions with which they are not normally associated.

---

77. Dictionary.com (2010). Definition of learning.
78. Tokuhama-Espinosa (2008b, p. 357).

Researchers such as Paul Bach-y-Rita make it clear that "we see with our brains, not with our eyes" (as cited in Doidge, 2007, p. 14). That is, the brain as a whole is responsible for sensory perception, not necessarily a single part of the brain. Bach-y-Rita explains this point using a simple metaphor: Let's assume that you are driving from point A to point B. You normally take the most efficient route, but if a bridge is down or the road is blocked, you take a secondary road. This secondary road might not be as fast as the "natural" route, but it gets you to point B all the same, and it may even become the preferred route if it is sufficiently reinforced.

Perhaps the author who has done the most to explain neuroplasticity to the public is physician Norman Doidge, who has documented studies that "showed that children are not always stuck with the mental abilities they are born with; that the damaged brain can often reorganize itself so that when one part fails, another can often substitute; that if brain cells die, they can at times be replaced; that many 'circuits' and even basic reflexes that we think are hardwired are not."[79] Neuroplasticity has implications for brains that have been damaged, but also for basic learning in classroom experiences and how we think about education. Whereas it was popular in the 1990s to think of the "crucial" early years, it is now acknowledged that learning takes place throughout the lifespan. Does this point speak against the privileging of early childhood educational practices? Not at all; it simply means that under the right conditions, the skills that identify normal developmental stages should be seen as benchmarks, not roadblocks, because humans can learn throughout the lifespan.

5. *The brain connects new information to old.*[80] Connecting new information to prior knowledge facilitates learning. We learn better and faster when we relate new information to things that we already know. This principle may sound like it needs no evidence—we experience it every day. For example, let's say you are going somewhere you have never been before. When someone gives you directions, it is very helpful if they offer you a point of reference that is familiar to you ("You'll see the post office; from there, turn right at the next corner"). Similarly, when a child learns, he or she builds off of a past knowledge; there is no new learning without reference to the past.

It is unfortunate that new concepts are sometimes taught in schools in a conceptual vacuum without anchoring the information to what students already know. This vacuum is the reason that students who have a poor foundation in a particular subject will

---

79. Doidge (2007, p. xv).
80. Tokuhama-Espinosa (2008b, p. 357).

continue to fail. How can a child who does not understand addition move on to understand subtraction? To use a house-building metaphor, if we have a weak foundation, then it is irrelevant how sturdy the walls are, or how well built the roof is; the structure cannot be supported. This is an argument for quality instruction in the early years. Without a firm foundation in basic mathematical conceptualization (or basic concepts in language, values, artistic or social content, for that matter), then a student will have a lot of trouble moving on to build more complex conceptual understandings.

The well-established concepts in MBE science are not new ideas. All five have been around for decades, if not centuries. What is new is that all five concepts have been proven without a doubt in neuroscience, psychology, and educational settings, adding to their credibility for use in planning, curriculum design, classroom methodology design, and basic pedagogy. What is new is their consistent application in best-practice classroom settings. These five "truths" should guide all teaching practices as well as future research on better teaching tools.[81]

In this chapter we defined MBE science in terms of its origins, its conceptual debates, and the "truths" accepted in this exciting new discipline. Before going into the classroom applications of this information, Chapter 3 takes a look back at the brief history of MBE science.

Suggested Reading

Arguments for the Creation of MBE Science

Ansari, D. (2005). Paving the way towards meaningful interactions between neuroscience and education. *Developmental Science, 8*(6), pp. 466–467.

Ansari, D., & Coch, D. (2006). Bridges over troubled waters: Education and neuroscience. *Trends in Cognitive Sciences, 10*(4), 146–151.

Battro, A., Fischer, K. W., & Léna, P. J. (Eds). (2008). *The educated brain: Essays in neuroeducation.* Cambridge, UK: Cambridge University Press.

Christoff, K. (2008). Applying neuroscientific findings to education: The good, the tough and the hopeful. *Mind, Brain, and Education, 2*, 55–58.

---

81. For a thorough review of each OECD category, readers are invited to read *The New Science of Teaching and Learning: Using the Best of Mind, Brain, and Education Science in the Classroom* (Tokuhama-Espinosa, 2010).

Fischer, K. W. (2009). Mind, brain, and education: Building a scientific groundwork for learning and teaching. *Mind, Brain, and Education, 3*(1), 3–16.

Fischer, K. W., Daniel, D. B., Immordino-Yang, M. H., Stern, E., Battro, A., & Koizumi, H. (Eds.). (2007). Why mind, brain, and education? Why now? *Mind, Brain, and Education, 1*(1), 1–2.

Geake, J. (2005a, Aug.). Educational neuroscience and neuroscientific education: In search of a mutual middle way. *Research Intelligence, 92,* 10–13.

Goswami, U. (2006). Neuroscience and education: From research to practice. *Nature Reviews Neuroscience, 7*(5), 406–413.

McNamara, D. S. (2006). Bringing cognitive science into education and back again: The value of interdisciplinary research. *Cognitive Science, 30,* 605–608.

Meissner, W. (2006). The mind–brain relation and neuroscientific foundations: II. Neurobehavioral integrations. *Bulletin of the Menninger Clinic, 70*(2), 102–124.

Organisation for Economic Co-Operation and Development. (2002). *Understanding the brain: Towards a new learning science.* Paris: OECD. Available online at *www.oecd.org.*

Organisation for Economic Co-Operation and Development. (2007). *The brain and learning.* Retrieved March 10, 2007, from *http://www.oecd.org/department /0,2688,en_2649_14935397_1_1_1_1_1,00.html.*

Pickering, S., & Howard-Jones, P. (2007). Educator's views on the role of neuroscience in education: Findings from a study of UK and international perspectives. *Mind, Brain, and Education, 1*(3), 109–113.

Rose, S. (2005). *The future of the brain: The promises and perils of tomorrow's neuroscience.* New York: Oxford University Press.

Tokuhama-Espinosa, T. (2010). *The new science of teaching and learning: Using the best of mind, brain, and education science in the classroom.* New York: Teachers College Press.

Willis, J. (2006). *Research-based strategies to ignite student learning: Insights from a neurologist and classroom teacher.* Alexandria, VA: Association For Supervision And Curriculum Development.

www.imbes.org

Journal of Mind Brain and Education: *www3.interscience.wiley.com/journal/117982931/home*

Transdisciplinary Fields and Disciplines

Davis, B., & Sumara, D. (2006). *Complexity and education: Inquiries into learning, teaching, and research.* Mahwah, NJ: Erlbaum.

della Chiesa, B., Christoph, V., & Hinton, C. (2009). How many brains does it take to build a new light? Knowledge management challenges of a transdisciplinary project. *Mind, Brain, and Education, 3*(1), 17–26.

Koizumi, H. (1999). A practical approach to trans-disciplinary studies for the 21st century. *Journal of Seizon and Life Sciences, 9,* 5–24.

McNamara, D. S. (2006). Bringing cognitive science into education and back again: The value of interdisciplinary research. *Cognitive Science, 30,* 605–608.

Posner, M. (2004). Is the combination of psychology and neuroscience important to you? *Impuls: Tidsskrift for Psyckhologi, 3,* 6–8.

Samuels, B. M. (2009). Can differences between education and neuroscience be overcome by Mind, Brain, and Education? *Mind, Brain, and Education, 3*(1), 45–53.

Schall, J. (2004). On building a bridge between brain and behavior. *Annual Review of Psychology, 55*(1), 23.

Ticker, P. (2007). The rise of brain-focused teaching: Teachers look to neuroscience for help in the classroom. *The Futurist, 41*(3).

Varma, S., McCandliss, B., & Schwartz, D. (2008, Apr). Scientific and pragmatic challenges for bridging education and neuroscience. *Educational Researcher, 37*(3), 140–152.

CHAPTER 3

A New Look at Old Problems in Education
A Brief History of the Science of Learning

"Knowing how something originated often is the best clue to how it works."
—Terrence Deacon, *The Symbolic Species: The Co-Evolution of Language and the Brain* (1998, p. 23)

Some questions have faced teachers for centuries. What is important to know? Who is prepared to teach? Who should be taught and how? Hints at answers to these questions can be found throughout history, and these answers point repeatedly to key concepts that are the cornerstones of the new science of teaching and learning.

From the Egyptians to the Greeks to the 1100s: The Roots of Formal Education

Humans are a complicated species, and exact records of many aspects of our common development are not so well known. The development of writing systems around 3500 B.C.E. aided in recording these lessons and served as a concrete record, replacing reliance on purely oral history. Some of the earliest written records show that formal education, in which basic communication skills, language, trading customs, and agricultural and religious practices were taught, began in Egypt some time between 3000 and 500 B.C.E. The earliest library known to man, in Babylonia, was built by Ashurbanipal, the king of the Neo-Assyrian Empire (685–627 B.C.E.). Texts in this library documented advances in math, reading, and writing, as well as common practices of warfare and hunting.

During the Zhou Dynasty (551–479 B.C.E.), Confucius, the famed Chinese philoso-pher, greatly impacted the overall curriculum focus of formal education and shaped educational values even through present-day systems. Though known better for moral and spiritual teachings, Confucius's focus on personal values determined what was impor-tant to teach as well as how this teaching was achieved in formal education settings. For example, self-control and respect were incorporated as aspects of the development of logical thinking. Additionally, Confucius was perhaps one of the first to think of differen-tiated instruction: "Teach according to the student's ability" (as cited in Chin, 2007, p. 1). This means that 2,500 years ago Confucius knew about the value of differentiated instruc-tion and its worth not only to the individual but also to society.

The content of formal education shifted with the Greeks, who sought to balance util-itarian skills with loftier contemplations about the origins of thought. Hippocrates (c. 460–370 B.C.E.), Socrates (c. 470–399 B.C.E.), and Aristotle (c. 384–322 B.C.E.) all speculated about what drives human will, motivation, and learning. While educators since the Greeks have contemplated how to influence human actions through formal education, it is relatively recent in human history that the focus has turned to brain func-tions that can be manipulated to enhance the teaching and learning process.[82] According to modern educational theorist Howard Gardner, "Greek philosophers may have been the first to raise questions about the nature of matter, living entities, knowledge, will, truth, beauty, and goodness. In recent centuries, however, philosophy has steadily been yielding ground, enthusiastically or reluctantly, to empirical science" (Gardner, 2000, p. 1).

The 10th–17th Centuries: The Senses and Learning

Starting in the 10th century, humanity gained a fundamental understanding about how sensorimotor perceptions are interpreted in the brain and translated into thought. Alhazen (or Al-Haytham; 965–1039 C.E.) was perhaps one of the greatest physicists of all times and a product of the Islamic Golden Age or Islamic Renaissance (7th–13th centuries). He made significant contributions to anatomy, astronomy, engineering, math-ematics, medicine, ophthalmology, philosophy, physics, psychology, and visual perception and is primarily attributed as the inventor of the scientific method,[83] for which author Bradley Steffens (2006) describes him as the "first scientist." Alhazen recorded some of the

82. Crivellato & Ribatti (2007).
83. The scientific method is the process by which research is conducted that involves the collection of data based on observable, empirical, and measureable evidence. Typically speaking, one makes a hypothesis, gathers data either through observation or experimentation, and then proves or disproves his or her hypothesis.

first ideas about experimental psychology and optical illusions and could be considered a Middle Eastern da Vinci. Alhazen's work helped move philosophical ponderings about intelligence to the realm of hard science. Alhazen established that learning is generated by our sensory perceptions of the world (even if only through memories of those perceptions and not actual perceptions themselves). Our senses feed information to our memory, and we compare new with old, detect patterns and novelty, and base new learning on past associations; new information is learned based on our past experiences.

From the Physical Body to the Learning Brain

Renaissance researchers posed similar philosophical questions to the Greeks, but sought answers based in physical evidence. Italy's Leonardo da Vinci's rendition of the human brain (1508) and Belgium's Andreas Vesalius's (1543) subsequent anatomical drawings not only created precise visual records, but they also began to name specific areas of the brain, creating consistent references and a shared vocabulary for future research. Da Vinci knew what current researchers today still struggle with: Without common terms of reference and vocabulary, it is impossible to compare findings (see Figures 3.1 and 3.2).

FIGURE 3.1
Leonardo da Vinci's rendition of the human brain, 1508

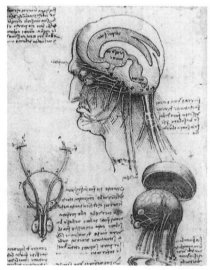

Source: http://www.drawingsofleonardo.org

FIGURE 3.2
Andreas Vesalius's depictions of the human brain, 1543

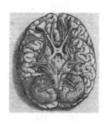

Sources: (a) http://exstaticfiles.wordpress.com/2007/04/andreas-vesalius.gif
(b) http://as.miami.edu/english/wiki105/images/e/e4/AndrerasVesaslius_Bas_of_The_Brain.jpg
(c) htt[://countyway.harvard.edu/chm/rarebooks/exhibits/gilt/images/vesalius.jpg

These creative scientists lived in an exciting era in Europe. "The first half of the seventeenth century saw the emergence of scientific groups whose members gathered to promote discussion and to disseminate the 'new' philosophy," (Becker, 2006, para. 1), which included study of learning and the human brain. In 1664, one of the most complete early versions of the brain was drawn by Christopher Wren (Willis, 1664) (Figure 3.3), who later designed St. Paul's Cathedral in London. It is poignant that the supreme example of human design, the brain, required a world-renowned architect to do justice to its form.

FIGURE 3.3
Christopher Wren's rendition of the human brain, 1664

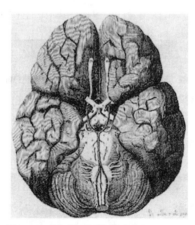

Source: https://eee.uci.edu/clients/bjbecker/NatureandArtifice/willisbrainb.jpg

René Descartes's proclamation *"Cogito, ergo sum"* (I think, therefore I am) in 1637 triggered a new reflection about the role of the individual and his or her mind and understanding of a worldview that has forever influenced Western concepts of education. Thinking, not just being, constituted the definition of one's purpose in the world. This idea implied that maximizing one's individual potential to think, create, and produce intellectually justified one's existence. In 1693, John Locke's *Some Thoughts Concerning Education* established the link between developmental psychology and human development. Locke made calls for a philosophy of education that encouraged a deeper self-regulation of metacognition and learning that continues to impact the way students are taught and how we observe what is learned even today. Locke suggested that a key to good teaching is to help students reflect more about their own thinking processes. By articulating their own mental steps in solving a problem, for example, Locke believed that learners would become better thinkers. This reflective process is a modern cornerstone of critical thinking[84] in which certain habits of mind that help students rehearse such reflective processes are basics of modern quality education.

The 18th and 19th Centuries: Widespread Formal Education

With the exception of the Islamic world, which had distinct academic institutions as early as the 10th century, a common phenomenon around the world was the use of religious institutions as locations for formal education. For the most part, churches and temples served as the first classrooms and, with few exceptions, generally only catered to the elite. Catholic schools were the first formal educational institutions in Norway around 1152, for example, and the Third Lateran Council (1179) officially mandated free education for the poor in England, though the classes were primarily devoted to religious readings. It wasn't until the 1500s, however, that widespread education began; some religious schools were converted into Latin schools (as in Norway and Denmark), and each market town was required to have a school.

Beginning in the 1600s, the trend toward the universalization of education became more democratically available, albeit with several shortcomings. Throughout the 17th century Zen Buddhist temples served as the educational structures in Japan. Similarly, in India in the 18th century, schools and temples were physically one and the same. Reading, writing, arithmetic, theology, law, astronomy, metaphysics, ethics, medical science, and

---

84. For a clear summary of this concept, see Bowell & Kemp (2002) and Facione (2007).

religion were taught to students of all classes in these institutions. Most educational institutions in the United States that were founded between 1640 and 1750 were started by religious denominations. However, beginning in the 1600s, many religious institutions gave way to nondenominational formal education around the world.

In 1633 the Parliament of Scotland approved a tax to provide for public education. Across the Atlantic in the late 1700s, Thomas Paine promoted the idea of free public education, though it wasn't until 1837 that Horace Mann managed to successfully create a tax to support public schools in the United States. In the 1880s public education became the norm in France, and by 1890 Japan also had full compulsory education. In 1919 compulsory and free education became standard in Imperial Russian and the ex-Soviet Union countries. Since 1950 China has had 9 years of compulsory education. Latin America began reforms in the 1960s to require between 6 and 9 years of basic education. In Africa, in 2009, less than 60% of all students were currently enrolled in formal education, despite its growing value in local communities and many countries' commitment to the "Millennium Development Goals"[85] for education, which include compulsory primary school completion as a minimum.

Put in this context it is easy to see how pedagogy, or the art of teaching, has had a relatively short history. The concept of creating formal education and the modern needs that have arisen due to the now varied student body are enormous. Whereas only a few hundred years ago few of our relatives were literate, it is now the norm that students of all socioeconomic and cultural backgrounds attend school. To make the setting more complex, it can be ventured that a wider variety of learning potentials (brains) also enters the modern classroom. When education became the norm, no longer were schools filled with obedient and religiously driven, wealthy students, as in the Middle Ages, but rather, they are now filled with students who are simply "normal" or even those with special needs who never would have attended school a hundred years ago. The evolution of widespread educational access was paralleled by discoveries in neuroscience that formed new beliefs about learning that impacted these more widely diverse classrooms.

Localizationism

Localizationalism is the belief that X skill is located in Y part of the brain. This idea is rooted in early studies, mainly in the 1700–1800s, which sought an association between

---

85. United Nations (2001).

certain parts of the brain and brain functions, as in language being in the left hemisphere. Localizationism implies that if for some reason X is damaged, then Y is lost forever. We now know that this is not necessarily true. However, in the 19th century the focus was on deciphering the map of brain functions; where patterns were found, generalizations about the brain were made. This had some good and other dubious results.

The 18th and 19th centuries were riddled with false convictions about the brain. These included the belief in phrenology, in which the bumps and crevices of the skull were measured to determine strengths and weaknesses of both academic prowess and personality traits.[86] When it was found that external traits of the skull did not reflect intellect, neuroscientists turned to the inner workings of the brain. In the mid-19th and early 20th centuries significant and highly credible new findings about the brain's functionality emerged.

Discoveries related to specific domain functions, such as language by Paul Broca (1862) and Carl Wernicke (1874), a general charting of the brain areas by Korbinian Brodmann (1909), and findings about the role of individual synapses or links between neurons in the brain by Santiago Ramón y Cajal (1911) generated a new and lasting excitement in the field. Broca and Wernicke established that most people (95% of right-handed people and 70% of left-handed people) have two main language areas in their left frontal (Broca) and parietal (Wernicke) lobes (see Figure 3.4). Brodmann devised an elegant system for charting primary visual motor and auditory pathways in the brain (see Figure 3.5). Brodmann's contemporary, Ramón y Cajal, made a lasting impact by showing that the neuron was the basic functional and structural unit in the brain. Each of these discoveries contributed to new definitions of the physical nature of learning and the brain. The turn of the 19th century brought a flood of new scientific theories of learning, including the now famous "nature versus nurture" debate.

The Biology of Learning and the Nature versus Nurture Debate

Just as formal education was getting underway around the world in the late 1800s, Francis Galton, the father of eugenics (1869), sparked the original debate on the nature versus nurture influence on learning and intelligence.[87] Are you who you are, and as intelligent as you are, based on the genes you received from your parents, or based on how you were raised? This question continues to be asked today and is at the root of many educational

---

86. van Wyhe (2006).
87. See Bulmer (2003) for a good recount of this amazing scientific saga.

FIGURE 3.4
Broca and Wernicke's Areas

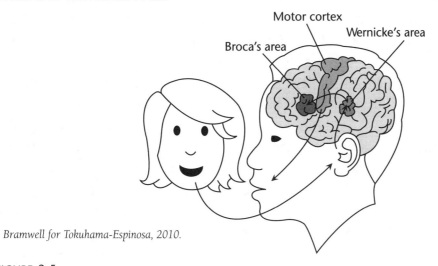

Bramwell for Tokuhama-Espinosa, 2010.

FIGURE 3.5
Brodmann's Areas

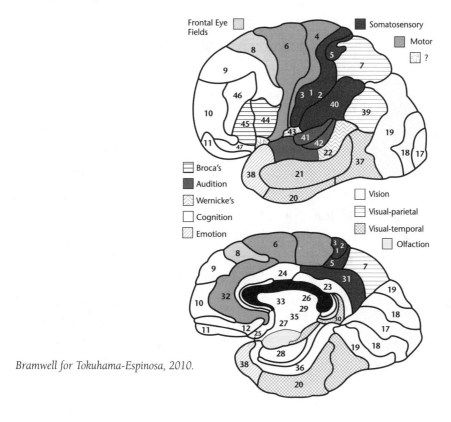

Bramwell for Tokuhama-Espinosa, 2010.

policy decisions. Are schools obliged to support all children, no matter how bright or dull (because it is not their fault, it's their genes; or because it is morally right to do so), and therefore required to invest resources into special education and programs for all learning differences (disabled, challenged, or gifted)? Galton was instrumental in calling attention to the role of biology in learning—a role that remains a major part of MBE science.

The theories of evolutionary psychology and sociobiology were given prominence by Mark Baldwin in the late 1800s in a theory that is known today as the Baldwin Effect, a proposed mechanism for specific evolutionary selection for general learning ability. The Baldwin Effect basically suggested that when learning occurs that is beneficial to the survival of a species, then it would be remembered in the genes passed on to the future descendents. This theory had profound influence on the belief that both biology and experience mutually impact learning outcomes. For example, in her eloquent book *Proust and the Squid*, Maryanne Wolf (2007) illustrates how reading has changed the human brain through dramatic evolutionary processes, a concept that is reinforced by Stanislas Dehaene's (2009) belief in neuronal recycling, or the reuse of evolutionarily older areas of the brain for new needs (as in reading, which has only been required for the past 5000 years or so). By the start of the 1900s there was a rush to link behavior to biology at every turn—for example, in studies of emotion and developmental psychology.

The 1900–1950s: Neurons That Fire Together, Wire Together

Donald Hebb made a daring link between brain science and learning through his ground-breaking book *The Organization of Behavior* (1949). In this book, Hebb wrote about how brain organization relates to behavior and posited the now-famous Hebbian synapse rule, a core of modern neuroscience: Neurons that fire together, wire together. This finding explained in biological terms what psychologists had witnessed for decades in behavior. In classical conditioning, associative learning results when a neutral stimulus is associated with conditioned stimulus, a concept first demonstrated by Ivan Pavlov (who won the 1904 Nobel prize in physiology and medicine for his work on the digestive system) when he discovered the basic principles of conditioning by the simple act of feeding his dogs: He typically rang a bell calling dogs to their food; he realized that soon after the first few rings of a bell, the dogs would begin salivating merely at the sound of the bell, without the food. In Hebb's terms, this was explained by the fact that the stimulus of the bell and the usual delivery of food created neuronal firings linking bell and food. The Hebbian synapse concept is fundamental to our current understanding of plasticity and learning as a whole.

The Hebbian synapse concept also explains anxieties related to learning. For example, if a student relates a negative emotion to a teacher of a certain subject, such as math, he or she may experience math anxiety, independent of the teacher, in the future due to the "wiring" of the negative experience with the subject matter. Although some teachers have begun to experiment with some of these concepts based on psychological models, widespread knowledge and use of the Hebbian synapse concept is still foreign to most teacher training programs. Other psychological theories of cognitive development were more successful in making their way into the classroom, however.

Stages of Cognitive Development

Jean Piaget, a contemporary of Hebb, also made profound contributions to the conceptualization of the new science of teaching and learning found today. Piaget was one of the most renowned developmental psychologists of the 1900s and is still recognized as one of its main figures today. Piaget was originally trained in the areas of biology and philosophy and considered himself a "genetic epistemologist."[88] Throughout his career, Piaget strongly grounded his work in biology and tied it to education.[89] Piaget's research was instrumental in defining four stages of cognitive development (sensory–motor stage, preoperational period, concrete operational stage, and formal operational stage) and also recognized the individual differences in reaching these milestones.

To understand Piaget's contributions, it is important to grasp the way in which he envisioned human development. Piaget perceived human development as a continuum with several sub-elements in each stage. The first of the four stages of development, the sensory–motor stage (0–2 years old), has six sub-stages: (1) simple reflexes; (2) first habits and primary circular reactions; (3) secondary circular reactions; (4) coordination of secondary circular reactions; (5) tertiary circular reactions, novelty, and curiosity; and (6) internalization of schemes.[90] The meticulous division and description of each of these stages can now be correlated to specific changes in the nervous system and particularly in brain development.

---

88. Huitt & Hummel (2003).
89. Piaget was known to have documented his work in a very detail-oriented fashion (see Piaget, 1928 1953, 1955, 1969/2000, 1971).
90. Santrock (1998).

In the second stage of cognitive development Piaget acknowledged two sub-stages: the emergence of a symbolic function (about 2–4 years old) and intuitive thought (about 4–7 years old). These are more complex to correlate to specific neuroscientific findings, but there is growing evidence of the maturation of certain brain areas related to complex thought (forebrain mechanisms) that experience a large amount of growth during these years.

In the third of Piaget's stages (the concrete operational stage), there are several processes, but no sub-stages. The complexity of human thought and development become evident in this stage, and many a neuroscientist has grappled with the implications of this division to date. These processes include:

- *Seriation*, or the ability to sort objects in an order according to size, shape, or any other characteristic;
- *Transitivity*, or the ability to recognize logical relationships or the relative relationship between objects[91];
- *Classification*, or the ability to name and identify sets of objects in terms of their varying characteristics;
- *Decentering*, in which the child approaches the problem from several angles in order to find the right solution;
- *Reversibility*, in which the maturing child comes to understand that numbers or objects can be changed, then returned to their original state;
- *Conservation*, in which the child grasps the idea that quantity, length, or number of items is unrelated to the arrangement or appearance of the object or items (as when water is poured from a short fat cup into a tall slim glass); and,
- The elimination of *egocentrism* and the possibility of becoming empathic (i.e., the ability to view the world from others' perspectives).

The beauty of Piaget's work is that we now know that all of these processes, which a child normally develops before the age of 12, relate to different mental tasks that can, indeed, be isolated in the human brain. That is, the systems needed to conduct seriation, transitivity, classification, etc., are all different (though sometimes overlapping) neural circuits in the brain. This means that they pose individual challenges for students as they develop.

91. Traill (1978).

The fourth stage of Piaget's conception of cognitive development is called the formal operational stage. This stage normally occurs as children move into adolescence (on average, around 13 years old or so) and begin to think more abstractly, which is related to their ability to reason logically and draw on existing information to develop hypothetical suppositions about situations. Piaget noted that an adolescent's verbal problem-solving ability was paralleled by the logical quality of his or her thought at this stage (as opposed to earlier stages when children work by a trial-and-error method). In the formal operations stage, humans begin to use a greater amount of hypothetical–deductive reasoning and systematically deduce or conclude choices as opposed to random guessing. In an interesting example, Piaget suggested that many "first loves" occur during early adolescence principally because teenagers are now able to contemplate possibilities beyond their immediate moment. The formal operations stage begins in adolescence, which explains teenagers' fascination not only with where they came from, but also with what they can possibly be in the future. In the 1960s Piaget was actually closer to the reality of the teenage brain than many modern theories (which suggest that hormones are to blame for their fickle behavior).

FIGURE 3.6
Piaget's Stages of Development

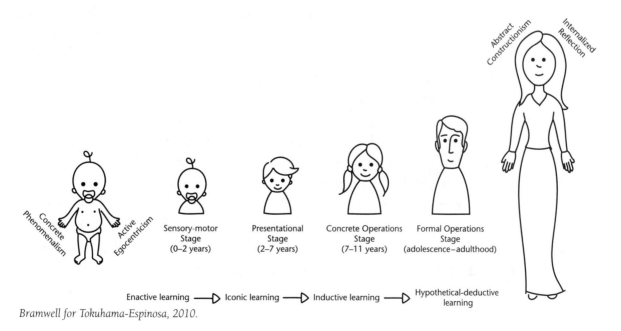

Bramwell for Tokuhama-Espinosa, 2010.

Both the theory of the stages of cognitive development as well as the individual variation with which students go through the stages are core elements of modern MBE science (see Figure 3.6). Piaget's keen observations allowed him to envision how developmentally observable behaviors are linked to changes in the brain over time. Through Piaget's experiments were based on observable behavior, his theories, like Freud's, presumed analogous physical changes in the brain that reflected the changes.

Social–Historical Psychology and Child Development

Another key contributor to the MBE science discipline was Lev Vygotsky, whose novel ideas on cognitive development and learning concepts (e.g., the Zone of *Proximal Development*, in which within a group there will always be someone who knows just a bit more than the others and through a *scaffolding* teaching–learning structure they will instruct one another) were fundamental in shaping modern pedagogy as well as subsequent theories of child development. Two of Vygotsky's core contributions still being debated today are related to cultural mediation and internalization as related to an individual's *"inner voice"* (Vygotsky, 1934). Cultural mediation begs the question as to whether there are "universals" related to human learning, versus the concept that all learning is filtered through one's culture (and therefore unique to each). Vygotsky's inner voice concept questions whether or not thinking is based on the words we know—that is, can we think without words? Both ideas are still points of contention in modern educational theory. Vygotsky's work was translated into curricula structure for school-age children by Vasili Davidov, whose work is also noted as influential in the emerging discipline related to its contributions of social attributes and learning.

One of Vygotsky's disciples, Alexander Luria (1968), made breakthroughs in his writings related to "cultural–historical psychology" and its influences on thought. While short-lived as a sub-discipline of psychology, the conceptual framework devised by these early thought leaders established the foundations for understanding how culture, especially as mediated through language, influences thinking. Luria's second large contribution was documentation of *The Mind of a Mnemonist: A Little Book about a Vast Memory* (Luria, 2006), which was the catalyst for a great number of studies related to the human memory system and questions on how memory impacts learning. Luria's work was important because by documenting the "curse of a flawless, synaesthetic memory"[92] he was able

---

92. Long (2006).

to demonstrate that there are various memory systems in the brain, not just a single entity called "memory." In this work, Luria documents the case of a man who was unable to forget, causing terrible difficulties in his life, such as the inevitable association of random concepts, which distracted him for "normal" exchanges with the people around him. Luria's documentation of memory led to a breakthrough concept for teachers, who began to understand that information could be recorded in different "formats" via distinct neural pathways and that memory is a vast and multilayered system, which can have many different types of flaws.

One extremely fascinating view of memory and different memory systems is related to synesthesia, or the ability to relate different types of information to different senses (e.g., something visual can be remembered through smell or texture; a taste can be remembered through a color or sound). Findings of some of the studies that were sparked by Luria's inspirational work included the acknowledgment that problems with memory can occur during stages of encoding (getting information into the brain), storage (maintaining links to the encoded information), or retrieval (being able to access and use memories stored in the brain). Other studies noted that different memory systems (e.g., short-term vs. long-term) have different, though often overlapping, neural pathways. Jerome Bruner, one of the 20th century's leading cognitive psychologists in educational psychology, lent his skills and insight to the foreword of Luria's work in a reprint in 1987 and helped reinforce the importance of the consideration of memory in all aspects of life and learning (Luria & Brunner, 2006). These contributions from psychology and education were complemented by stunning findings in the neurosciences around the same time.

From the 1960s to the 1980s: Enriched Environments?

In 1958, Mark R. Rosenzweig and colleagues published results of rat experiments that opened a new field of discussion related to the neurobiological basis for behavior and the influence of enriched environments. Building off of Rosenzweig's findings at the University of California, Berkeley, colleague Marian Diamond's work examined differences between rats' brains (dendrites and synaptic growth) based on a comparison of impoverished versus enriched environments.[93] Rosenweig's and Diamond's work started the discussion of how enriched learning environments could enhance neuronal growth in humans and the subsequent debate as to whether increased synaptic growth translated

---

93. For a complete reading on this scientific reflection, see Diamond et al. (1964, 1980, 1987, 1988).

into better learning (see Figure 3.7). As mentioned in an earlier chapter, the authors of the original studies now believe that the "enriched" laboratory environments were actually more like "normal" rat environments (i.e., sewers), which does not prove that enriched environments are better, but rather that poor environments are worse than normal environments.[94] Despite this new knowledge, there is a million-dollar industry dedicated to training parents and teachers to design "enriched" environments.[95]

FIGURE 3.7
Enriched Rat Environments and Synaptic Growth

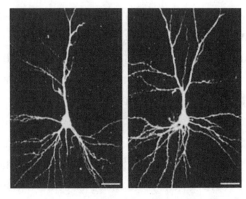

Source: Barbro, Johansson, and Belichenko (2001), *Environmental Enrichment on Intact and Postischemic Rat Brain.*

William Greenough, in turn, built off of Diamond's work as he explored how experience affects the developing and the mature brain.[96] Greenough understood that plasticity, commonly known in the field today but new a dozen years ago, related to the brain's capacity to change and build new synapses with experience. We know that "synapses form in situations in which animals are learning; synapses typically do not form as a result of non-learning-related neural activity"[97]; therefore, more synaptic activity is an indication of learning. His current work focuses "upon cellular mechanisms underlying learning and memory and other brain information storage processes"[98] using his knowledge of how plasticity works.

The discussion about what constitutes an "enriched environment" continues today and is accompanied by a vibrant debate as to whether babies and children should or

---

94. Reported in Diamond (1997, 2001b).
95. Reported in Hall (2005) and the OECD (2002).
96. Greenough (1987).
97. Greenough (n.d.). Available online at *http://www.psych.uiuc.edu/people/showprofile.php?id=61.*
98. Ibid.

should not be sent to early stimulation classes. As Greenough and others showed, while there is no doubt that enriched environments change the brain and that new learning occurs, the main discussion related to enrichment revolves around the definition of the term: what may be enrichment to one person (or rat) may not be enrichment to another. Enrichment is discussed in the following chapters; what is important to note here is that the excitement in the emerging discipline at the end of the 1960s led to a number of academic initiatives.

The Pre-MBE Science Stage

Dartmouth College's doctorate program in psychological and brain science was started in 1968,[99] and Dartmouth's undergraduate educational degree in educational neuroscience is also one of the oldest in the nation, founded in 1990.[100] The Dartmouth program continues to grow today as more and more applicants seek academic programs that promote MBE science principles. Both the undergraduate and graduate programs merged knowledge bases from psychology and neuroscience and subsequently education before others recognized the truly complementary nature of the fields. Dartmouth was an early starter; most other programs did not formally begin until the early 2000s.

A number of academic researchers began explicitly linking brain functioning to learning and education starting in the 1970s. Michael Posner, author of some 280 books and articles on attention and memory, wrote his earliest works beginning in the 1970s. Posner has been a key contributor to the continual evolution of the discipline of MBE science, and his most recent work has been fundamental in bridging psychology and neuroscience for the application in education. The work at Dartmouth and by people such as Michael Posner in the 1970s came principally from developmental neuropsychology and can be called a "pre-MBE stage."

Between 1973 and 1979 there was a rise in interest in defining and promoting educational neuropsychology, another forerunner to MBE science.[101] The discipline of educational neuropsychology seeks to merge education, neuroscience, and psychology, but unlike MBE science, emphasizes the study of learning rather than teaching. For teachers, educational neuropsychology was a leap forward in merging the common goals of education with those of developmental psychology in the school setting, but still did not serve

99. Dartmouth (2008).
100. Ibid.
101. Representative works of this period can be found in Kral & Maclean (1973); O'Keefe & Nadel (1978); Selye (1974).

teachers' needs completely (how to teach better). Educational neuropsychology was an improvement over simple developmental psychology because neuroscientific studies were given more prominence. The lack of neuroscientific support for some of the studies in developmental psychology meant than many studies were about the "mind" rather than the "brain," which some argued detracted from their applicability in teaching. However, educational neuropsychology is quickly giving way to MBE science at the time of this writing for two primary reasons. First, as noted above, MBE science studies teaching, not just learning processes, and second, due to the syntax of the term *educational neuropsychology*, education and neuroscience are considered a sub-field of psychology—whereas in MBE science there is equal input from all three parent fields. Several studies in this pre-MBE stage considered life skills, such as the role of motivation or emotions, and how they impact learning.

Emotions and Learning

One of the first links between emotions and learning was introduced in the language context in the form of the *affective filter hypothesis*[102], which basically suggests that how we feel influences what we are able to learn. That is, emotions impact how, what, and why we learn. Currently this hypothesis is correlated with amygdalar neuroimaging studies that, in some cases, show how stress and emotional states influence learning. What is important for teachers to accept is that emotions impact decision-making and that decision-making is core to learning. The role of emotions and their impact on learning is discussed in more detail in Chapter 6.

In the 1960s, American public education went into an existential crisis. Myron Lieberman's book *The Future of Public Education* was representative of a general review of core concepts related to educational practice, including teacher education of the basics of learning. The National Education Association, the largest professional organization of teachers in the United States, began to take interest in the application of neuroscience findings to the classroom in the late 1970s. In 1978, *Brain Research and Learning* (National Education Association, 1978), and Chall and Mirsky's work *Education and the Brain* (1978) were both published. These two books were serious and well-researched attempts to integrate neuroscience and education and rode on the heels of many breakthroughs about human learning. This was to be the beginning of a general popularization of information

---

102. Dulay & Burt (1977).

on neuroscientific research for teachers and a general marriage of neuroscience, education, and psychology, and it came at a time when policy makers began to focus on reaching all students in a more equitable way. How can we serve not only the highest-achieving students, but also respond to the needs of the lower- achieving ones? America and many other countries around the world began to realize that a chain is only as strong as its weakest link; public education had to do more to reach all of the members of society.

The 1970s saw a huge surplus of teachers in the United States as budget cuts meant that classes grew larger and only core subject-area teachers were hired. The larger class sizes meant less individualized attention for students, but also drew focus to attention-related difficulties on the whole. Discoveries about neurotransmitters related to attention mechanisms in the brain led to the introduction of Ritalin in 1971, which was meant to aid general treatment of minimal brain dysfunction, which manifested itself in the form of hyperkinetic activity.[103] The end of the 1970s witnessed the crystallization of many concepts about learning related to attention and memory, and to other areas as well. Perhaps two of the most important developments emerged from Michael Gazzaniga's call to bring functional neuroscience to the forefront of teaching in his text *Neuropsychology: Handbook of Behavioral Neurobiology*, and Michael Posner's move toward the integration of neurosciences and psychology for the benefit of understanding learning in a more holistic fashion.[104] Both of these efforts tried to put a more "utilitarian" face on neuroscientific findings and brought the information out of laboratories and into classroom settings. The back-to-basics approach in public education was mirrored in the emphasis of what was considered important in the science lab; if it could not be applied in authentic settings, there was less funding available for research. Gazzaniga's and Posner's contributions in the late 1970s to the applicability of science findings for classroom became norms for future studies, and their earlier works remain important for researchers today.

Some Pioneering Institutions

Three pioneering neuroscience societies were also formalized in the late 1970s. In 1977, the Japan Neuroscience Society was founded as "an academic organization of scientists who study the brain and nervous system and wish to publish their findings in order to promote the welfare and culture of humans."[105] Also in 1977, the Centre for Neuroscience

---

103. Clements (1966).
104. See Gazzaniga (1979); Gazzaniga, Steen, & Volpe (1979); Posner (1989).
105. See the Japan Neuroscience Society website (*www.jnss.org/english/index_e.html*).

(CNS) was established as an institute of Flinders University in Adelaide in South Australia, and was "the first such multidisciplinary centre in the neurosciences to be established in an Australian university."[106] CNS members were instrumental in establishing the Australian Neuroscience Society later in 1979. These societies promoted new findings about the brain that were fueled by growing information from improved imaging techniques. These Austro–Asian institutions were early leaders; most other such institutions came along in the late 1990s.

Neuroimaging Boosts Knowledge about the Brain

Technology funding was given a boost in response to the first modern computer developments in the 1970s. The use of automated robots on assembly lines in Japan in the 1970s triggered new discoveries in other fields, such as medicine. In the 1980s improvements in neuroimaging and eventually the development of in vivo imaging techniques enabled observation of the learning brain, providing insights into the brain's perceptual, cognitive, and emotional functions, with clear relevance for education. Despite the existence of electroencephalographs (EEGs) since 1929 and early computerized axial tomography (CAT) scans and magnetic resonance imaging (MRI) (both 1973), neuroimaging did not reach broad use until the introduction of positron emission tomography (PET) scans in 1979, transcranial magnetic stimulation (TMS) in 1985, and functional magnetic resonance imaging (fMRI) in 1990, when there was an explosion of studies. With more refined neuroimaging tools, more and more work was done on healthy patients, not only those who had suffered traumas or lesions. Much of the earlier work with brain imaging techniques on healthy patients focused on the areas of language and attention. The excitement over increased empirical evidence on learning mechanisms triggered further interest from teacher practitioners in education.

Writings and Early Attempts at MBE Science

The first dissertation on MBE science was written in 1981 (O'Dell, 1981), entitled *Neuroeducation: Brain Compatible Learning Strategies*. O'Dell was ahead of his time and probably unaware that his visionary view of the teaching and learning process would become the norm 30 years later. Speculation about neural mechanisms involved with cognition and

---

106. See Flinders University website (*http://www.flinders.edu.au/*) by Professor Simon Brookes.

consideration of applications to education began in earnest in the early 1980s.[107] The implications of selective brain research on the philosophy of education[108] also hinted at the first considerations of what is known today as *neuroethics*: how choices are made with new knowledge about brain functions. The link to educational practice was encouraged further by the attempt to label the emerging learning science as "applied educational psychology" in the early 1980s.[109] It can be speculated that the reason this title did not enjoy popular support is due to the lack of neuroscientific backing used to support claims.

> *"Education is discovering the brain and that's about the best news there could be. . . . . Anyone who does not have a thorough, holistic grasp of the brain's architecture, purposes, and main ways of operating is as far behind the times as an automobile designer without a full understanding of engines."*
> —Leslie Hart, *Human Brain and Human Learning* (1983/1999, p. xi)

Two popular books for educators that were published at this time were Howard Gardner's *Frames of Mind* (1983) and Leslie Hart's *Human Brain and Human Learning* (1983). These two books are considered influential in educational circles because they marked the start of interest in the brain–learning connection in the teaching profession. Though Gardner was inspired by his work with "shattered brains" at Boston Veteran's Hospital in the 1970s,[110] he did not claim that his *theory of multiple intelligences* related to specific brain areas, nor that it was supported by neuroscience, though he has clearly documented that at least some of the intelligences (language, music, arithmetic) can be isolated by a neuronal lesion. Gardner's work struck a cord with teachers, parents, and educational psychologists because he challenged the accepted view of "intelligence" and, in doing so, Gardner invited a general questioning of what we believe to be true about all educational measurements. In contrast, Hart's work was, indeed, focused on how the brain learns. Hart was one of the first to call attention to the *lack of attention* given to the brain in educational practice. Hart said that designing educational experiences without an understanding of the brain was like designing a glove without an understanding of the

---

107. See Posner (1981).
108. See McDonnold (1981).
109. Gaddes (1983).
110. See Gardner's first book (1974), *The Shattered Mind*, for a better understanding of how his theory evolved. Also see Battro and Denham's work (2007) on digital intelligence (*La Inteligencia Digital*), which gives a good overview of the definition of intelligence in this broader perspective.

human hand (1983), and he called on teachers to become savvier in their practice. Hart's work was monumental in emphasizing the "why" as well as the "how" of teaching. If there is one book that likely laid the groundwork for a new genre in writing about the brain and learning, it was most likely Hart's.

Connectivity, Cognitivism, and Constructivist Models

In parallel with the new view of the brain and learning offered by Hart, and the new understanding of intelligence proposed by Gardner, the mid-1980s marked the beginning of discussion on the *connectivist model* in psychology.[111] These models began to offer a more sophisticated view of the brain as a complex integration of various systems (thus the connectivist idea), rather than just the simple localization theories of the past (which believed that X function was located in Y spot of all brains). The 1980s also noted a shift from behavioral studies in educational psychology to those of *cognitivism* and constructivist theories. The general idea of cognitivism is that mental functions can and should be explained by evidence of brain activities that can be measured through experimentation. On the other hand, the *constructivist* model of learning, often attributed to Piaget, suggests that people construct their own knowledge based on their experiences. Viewed together, cognitivism and constructivist models of learning pointed to the increasingly complex understanding of how human mental capacity grows over the course of one's lifetime, and how this growth can be measured both in relative and absolute terms. Since this early movement away from *behaviorism* (the belief that all things organisms do can and should be regarded as behaviors) toward cognitivism, psychology took a turn toward the hard, rather than soft, social sciences. The interdisciplinary view of learning and its natural counterpart of teaching were firmly established in the 1980s.

New Organizations

The interdisciplinary nature of MBE science was reflected in the mission statements of many new organizations in the 1980s. In 1983 the Economic and Social Research Council (ESRC) in the United Kingdom and the Medical Research Council (MRC) were founded to encourage "innovative and multidisciplinary research proposals that link basic or

---

111. See McClelland, Feldman, Adelson, Bower, & McDermott (1986).

health-related neuroscience to social factors and social behaviour."[112] The ESRC focuses on "links between the mind, brain, innate traits, society, culture and behaviour, whether normal or abnormal."[113] The social research angle promoted by these groups was complemented by a return to an appreciation of the natural sciences in the mid-1980s. The influence of genetics and heritability on general intelligence refocused attention on the roles that both nature and nurture play in learning,[114] maintaining a firm spotlight on the link between biology and pedagogy.

The Birth of Neuroscience

Between 1984 and 1989 the birth of neuroscience began with the projection of the new field,[115] and then books about neuroscience itself.[116] For some, neuroscience, rather than educational neuropsychology, is the true birth mother of MBE science. Neuroscience was one of the first truly transdisciplinary fields, and some authors, such as Gardner (1987), included fields as obvious as psychology and as distant as linguistics, artificial intelligence, and philosophy. Neuroscience gave theorists a large conceptual umbrella under which they could posit hypotheses about the biological foundations of thinking at all levels. The emergence of neuroscience was not lost on educators, who quickly unified around the new information.

Education's Interest in the Brain

Whereas education had been discussed in social–political terms during the greater part of the 1960s and 1970s, in the 1980s the focus changed from "equity" to "excellence,"[117] and in doing so, there was a stronger emphasis on learning mechanisms in the brain more than on legislation. The Brain, Neurosciences, and Education Special Interest Group (SIG) of the American Educational Research Association (AERA) was formed in 1988. This SIG of the AERA was originally formed as the Psychophysiology and Education SIG and is the oldest organizational entity specifically dedicated to linking research in the neurosciences and education in the United States. It was once the only organizational group in the world

---

112. See the ESRC Society Today website (*http://www.esrcsocietytoday.ac.uk/ESRCInfoCentre/about/CI/CP/Social_Sciences/issue 63/neuroscience.aspx*).
113. Ibid.
114. See Fancher (1985) for details.
115. Gazzaniga (1984) and Posner (1984).
116. See Gardner (1987) and Posner (1989).
117. Brown Foundation for Educational Equity, Excellence, and Research E-notes.com (2009).

that hosted an annual peer-reviewed venue for authors to present papers linking research and theory in the neurosciences and education. The purpose of the current SIG remains to promote an understanding of neuroscience research within the educational community, and it achieves this goal by promoting neuroscience research that has implications for educational practice and by providing a forum for the issues and controversies connecting these fields.[118] In many ways the AERA's established focus on the psychophysiology of learning was slightly ahead of its time when founded. Shortly after the SIG's founding, an avalanche of findings marked the Decade of the Brain.

The Early 1990s: The Decade of the Brain

The *Decade of the Brain* (1990–1999) spurred the development of thousands of new findings and dozens of theories about the brain and learning. Two basic types of learning theories were strengthened at this time: modular, domain specific versus global theories.

Modular, domain-specific theories mainly focus on explaining the neural mechanisms of skills such as mathematics,[119] reading,[120] attention,[121] and memory.[122] These reviews tend to be very precise studies of very specific skills, such as how the brain perceives phonemes, or how a specific aspect of the brain is responsible for human face memories. These are discussed in further detail in Chapter 6 on Topics in MBE Science.

Global theories of learning provide overarching beliefs about how the brain learns best. Kurt Fischer and others, for example, recognized the value of neuroscience research in education and began to envision an independent field at this time. Cognitive neuroscientists such as Bruce McCandliss and Sally Shaywitz and researchers at the U.S. National Institutes of Health (NIH) and the U.S. National Institute of Child Health and Human Development (NICHD) began doing experiments in neuroscience labs that had more direct applications to education based on global theories of how the brain worked in terms of teaching and learning experiences.

The 1990s were also the beginning of the move to bring more accountability to American education. Who was responsible for good (or bad) educational efforts? Were the states individually responsible for the country as a whole? How about teachers? Account-

---

118. AERA Brain, Neurosciences, and Education (2008).
119. For good examples, see Dehaene (1999a, 1999b).
120. See Klein & McMullen (1999).
121. For exemplary work, see Posner & Rothbart (1998a, 1998b).
122. For an example, see Anderson (1995).

ability measures put a great deal of pressure on local educational systems to find the root causes of success or failure in their school system. What began as finger-pointing from the macro-level eventually reached the most micro-level possible: the individual student and his or her brain. Many states began taking a hard look at their local populations and considered how certain characteristics, such as low socioeconomic status, poverty, poor nutrition, and lack of early educational support impacted the general learning levels achieved by their students. Even well-off states realized that, once again, the chain was only as strong as its weakest link. Educational interventions moved from the state level to the individual, which created the demand for increasingly personalized measures.

Early attempts by scientists to move closer to teacher-friendly information and products began to escalate in the early 1990s. Experimental psychologist Paula Tallal, originally at Cambridge University (now at Rutgers), and neurophysiologist Michael Merzenich, originally from Johns Hopkins University (now at the University of California at San Francisco), began organizing brain-based conferences for educators through their Scientific Learning Corporation (best known for the Fast ForWord language program). These meetings resonated well with teachers and school districts alike who clamored for interventions that were closer to their realm—that of the individual student. Teacher enthusiasm led to more innovations in the classroom. Though some of this work was of high quality, in some cases "innovation" was not tempered by reality checks in research, and in others it meant promoting neuromyths.

International Cooperation in MBE Science and New Institutions

The early 1990s also saw international, interdisciplinary cooperation in the discipline increase. In 1990 the James S. McDonnell Foundation, based in St. Louis, and the Pew Charitable Trusts of Philadelphia, helped found the Centre for Neuroscience at the University of Oxford. The Centre "encourages work in all areas of neuroscience across all relevant disciplines and embraces research on experimental, theoretical, and clinical studies of perceptual analysis, memory, language, and motor control, including philosophical approaches to cognition."[123] In 1994 The Max Planck Institute for Human Cognitive and Brain Science (MPI CBS) in Germany was founded and "revolves around human cognitive abilities and cerebral processes, with a focus on language, music, and action."[124] According to the MPI website: "In 1917, the first interdisciplinary brain research institute

123. Oxford Centre for Cognitive Neuroscience website (*www.cogneuro.ox.ac.uk/centre/about.html*).
124. Max Planck Institute website (*www.mpg.de/english/portal/index.html*).

in the world was established in Munich, the *'Deutsche Forschungsanstalt für Psychiatrie'* (German Research Institute of Psychiatry)." Both of these centers are pioneers in the study of neuroscience and its application in education. For the first time there was significant funding available to focus on the brain in educational settings. However, with increased research and formalization of the discipline came doubts about the lofty goal to link education and neuroscience, and along with these doubts, a good deal of skepticism.

Late 1990s: Healthy Skepticism of the Emerging Discipline of MBE Science

Healthy skepticism of the discipline was flamed by John T. Bruer's article "Education and the Brain: A Bridge Too Far" (1997), which was followed by a discussion of the educational relevance of research in neuroscience by James Byrnes and Nathan Fox in two seminal articles: "The Educational Relevance of Research in Cognitive Neuroscience" (1998a) and "Minds, Brains, and Education: Part II. Responding to the Commentaries" (1998b). Byrnes and Fox's articles and the peer commentary that followed stimulated the beginning of a vibrant debate about what could and should link neuroscience and education. Educators who agreed with Bruer (1997) noted that teachers could not translate neuroscience research directly into practice. Many of those in agreement with Bruer believed that teachers should rather embrace cognitive psychology to enhance their understanding of learning or other preexisting fields.[125] Calls for "making neuroscience educationally relevant"[126] and the need for "creating bidirectional collaborations between educational psychology and neuroscience"[127] were numerous at the end of the 1990s. Faculty seminars, such as the one held in 1998 at the University of Cambridge, considered the implications of neuroscience for education,[128] and more and more teachers began to become more directly involved in MBE, rather than simply being blind consumers of neuroscience publications, which often did not have direct application in the classroom.

Educational Use of MBE Tools

In 1998 the Education Commission of the States published a consideration of how neuroscience could have educational policy implications. There was a boom in pedagogical rethinking at the end of the 1990s, including attempts to unite teachers around a set of accepted

125. For an example, see Caine, Nummela-Caine, & Crowell (1999).
126. This is the title of an article by Berninger & Corina (1998).
127. This is the title of an article by Schunk (1998).
128. For documentation of this event, see Geake & Cooper (2003).

best-practice teaching elements[129] and curriculum/lesson planning.[130] While these methods were not the product of neuroscientific research, they knowingly or not applied MBE standards, thus giving them credibility beyond the field of education. This point is very important because it makes the distinction between information *produced* by the new MBE discipline and information that is used in the field of education that adheres to MBE principles. For example, it is important to note that curriculum planning in Wiggins and McTighe's *Understanding by Design* is structured around attention spans and memory, two aspects that are fundamental to MBE science, though the authors do not claim to base their theory on MBE principles.

Some teachers began hearing certain messages from neuroscience, such as the belief that there are no two brains alike, and began formulating their practice around these neuroscientific findings. For example, there was a movement to differentiate instruction based on the recognition of individual learning abilities and needs.[131] One of the most influential books related to learning was sponsored by the National Research Council[132] and updated in 2003 by Bransford, Brown, and Cocking. Their *How People Learn* (2003) remains an invaluable reference for teachers. Other high-quality research was also produced at this time, resulting in teaching interventions that were proven in the lab and applied in classrooms and homes around the United States. For example, new neuroscientifically based reading curricula, such as the Fast ForWord,[133] and RAVE-O (retrieval, automaticity, vocabulary, engagement with language, orthography),[134] were developed by neuroscientists and have been applied in the classroom successfully since the late 1990s (see Chapter 7). The initial evaluations of these programs indicated very favorable results, demonstrating that collaborative endeavors between neuroscientists and educators can, indeed, prove fruitful. By the late 1990s global learning theories sought to offer an overarching explanation of the human teaching–learning process. One such concept was the universal design for learning (UDL), which is "defined by research on diversity, brain-based research, multiple intelligences, and the flexibility of digital media," (Gray Smith, 2008, p. vii). UDL is meant to guide the creation of "flexible learning environments" that are conducive to differentiated learning structures in the classroom. UDL not only joins neuroscience and education but also integrated technology as well as having an eye toward the psychological well-being of all students in the classroom.

129. This extremely important pedagogical feat was conducted by Zemelman, Daniels, & Hyde (1998).
130. The most important attempt in this area that coincides with MBE science is that of Wiggins and McTighe (1998) in their groundbreaking book *Understanding by Design*.
131. An excellent example of work in this area is Carol Ann Tomlinson's work (1999).
132. Bransford, Brown, Cocking, Donovan, Pellegrino, & National Research Council (Eds.) (1999).
133. For more details on this program, see Chapter 7 and articles by Gillam (1999); Lavin (2005); Loeb, Store, & Fey (2001); Scientific Learning Corporation (n.d.).
134. See Wolf (2008) for a complete explanation.

Popular Press Tries to Fill the Void with Varying Degrees of Success

Teacher interest in the brain grew, but few professional programs in universities offered courses in this discipline, and thus popular-press books about brain-based learning flourished to fill the void at the end of the 1990s. One of the best selling books of all time aimed at teachers, *Teaching with the Brain in Mind*, was published in its first edition at this time.[135] In 1999 the first Learning Brain EXPO in San Diego gathered over 700 teachers and scientists, attesting to the popularity of anything labeled *brain-based* at the time.

The first "Learning & the Brain Conference" took place on the Harvard University and MIT campuses in 1997 and sought to elevate the caliber of teacher–neuroscientist encounters and began formal meetings at the end of the 1990s. The 26th conference in this series took place in May 2010 and drew over 2,000 people in attendance, mostly educators, pointing to an increasing interest by teachers in the emerging discipline. The current conference series is cosponsored by the Mind, Brain, and Education Program at Harvard Graduate School of Education, the School of Education at Johns Hopkins University, the Comer School Development Program (Yale University School of Medicine), the Neuroscience Research Institute (University of California, Santa Barbara), the School of Education at Stanford University, the Center for the Study of Learning at Georgetown University, the Dana Alliance for Brain Initiatives, the Cognitive Control and Development Lab (University of California, Berkeley), the National Association of Elementary School Principals, the National Association of Secondary School Principals, and others. The wide range of high-quality sponsors of this conference series demonstrates a deep interest by learning institutions to incorporate more neuroscience understanding into their teacher education.

The growth in publications during the 1990s shows the impact that the Decade of the Brain had on encouraging research in the discipline, as well as the great impact that technology has played in providing continually improved means of observing healthy, functioning human brains. By 2010 the important work directly related to MBE science—rather than that derived from the parent fields of neuroscience, psychology, or pedagogy—was numerous, signaling growing interest, research, and application of concepts in the emerging discipline. However, many questioned the quality of the information to which teachers were being exposed.

135. Jensen (1998b).

New Academic Programs in MBE Science

In the late 1990s many formal associations were launched around the emerging discipline in order to try and put parameters on quality-control questions. Cornell University's Sackler Institute for Developmental Psychobiology was founded in 1998 and has increasingly focused on educational neuroscience. Across the Atlantic, the Belgian Society for Neuroscience was founded in the same year, showing that the interest in the brain and learning was, indeed, an international phenomenon. Academic programs also began to grow at this time. After several years of planning (1997–2001) Harvard University launched its Master's Program in Mind, Brain, and Education in 2001–2002. In a like fashion, the University of Cambridge's Program in Psychology and Neuroscience in Education started in 2004. The Transfer Centre for Neuroscience and Learning in Ulm, Germany (2004), Bristol University's Centre for Neuroscience and Education (2005), and the start of The Learning Lab in Denmark (2005) were all landmark beginnings in an attempt to structure the emerging discipline. Other programs available in MBE science by 2005 included those at the University of Texas at Arlington, the University of Southern California, Beijing Normal University, and Southeast University in Nanjing.

The 2000s: (Mis)Interpretations of Neuroscience in Education

From 2000 to 2005 there was a refinement of knowledge about the developmental processes of learning,[136] which led to a proliferation of neuroscientific information written for and by educators.[137] While some educators shared measured, quality advice to teachers, popular press writers promoted commercially attractive but neuroscientifically inaccurate claims. For example, discussions about *right-brained children in a left-brained world,*[138] or guides on how to use *right-brain styles for conquering clutter, mastering time, and reaching your goals,*[139] which were popular in the 1990s, continued to be bought in the thousands, as in the case of *Boost Your Brain Power Week by Week: 52 Techniques to Make You Smarter.*[140] This easy acceptance of false information earned many teachers a bad reputation in hard science circles. Teachers were accused of looking for "quick fixes" rather than respected as quality researchers themselves. This poor reputation led to the rejection

136. An excellent example of this can be found in Posner, Rothbart, Farah, & Bruer (2001).
137. Examples of these kinds of work include Jensen (2006a); Levine (2000); Sousa (2000); Weiss (2000a); Westwater & Wolfe (2000); Wolfe (2001a); Zull (2002).
138. Freed & Parsons (1998).
139. Luhmkuhl (1993).
140. Lucas (2006).

of the label "brain-based education" because it was associated with many false claims about the brain and learning.

Cutting-Edge Technology

Brain imaging technology took a leap at the turn of the century with Hideaki Koizumi's development of Optical Topography™, which was announced in 1995 and commercialized by Hitachi Medical Corporation in 2001 as "a safe, patient-friendly brain imaging technique that uses light to measure hemodynamic changes in the brain."[141] This technology was revolutionary in that "there is no need for a special measuring environment or patient restraint during examinations, [so] brain functions can be measured in a natural state."[142] This technology made it possible to image brain functions of babies, for example, previously thought impossible, which opened a myriad of possible "application[s] in studies of learning and education."[143] This technological advance was a huge stepping-stone along the path toward better links between the laboratory and the classroom. Koizumi's invention is a great move towards moving laboratory accuracy into realistic classroom settings.

FIGURE 3.8
Hideaki Koizumi and Hitachi's New Brain Imaging Technology: Optical Topography

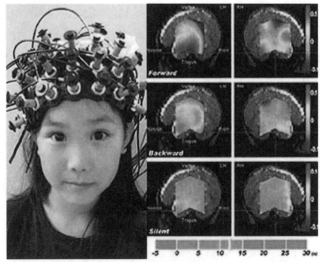

Source: World Press Report of Hitachi Brain Machine Interface.

141. Hitachi (2008).
142. Ibid.
143. Ibid.

The Birth of a New Discipline: MBE Science

It can be said that the MBE discipline was "born" in several different places at once, all across the globe. At the turn of the 21st century formal attempts to unify interdisciplinary concepts in learning and teaching were numerous. In 2000 the Australian National Neuroscience Facility was founded to synthesize and integrate various institutional findings in order to elevate the level of neuroscience and education research. In 2000 the Neurosciences India Group was also founded with the mission to "empower through education" by pursuing cutting-edge research on learning. Both realized the usefulness of MBE research for classroom purposes. Many universities, such as the University of Melbourne in its Mind, Brain and Behaviour forum series, led global reflection on the relationship between intelligence and education from a neuroscientific perspective.[144]

Some of the earliest formal organizations promoting MBE beliefs around the world included INSERM's (French National Institute of Health and Medical Research) Cognitive Neuroimaging Unit in France (2001), and the Oxford Neuroscience Education Forum (2001) in the United Kingdom. But perhaps the greatest leader in this movement was the consorted effort of the Organisation for Economic Co-operation and Development (OECD), which conducted three international conferences at this time to synthesize opinions and concerns and to design agendas for research in the emerging discipline at the intersection of neuroscience, psychology, and education. These conferences took place in New York (2000), Granada, Spain (2001), and Tokyo (2001) and served to identify leaders, as well as the major challenges facing them. The 400th anniversary meeting of the Pontifical Academy of Sciences in November 2003 also focused on mind, brain, and education and provided historical context for understanding the significant changes in education that would result from the birth of this new learning science.

Government Efforts to Unite the Brain and Learning Initiatives

Several government programs related to the emerging discipline started in the early 2000s as well. The Japan Research Institute of Science and Technology (2001) and the subsequent creation of the RIKEN Institute in Japan (2002) emphasized flexible, interdisciplinary research about the brain and learning. At the end of 2002, the Dutch Science Council, in consultation with the Dutch Ministry of Education, Culture and Science, set up the Brain and Learning Committee. The Dutch Science Council undertook initiatives

---

144. For a more complete history on this entity, see Geake (2000).

to stimulate an active exchange among brain scientists, cognitive scientists, and educational scientists about educational practices. This exchange culminated in a book of state-of-the-art findings, *Learning to Know the Brain* (Jolles, 2005). The trend toward applying neuroscientific concepts in educational settings was paralleled by an increasingly receptive society, eager for new tools to combat problems in education.

The First International Society Related to MBE Science

In 2004 the formation of the International Mind, Brain, and Education Society (IMBES) was announced at the conference on Usable Knowledge in Mind, Brain, and Education at Harvard University. Since its inception, IMBES has held increasingly larger society meetings, a fact that speaks to the willingness of members to wear the MBE "hat," as opposed to remaining solely in their field of formation (as educational psychologists, cognitive neuroscientists, or otherwise). In 2005 the Mexican Society for the Neurosciences was founded, demonstrating the spread of MBE values in places other than Europe, Japan, and the United States. This was followed by an innovative doctorate program in the same year: The Joint International Neuroscience PhD Program united various world perspectives on the emerging discipline and was sponsored by the University of Bologna (Italy), Université Claude Bernard (Lyon, France), University College of London (U.K.), University of Bangor (Wales, U.K.), and Wake Forest University, School of Medicine (North Carolina, U.S.A.). Innovations in the discipline began to snowball by 2010s.

The New Challenge: Transdisciplinary Communication

These various initiatives converged to create the global transdisciplinary discipline of MBE science. Between 2004 and 2006 many concrete suggestions circulated about how to improve interdisciplinary communication in the emerging discipline.[145] Activists promoting a formal union called attention to the lack of common vocabulary and the challenges different worldviews placed on advancements in the discipline. This challenge was faced, head on, by a handful of professionals who studied within two, if not all three, of the parent disciplines (some of their suggestions are found in Chapter 9). An increasing number of individuals who were formally trained in both pedagogy and neuroscience began to publish work that is acceptable to neuroscientists, useful to educators, and with

---

145. Some of the most convincing and articulate of these arguments can be found in Ansari (2005a); Geake (2005a); Goswami (2004, 2005a, 2005b); Howard-Jones (2005); Wunderlich, Bell, & Ford (2005).

an appeal to psychologists as well. Usha Goswami and Judy Willis are examples of neuro-scientists-turned-educators in the new profession of MBE science.[146] Their expertise on the brain and their clear and coherent friendly writing styles brought many a teacher to the MBE flock. Similarly, Patricia Wolfe and David Sousa went from teacher status to MBE experts. They, too, provide coherent and easy-to-read evidence-based information to teachers and help neuroscientists view learning problems in the more practical light of the classroom setting.

Institutes and organizations devoted exclusively to the goals of the emerging discipline continued to grow, as with the Oxford University Institute for the Future of the Mind (2006), evidence of the continual formalization of the discipline. The short but elegant book, *The Birth of a Learning Science* (OECD, 2007), added to the global recognition of a new discipline as a shared view by the 30 OECD member countries (Australia, Austria, Belgium, Canada, Czech Republic, Denmark, Finland, France, Germany, Greece, Hungary, Iceland, Ireland, Italy, Japan, Korea, Luxembourg, Mexico, Netherlands, New Zealand, Norway, Poland, Portugal, Slovak Republic, Spain, Sweden, Switzerland, Turkey, United Kingdom, United States). In a landmark event, the new discipline of MBE science launched the first issue of the international *Mind, Brain, and Education Journal* in March 2007, thanks to efforts by Kurt Fischer and David Daniel. This scholarly journal managed what few publications before had done: Establish a readership that included cognitive neuroscientists, teachers, and educational psychologists all in one.

Uniting the Discipline: Teachers, Psychologists, and Neuroscientists Working Together

Starting about 2007 there were many concerted efforts to further integrate teachers into the research process through conferences and society meetings, as with Sue Pickering and Paul Howard-Jones's *Educator's Views on the Role of Neuroscience in Education: Findings from a Study of UK and International Perspectives* (2007), and the first International Mind, Brain, and Education Society conference in 2007 in Fort Worth, Texas, organized by Marc Schwartz and the Southwest Center for MBE at the University of Texas at Arlington. Developmental psychology, neuroscience, and learning theory became a more common combination in publications such as *Human Behavior, Learning, and the Developing Brain: Typical Development* (Coch, Fischer, & Dawson, 2007), and *The Jossey-Bass Reader on the*

---

146. Excellent examples of this interdisciplinary approach can be found in Goswami (2006); Willis (2006).

Brain and Learning (Wiley, 2008). The second conference of the International Mind, Brain, and Education Society was held in Philadelphia in May 2009, with membership steadily on the rise. With both publications and society meeting attendance increasing, it seems that MBE professional formation is growing. With increased acceptance, however, comes an increased responsibility. Starting around 2004 questions of neuroethics began to emerge.

Neuroethics and Self-Criticism in MBE Science

As the discipline became more established, consequences of its work were considered and there was a growing concern about *neuroethics*.[147] Calls for neuroethical decisions began to increase as the proper use of information about individual brains became more publicly available. For example, there are increased calls for position statements on memory-enhancing drugs, the benefits and potential drawbacks of scanning students' brains for "defects," and the responsibilities that teachers and parents have for the proper care of children's brains.[148] All of these different ethical areas pose complex challenges to practitioners in the future. The discipline as a whole, as well as each individual professional, will have to reflect upon these issues.

Linked to ethical concerns were articles that challenged findings in the 1990s related to learning concepts in the developing discipline.[149] New self-criticisms are reflective of maturation, which is now old enough to look back at its own research and critique itself. Numerous articles began to appear that gave a slap on the wrist to those who dared to promote half-truths and neuromyths about the discipline. This healthy judgment of research in the discipline helped to elevate standards, but it also increased tensions in the relationships formed by professionals in education, psychology, and neuroscience. Pleas from all sides called for improved communication and sharing by the early 2000s. Teachers begged neuroscience to tell them which information was "good" and what was "bad" during the IMBES conferences (2007). Neuroscientists reacted to criticisms that their work related to laboratory animals, not to teachers and their students, and asked teachers for "real-life" problems upon which to structure future research. Psychologists began to react to educators' calls to ground theory in more practice.

---

147. Excellent coverage of the neuroethic theme can be found in the Farah (2007); Glannon (2007); Illes (2005); Illes & Raffin (2002).
148. These specific examples are found in Sheridan et al. (2005); Iles (2005).
149. An example can be found in Cole (2004).

A Pendulum Swing from the Mind to the Brain and Back Again

By the end of 2007 it became clear that MBE science had experienced a pendulum swing. From the time of the Greeks through the Decade of the Brain in the 1990s there was a demand to ground teaching in science, or more specifically, in information about the brain. Around the start of the 21st century, there was a change, however. Many scientists reminded the discipline that it was "losing its mind in favor of the brain,"[150] and that a move toward "biological determinism"[151] was unbalanced, at best, and dangerous, at worst. These observations returned a more human face to the emerging discipline and demanded a happy medium between research and practice as well as between the laboratory and the classroom. This pendulum swing brings the balance back to the middle and values both the science as well as the art of teaching.

In 2008 an international Delphi panel of 20 experts in the emerging discipline sought to create a framework for standards.[152] The concerted efforts by neuroscientists, psychologists, and educators on this panel brought many key questions from the backburner into the spotlight. Who should teach and how and what should be taught to take advantage of knowledge about the brain became the key issues in education. These issues included the creation of standards and a shared language as well as core topics and themes in the new science of teaching and learning, all of which is discussed in the following chapters.

By the end of the first decade in the new millennium the numbers in MBE science increased from a handful of enthusiasts to thousands. International gatherings such as "Explorations in Learning and the Brain"; "Learning and the Brain"; "The International Mind, Brain, and Education Conference"; "Learning Brain Europe"; "Primary Teacher UK: Learning Brain Europe Conference," and the "Behavior and Brain Conference" were just a few of the society meetings that took place in the United States and the United Kingdom in 2008. For the first time, books used the "mind, brain, and education" label in their titles: *The Developmental Relations between Mind, Brain and Education: Essays in Honor of Robbie Case*;[153] *Mind, Brain, and Education in Reading Disorders*;[154] and *The New Science of Teaching and Learning: Using the Best of Mind, Brain, and Education Science in the Classroom*[155] were all published between 2009 and 2010.

---

150. Siegel (1999, p. xii).
151. Siegel (1999, p. xiii).
152. To see the complete study, see Tokuhama-Espinosa (2008b).
153. Ferrari & Vuletic (2010).
154. Fischer, Bernstein, & Immordino-Yang (2007).
155. Tokuhama-Espinosa (2010).

MBE science has its roots in thousands of years of academic reflection. This brief history of MBE science tracks its parallel development around the world in psychology, education, and neuroscience—a development that became an integrated effort in the 1990s and a new academic discipline around 2004–2006. Once unified, the new discipline asked some obvious questions of its membership: Most importantly, what are the goals of the new discipline, and by what standards are members bound? These questions are addressed in Chapter 4.

Suggested Reading

General Introduction to Mind, Brain, and Education Concepts

Battro, A., Fischer, K. W., & Léna, P. J. (Eds). (2008). *The educated brain: Essays in neuroeducation.* Cambridge, UK: Cambridge University Press.

Blakemore, S., & Frith, U. (2007). *The learning brain: Lessons for education.* Malden, MA: Blackwell.

Bransford, J., Brown, A. L., & Cocking, R. R. (Eds.). (2003). *How people learn: Brain, mind, experience, and school.* Washington, DC: National Academy Press.

Byrnes, J. (2007). Some ways in which neuroscientific research can be relevant to education. In D. Coch, K. W. Fischer, & G. Dawson (Eds.), *Human behavior, learning, and the developing brain: Typical development* (pp. 30–49). New York: Guilford Press.

Doidge, N. (2007). *The brain that changes itself.* New York: Penguin Group.

Ferrari, M., & Vuletic, L. (2009). *The developmental relations between mind, brain, and education: Essays in honor of Robbie Case.* Holanda: Springer.

Fischer, K., Bernstein, J., & Immordino-Yang, M. H. (2007). *Mind, brain, and education in reading disorders.* New York: Cambridge University Press.

Geake, J. (2005b). The neurological basis of intelligence: Implications for education: An abstract. *Gifted and Talented, 9*(1), 8.

Geake, J. (2009). *The brain at school: Educational neuroscience in the classroom.* England: Open University Press.

Kandel, E., & Squire, L. R. (2000). Neuroscience: Breaking down scientific barriers to the study of brain and mind. *Science, 290,* 1113–1120.

Levine, M. (2000). *A mind at a time.* New York: Simon & Schuster.

Pickering, S., & Howard-Jones, P. (2007). Educator's views on the role of neuroscience in education: Findings from a study of UK and international perspectives. *Mind, Brain, and Education, 1*(3), 109–113.

Posner, M., & Rothbart, M. K. (2007). *Educating the human brain*. Washington, DC: American Psychological Association.

Tokuhama-Espinosa, T. (2010). *The new science of teaching and learning: Using the best of mind, brain, and education science in the classroom*. New York: Columbia University Teachers College Press.

Wiley. (2008). *The Jossey–Bass reader on the brain and learning*. San Francisco: Wiley.

Wolfe, P. (2001). *Brain matters: Translating research into classroom practice*. Alexandria, VA: Association for Supervision and Curriculum Development.

CHAPTER **4**

Sorting the Science from the Myths:
Establishing Goals and Standards

"The central question is whether we can create a true learning society by means of the normal processes of gradual reform, so as to adapt our existing models and patterns of provisions to meet the needs of the new century, or whether we need to think rather in terms of replacing them with something distinctly different."
> —Organisation for Economic Co-Operation and Development (2002, p. 25)

"What standards are upheld by the scientific community affect the community internally, and also affect its relations with society at large."
> —Serge Lang, mathematician (1927–2005), *Challenges* (1997, p. 243)

Half the battle in establishing MBE science has been related to its parameters. By what rules do we play? Should all research and practice in the new science of teaching and learning be subjected to the combined standards in the parent fields of neuroscience, psychology, and education, or to its own standards? Gardner and colleagues (2005) framed the concern for standards by asking some overarching questions of MBE science as they relate to the application in the classroom: "What is the quality of evidence purporting to be relevant to education, and by which standards of education? What use should be made of new knowledge and advances? By whom and with what safeguards? How do we respond to unanticipated consequences of research? Who has responsibility?"[156] At least two important pairs of conceptual marriages in the emerging discipline lead to answers to these important questions.

---

156. See Sheridan et al. (2005 p. 11) for the complete article.

The first important conceptual marriage has to do with the relationship between *evidenced-based learning theory* and *classroom practice*. This relationship calls attention to the disconnection often found between what happens in neuroscientific laboratory studies and the reality of what happens to students in schools. This relationship sends warning signals to MBE practitioners to, on the one hand, reject lab studies that can't be proven in the classroom, and on the other, to be suspicious of classroom practices that cannot be substantiated by scientific evidence. This means that studies proving brain functions in lab animals, for example, can (and in some cases should) be a starting point in research, but should not be accepted as final evidence in dictating practices related to children in classrooms. Likewise, "what seems to work" to teachers based on gut feelings should not be accepted until there are documented observations or evidence. Having said this, however, it should be remembered that scientific evidence alone isn't the whole story.

> *"Everything that can be counted does not necessarily count; everything that counts cannot necessarily be counted."*
> —Albert Einstein (1879–1955), quoted in Patton (2008, p. 420)

Albert Einstein made the keen observation that everything that can be counted does not necessarily merit attention, nor does that which cannot be counted deserve rejection. Einstein's comment is a reminder that simply "biologizing" educational practice is not the solution;[157] measurable, scientific data are not the only ways to gauge student learning or evaluate successful teaching. Teachers who "know" that something works based on years of experience and on gut feelings should not be asked to reject this type of professional intuition outright, but rather should be encouraged to find ways to explain it in empirical form. Some of the best practices in classroom settings have yet to be confirmed by science.[158] Our role as responsible teachers is not to reject these practices, but to help establish what level of backing each of them has. One way we can do this is by deciding where such practices fall in terms of the *OECD continuum*, which ranges from information that is well established to information that is simply a myth about how learning takes place (explained in the next section in Table 4.1).

This conceptual marriage between evidenced-based learning theory and classroom practice is epitomized by much of the interesting research in neuroscience that considers behaviors that are not typical of normal human subjects. Such research is quite curious,

157. Brown & Bjorklund (1998).
158. For excellent arguments to this effect, see Howard-Jones (2007).

though it brings very little to the teachers' banquet of options. Unfortunately, it is far too common to find studies in neuroscience about learning that are extremely well designed, use proper data collection, analyze the data in a thorough way, and present findings in a reflective and thorough manner, but which prove absolutely contrived human brain functions. This issue leads to a simple but important idea: MBE science findings should be judged not only on the quality of the research itself, but also in terms of the quality of the research question. Some studies stretch the imagination. For example, research testing the brain's ability to learn strategies to recognize "pseudo words"[159] may be interesting as a novel activity, but in practical terms, the findings of such studies are limited in their usefulness in the classroom. In relative terms, how important is it for teachers to know how the brain does not read words that do not really exist in English? Likewise, literacy skills that are not actually found in the human repertoire of abilities are often included in brain-based learning research. One has to use a lot of imagination to see how such studies are relevant when explaining normal human reading behavior. For example, an article in a prestigious psychological journal demonstrated how "readers structure narrative text into a series of events in order to understand and remember the text" (Speer, Zacks, & Reynolds, 2007, p. 449) a finding that potentially has a great deal of merit. After all, a better understanding of how the brain divides information in order to remember more successfully can help teachers improve their instruction of reading skills. What is unfortunate is that upon closer examination it becomes apparent that the experiment, despite its excellent execution, is based on a completely contrived mental process, which is alien to normal human experiences during the reading process. This means that the experiment "proved" something that the brain does not normally do; again novel but useless information for teachers. When we review the conceptual marriage between evidence-based learning and the classroom, we are reminded that useful studies should begin with student experiences in natural learning environments, and then move into the lab for support.

This first conceptual marriage of evidence-based learning theories and classroom practice is related to a second. There is juxtaposition between *natural brain learning processes* and *existing educational policies* that points to the parameters for standards in the new MBE discipline. This second conceptual marriage calls attention to the fact that many of the things that are dictated by school norms are contradictory to what we know is best for the brain in learning contexts. There are at least four clear examples of this fundamental contradiction related to sleeping, eating, classroom management, and teaching

159. For this precise study, see Munte & Matzke (1997).

methods. First, school start times have evolved to meet modern work schedule needs of parents rather the alert mental stages of students.[160] If educational systems were more attuned to the sleep needs of students, later school start times that coincide with adolescent brains (due to changes in the timing of the sleep-related hormone, melatonin) would be the norm, not 8:00 A.M. first bells. Second, we know that nutrition impacts the brain's readiness to learn, yet french fries and colas are the norm in many school cafeterias. Though there are some calls to change the way we feed our children,[161] and the new Safe Food for Schools Act in the United States promises to make some dietary changes in schools, at present, many cafeterias sell what is economically more viable and easier to prepare—fast food. Third, some teaches do not have strong classroom management skills, which are recognized as a vital element in student success, according to evidence-based educational researchers Robert Marzano and colleagues (2003). Teachers with poor classroom management skills often subject students to frequent humiliation in front of their peers, causing a sense of insecurity, which impedes learning. The inadequate preparation of teachers to manage challenging classroom situations means many students don't learn, despite beautiful infrastructure, good curriculum, and sufficient materials. Finally, it is also clear that traditional teacher-centered practices that revolve around rote memory skill acquisition are contrary to the "natural" way the brain learns.[162] Modern teachers who integrate a variety of teaching methods that are student-centered and placed in the student's own context are more successful than activities that are passive and instructor-oriented.

Given the state of sleep and eating habits, poor classroom discipline practices, and inadequate methodologies, we should ask ourselves if there should be policies that protect students from school or teacher practices that have been shown to be ineffective or counterproductive. While we know that it is nearly impossible for the brain not to learn, as it naturally seeks to do for evolutionary-based survival reasons, we do see problems in schools that offer less than optimal conditions for learning.

The conceptual marriage between evidenced-based learning and classroom practice and the contradiction between natural learning processes and school policies offer a framework within which we can begin to categorize the worth and applicability of certain ideas in education. The big ideas in MBE science revolve around what we know as a fact (well established) and what is probably so (information that will likely be proven correct

160. For convincing studies on this point, see Carskadon, Acebo & Jenni, (2004); Carskadon, Wolfson, Acebo, Tzischinsky, & Seifer (1998).
161. See Cooper & Holmes (2006).
162. For this argument, see Given (2002); Gunn, Richburg, & Smilkstein (2006).

TABLE 4.1

Four OECD Categories Compared with Best Evidence Encyclopedia and What Works Clearinghouse

Four Categories of Information in the Emerging Field of Educational Neuroscience/Mind, Brain, and Education Science	Best Evidence Encyclopedia	What Works Clearinghouse
WHAT IS WELL ESTABLISHED (A) A1. "Human brains are as unique as faces; while the basic structure is the same, there are no two which are identical. While there are general patterns of organization in how different people learn and which brain areas are involved, each brain is unique and uniquely organized." A2. "All brains are not equal in their ability to solve all problems. Context as well as ability influence learning. Context includes the learning environment, motivation for the topic of new learning, and prior knowledge." A3. "The brain is a complex, dynamic, and integrated system that is constantly changed by experience, though most of this change is only evident at a microscopic level." A4. "Human brains have a high degree of plasticity and develop throughout the lifespan, though there are major limits on this plasticity, and these limits increase with age." A5. "Connecting new information to prior knowledge facilitates learning."	STRONG EVIDENCE OF EFFECTIVENESS At least one large randomized or randomized quasi-experimental study, or multiple smaller studies, with a median effect size of at least +0.20. A large study is defined as one in which at least 10 classes or schools, or 250 students, were assigned to treatments. Smaller studies are counted as equivalent to a large study if their collective sample sizes are at least 250 students. If randomized studies have a median effect of at least +0.20, the total set of studies need not have a median effect size.	POSITIVE EFFECTS Strong evidence of a positive effect with no overriding contrary evidence. Two or more studies showing statistically significant positive effects, at least one of which met WWC evidence standards for a strong design. No studies showing statistically significant or substantively important negative effects.
WHAT IS PROBABLY SO (B) B1. "Human brains seek and often quickly detect novelty (which is individually defined)." B2. "Human brains seek patterns upon which they predict outcomes, and neural systems form responses to repeated patterns of activation (patterns being individually defined)." B3. "Human learning is achieved through developmental processes which follow a universal pattern for most skills, including academic skills shared across literate cultures, such as reading, writing, math." B4. "The rehearsal of retrieval cues aids in declarative memory processes." B5. "The elaboration (overt teaching) of key concepts facilitates new learning."	MODERATE EVIDENCE OF EFFECTIVENESS One large matched study or multiple smaller studies with a collective sample size of 250 students, with a median effect size of at least +.0.20.	POTENTIAL POSITIVE EFFECTS Evidence of a positive effect with no overriding contrary evidence. At least one study showing a statistically significant or substantively important positive effect. No studies showing statistically significant or substantively important negative effects and few or the same number of studies showing

B6. "Declarative knowledge acquisition depends on both memory and attention."

B7. "Nutrition impacts learning (good eating habits contribute to learning and poor eating habits detract from the brain's ability to maximize its learning potential)."

B8. "Sleep is important for declarative memory consolidation (though other types of memories, such as emotional memories, can be achieved without sleep). Sleep deprivation also has a negative impact on memory."

B9. "Stress impacts learning: 'good' stress (eustress) heightens attention and helps learning, while 'bad' stress detracts from learning potential."

B10. "The human brain judges others' faces and tones of voices for threat levels in a rapid and often unconscious way, influencing the way information from these sources is perceived (i.e., valid, invalid, trustworthy, untrustworthily, etc.)"

B11. "Feedback and meaningful assessment is important to human learning, though the importance and role of feedback vary greatly across domains and processes."

B12. "Self-regulation (monitoring oneself via executive functions) is an integral part of higher order thinking skills."

B13. "There are 'sensitive periods' (not critical periods) in human brain development in which certain skills are learned with greater ease than at other times."

B14. "Emotions are critical to decision making."

B15. "Support (academic, moral, or otherwise) from others (often teachers, peers or parents) is critical for optimal academic performance, which includes learning."

B16. "When knowledge is actively constructed by a learner, the learner will be motivated and engaged in learning."

B17. "Educators should use strategies that optimize neurogenesis (lower stress, improved social contacts, enrichment and exercise)."

B18. "Water is 'brain food.'"

B19. "The search for meaning is innate in human nature."

indeterminate effects than showing statistically significant or substantively important positive effects.

WHAT IS INTELLIGENT SPECULATION (C)

C1. "Different memory systems (i.e., short term-, long term-, working-, spatial-, motor-, modality-specific-, rote-, etc.) receive and process information in different ways and are retrieved through distinct, though sometimes overlapping, neural pathways."

C2. "In terms of synaptic growth, the most active synapses are strengthened, while relatively less active synapses are weakened. Over time, this shapes brain organization. This has been referred to as the 'use it or lose it model,' whereby synapses that are most active are strengthened, while relatively less active synapses are weakened (and sometimes eliminated)."

C3. "Differentiation (allowing students to learn at different paces) in classroom practice can be justified by the fact that students have different intelligences and cognitive preferences."

C4. "Human brains seek patterns (which are individually defined) upon which they predict outcomes."

C5. "Learning is enhanced by challenge and is typically inhibited by threat (in which threat is individually defined)."

C6. "Human learning is a constructive process in that humans construct meaning from existing knowledge structures. Such existing knowledge structures are individually defined."

C7. "The development of personal relevance to new knowledge makes learning easier."

C8. "Self-esteem impacts learning and academic achievement."

C9. "The brain learns best when content information responds to survival needs (social, emotional, economic, and physical)."

C10. "The brain is not designed for typical passive classroom instruction, rather it enjoys multimodal, experiential and diverse learning experiences."

C11. "There is a positive correlation between instructional time (including homework) and student achievement."

C12. "The human brain learns best when facts and skills are embedded in natural contexts (or concrete examples), in which the learner understands the problems he/she faces, and recognizes how the facts and/or skills might play roles in solving that problem. This is due to the fact that motivation tends to be higher when facts and skills are embedded in natural context."

LIMITED EVIDENCE OF EFFECTIVENESS

At least one qualifying study with a significant positive effect and/or median effect size of +0.10 or more.

MIXED EFFECTS

Evidence of inconsistent effects as demonstrated through either of the following: at least one study showing a statistically or substantively important positive effect and at least one study showing a statistically significant or substantively important negative effect, but no more such studies than the number showing a statistically significant or substantively important positive effect, or at least one study showing a statistically significant or substantively important effect than showing a statistically significant or substantively important effect.

C13. "The brain does not learn in a linear, structured and predictable fashion. This implies the need to use various sensory channels at the same time, including audiovisuals, readings, group work, reflection, and novel activities."

C14. "The brain learns complex concepts best when they are taught and experienced through various sensory stimuli."

C15. "'Best practice' activities in education are activities that are student-centered, experiential, holistic, authentic, expressive, reflective, social, collaborative, democratic, cognitive, developmental, constructivist, and/or challenging. Students learn better and faster using best practice activities."

C16. "Good learning environments—defined within this survey as being those which are safe, offer intellectual freedom, paced challenges, ample feedback, a level of autonomy, respect, and include active learning activities—are better than learning environments that do not have these characteristics."

C17. "Humans build knowledge and skills through actions."

C18. "Humans can learn new information while sleeping."

C19. "All people use kinesthetic, visual and auditory pathways to take in new information, and there is strong evidence that different people use different processing strategies at different times depending on the context of the learning."

C20. "Music can influence learning (though it is as of yet unclear how and why this occurs and varies by individuals)."

C21. "Movement can enhance learning of academic subjects (though it is unclear as to exactly what the mind-body mechanism is that influences this)."

C22. "Humor can enhance learning (though it is unclear as to exactly what the mind-body mechanism is that influences this)."

C23. "Children learn certain skills (such as language) effortlessly."

C24. "Male and female brains learn in different ways."

C25. "Enriched environments make children smarter."

WHAT IS A POPULAR MISCONCEPTION OR A NEUROMYTH (D)

D1. "On average, most people use about 10% of their brains."

D2. "Brain Gym™ ('a series of simple body movements to integrate all areas of the brain to enhance learning,') is an effective way to enhance young children's learning potential."

D3. "There are brain differences by race."

D4. "Brain parts act in isolation from one another."

D5. "Differences between the male and female brain have been proven to map onto specific functional consequences."

D6. "You can't change the brain."

D7. "Learning more than one language at a time will permanently disrupt learning of a native language."

D8. "Everything important about the brain is determined by the age of three."

D9. "Memory is like an objective recording of a situation, and reality exists in an abstract form for all to perceive."

D10. "Unstructured discovery learning is preferable to structured, teacher-centered instruction because of neurological functioning."

D11. "The Theory of Multiple Intelligences is validated by neuroscience research."

D12. "The brain has an unlimited capacity."

D13. "Memorization is unnecessary for complex mental processing."

D14. "There are optimal periods associated for learning associated to neurogenesis."

D15. "The brain remembers everything it has ever experienced; forgetting is simply an absence of recall ability."

D16. "Neurons are never replaced (you can't grow new brain cells)."

D17. "The brain is different from the mind."

D18. "Human infants are born with a 'blank slate' and knowledge just needs to be provided for them to learn."

D19. "Gender differences outweigh individual differences when it comes to learning abilities."

D20. "Neural plasticity is due to good pedagogy."

D21. "Learning only occurs in the classroom."

D22. "Learning is independent of a learner's history."

D23. "Learning can be isolated from the social/emotional content."

D24. "Teens 'act out' and are irresponsible because the prefrontal cortex doesn't develop until the mid-20s."

INSUFFICIENT EVIDENCE

Studies show no significant differences.

NO QUALIFYING STUDIES.

NO DISCERNIBLE EFFECTS

No affirmative evidence of effects. None of the studies show a statistically significant or substantively important effect, either positive or negative.

Or

NO QUALIFYING STUDIES.

Or

POTENTIALLY NEGATIVE EFFECTS

Or

NEGATIVE EFFECTS

D25. "Some people are more 'right-brained' than others, and other are more 'left-brained.'"
D26. "Left and right hemispheres as separable systems for learning."
D27. "Language is located in the 'left brain' and spatial abilities are in the 'right brain.'"
D28. "More will be learned if teaching is timed with periods of synaptogenesis."
D29. "Reasoning and decision-making can be divorced from emotion and feeling, and doing so improves the quality of thought in which one engages."

Source: Tokuhama-Espinosa (2008b, pp. 108–111).

or incorrect in the near future with more research, or information that is true for all learners but has individual variations). The big ideas also try to explain information that is, at this point in time, intelligent speculation and that has been placed in this category either because there are too many individual variants related to the idea, or because it is information that seems logical but has little or no scientific backing. The big ideas also call attention to the misinformation that is often commercialized and that is labeled as neuromyths or false beliefs about the brain and learning. These four categories of information were suggested by the Organisation For Economic Co-Operation and Development (OECD), formed by participants from 30 nations around the world, in their book *Understanding the Brain: Towards a New Learning Science* (2002). The OECD offers some examples of the four categories, as follows (based on OECD, 2002, p. 29):

- *What is well established*: These are essential concepts that form the basic foundations of best-practice teaching (e.g., *plasticity*, or the malleable nature of the brain and its ability to form new connections throughout the lifespan, which now has hundreds of credible human studies behind it).
- *What is probably so*: There are important concepts or practices that we need to keep our eye on because they may soon become well established but still lack unanimous backing from at least one of the three disciplines (neuroscience, psychology, and/or education) (e.g., *sensitive periods*, which have hundreds of studies behind them, though not all conducted on humans and few related to academic subjects).
- *What is intelligent speculation*: These tend to be concepts that we want to believe are true, but which just don't have the science behind them to support the weight of claims attached to them. Some of these concepts may eventually become well established after more research is conducted or if terms are better defined, or they may simply fall into the category of a neuromyth (e.g., *gender differences and learning*, which has thousands of studies behind it, albeit of mixed quality and sometimes with contradictory findings).
- *What is popular misconception or a neuromyth*: These tend to be "sexy," attractive, and highly marketable concepts about the brain and learning that have little or no evidence behind them. They either reflect the ignorance of their promoters about the brain, or they are knowingly promoted misinterpretations about the brain sold to the public by unscrupulous consultants (e.g., "*right brain*" and "*left brain*" discussion,

which has been the target of thousands of books and articles, some of which promote the term, but most of which criticize the lack of factual accuracy of the claim).

The OECD scale is an excellent tool for sorting good information from bad in MBE science because it is an evidenced-based tool agreed upon by MBE scientists around the world. To add to the descriptive design of the OECD continuum and to further help teachers and researchers sort through the vast array of information and its varying level of quality, the OECD continuum is juxtaposed in Table 4.1 with Briggs's *Best Evidence Encyclopedia* and *What Works Clearinghouse* comparison.[163] Both the *Best Evidence Encyclopedia* and the *What Works Clearinghouse* are attempts to categorize the quality of evidence in educational research. This comparison places dozens of concepts considered in education on the OECD continuum and adds two qualitative scales for comparison that helps us understand just how we can measure if an idea being used in education is really "good" or "bad" information in practice.

The list of concepts expressed in Table 4.1 is as complete as possible in 2010. However, other concepts are sure to emerge in the literature, and these will need to be rated and added in the future, and it is also likely that more neuromyths will be invented. Additionally, and perhaps even more important for readers to understand, some of these concepts are likely to change categories as more research is conducted. For example, many savvy readers will find much of the information in the "Probably So" category ideas that appear to be best-practice teaching (e.g., "Enriched environments make children smarter" or "The development of personal relevance to new knowledge makes learning easier"). The reason many concepts fall into the Probably So category are because they refer to highly individual traits and are very difficult to measure or prove in comparative studies. For example, what conditions constitute an enriched environment—and for whom? Or just how can we test for personal relevance? In many cases it may be possible to design experimental research that can confirm some of these ideas, but in others, the highly individual nature of some aspects of learning make it impossible to do so. Does this mean that the concept is not worthy of recognition in education? Absolutely not; as noted above in Einstein's quote, simply because something cannot be quantitatively measured does not mean it is unworthy or useless. It does mean that such concepts have less empirical grounding and need to be implemented with a focus on their far more personal nature. Despite its shortcomings, Table 4.1 is a good initial guide for helping the general

163. Briggs (2008).

public and teachers, in particular, understand the quality of information being marketed toward teachers.

It behooves all teachers to think critically about all of the information available: "We are approaching a new age of synthesis. Knowledge cannot be merely a degree or a skill. . . . it demands a broader vision, capabilities in critical thinking and logical deduction without which we cannot have constructive progress."[164] As Antonio Battro, past President of the International Mind, Brain, and Education Society noted, unless teachers think critically about the information they are applying when they design their classes, it is unlikely that students will learn to think critically in their own lives (2003); good models are highly influential in this area. There is a great deal of information being sold to teachers that is trendy and attractive, but which has no sustenance. One of the ways to avoid bad information is by clearly understanding the goals and standards of MBE science as a discipline.

Goals in the New Discipline

Like all disciplines, the goals of MBE science can be divided into three categories: research, practice, and policy. These goals help put the parameters around what, how, who, when, where, and why studies are conducted, thus serving as basic guidelines for researchers, practitioners, and policy makers. Teachers can use the goals to ensure that they ground their practice in solid principles. Students of MBE science can use these goals to develop new research questions. Leaders in the discipline can use the goals to guide policy decisions. The goals give MBE scientists a "north" by which to guide their work. Goals, however, are meaningless unless they are matched with standards, which are also explained below.[165]

Research Goal

The research goal of the emerging discipline of MBE science is to:

Establish a working understanding of the dynamic relationships between how we learn, how we educate, how the brain constructs new learning, and how the brain organizes and processes information.

HOW?

• Study how brain mechanisms contribute to education and learning.

---

164. Shing (2003).
165. Tokuhama-Espinosa (2008b).

- Study relationships between human development and the biology of the brain.
- Develop insights into the neuroscientific and cognitive scientific determinants of normal, successful, and borderline/pathological learning and apply these in the field of education according to evidence-based principles.
- Study context and psychosocial factors (e.g., socioeconomic factors, levels of parental education, intellectually stimulating environments, culture) as they interact with biological influences on learning.
- Study how biopsychological factors (e.g., sleep, nutrition, stress) can modulate learning and the efficiency of teaching.
- Study lifelong learning in the context of the developing teacher, including how teacher self-efficacy impacts student learning, teacher experience contributes to classroom experiences, and information processing in teachers at different ages.
- Study how student self-regulation, metacognition, and higher-order thinking skills can be best developed.
- By determining how and why certain pedagogical practices are successful.

This research goal and its eight sub-elements make it clear that MBE science considers the entire range of human learning and the consequences of teaching, ranging from neuroanatomical to socioeconomic factors, from normal to pathological development, from infant to adult learning processes, and from the role of the teacher to the role of the student.

Practice Goal
The practice goal of MBE science is to:
> Align learning and teaching with how human beings are biologically organized for learning.

HOW?
- Reciprocally connect research with practice on processes of learning and teaching.
- Apply neurobiological principles to the theory and practice of education.
- Study and evaluate how findings from research in neurosciences can be applied to educational practice.
- Apply research findings in cognitive neuroscience to educational practice and theory.

- Use successful classroom experiences as points of departure for continued research in the neurosciences.
- Apply our understanding of the brain to education.

In real-life application, this list of how to implement the practice goal means that teachers use all they can glean from quality information about the brain to devise best-practice instructional methods. From a researcher's perspective this means using what works in classrooms as a point of departure for lab study. On the whole, implementing this list bridges the gap dividing neuroscientific lab studies and the classroom setting.

Policy Goal

The policy goal of the emerging discipline is to:

Continually encourage the pursuit of neuroscientifically substantiated beliefs founded in educationally-inspired research questions, the results of which have potential application to educational practice.

HOW?

- Inform educational policy and practice with research on the science of learning.
- Improve the efficiency of educational policies, both for normal and for at-risk children, by relying on scientific principles of how the child's brain/mind operates, both for the design and for the evaluation of education strategies.
- Inform neuroscientific research directions through experiences in education.

The points in this list mean that policy decisions in MBE science walk the fine line linking neuroscience, psychology, and education. This balance is achieved in such a way as to approach educational strategies for both normal and at-risk students using the refined multiple-lens of the new discipline. Once the goals of the new discipline have been clarified, it is important to see how they translate into both practice and research standards.

New Standards for Education

Standards are considered to be generally accepted principles that guide best practice. In legal terms, standards are considered to be the criteria and rules that guide behavior,[166]

---

166. Ropper & Brown (2005).

especially as they relate to protecting the rights of participants, patients, or students.[167] In education, standards identify what a student is expected to know and be able to do once he or she has completed a certain level of study.[168] According to the Association for Supervision and Curriculum Development (ASCD)[169] in the United States, standards embody several sub-components, such as content standards, performance standards, opportunity-to-learn standards, and world-class standards. Standards in MBE are the principles that guide best practice, are legally or morally binding, and help define both content and performance guidelines. In short, those being guided into this new discipline, be they teachers or researchers or their trainers, must adhere to certain principles.

Neuroscience, psychology, and pedagogy each has its own standards. It might seem logical to presume that MBE standards would be the intersection of these disciplines. But this is erroneous. There are two possible ways to conceptualize standards that emerge from combining existing disciplines. The new standards can either represent the minimum common denominator within neuroscience, psychology, and pedagogy, or alternatively, they can be the sum of the standards in these disciplines. In the first case, the standards are the points of commonality; in the second, the standards are the points of commonality as well as diversity across the fields of neuroscience, psychology, and pedagogy (see Figure 4.1).

The vast majority of experts in the new MBE discipline said that standards in the new discipline should represent an appropriate and rigorous synthesis of standards in neuroscience, psychology, and pedagogy, and, in addition, should include a set of ethical guidelines for evaluating not only the soundness of information but its usefulness, appropriateness, and applicability to learning environments.[170] In other words, people working within the new discipline are willing to submit themselves to the scrutiny of the standards in all the parent fields, plus a set of ethical guidelines that judge the appropriate use of information before it is used in teaching settings. By adhering to such high standards, the teacher-practitioner in MBE science gains a high level of respect for both the quality and execution of activities in the research, teaching, and learning processes. These standards protect teachers from half-truths in classrooms. Half-truths or neuromyths (myths about the way the brain works) are the greatest enemies of quality work in teaching and should be avoided at all costs. To place this information in context, 24 of the most common neuromyths found in the literature are explained below.

167. For the structure of standards in neuroscience, psychology, and education, see the American Academy of Neurology (2007), the American Psychological Association (2007b), the British Psychological Association (2006), and Gordon, Cooper, Rennie, Hermens, & Williams (2005), respectively.
168. For a good explanation of this, see the Association for Supervision and Curriculum Development website (2007).
169. ASCD (2007).
170. See Tokuhama-Espinosa for a full explanation of this discussion (2008b, p. 82).

FIGURE 4.1
Standards in MBE Science: The Common Denominator or the Sum?

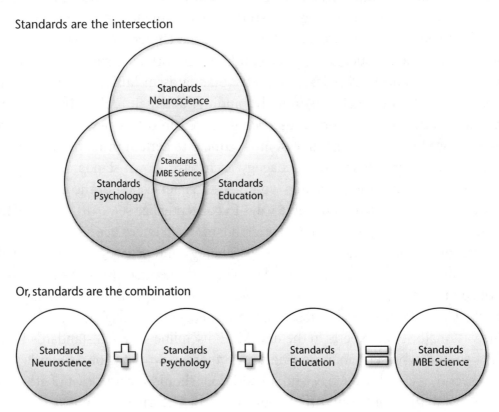

How New Standards Alert Us to Neuromyths

Neuromyths are typically born of a partial fact or a single study and are overgeneralizations about the brain—or in some cases, outright misinterpretations of data. According to the OECD (2007), neuromyths are "hypotheses which have been invalidated, [but which] nevertheless leave traces and if these have captured a wider imagination, 'myths' take root" (OECD, 2007, p. 108). Several broad categories of neuromyths are commonly found in the teaching literature but for which there is no evidence: misinterpretations of data and unsubstantiated beliefs; misinterpretations about brain processes; folk myths about the brain; myths about memories and learning; and myths about where learning takes place in the brain.[171] When these types of myths are applied in the classroom, they give teaching

171. The information below is taken, in part, from *The New Science of Teaching and Learning: Using the Best of Mind, Brain, and Education Science in the Classroom* with permission from the author (Tokuhama-Espinosa, 2010).

a bad name. Teachers should be aware of these neuromyths and be sure to steer clear of their use when planning class content, activities, or designing instructional methods. Below are common myths that plague educational literature.

Myth 1: Humans Use 10% of Their Brains

It was thought that once we had better neuroimaging techniques, we would be able to show exactly how much of the brain was being used. Science fiction series have always called attention to the unused parts of the brain, hinting at the fact that humans, as a species, are just not living up to their potential. Despite advances in technology, it is impossible to measure exactly how much of the brain is being used for a number of reasons. First and foremost, the amount of brainpower needed to complete a task (to think, use a formula, play an instrument, etc.) changes with the learning processes. The brain uses more energy, for example, when it learns to read than once it has mastered that task. This means that brain scans taken when a person is in the process of learning a task will look more occupied than a scan of the same brain after the person has mastered the task. Second, not all parts of the brain should be working on all tasks. If we view a brain scan of someone labeling pictures and see only about 10% of the brain active, this might actually be 100% of the areas of the brain that should be functioning. The bottom line is that it would be inaccurate to say that humans use only a small percentage of their brain-power. This is not only untrue, it is also discouraging to students to be told that they are not living up to their potential.

Myth 2: The Brain Has an Unlimited Capacity

As a physical entity, the brain has a finite capacity. There is no denying that the human brain is the most amazing structure in the universe; nevertheless, it is not boundless. Many will argue that there is really no telling what the actual limits of the brain are, as far as imagination goes. However, *imagination* and *capacity to learn* are not one and the same. It is unfair to students to make promises of intellectual prowess when we know that limits placed on the brain—by genetic inheritance, nutrition, socioeconomic status, as well as the quality of one's teachers—do indeed have an impact. Some teachers may feel that students should be told that they have unlimited capacity as a way to stoke motivation; however, it is perhaps even more encouraging to hear that they can and should live up to their individual potential.

Myth 3: There Are Brain Differences by Race

A child's potential to do well on intelligence tests is impacted by his or her culture, socioe-conomic status, interest level, test preparation, previous schooling, familiarity with test content, and a myriad of other factors. However, there are no studies showing that there are physical differences in the brain, based on race, that are the cause of high or low intelligence. This myth harkens back to the old days of phrenology when it was thought that a person's intelligence and temperament could be determined by the observable differences in skull protrusions or other external physical differences. This myth is incredibly damaging to students who have been told that they are not as smart as children of other races, and it should be removed from all literature and teacher belief systems, as it lowers both the self-esteem and perceived potential of students. One of the most intriguing sets of data that demonstrates that performance is more related to psychological (rather than neurological) differences is the so-called "Obama Effect." It was found that African American students have always scored slightly lower than their European American peers in standardized tests in the United States. However, the month after Obama won the election for president, the scores of African Americans elevated to the same level of their European American counterparts; apparently, simply being shown that race was not a factor in achievement helped them overcome this perception.[172]

Myth 4: Everything Important about the Brain Is Determined by the Age of 3

The importance of good nutrition in the early years is undeniably important in the healthy development of the brain. However, this does not mean that all the raw material is in place by the age of 3. It is clear that a child who has been malnourished will not have the same possibilities as a child who is well nourished, but this does not mean that a child who has not participated in early stimulation programs by the age 3 it will be "lost" intellectually forever. This myth was debunked in Bruer's book *The Myth of the First Three Years* (2002), which articulately challenged the artificial limits put on the brain's potential to learn throughout the lifespan. MBE science notes that there are no critical periods for any academic skill (e.g., math, reading). That is to say that if addition is not learned by age 6, then it can still be learned by 7, 8, 9, or 90 years of age. (There may be critical periods for non-academic skills, however, such as learning to walk or to speak one's first language.) It is damaging to children's ego (and subsequently to their potential for new learning) for parents to believe that if they have not provided their children with early

---

172. Studies conducted by Ray Friedman (Vanderbilt University), David M. Marx (San Diego State University), and Sei Jin Ko (visiting professor at Northwestern University) in *The Journal of Experimental Social Psychology*, January 2009 as cited in the *New York Times* (Dillon, 2009).

stimulation classes from birth, they will not be able to reach the same potential in school as those who have done so.

Myth 5: Brain Parts Work in Isolation

When brain imaging first became more common in studies published in the 1990s, many educators leaped to identify which parts of the brain were "language parts" or "math parts" with the hope that, in doing so, ways to stimulate these areas would become clearer. We now know that brain parts do not work in isolated functions; rather they work as complex systems, often using pieces from all of the different lobes (frontal, parietal, occipital, and temporal) at once. Localizationism has been rejected in favor of systems thinking. This type of myth leads to other misinterpretations about brain functions. Teaching is a complex and difficult process, and there is no one-size-fits-all solution to any learning challenge, such as the idea that "the reading center" of the brain can be stimulated by doing such-and-thus an activity. Reading, and all other skills taught in school, involve a complex array of sub-skills that draw on more than one part of the brain. Pretending to make learning simple by parceling out subjects to different parts of the brain only conceals the multifaceted difficulties that can occur in educational processes. Teachers should be aware of the many sub-areas involved in learning specific skills in order to be better prepared to enhance each student's abilities.

Myth 6: Some People Are More "Right-Brained," and Others Are More "Left-Brained"

One of the biggest market hypes in brain-based learning has involved convincing teachers that they should stimulate the "under-used right hemisphere" of the brain and design classroom experiences that help "right-brain learners." This myth is purported in part by people who would like to see more of the arts in schools—an admirable goal—but which should be pursued on its own merits, not because of the belief that some learners are being deprived of a good education due to their hemispheric preferences. First, it should be acknowledged that humans have only one brain, comprised of a right and left hemisphere, which they use in concert; people are not "right-brained" or "left-brained" from birth or due to schooling. Rather, we all use integrated systems involving both hemispheres for almost all tasks. It is misleading to tell children that they are right- or left-brain oriented because it puts false limitations on their development. While many people do process spatial abilities and intonation perception areas in their right hemispheres, for example, this is not true for all, nor it is a complete vision of how the brain learns.[173] While it is admirable to encourage more arts, music, creativity, and spatial activities (geographical locations, geometry, etc.) in school settings, using the "right-brain" argument is naïve.

Myth 7: Left and Right Hemispheres Are Separable Systems for Learning

Related to Myth 6 is the false belief that learning systems in the brain are divided into the two hemispheres. For example, some say that language is processed in the left hemisphere and creativity in the right. Although Broca's and Wernicke's (language) areas are in the left hemisphere for 95% of right-handed people and 70% of left-handed people, other aspects of language use a great deal of the right hemisphere (e.g., understanding metaphors and humor) in these same individuals, which means that the language system is spread throughout the right and left hemispheres. Additionally, it is misleading to tell children that they can "stimulate their right brains" by doing certain activities as suggested by some commercial ventures. The brain is a singular and complex system and should be appreciated for its conglomerate organization, rather than "dummied down," which only leads to long-term problems in the actual teaching–learning process.

Myth 8: Brains Objectively Record Reality

This myth suggests that there is such a thing as an objective recording of reality that everyone shares. However, the truth is that people's memories are actually subject to misinterpretations or false recollection, which is why people often remember the same event in different ways. Memories stored in the brain are subject to the same filters of experience through which all aspects of "reality" pass. This reality is based on the learner's past as well as the "filter" of his or her sensory perceptions. The subjectivity of memory is an important concept for teachers to share with their students because it helps students recognize their own personal biases in recollection. This type of intellectual empathy is a key element in critical thinking.

Myth 9: Memorization Is Unnecessary for Complex Mental Processing

Some teachers have been led to believe that memorization is somehow "bad" when it comes to modern classroom experiences—which should, at all costs, be more entertaining. This notion presumes that memorization is only part of sheer rote learning, in which lists of concepts are presented out of context (as occurs in some classrooms). This is false. Memorization can take place in authentic and enjoyable contexts as well (e.g.,

173. See Voyer, Voyer, & Bryden (1995).

when something new is memorized, thanks to a clear association with a past experience). However, the acquisition of declarative knowledge depends on both memory and attention, which means that complex mental processing is impossible without memorization. Pretending that memorization is unnecessary for complex mental processing, such as that which occurs in new learning, perpetuates a dangerous myth in the classroom. Learning depends on memorization, which is necessary for complex mental processing.

Myth 10: The Brain Remembers Everything That Has Ever Happened to It

There is a myth that suggests that the brain remembers everything that has ever happened to it, which is false. Forgetting occurs when we no longer have access to a memory. The brain does not remember everything it has ever experienced, only those experiences that have successfully passed from working to long-term memory, and for which retrieval has been made possible through practice. We forget something when (a) we never memorized it in the first place (it didn't get to long-term memory), or (b) when we have not strengthened the neural pathways for retrieval, and thus access to a memory is lost.

Myth 11: Optimal Periods of Learning Are Connected to Neurogenesis

There is a myth that there are optimal periods for learning that can be timed with neurogenesis, or the creation of new cells in the brain. This is a myth because neurogenesis is all but impossible to predict with current technology and because learning takes place outside as well as within moments of neurogenesis.

Myth 12: Teaching Can Be Timed with Synaptogenesis

Some popular press books suggest that more will be learned if teaching is timed with periods of synaptogenesis, the times at which new synapses are formed. This statement is a myth for two reasons. First, learning causes synaptogenesis, not the other way around. Second, this statement presumes that (a) we can anticipate moments of synaptogenesis, and that (b) better learning occurs with "new" brain cells than with older ones. Neither of these statements has been proven.

Myth 13: Brain Cells Cannot Be Replaced

As mentioned earlier in this book, one of the most exciting discoveries in the past few decades relates to the confirmation that new brain cells are indeed generated. The myth that you can never replace brain cells has been dispelled by the documentation of human neurogenesis (see Eriksson and colleagues' work in 1998 for more information on this fascinating topic).

Myth 14: The Brain Is Immutable

There is a very dangerous myth that suggests that we can't change the brain. This is a neuromyth because not only can we change the brain, it is impossible not to do so. As we saw earlier, the brain is a complex, dynamic, and integrated system that is constantly changed by experience. These changes are the results of new learning and the physical alterations that occur at the molecular level in the brain in response to experiences.

Myth 15: Learning Foreign Languages Disrupts Knowledge of Students' Native Language

In the 1960s it was thought that only a single part of the human brain is dedicated to language. The myth sprang up that if people were to learn more than one language, they would, in effect, be dividing this potential. We now know that there is an overwhelming number of benefits to bilingualism and that this myth has no grounding. Teachers should work hard to help their students understand the general cognitive, social, cultural, economic, and academic benefits of speaking more than one language, and dispel this myth entirely as soon as possible.

Myth 16: Children Are Blank Slates

In the 17th century it was believed that children were born into the world ignorant, with minds as blank slates ("tabula rasa") upon which their parents and educators had to write in all necessary knowledge. We now know that children are born knowing certain skills as basic to human survival as language, which may be "preprogrammed" in the genetic makeup, as well as with a battery of life experiences that take place during pregnancy. Children are not born with blank slates for brains. Yeats (1923) was a bit closer when he said, "Education is not the filling of a pail, but the lighting of a fire."[174]

Myth 17: Brain and Mind Are Separate

There is a longstanding philosophical argument about the dualistic nature of the mind and the brain, which has purported the myth that they are separate entities. The brain is a physical organ, while the mind is an intangible representation of self; the brain generates the concept of the mind, without which neither would exist.

---

174. Quote attributed to William Butler Yeats, poet (1865–1939).

Myth 18: Incomplete Brain Development Explains Teenagers' Behavior

This myth is based on the idea that teens act out and are irresponsible because the prefrontal cortex doesn't develop fully until the mid-20s. While it is true that the prefrontal lobes (which are responsible for executive functions) are still developing during the teen years, teenagers act out for a great number of reasons, among which include changing brain structures, but which should also consider poor home environments, bad models, hormonal challenges, and peer pressure.

Myth 19: Reasoning Is Contrary to Emotion

There is another longstanding myth that people with a "cool head," who are able to divorce emotions from their reasoning, are more successful. We now know, however, that emotions are vital to good decision-making and that it is impossible to reason without the influence of emotions. Although reasoning and emotions appear to be on different ends of the spectrum, they are actually complementary processes. Emotions are a part of all decision-making processes.

Myth 20: Unstructured Learning Is Superior to Structured
Learning Due to Improved Neurological Functioning

Unstructured discovery and self-paced learning are excellent techniques, which work well in modern classrooms. They work, however, not due to improved neurological functions, but rather because unstructured learning improves self-efficacy (a psychological concept) and is based on active learning principles (a pedagogical concept). The brain can and does learn in unstructured as well as structured classrooms.

Myth 21: Plasticity Is the Product of Good Pedagogy

Some popular press books suggest that neuroplasticity is due to good teaching practices (pedagogy). Plasticity is the attribute of the brain that makes it malleable and allows it to change in response to all new learning. This means that plasticity occurs in all instances of learning, with or without good teaching.

Myth 22: Learning Occurs Only in the Classroom

With the advent of formal education, classrooms became the dominant location of school-based instruction, which led to the myth that all learning occurs in schools. It is vital for teachers to help their students understand the value of learning that occurs outside of the classroom and to use these experience to enhance their own in-class learning. It is also important for people to remember that learning occurs across the lifespan, far beyond the school-age years.

Myth 23: A Student's History Does Not Affect His or Her Learning

It was once thought that we could teach anything to anybody, given the right techniques. We now know that a learner's past will always impact new learning. What a student already knows will influence the way he or she perceives new information. This means that expecting the same results from all students is misguided; students enter the classroom on an uneven playing field due to their histories.

Myth 24: Learning Can Be Isolated from Social and Emotional Content

It was once thought that learning could be separated from how the person feels about others (including the teacher). This myth led to the mistaken belief that the way classroom instruction was provided made little difference to the quality of the learning. We now know that learning is always influenced by the social and emotional contexts in which it occurs; the conscientious formation of group activities, for example, has a greater impact than once thought upon the quality of learning.

Irresponsible communicators tend to overgeneralize a single fact that ends up promoting neuromyths (e.g., language is a left-hemisphere activity). All educators need to be aware of the neuromyths that permeate the discipline and to be trained in the basic principle, tenets, and instructional practices of MBE science (see Tokuhama-Espinosa, 2010), not only those who profess affiliation to the new discipline. This is not presumptuous of the discipline's promoters; it is simply being responsible to students. Prudence about overgeneralization of information is advised because too much is at stake for such poor quality data to remain in the literature. There is a simple guide to improve the quality of information in MBE science.

Distinguishing Good Information from Bad

> *"Make a habit of two things: to help; or at least to do no harm."*
> —Hippocrates, *Epidemics*, Book I (Chapter 2, translated by Francis Adams, 1849)

All teachers should embrace medicine's first rule, which is *do no harm*. If we teachers are always reminded to do no harm before undertaking research, practicing our trade in classrooms, or designing policy, then the discipline will be in better hands. It may, indeed, *do harm* if teachers "throw out the baby with the bathwater" by rejecting everything in educational practice that cannot be proven by neuroscience. Similarly, it might be harmful to neuroscientists to dismiss teacher instinct. During the first inaugural International Mind, Brain, and Education Society Conference in 2007, many participants asked for help distinguishing "good" information from "bad" in the emerging discipline. Teachers are often overwhelmed by popular press titles that claim to help develop "better brains" and are at a loss to evaluate the quality of the information presented. There are two key tools that help distinguish good information from bad in MBE science. The first was seen earlier in this chapter on the OECD continuum. The second is a checklist of steps that have been devised using the input of the experts.

According to Patricia Wolfe (2006), one of the best ways to judge the quality of information is by using conceptual frameworks. Wolfe herself suggests one, which is seen below combined with the opinions of the international expert panel's steps (Tokuhama-Espinosa, 2008a). Together they make a useful set of questions we teachers and researchers can use to determine the level of credibility of the information found in education. Wolfe suggests that we must read about information on the brain critically before applying it to classroom practices. To do this, she suggests asking oneself the following questions:

- How many subjects were in the study? (That is, is it a representative study?)
- What were the ages and characteristics of the subjects? (That is, do these match the students with whom you work?)
- Was there a control group of subjects who were matched with the subjects in the experimental group?
- What was the methodology used for this study?
- Has the study been replicated by other scientists using the same methodology?
- Are there similar studies that have contradictory findings?

In a similar vein, the OECD (2002, p. 49) says that a critical community will also ask:

- What was the original study and its primary purpose? (That is, are the results being interpreted in the right context?)

- Is this a single study or a series of studies? (That is, are findings in context?)
- Did the study have a learning outcome? (That is, was an application in a real classroom setting part of the study?)

The MBE experts suggested five additions:

- Are the classroom interventions evidence-based, and if not possible, are they practice-based in order to justify their contextual validity? (*Evidence-based* means that there is a study that proves this; *practice-based* means that good results have been achieved over time using that intervention.)
- Are qualitative as well as quantitative research norms valued equally? (That is, equal weight should be given to qualitative studies as to quantitative ones.)
- Is the study or recommendation being applied up-to-date? (Information about the brain changes so quickly that "yesterday's news" may actually be proven ineffective.)
- Is the information viewed with enough critical thinking skills to ascertain how to "connect the dots" in MBE science? (Teachers have to show a high level of intellectual perseverance and work hard to think through all of the information possible before acting.)
- Is the information judged using a transdisciplinary lens? (It is not enough to have information from education; we need to nurture our understanding of how to teach with information about how the brain learns and how the mind processes new ideas.)

All of these steps together create a type of checklist that teachers and researchers can follow to ensure the quality of their information (see Figure 4.2). This checklist, combined with the OECD continuum, are two powerful tools to help teachers determine the quality of the information they are seeking to apply in their teaching. But how are these tools actually put into practice? An example of a common teaching practice shared in light of these tools helps illustrate the point.

Does the Use of the Socratic Method Complement MBE Standards?

It is useful to see how MBE science goals and standards relate to existing structures in

FIGURE 4.2
Steps to Ensure Quality Information

How to distinguish "good" information from "bad" in the emerging field

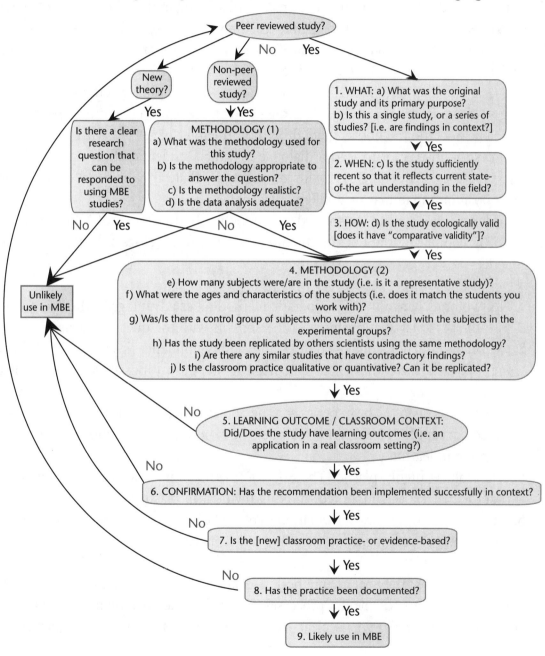

education. Perhaps the oldest teaching strategy in use is the Socratic method, a successful approach in the teaching and learning process that has proven itself in classrooms over the past 2,500 years (c. 490 B.C.E.). As such, it is a prime subject for comparison with MBE science standards. This means that, instead of starting in the laboratory and arriving in the classroom with a proposal for better teaching, we can run the process backwards. What happens when we take a successful classroom practice and put it to MBE science scrutiny? First it is important to define the Socratic method.

The Socratic method, named after the Greek philosopher Socrates, is a way of engaging students in discussion by encouraging their acknowledgment of gaps in understanding. The Socratic method is guided by the principle "never tell what you can ask," which forces the instructor to lead a dialogue in which students reflect upon their own thinking processes.[175] In some cases this results in a debate in which one or both sides defends a position unfamiliar or unlikely.

In order to evaluate the worth of the Socratic method in terms of MBE science, we can begin by comparing the Socratic method with the five well-established concepts in MBE science, as seen below:

1. No two brains are alike: The Socratic method takes advantage of this fact to delve into the personal relationship each person has with the question at hand.
2. All brains are not equal—context and ability influence learning: The Socratic method recognizes that there is a need to iterate a process to the level of the learner.
3. The brain is changed by experience: The Socratic method relies on this well-established concept for its existence; without the expectation of change, there would be no point in learning.
4. The brain is highly plastic: The Socratic method serves as a type of intellectual therapy that expects modified thinking (evident in plasticity).
5. The brain connects new information to old: The Socratic method relies on an individual's use of past memories to relate new concepts.

One of the reasons that the Socratic method is so successful is that it requires higher-order thinking. If we compare the mental processes involved in the Socratic method with those of *Bloom's Taxonomy* (1956), it is clear that students are working at a higher level of

175. Bain (2004).

thinking when they participate in a Socratic discourse, for example, than when they are passively lectured. Bloom's original taxonomy had six levels: knowledge, comprehension, application, analysis, synthesis, and evaluation. In a new look at Bloom (Figure 4.3), we see how knowledge and comprehension are combined (as being able to remember and understand), and how synthesis is exchanged for the creative process (to be creative, one has to synthesize past ideas and concepts to develop something new). By demanding higher-order thinking skills (analysis, creativity, and evaluation) through Socratic dialogue, students develop metacognition, exercise different memory systems, and pay attention to their own thinking processes[176] as well as those of others (all of which are MBE concepts, as seen in Chapter 9).

FIGURE 4.3
A New Look at Bloom's Taxonomy

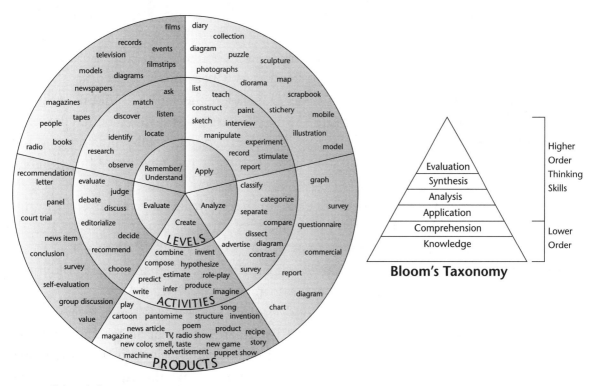

Bramwell for Tokuhama-Espinosa, 2010.

176. Meltzer (2007).

When students are lectured to in class, at best they manage to gain basic knowledge about core concepts, which in some instances turns into actual comprehension (as opposed to rote memorization). However, unless they are asked to do something with the information, students will never reach Bloom's midstage of applying that new concept during a lecture, let alone be able to analyze it. True synthesis of information only comes after an individual can analyze a variety of different situations in which the concept exists, as in how a certain math concept is manifested in many different contexts or examples. If synthesis is reached, then the individual can potentially produce a creative product and evaluate the concept for its intrinsic worth or utility. In the Socratic method the student is the protagonist of his or her own learning process, guided by the teacher's carefully chosen questions to reach new ideas.[177] This method is recognized as best practice in many schools, most notably many prestigious law and medical institutions around the world, and it is used in thousands of middle and high schools as well. The Socratic method is not designed to help students simply learn facts or memorize lessons; rather it is successful because it focuses more on the "whys" of information then the "whats."

The Socratic method embodies several well-researched areas in education. First, the study of executive functions and decision-making is a heavily researched area in MBE science. Executive functions include a wide range of higher-order thinking skills: for example, goal setting and planning, organization of behaviors over time, mental flexibility, attention and memory systems (including working memory), and self-regulation and self-monitoring processes.[178] To go further, it has also been shown that executive functions can be improved via the Socratic method of questioning. Executive functions have been the focus of developmental cognitive neuroscience for several years, attesting to their importance for inclusion in MBE science. Finally, executive functions are also related to the development of empathy, a vital component of the Socratic method (being able to put oneself in another's shoes).[179] Intellectual empathy is a key characteristic of critical thinkers as a whole. Empathy has also been researched in MBE science.

Given this analysis, the Socratic method appears to be a classroom format that is highly compatible with MBE science goals and standards. But not all teaching methods used in class can stand up to this type of scrutiny. For example, we mentioned lecture earlier on. It is clear that lecturing to students does not achieve the same level of results

---

177. Holmboe & Johnson (2005).
178. Nelson & Luciana (2001).
179. This is based principally on works by Facione (2007) and Paul & Elder (2005).

as the use of the Socratic method because it does not manage to stand up to MBE standards.[180] In Chapters 5 and 6 we further explore exactly who, how, why, and what is studied in MBE science and just how teaching is improved through this new discipline.

Suggested Reading

Teaching in MBE Science

Cohen, M., & Ranganath, C. (2007). Reinforcement learning signals predict future decisions. *Journal of Neuroscience, 27*(2), 371–378.

Crawford, M., & White, M. (1999). Strategies for mathematics: Teaching in context. *Educational Leadership, 57*(3), 34–39.

Goswami, U. (2008). *Cognitive development: The learning brain.* London: Taylor & Francis.

Harvey, S., & Goudvis, A. (2007). *Strategies that work: Teaching comprehension for understanding and engagement* (2nd ed.). Portland, ME: Stenhouse.

Holmboe, K., & Johnson, M. H. (2005). Educating executive attention. *Proceedings of the National Academy of Sciences of the United States of America, 102*(41), 14479–14480.

Marzano, R. (2003). *What works in schools?: Translating research into action.* Alexandria, VA: Association for Supervision and Curriculum Development.

Marzano, R. (2007). *The art and science of teaching: A comprehensive framework for effective instruction.* Arlington, VA: Association for Supervision and Curriculum Development.

Marzano, R., Pickering, D. J., & Pollock, J. E. (2004). *Classroom instruction that works: Research-based strategies for increasing student achievement.* New York: Prentice Hall.

Ronis, D. (2007). *Brain-compatible assessments* (2nd ed.). Thousand Oaks, CA: Corwin Press.

Sousa, D. (2000). *How the brain learns.* Thousand Oaks, CA: Corwin Press.

Willis, J. (2006). *Research-based strategies to ignite student learning: Insights from a neurologist and classroom teacher.* Alexandria, VA: Association for Supervision and Curriculum Development.

Willis, J. (2007). *Brain-friendly strategies for the inclusion classroom.* Alexandria, VA: Association for Supervision and Curriculum Development.

180. Zemelman, Daniels, & Hyde (1998).

CHAPTER **5**

The Scientifically Substantiated Art of Teaching, Part 1
Lessons from Research

"If we knew what it was we were doing, it would not be called research, would it?"
—Albert Einstein (1879–1955), as cited in Mitchell & Jolley (2009, p. 73)

Where does evidence relevant to MBE science come from? The emerging discipline of MBE science is a complex union, as we have seen. Studies can originate from many different sources and disciplines. The transdisciplinary nature of the new science of teaching and learning implies that it draws not only from the three parent fields (neuroscience, psychology, and pedagogy), but also from their sub-disciplines, which include cognitive neuroscience, psychological neuroscience, educational neurosciences, educational neuropsychology, psychobiology, microbiology, neuropsychology, as well as others. Additionally, in many instances, studies about specific skill sets, such as reading and math, contribute to knowledge about how to teach best. Finally, because teachers should be aware of the general way in which knowledge and intelligence are defined, a consideration of studies from the fields of philosophy and epistemology, as they relate to questions of how we know (or how we think we know) about the world around us, is also important. The range of MBE science literature seems complex, and it is, but with good reason.

To understand MBE science literature in proper context, "one must 'level jump'—that is, simultaneously examine the phenomenon in its own right (for its particular coherence and its specific rule of behavior), and pay attention to the conditions of its emergence (e.g., the agents that come together, the contexts of their co-activity, etc.)" (Davis & Sumara, 2006, p. xi). Several broad categories of studies help divide the information into easy-to-understand units: *who* is studied relevant to MBE science; *what is* studied in this new science of teaching and learning; *how* studies are conducted; and *which dimensions* are important to teachers. Each of these categories of studies is explained below.

Who Is Studied and Why

MBE science studies and serves all age groups and people of all mental abilities in its efforts to consider human learning across the lifespan. The use of longitudinal studies in many cases reflects an important perspective of MBE practitioners: Human learning can and does occur across the lifespan and should be viewed on a continuum and in relation to important individual developmental measures throughout life rather than on neatly fixed school levels.

While all age groups are considered relevant to MBE science, by far the most studied age group, based on the number of publications, is the birth to 5-year-old group.[181] Although there are currently more studies in these early years, it is likely that this will change in the near future because the practice of learning throughout the lifespan encourages increasing studies in older populations. In terms of total number of publications, the 0–5 age group is followed by primary school children, middle school children, high school students, and last of all, college students and adults. That is, the amount of available studies is in direct proportion to age. This is probably true for two reasons. First, interest in younger students may be due to the discipline's partial roots in developmental psychology and developmental neuroscience, which focus on younger humans. Another reason for the emphasis on the early years could be the belief that the first 3 years of life have a particularly influential impact on future learning—a claim that has recently been refuted by studies on neuroplasticity and neurogenesis, which demonstrate that the brain can and does learn throughout the lifespan[182] (although nutrition in the early years has a profound impact on potential).

Another reason that the majority of studies focus on younger children is that many false limits have been placed around certain abilities. For example, it was once hypothesized that if a person did not learn a foreign language before the age of 3, then he or she would never become proficient. This view was modified in the 1960s, and the limit was set at adolescence. We now know that people can (and probably should) learn foreign languages well into old age. In fact, Ellen Bialystok (2007) found that learning a foreign

181. Tokuhama-Espinosa (2008b).
182. Bruer (1999c).

language in the elder years stimulated the brains of the learners, staved off the effects of dementia, and was reported to provide a greater sense of fulfillment. The adage "use it or lose it" holds true for older learners; the more they use their brain, the more likely their brain will stay in shape. The challenge to society is to accept this new understanding that learning is a lifelong process that is by no means limited to the school-age years. It is likely that the age focus will shift in the near future toward older learners for the simple reason that populations are living longer, and geriatric studies indicate that part of the key to quality of life into old age relates to staying busy, both physically as well as mentally.

Another group of studies that is relevant to MBE science and important for teachers to know about are longitudinal studies that seek to track changes in the developing brain over the lifespan.[183] Jay Giedd, Chief of Brain Imaging at the Child Psychiatry Branch National Institute of Mental Health, has done a tremendous service in his longitudinal research by advancing ideas about the way we look at learning across the lifespan. By studying children's brains through adulthood, Giedd has demonstrated that radical changes occur in the adolescent brain that rival changes in newborns to 3-year-olds.[184] The restructuring of the architecture of the human brain during adolescence explains a great deal about teenage behavior, which is now known to be heavily influenced not only by hormonal and social changes but also by the physical reorganization of the brain. These studies have provided a more complete understanding of age-related behavioral attributes, giving parents and teachers new insight about how and why individuals act the way they do at different stages in their lives. These studies also give teachers a more complete understanding about the changing needs of the brain, from childhood to adolescence and through adulthood, related to nutrition, sleep, exercise, social stimulation, and emotional regulation (more on this topic in the coming pages).

Another category of studies relevant to MBE science investigates brain anomalies, rarities, or uncommon developmental trajectories. We teachers can learn a great deal from studies of individuals who are savants, gifted, have autism, are mentally retarded, have only half a brain, or have other congenital learning disabilities such as attention deficit disorder (ADD) or dyslexia. In some cases these special brains are the cause of learning problems, and in other cases they simply explain brains that work "a little bit differ-

183. For an example of a well-executed longitudinal study that supports MBE science principles, see Sowell, Thompson, Leonard, Welcome, Kan, & Toga (2004).

184. Documentation of this research can be found in the following articles: Giedd, (2004); Giedd, Blumenthal, Jeffries, Castellanos, Liu, & Zijdenbos (1999); Giedd, Snell, Lange, Rajapakse, Casey, & Kozuch (1996); Gogtay, Giedd, Lusk, Hayashi, Greenstein, & Vaituzis (2004); Thompson, Giedd, Woods, MacDonald, Evans, & Toga (2000).

ently."[185] The consideration of this wide variety of mental abilities allows us to establish what is "normal" and "abnormal" for the majority of people, as well as to explore the vast potential of the human brain in learning contexts.

This group of studies on atypical brain structure and function complements information that is known about typical brains and helps researchers to speculate about learning mechanisms in general, including those of the children in our classrooms. One of the ways these kinds of studies have helped teachers is that research about brain anomalies is easier to access and less ethically charged than studies of normal schoolchildren's brains. It is interesting to note that between the 1400s and 1900s, much of what was known about the brain was gleaned from examining damaged brains. Most healthy brains were buried with their owners, whereas "damaged" ones were studied as a way to find answers to illnesses and dysfunctions. Now, with the advent of imaging technology in the 1990s, we have gained glimpses into healthy functioning brains, and these glimpses have highlighted the individual variances between brains. These individual differences guide researchers in understanding subtle disparities in brain functioning between people who suffer from dyslexia, for example, and those who process language in a "normal" way. This information is key to teaching all students more effectively.

By studying the way people with certain problems approach learning challenges, we gain knowledge of how both "normal" and "different" brains work. For example, a brain scan of a person who has a language loss following a stroke may reveal the areas of the brain that relate to language processes (in both healthy and damaged brains). In a similar way, information from neuroimaging studies of people with different problems can help us understand which "normal" processes are being disturbed.[186] Exactly what is the brain capable of achieving, and under what conditions is this achieved? Learning differences are not seen as a negative in MBE science, but rather as a way to understand all brains better. Some of these different brains and their contributions are noted below.

• *Savants.* Savant syndrome is a rare condition in which an individual possesses an island of genius within an ocean of deficit. In some cases this means a severely retarded individual who is a genius in math skills, or an autistic individual with prodigious music skills, for example. Darold Treffert is perhaps the world's leading expert on the study of savant syndrome. According to Treffert, savantism is six times more frequent in males than

185. This is the title of the book by Bragdon & Gamon, (2000). For a good review of the wide range of differences, see Devinsky & D'Esposito's *Neurology of Cognitive and Behavioral Disorders* (2003).
186. A excellent review of many learning disabilities typically found in schools can be found in Coch, Dawson & Fischer, (2007).

females.[187] While typically genetic, in rare cases, sanvantism can also be acquired via traumas to the head. All savants have fascinating memory skills, which should make them of extreme interest to teachers, because we now know that there is no new learning without memory. A better understanding of exactly how savants access their apparently infinite memory systems may someday unlock the way average people do so. Some of these studies have helped us learn that there is a close link between the average savant's highly developed memory system and his or her close attention to minute detail. Can explicit teaching of detail enhance nonsavant memory? More research and a better understanding about how attention and memory are related will help teachers enhance student learning.

• *Gifted students.* Giftedness is normally defined as superior intelligence, though Robert Sternberg and Janet Davidson note in *Conceptions of Giftedness* (2005) that although high IQ scores may be an indication of giftedness, other factors are usually present, such as superior emotional, psychomotor, and creative abilities, spurred on by high self-concept and motivation.[188] Studies of giftedness help demonstrate physiological differences between typical and atypical brain structures and how those structures mediate executive function activities (higher-order thinking), for example.[189] By studying gifted students' frontal lobes and how their brains process, analyze, synthesize, and judge information, we get a better idea of how nongifted children can be taught to enhance these skills. For decades gifted students have been misdiagnosed or ignored in educational settings, and even, in some cases, seen as being as "troublesome" as students with learning deficits. As a group, we teachers are just beginning to learn what to do when a child has a learning problem that slows him down, but we have really little idea of what to do for those who excel and finish before everyone else for inexplicable reasons and then sit angry and bored for the rest of the class (see Table 5.1). We can improve our teaching—devise better teaching methods that can reach more students across the spectrum—by better understanding how the brains of gifted students work.

• *Autism* is a brain development disorder that affects approximately 6 per 1,000 people in the general population and occurs about four times more frequently in boys than girls. The chief characteristics of children with autism involve repetitive behavior (compulsive and/or ritualistic) as well as low levels of social interaction, lack of eye contact, and inability to react to the emotions of others. An important new area of research relevant to

187. See Treffert (2009) for a thorough explanation of savant syndrome.
188. For good reviews of studies on giftedness, see Mendaglio (2002); Sternberg & Davidson (2005).
189. Some excellent work in this area can be found in Geake (2005b); Sabatella (1999); Ziegler & Goswami (2005).

TABLE 5.1
Gifted Criteria

Level	Standardized Intelligence Test	Within General Population
Bright	115–129	1 in 6 (84th percentile)
Moderately gifted	130–144	1 in 50 (97.9th percentile)
Highly gifted	145–159	1 in 1000 (99.9th percentile)
Exceptionally gifted	160–174	1 in 30,000 (99.997th percentile)
Profoundly gifted	175+	1 in 3 million (99.99997th percentile)

Source: Based on Miraca Gross (2004) and Deborah Robson, Judy Fort Brenneman, and Kiesa Kay (2007).

MBE science relates to the discovery of mirror neurons as the physiological basis of empathy and to their dysfunction in children who have autism. Mirror neurons "show activity in relation both to specific actions performed by self and matching actions performed by others, providing a potential bridge between minds."[190] Simply observing another implementing an action activates these neurons. Studies have shown that people with autism, who tend to have problems with social cognition and empathy, are lacking in the production of mirror neurons, pointing for the first time to physical evidence of the root causes of this disorder.[191] These studies point not only to explanations for how autistic and gifted minds work, but they also offer a more complete understanding of how the brain works in normal populations. Our classrooms are more and more diverse, perhaps more in terms of mental abilities as in any other way. The 21st-century teacher needs to know how to, at a minimum, recognize these special, autistic brains and be able to guide parents toward specialists. Teachers who are aware that autism may be caused by a malfunctioning mirror neuron system can rethink strategies for intervention.

• *Students with ADD.* Attention deficit (hyperactivity) disorder is a learning problem that affects more children in the United States than any other. There is now information that explains the complex neural circuitry in the brain required to maintain attention, judge the importance of what is being attended to, process this assessment, and act

190. Williams, Whiten, Suddendorf, & Perrett (2001, p. 287).
191. Hadjikhani, Joseph, Snyder, & Tager-Flusberg (2006).

accordingly. By identifying where the regular attention circuitry goes awry in people with ADD, either due to neurotransmitter imbalances[192] or the circuit physiology itself,[193] we can then make recommendations about treatment.[194] Studying people with ADD also helps create hypotheses about how brains without ADD manage attention. This knowledge can help teachers better diagnose attention problems in their students and then guide them with varying levels of attention circuitry management abilities, as well as help students develop a better metacognitive understanding of just how they pay attention. Interesting longitudinal studies have compared developmental traits in ADD over many years. For example, some very interesting research has tracked people over their lifetimes and reported that 30–50% of those with ADD in childhood continue to have ADD in adulthood.[195] Do some people simply "grow out" of ADD? If so, why? What are the physiological changes in the brain architecture or chemistry that cause this improvement? What happens in the brains of the 30–50% of people that fail to shed ADD after the early school years? Should treatment for adults be different from that of younger patients with ADD? All of these questions should be studied further in MBE science with an eye toward maximizing the quality of life as well as the potential to learn. We as teachers need to know the state of the research in order to be as effective as possible in the classroom.

• *People with half a brain: Hemisphericity*. Despite the rareness of the condition, there is a surprising number of studies related to hemisphericity and interhemispheric integration, or the study of individuals with only half a brain.[196] These studies show how a person with just one of the two hemispheres in the brain can grow up relatively normally. This fact demonstrates the brain's plasticity and flies in the face of the idea that certain areas of the brain are programmed for just one type of learning (e.g., the left hemisphere is solely responsible for language). Hemisphericity studies[197] are testaments to the flexibility of brain structures and suggest that complex systems, rather than single specific areas of the brain, manage learning. The importance of these studies is immense as they point to the overall potential of the human brain to rewire itself for efficiency.

---

192. For examples of these kinds of studies see Scholes, Harrison, O'Neill & Leung (2007).
193. For some examples, see Qiu, Crocetti, Adler, & Mahone (2009); Vance, Silk, Casey, Rinehart, Bradshaw, & Bellgrove (2007).
194. Volpe, DuPaul, Jitendra, & Tresco (2009).
195. For examples, see Biederman, Petty, Dolan, Hughes, Mick, & Monteaux (2008); Miller, Miller, Newcorn, & Halperin (2008).
196. Perhaps the most renowned studies in this area come from the excellent documentation by Battro (2000) and Immordino-Yang (2004, 2007a).
197. Such as those conducted by Battro, 2000; Immordino-Yang, 2004; Immordino-Yang & Fischer (2007).

• *Dyslexia*. A challenging condition that has produced a great deal of research in recent years is dyslexia.[198] Evident in problems related to reading and spelling, dyslexia is a learning disorder that impacts between 5 and 17% of the U.S. population.[199] There are many theories about dyslexia (see below) as well as a myriad of ideas about dyslexia's roots (evolutionary vs. acquired), and several proposed programs to treat this language disorder. Nevertheless there is no full consensus about treatment. According to the Dyslexic Research Institute (2009), "Ten to fifteen percent of the U.S. population has dyslexia, yet only five out of every one hundred dyslexics are recognized and receive assistance," due in part to teachers' inabilities to grasp the scope of the problem.[200]

Some studies have identified the different brain structures and processes in people learning to read and write with dyslexia compared to those without dyslexia. By learning about the different ways people with dyslexia process words, researchers are learning about reading processes in normal children, as well as developing the tools to design more effective interventions. Specific interventions are being tested in different universities around the world. For example, Todd Richards and Virginia Berninger's research at the University of Washington emphasizes not only the phonemic relations between words, but also the familiarity of the form of the word (physical appearance), and creates drills that group words accordingly. The researchers found that these interventions helped the majority of children, but as with interventions in medicine, although the treatment has been effective with many, it has no effect on others.[201] What does this tell us? The simple fact that the complexities of dyslexia mean that some individuals respond to some interventions, but there is no single intervention that helps everyone. The interventions considered by the National Academy of Sciences to prevent reading difficulties[202] concluded that the same interventions were recommended for students with dyslexia as for regular readers: systematic phonics combined with many opportunities to practice new words in meaningful text and opportunities to write in the classroom. This recommendation implies that dyslexic brains are more alike than different from brains without dyslexia, which is of no surprise. The information about dyslexia does tell us, however, that there is a wide range of sub-components to reading, and these sub-components have

198. Some representative works include: Aylward, Richards, Berninger, Nagy, Field, & Grimme (2003); Corina, Richards, Serafín, Richards, Steury, & Abbott. (2001); Shaywitz & Shaywitz (2005).
199. Birsh (2005).
200. This figure is debated because others say that this disability hinders just 3–6% of the United States population (Joseph, Noble, & Eden, 2001). The lower figure is more in alignment with other country studies.
201. For the results of this research, see Aylward, Richards, Berninger, Nagy, Field, & Grimme (2003).
202. *Preventing Reading Difficulties in Young Children*, edited by Snow, Burns, & Griffin (1998).

led to theories about their possible deficits in dyslexia: phonemic awareness and the ability to "hear" written words in our heads (phonological deficit theory of dyslexia); the speed with which we can "hear" (rapid auditory processing theory); the accuracy with which we can decode the visual patterns of words (visual theory); the way we block out distractions to focus on written words (perceptual visual-noise exclusion hypothesis); the way we articulate (speak) and write using specified motor function (cerebellar theory); and the general way that the brain integrates its ability to see, hear, process, decode, pronounce, and finally read (magnocellular theory).

The information about brains that work a little bit differently helps teachers not only to recognize specific learning problems, such as dyslexia, but also to grasp how the brain works as a system. Reading is not a simplistic processes; it involves a complex combination of abilities that culminates in the possibility of reading and writing. By learning more about each of these special brains, teachers are better prepared to meet the individualized needs of their students.

In summary, MBE science studies just about everyone: all age groups and all mental abilities. This global approach might seem counterproductive in that specialist knowledge of different age groups or ability levels might yield more precise findings. However, this global overview is useful in making overarching comparisons about what is considered "normal" versus "atypical" in the human repertoire of skills, which in turn points to a clearer understanding of what it truly means to reach personal potential through good teaching.

What Is Studied and Why

All dimensions of human learning are studied in MBE science, so it is a bit ingenuous to limit the scope in this book to the few entries here. To select the elements most deserving of description, we first consider information to which teachers are not normally exposed and which is of vital importance in understanding the teaching–learning dynamic. In the broadest sense, these studies are broken down into two large groups: studies related to specific skills, abilities, or domains (e.g., reading or math), and those that are focused on cognition as a whole (e.g., theories of intelligence). Additionally, there are three broad categories of studies related to the biological aspect of learning that are essential to an understanding of MBE science: studies on neurogenesis, plasticity, and the mind–body connection (which includes studies on sleep, exercise, and nutrition, and the impact of each on learning).

Isolated Skills Studies

Studies related to specific skills, abilities, or domains are described below in general terms, and several specific examples are given in Chapters 6 and 7 of this book. Studies in this category document metabolic changes in the brain based on certain stimuli, as in learning to play the guitar or to read, for example.[203] The fascinating aspect of these studies is that they help teachers understand that there are no simple classroom subjects or skill sets; rather, each is comprised of a myriad of sub-skills. For example, to play a guitar and sing, an individual needs to be able to coordinate specific finger movements while interpreting the symbols on the page to read the music, and simultaneously considering the rhythm, intonation of voice, and speed with which to play. What does this breakdown into sub-skills mean for teachers? It helps us understand that each skill that a student learns can and should be broken down into its smaller pieces for better management. One of the most effective war tactics is to divide and conquer. Why? Because once the whole is broken down into more manageable smaller pieces and isolated, the pieces can be dealt with in a more efficient manner. Some of the best-practice teaching methods embrace this idea—and it is common knowledge among the good teachers. In a concrete example of this practice, Zemelman and colleagues (2005) suggest that teachers should correct writing assignments in parts: First for content idea, then for spelling, then for grammar, then for organization, etc., in order to make the challenge of writing well more manageable for students, and to call their attention to the types of problems they may be facing. It is much easier for students to deal with one type of correction at a time than with a lot of red all over the paper at once. This approach also helps them recognize their strengths and weaknesses related to aspects of writing. Receiving a page full of errors leaves students at a loss as to how or where to begin improvement. The intricacies of many academic skills, including reading and writing sub-skills, are explained in more detail in Chapter 7. Suffice it to say now that studying the brain as we learn how to teach widens teacher appreciation of the many intricacies of academic instruction of as well as life survival skills.

Remediating skills requires accurate diagnosis; therefore, the more we know about how the brain learns, the better we become at identifying and resolving children's learning challenges. A wealth of imaging studies has demonstrated how the brain learns to read,[204]

203. For examples, see Bluestone, Abdoulaev, Schmitz, Barbour, & Hielscher (2001).
204. See Noesselt, Shah, & Jancke (2003) for a good example.

do math,[205] pay attention,[206] remember,[207] and control itself using executive functions,[208] not to mention lesser-known studies on how the brain interprets humor. Recent studies at Stanford Psychiatry and Neuroimaging Laboratory (2003), for example, sought to identify how humor and reward systems in the brain are related.[209] Why is this important to teachers? Because an appreciation of the complex nature of learning and an understanding of the many sub-components involved in a specific learning task helps us teach more effectively, pinpoint problem areas more accurately, and differentiate instruction with more precision. Related to humor, for example, researchers found that the areas of the brain involved in the rewarding feelings that follow the use of some addictive drugs and alcohol, or monetary gain in gambling addiction (the nucleus accumbens, ventral tegmental area), as well as brain areas that process fear and other emotions (amygdala), are all involved in the brain's interpretation of humor.[210] What does this say about class clowns? About relaxed and fun class environments? About teachers who "can't take a joke"? The specifics of these skill areas, both in academic and human survival realms, are the focus of Chapter 6.

In summary, studies about domain-specific skills such as reading, writing, guitar playing, or humor help teachers understand how to break down skills into their smaller parts. In doing so, teachers are better equipped to diagnose problems with greater accuracy. By understanding the disaggregated elements of reading, for example, teachers can develop more accurate interventions (see Chapter 7). The other large groups of studies that help teachers do their job better are related to global theories of intelligence and cognition as a whole.

Studies on Cognition as a Whole

Studies that focus on cognition as a whole establish "normal" boundaries for different cognitive activities. These texts seek to "map the mind"[211] in images using new technology. The most substantial contributions to understanding general intelligence, with direct rele-

---

205. See Rickard, Romero, Basso, Wharton, Flinton, & Grafman (2000) for a sample of this concept.
206. For an example of this, see Iidaka, Aderson, Kapur, Cabeza, & Craik (2000).
207. See Schacter & Wagner (1999).
208. An example of this type of study can be found in Weiskopf, Scharnowski, Veit, Goebel, Birbaumer, & Mathiak (2004).
209. This study showed "new evidence that humor engages a network of subcortical regions including the nucleus accumbens, a key component of the mesolimbic dopaminergic reward system. Further, the degree of humor intensity was positively correlated with BOLD signal intensity in these regions. Together, these findings offer new insight into the neural basis of salutary aspects of humor" (Mobbs, Greicius, Abdel-Azim, Menon, & Reiss, 2003, p. 1041).
210. *ScienceCentral Archives* (2007).
211. Examples of these types of studies can be found in Cabeza & Kingstone, (2001); Cabeza & Nyberg (2000); Carter (1998); Friston (2005); Debener, Ullsperger, Siegel, & Engel (2006); Gazzaniga (2005b); Martin, 2003; Nuñez, 2005; Tamraz & Comair (2005).

vance to MBE science, occurred in the last few decades, between 1985 and the present. The documentation of "normal" patterns of thinking has led to new theories of intelligence. Those theories relevant to the MBE science literature ground intellectual abilities in neurological explanations.[212] For example, Fischer and Rose's webs of skills (2001); Atherton's neurocognitive model for students and educators (2002); Connell's attempts to define the foundations of educational neuroscience by integrating theory, experiment, and design (2005); and Fischer's dynamic cycles of cognitive and brain development (2007) each establishes cognitive development in a system that explains how the brain creates the mind and how each mind is unique and constantly changing. While it is unclear as to whether any of the aforementioned theorists overtly aspired to unite their theories with that of the emerging discipline, it is testament to the increasing needs of education that there are so many new theories in recent times. Other studies relevant to MBE science ground human intellect in evolutionary processes and suggest that humans will continue to increase their overall mental abilities as new challenges in the environment are met. The evolutionary view reminds teachers that some skills, such as reading, for example, are not as "natural" as skills such as scanning the horizon for the enemy, but rather imposed on the brain—which might explain why there are more problems with some skill sets than others.[213]

Perhaps the group of studies that is most relevant to teachers is that related to theories of intelligence. Some of these studies jibe at the simplistic ways we once presumed to measure intelligence in schools.[214] Historically, the studies on intelligence have evolved from a consideration of "g," or pure intellectual potential, to a broader view of intelligence based on individual potential.

The first challenge to the single intelligence model ("g") came from Howard Gardner's theory of multiple intelligences,[215] which has dominated educational discussions over the past 25 years, most likely due to the attractiveness of seeing a variety of ways (eight, at last count) in which people can be intelligent, not simply one. Gardner's newer work, *Intelligence Reframed* (2001), Hawkins' *On Intelligence* (2004), and Sternberg's *Triarchic Theory of Intelligence* (1985) are all models that seek to break out of the once-limited way of estimating human ability.[216]

212. See Blair (2006); Haier & Jung (2007).
213. See Calvin (1996); Dehaene (2009); Schultz (2001).
214. As in work by Perkins (1995).
215. Gardner (1993a).
216. See Mayer (2007).

Another example of theories of intelligence that are relevant to MBE science is found in Mel Levine's work. Levine (2000) divides human potential into systems or neurodevelopmental constructs. He believes that just as the body has seven systems (digestive, reproductive, respiratory, circulatory, nervous, skeletal, muscular), the brain has eight: memory, attention, temporal-sequential ordering, spatial ordering, language, neuromotor function, social cognition, and higher-order cognition. Just as the body suffers if any one of the seven systems is not working well, the brain's potential can be limited if one of the eight systems in question is not functioning fully. For example, Levine argues that memory and attention are the driving processes involved in learning. If a child has a problem with any aspect of memory (working, short-term, or long-term), or suffers from attention deficits at any level, learning is impaired. His theory also suggests that if a student has a poor temporal-sequential ordering system, he will be challenged to comprehend mathematical formulas or grammatical rules as sequential ordering relates to formulas and rules. A deficit in any of the neurodevelopmental constructs impacts the student as a whole and effectively impairs his or her potential learning abilities. Levine's work bridges the gap between purely psychological models of intelligence and biologically based ones. Though less well known than Gardner, Levine's theory of neurodevelopmental constructs finds support from neurologists and will most likely be the start of a new genre of thinking about intelligence in the future, especially with relevance to MBE science.

Biological Aspects of Learning
Certain biological aspects of learning are highly relevant to teachers, but rarely mentioned in education training programs. These include how specific processes—neurogenesis, plasticity, and the mind–body connection (sleep, nutrition, and exercise)—influence learning.

• *Neurogenesis.* Another way we as teachers can understand the brain better is through an understanding about the existence of neurogenesis,[217] or the generation of new brain cells. Neurogenesis, proven only in the past decade, shows that brain cells can and do regenerate not only in animals,[218] but also in humans.[219] The neuromyths that have mushroomed around this process were discussed in a previous chapter. It is vital that teachers accept that a true understanding of this concept is still in its infantile stages and

217. For the variety of theories related to neurogenesis, see Becker, S. (2005); Aimone, Wiles, & Gage (2006); Shors, Townsend, Zhao, Kozorovitskiy, & Gould (2002).
218. As demonstrated by studies such as that of Luzzati, De Marchis, Fasolo, & Peretto (2006).
219. See the documentation of this groundbreaking finding in Bruel-Jungerman, Davis, Rampon, & Laroche (2006); Ortega-Perez, Murray, & Lledo, (2007); Society for Neuroscience (2007a); Tashiro, Makino, & Gage (2007).

there are many false claims that neurogenesis is related to good teaching.[220] Here we focus on what is actually established at this point in time. Neurogenesis happens as a cycle somewhat like menstruation. It occurs more or less monthly: About half of the cells die immediately, and about half of the surviving cells attach to existing ones, while the final fourth create new links. Some studies have indicated that exercise or high levels of oxygenation help the survival rates of new brain cells, though this has only been proven in rats.[221]

Teachers should know that adult neurogenesis of hippocampal cells (the hippocampus is a structure that mediates long-term memory) is important for learning. These studies contribute to the understanding that humans can and do learn throughout the lifespan. Other studies on neurogenesis focus on the implications, facts, and limitations of this knowledge.[222] Does neurogenesis ensure learning into old age? Apparently not, but it does explain how deterioration of mental skills can be staved by activity. Adults who remain active (e.g., by doing Sudoku or crossword puzzles, learning a foreign language, or engaging in any mentally stimulating activity) can counteract the natural decline of memory loss by taking advantage of the new brain cells that are produced, especially in the hippocampal region. What is key for us as teachers about studies on neurogenesis is the understanding that both the proliferation and survival of new brain cells can be impacted by activity, nutrition, and other lifestyle choices.[223] Future studies in neurogenesis may possibly identify more concrete ways to enhance new cell growth in the brain, curtailing the negative downturn of abilities generally related to advancing age. Current studies in neuroplasticity and neurogenesis give teachers and learners evidence that learning can and does occur throughout the lifespan, not just during early childhood as was once speculated until recently,[224] which may eventually influence educational policy and lifelong learning programs.

• *Plasticity*. Brain plasticity (neuroplasticity) is a term that sounds odd to the average person, for whom the word *plastic* brings up images of Tupperware, rubber bands, and Saran Wrap. Among neuroscientists, though, *plasticity* refers to the brain's ability to change—for better or worse—throughout life. Plasticity—the reorganization of connec-

---

220. See Bruel-Jungerman, Rampon, & Laroche (2007); Kitabatake, Sailor, Ming, & Song (2007).
221. van Praag, Christie, Sejnowski & Gage (1999).
222. Kim, Shirvalkar, & Herrera (2003).
223. Examples of these types of studies can be found in Bruel-Jungerman, Davis, Rampon, & Laroche (2006); Eriksson, Perfilieva, Njork-Eriksson, Alborn, Nordborg, & Peterson (1998); Kornack & Rakic (1999); Santarelli, Saxe, Gross, Surget, Battaglia, & Dulawa (2003); Tashiro, Makino, & Gage (2007); Luzzati, De Marchis, Fasolo, & Peretto (2006); Thomas, Hotsenpiller, & Peterson (2007).
224. As seen in Shore (1997).

tions in the brain—is perhaps the most fascinating aspect of the human brain to teachers, because it is the epitome of learning. All learning is characterized by plasticity, or the connection of brain cells that were not previously linked. Plasticity challenges old views that the brain is a fixed structure; instead, we now know that it is malleable and that different parts can be used for different things.

In extreme cases, plasticity allows the brain to readjust and relocate brain functions from one area to another due to damage. Brain plasticity is a concept that is at once extraordinarily complex and very simple: "That the brain is not static; that it responds to circumstances, to new learning, is fairly easy to grasp."[225] Neural plasticity is actually the essence of learning. Every time the brain learns something, new it experiences physical changes and demonstrates its plasticity.

Some of the studies on plasticity focus on specific processes such as memory.[226] These studies show how the brain physically changes with the creation of new memories. Other research points to the drastic changes in plasticity that occur in the brain during certain ages.[227] Studies related to growth periods hint at the idea that the brain has certain *sensitive periods* for growth in which some cognitive skills may be easier to learn (this does not suggest a *critical period*, however, in which new learning must occur or the possibility to learn is lost). Actually, other studies on neuroplasticity point to the ability of the human brain to learn into old age,[228] which debunks concepts of critical periods for skill acquisition.[229] Teachers should also know that longitudinal studies have demonstrated both plasticity and neurogenesis as manifested in life changes,[230] or literally how life changes the brain. Research in neuroplasticity offers evidence of how behavioral changes are actually reflections of physical changes in the brain, including the documentation of how therapy changes the brain.[231] Plasticity is one of the most exciting discoveries in modern times and one of the truly optimistic findings related to the brain.

• *Mind–body connection.* Recognition of the mind–body connection harkens back to the Latin saying *Corpus sanus in mente sana* ("fit body, fit mind"). The basic idea is that

---

225. Merzenich (2008, p. 1).
226. See Benfenati (2007) and Society for Neuroscience (2007c) for examples.
227. Some key studies in this area include Eliot (1999); Elman, Bates, Johnson, Karmiloff-Smith, Parisi, & Plunkett (1996); Fischer & Rose (1998); Jernigan, Trauner, Hesselink, & Tallal (1991); Strauch (2003); Thompson, Vidal, Giedd, Gochman, Blumenthal, & Nicolson (2001).
228. See Sowell, Peterson, Thompson, Welcome, Henkenius, & Toga (2003).
229. Key studies can be found in Bruer (1999b); Chungani (2005); D'Arcangelo (2000); Ellers (2004); Lewis (1997); Pediatric Services (2002); Ramscar & Gitcho (2007); Schwartz (2003).
230. For some of the more extraordinary studies, see Giedd, Blumenthal, Jeffries, Castellanos, Liu, & Zijdenbos (1999); Gogtay, Giedd, Lusk, Hayashi, Greenstein, & Vaituzis (2004); Sowell, Peterson, Thompson, Welcome, Henkenius, & Toga (2003).
231. Doidge (2007).

what happens to the body impacts the brain's ability to function.[232] Teachers and educational policy makers need to be aware of the rich and growing list of findings in this area in order to be more effective in the classroom. How does the brain manage the body, or conversely, how does the body impact the brain? (See Figure 5.1 for Leonardo Da Vinci's answer to this question.) There are at least three specific foci of MBE research on the mind–body connection: sleep, exercise, and nutrition.

FIGURE 5.1
Da Vinci's Interpretation of the Mind–Body Connection

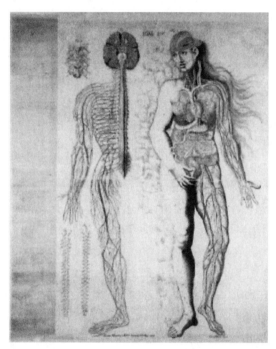

Source: British Science Museum online resources (http://www.sciencemuseum.org.uk/hommedia.ashx?id=7252&size=Small).

Related to the previous point about plasticity, there are several studies that show how sleep can impact brain plasticity.[233] These studies imply that those who sleep well use their brains more effectively and may even use more areas. This finding has great implications for teaching. In order to make the most of this knowledge, teachers should educate parents about the studies that show how sleep deprivation impacts cognitive func-

232. See Meissner (2006) for a good representational study in this area.
233. Dang-vu, Desseilles, Peigneux, & Maquet (2006); Maquet (2003).

tioning.[234] While the impact of lack of sleep on student performance is obvious to many classroom teachers and parents, it is now fully documented that not only is the body affected when people don't sleep, but also the mind's potential to learn.

Sleep not only rests the body and mind, it is also fundamental to the consolidation of long-term memory.[235] Sleep deprivation has a negative impact on memory; people who do not get sufficient rest cannot pay attention, nor can they consolidate memories effectively. Many of the documents in this sub-field explain the importance of sleep for school success.[236] Although most of us know this instinctively, it can be impressive to read the actual research. Numerous studies have investigated the role of physical well-being on mental achievement,[237] including the impact of student sleep cycles on learning potential.[238] Some studies in this category note the overall importance of rest on learning prowess,[239] specifically noting which neural networks are impaired by sleep deprivation and the consequences for learning.[240] Longitudinal studies on sleep patterns in children also clearly identify sleep needs as well as the consequences that a lack of sleep can have on student learning.[241] But why does sleep impact learning? One answer is related to attention spans; simply put, tired people can't pay attention. However, there is another more intriguing answer relevant to MBE science.

How and why do sleep needs change from infancy through adulthood? Why do newborn babies sleep far more than adults (averaging 17 hours a day) and spend an inordinate amount of time in REM (rapid eye movement) sleep (between 50 and 60%), when adults sleep between 7 and 8 hours a day and spend just 20–25% in REM? What is it about REM sleep in infancy that is so important to brain formation? Why does this need for sleep slowly reduce in childhood, but then once again increase in adolescence (when it often isn't satisfied)? Why do young adults need more sleep than people over 60? While there are no clear answers at this stage, there are hints at the answers to these questions in the chemical structure of sleep.

234. As in work by Hobson (2004); Killgore, Blakin, & Wesensten (2005); Wamsley (2007); Wolfson & Carskadon (1998).
235. For some of the very important work in this area, see Hobson (2004); Mednick, Nakayama, & Stickgold (2003).
236. See Carskadon, Wolfson, Acebo, Tzischinsky, & Seifer (1998).
237. A representative sampling of these kinds of studies can be found in Hillman, Castelli, & Buck (2005).
238. Pérez-Chada, Pérez Lloret, Videla, Cardinali, Bergna, & Fernández-Acquier (2007).
239. Wamsley & Antrobus (2006).
240. See Bell-McGinty, Habeck, Hilton, Rakitin, Scarmeas, & Zarahn (2004). Also, for a general overview of "chronoeducation," or the impact of sleep cycles on learning, see the *Mind, Brain, and Education Journal, 2008, 2*(1), pp. 29–47, available online at *www3.interscience.wiley.com/journal/117982931/home*.
241. Andrade, Benedito-Silva, Domenice, Arnhold, & Menna-Barreto (1993); Pérez-Chada, Pérez Lloret, Videla, Cardinali, Bergna, & Fernández-Acquier (2007); Taylor, Jenni, Acebo, & Carskadon (2005).

TABLE 5.2
Sleep Needs Newborns to Adults

Age	Newborns					Children			Adolescents			Adults			Over 60s		
	1w	1m	3m	6m	9m	2y	5y	7y	9y	11y	13y	14y	15y	16y	18	18+	60+
Average hours of sleep	17	15.5	15	14.25	14	13	11	10.5	10	9.5	9.5	9.5	9.25	9	8.5	7–8	6.5

Source: Based on information from Hobson (2000), Carskadon, Acebo & Jenni (2004) and Carskadon, Wolfson, Acebo, Tzischinsky, & Seifer (1998).

A vast number of studies demonstrate the role of dreaming—primarily the REM stage—in memory consolidation.[242] These studies show that people need adequate sleep in order to consolidate memories. Teachers need only reflect for a moment to think of the many implications this finding has for school. According to researchers in this field, the main reason for this effect relates to the types of memories being acquired in a school (i.e., declarative or explicit memories) and the unique structure of REM states versus other stages of sleep (including the combinations of neurotransmitters that are active in this particular stage of sleep).

• *Physical exercise.* The role of movement in learning has been well documented in the active-learning literature that shows how movement can enhance learning.[243] The major tenets of active learning involve increased movement, which results in better oxygenation of the brain, leading to better attention spans and retention.[244] As the brain uses roughly 20% of the body's oxygen supply, better oxygenation translates into "clearer thinking."[245] When the body is inactive, less oxygen flows through the brain, and drowsiness can occur. These studies are relevant to teachers because they provide evidence against certain teaching methodologies, such as extremely passive ones, due to the lack of oxygenation experienced by students. One of the reasons that recall is so low for lecture techniques, for example, is that passive reception of information does not involve any energy on the part of the student.[246] In contrast, when a student is involved in active learning (e.g., in small-group discussion, debates, physical construction of models, composition of narratives), he or she is more likely to remember the content.

242. Some of the seminal work in this area is documented in studies by Best, Diniz Behn, Poe, & Booth (2007); Fogel, Smith, & Cote (2007); Hobson & Pace-Schott (2002); Hobson, Pace-Schott, & Stickgold (2000); Stickgold, (2005, 2006); Yoo, Hu, Gujar, Jolesz, & Walker (2007).
243. See Greenleaf (2003); Moss & Sholey (1995); Sibley & Etnier (2003).
244. In Moss & Sholey (1995); Wolfe (2001a).
245. See Nunley (2002a).
246. For more information, see Sousa (2000).

In short, static, inactive classrooms are out, and dynamic, active classrooms are in. We have all experienced interminable, passive lecture situations in which learning is meant to emerge from a magical transmission of oral communication and auditory perception. This works for some learners, in some situations with some subjects, but for most learners, attention cannot be maintained beyond a 10- to 20-minute span. The bottom line: If there is no movement (change of person, place, or activity), then learning is jeopardized. Short moments of movement between lessons or a shift to concepts dedicated to the body in order to refresh the mind can enhance the retention of new concepts. Such breaks can be as simple as changing seats in a class.[247] There is no conclusive evidence as to whether "brain breaks" appear to work due to better oxygenation[248] or simply because they refocus attention and break up the monotony of lessons. Great teachers also know that when students interchange movement activities with thinking activities, they are able to maintain clear attention for longer periods.[249]

Other physiological studies report on the chemical changes in the brain. Major proponents of active learning include Greenleaf, whose article "Motion and Emotion in Student Learning" (2003) demonstrated the link between movement and brain-based learning concepts. According to Greenleaf, "brain-body-environment relationships . . . are expanding and sharpening our capacity to become more effective educators" (Greenleaf, 2003, p. 37). Active and passive brains display different blood flow and chemistry.[250] Active brains have a physiology that is more conducive to better attention and long-term memory. Several studies document that physical exercise can actually enhance memory and recall due to the neurotransmitters that are activated in the process.[251] Moss and Sholey supply "evidence demonstrating that oxygen administration improves memory formation" (Moss & Sholey, 1995, p. 255). Teachers who are armed with this knowledge know to include active learning tasks in class and to vary instructional methods in ways that allow students to physically change position with frequency.

• *Nutrition.* Many studies about nutrition are relevant to MBE science.[252] Good eating habits contribute to learning, and poor eating habits detract from the brain's ability to maximize its learning potential. "A student's diet contributes toward both poor attention and its opposite, improved concentration. What our students eat influences how well they

247. Keuler & Safer (1998b).
248. It stands to reason that the more physical activity a student is engaged in, the more oxygen is flowing through his or her bloodstream.
249. Chatterjee (2004).
250. For a more detailed explanation, see Gazzaniga (2005b).
251. See Winter, Breitenstein, Mooren, Voelker, Fobker, & Lechtermann (2007).
252. See Peretta (2004).

do in our classrooms."[253] Several studies discuss the specific impact of nutrition on learning[254] or its impact on states of mind; the state of the body impacts the potential of the brain to learn.[255] Marcason's (2005) studies, for example, demonstrated how diet might have an impact on neural tissues that affect executive function and attention. This means that fatty foods or high-sugar soft drinks, which often make up part of teenage diets in the United States, may be a contributing factor not only to obesity, but also to learning problems.[256] Yet other studies in this group relate to how diet may impact certain learning deficits. Poor nutrition can impact the brain through the balance of chemicals, sugars, fats, and other ingredients found in the foods children eat, and can also explain the highs and lows of attention many students experience in class. Other studies in this field consider how specific aspects of diet, such as overuse of polyunsaturated fatty acids, can impact the brain, memory, and learning networks.[257]

Knowledge about the link between mental and physical health has implications for school policy (e.g., cafeteria options) as well as national health policies. As with all of the other tenets in MBE science, the difficult aspects of nutritional issues are in their relative nature. To a certain extent, different people have different nutritional needs and will react differently to specified diets, which makes it hard for teachers to know whether they should intervene in student choices or not. Minimally, great teachers should know the potential impact of dietary choices on classroom learning and try to model best behavior themselves.

Evidence from biology and the neurosciences shows how neurotransmitters that are influenced by nutrition impact learning[258] (often via impediments to attention and memory).[259] What students eat can impact the way certain neurotransmitters are released in the brain, all of which can influence learning conditions toward optimal or sub-optimal levels. It is well known that "[f]ood intake and energy expenditure are controlled by complex, redundant, and distributed neural systems that reflect the fundamental biological importance of adequate nutrient supply and energy balance" (Berthoud & Morrison, 2008, p. 55). Teachers, parents, and policy makers need to be informed about what types of diets are more conducive to general mental well-being. A rule of thumb for the time

253. Tokuhama-Espinosa (2010).
254. See Liu (2004).
255. In Lesser (2003).
256. Molteni (2002, p. 308).
257. Petursdottir, Farr, Moreley, Banks, & Skuladorrtir (2008).
258. As in the work by Marcason (2005).
259. See Posner (2004a).

being is that what is good for the heart is good for the brain.[260] That is, a low-fat diet supplemented with (dark-skinned) fruits and vegetables, fish high in omega-3 fatty acids, and nuts in place of candy bars are good basic guides in terms of appropriate food intake. The body–mind connection is important to MBE science because students who receive less than adequate sleep, exercise, and/or nutrition do not fare as well in formal learning environments.[261] The mind–body connection in the literature demonstrates that students learn better when the body's needs are taken into account.

The "what and why" of research foci in MBE science are broad and range from isolated, domain-specific skills to global theories of intelligence. The more biological aspects of learning are also included, such as neurogenesis, plasticity, and the mind–body connections as seen in studies on sleep, exercise, and nutrition. All of these areas are important to MBE science because they show how classroom learning is impacted by a myriad of factors, many of which are not yet taught in teacher training schools. Another way to understand MBE science better is by reviewing exactly *how* studies are conducted.

How Studies Are Conducted

There are many ways to learn about the brain. Two basic ways are through observation and through the use of technology. In education and psychology we primarily use observation of externally visible changes in behavior. A teacher tries a new reading intervention and then watches for results; a psychologist guides a child through a specific therapy and looks for changes in behavior. Observation of behavior in education and psychology is now complemented by brain imaging techniques from neuroscience to determine with more precision exactly how the brain learns and what type of teaching or stimulus brings this about in the most efficient way. While historically observation has provided one type of information about learning, and imaging technology another type, in MBE science these two methods are combined to create a more powerful means of understanding learning processes. Psychologists are already trained in basic observational skills as undergrads, which is also the norm in some teacher colleges. As John Oates at the Center for Childhood, Development and Learning in the United Kingdom notes, "The skills of systematic observation and assessment of behaviour are generally recognised as central

---

260. Readers are also encouraged to read the complete, albeit technical, studies by Mark P. Mattson of the National Institute on Aging cited in Restak's work (2009).
261. Society for Neuroscience (2007i).

components of undergraduate research methods training in psychology and form a major element of the defined core competencies . . ."[262] Such observation skills should be a core element of pedagogical training around the world as well. Teachers should be taught to pair observable student behavior with knowledge about the brain to reach a better diagnosis of problems, and to then devise improved personal educational plans. But in practice, what does this improved teacher process look like?

One way we teachers can improve our work is by systematizing the notes we take on our students' progress. While many teachers "jot down ideas" about certain students and often reflect for long hours about how to "reach" one kid or another, MBE science suggests that doing this in a more structured manner would lead to better results. For example, random note-taking can be replaced with a more organized approach through the use of three constructs—coding, reliability, and validity—that are all core attributes of careful observation and comprehensive note-taking in psychology and pedagogy.

• *Coding* is the ability to select core concepts and to code replies to questions or observable behavior into these core categories. For example, a teacher might choose to hone in on aggressive behavior in class to see what triggers these problems in her group.

• *Reliability* relates to the actual quality of the information being accessed. For example, the teacher will *not* note down situations based on hearsay, but rather only when he or she is witness to the actual behavior.

• *Validity*, or *ecological validity*, as some call it, means that the context in which the behaviors were observed was as authentic as possible. This means that the teacher probably would code aggressive behavior toward peers in a different way from aggressive behavior toward inanimate objects (though both would be recorded). Validity also relates to time-and-event processing (whether the time in which an event was observed influenced outcomes). For example, is aggressiveness more prevalent at specific times, such as when one parent or another drops off the child? Or right after break periods? All of this information will offer a better diagnosis of the root causes of the child's problem and will help the teacher choose more appropriate interventions.

It should be noted that ecological validity is one of the most controversial constructs in MBE science studies—more specifically, whether it is present to a sufficient degree, as what occurs in a lab situation does not necessarily reflect what happens in classroom settings (a wonderful summary of this dilemma can be found in Daniel & Poole, 2009). Let's say that in a lab a rat behaves erratically after ingesting a glucose substance. This does

---

262. Oates (2004).

not necessarily mean that a child would act the same way in a classroom—or does it? Though laboratory studies on animals do not always reflect the life of human children in classrooms, laboratory research protocols often offer a level of precision that subjective classroom observations cannot achieve. It is for this reason that both observations as well as imaging techniques are fundamental to MBE science.

Aside from observation, which has traditionally been used in psychology and now in education, there are now other tools with which teachers should become more familiar in order to better understand the brain and learning that come from neuroscience.

Neuroimaging

Neuroimaging helps teachers "see" the brain and understand its structure, functions, and how pharmacology affects it. By understanding (and in some cases using) neuroimaging studies, teachers can become more aware of the fact that different combinations of brain parts work at different times as systems, which helps explain the complexity of learning each skill and its subsets (more detail on imaging in the following section).

Neuroanatomy

Studying which areas of the brain are active during which learning processes requires a working knowledge of *neuroanatomy*, or the study of the brain's different parts. This includes not only the primary cortical lobes, but the neural networks as well. The study of the basic gross structure of the brain is useful to all teachers who want to have access to the best information possible about learning.

With this goal in mind, we would all do well to be able to distinguish the *frontal lobes* (involved in decision-making and higher-order cognition) from the occipital lobes (which are related to vision), for example. Neuroanatomy is the study of the anatomical organization of the brain. This includes not only the primary lobes, but the neural networks as well.

In order of interest (i.e., number of published studies), it was found in a meta-analysis of the literature I conducted in 2008 that the brain part of choice in studies of teaching and learning was, not surprisingly the *hippocampus*, known for its role in long-term memory storage. The hippocampus was followed in popularity by studies of the *amygdala*, related to emotional memory processing, and the *pre-frontal cortex*, related to executive functions and decision-making. Other areas related to sensory perception, such as the *occipital lobes* (as noted are related to the vision system), the *parietal lobes* (hearing system), and the *corpus callosum* (known for bridging communication between the two hemispheres of the brain) were also popular brain areas for studies. All of these anatomical studies offer pieces to the puzzle that unravel the mysteries of the brain and how it learns. Teachers don't need to be experts in neuroanatomy, but it is recommended that they become familiar with basic terms in order to understand studies that are useful in bettering practice (see Figure 5.2).

FIGURE 5.2
Basic Neuroanatomy for Teachers

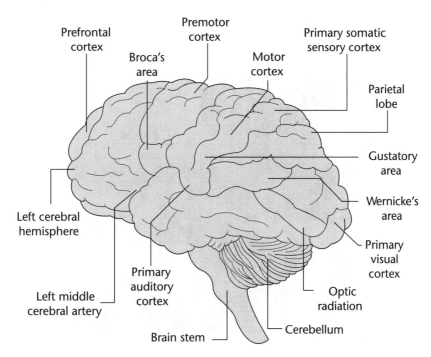

Bramwell for Tokuhama-Espinosa, 2010.

Applying Neuroanatomy in the Classroom
The systems view of the brain means that distinct parts are involved in different aspects of, for example, the learning and processing of language. Teachers should know that different neural mechanisms mediate the processing of metaphors[263] than the learning of

263. For more information on this, see Argyris, Stringaris, Medford, Giampietro, Brammer, & David (2007); Kacinik & Chiarello (2007).

spelling,[264] for example. Teachers who know this understand why students may master one aspect of language without being able to master another (e.g., good at metaphors but clueless in spelling), and in doing so, are more effective instructors. In other cases, a student may be able to spell perfectly, but may have no memory for the meaning of the word he or she spells, or, in other instances, may have great spelling (see Figure 5.3) but no idea about prosody, or what intonation to give the word.[265] Studies conducted by Laura Ann Pettito of Dartmouth College are beginning to show how the brain processes phonetically "regular" words versus those that are irregular (such as *yacht* in English). Other studies, at the University of Glasgow, demonstrate how the brain decodes the neural activity of spelling.[266]

FIGURE 5.3
Spelling and the Brain

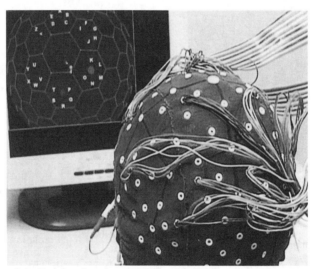

Source: Glasgow University and the Hamilton Institute, NUI Maynooth (2009).

Studies have clearly demonstrated that the sub-components of language enter the brain through different neural pathways. For example, orthographic learning enters the brain in a different way from phonological processing.[267] This is why it is inaccurate to say that a child has "language problems" because unless the specific sub-component of language can be identified, the teacher has not really isolated the problem. To make matters

264. Henry, Beeson, Stark, & Rapcsa (2007).
265. See Friedrich (2003) for more on this topic.
266. Blankertz, Krauledat, Dornhege, Williamson, Murray-Smith, & Müller (2007).
267. Booth, Burman, Meyer, Gitelman, Parrish, & Marsel (2004).

more complex, the brain changes daily with experience.[268] As mentioned earlier, researchers using imaging techniques found that the way the brain works when it is *learning* to read is different from how it works when it already *knows* how to read.[269] Other aspects of reading, as they relate to the MBE science literature, are discussed in Chapter 7.

In addition to understanding the basics of the brain's anatomy, teachers should also be informed about the definition and role of neurotransmitters as they relate to learning.

Neurotransmitters and Their Impact on Learning
In a preceding section we already considered how nutrition impacts neurotransmitter function. Here we consider other influences, such as various emotional states.

Neurotransmitters are chemicals (hormones, peptides, molecular systems) that transmit signals from one part of the brain to another (actually, from neuron to neuron). Synapses (the junctions across which nerve impulses pass) can be electrical or chemical exchanges between neurons. Chemical exchanges are called neurotransmitters (as they transmit messages from one neuron to another). Neurotransmitters can be triggered by messages from the brain related to emotions ("*I feel good! Release more dopamine!*"), or due to experiences ("*I just had a learning experience—release more acetylcholine to help plasticity!*"). In some cases, the lack of certain neurotransmitters in the brain can be blamed for certain behavior. For example, melatonin is a neurotransmitter related to regulating circadian rhythms. Let's say we catch a plane from New York to London and our biological clock is thrown off. The only way for the brain to adjust to the change in time zones is to readjust when and in what amounts melatonin is released. To put this in a classroom context, it is now known that the balance and release of melatonin changes its pattern in adolescence, causing teens to want to stay up later and wake up later. Teachers need to understand how some behaviors are influenced by certain neurotransmitters. Some neurotransmitters are also key to forging memories. This information helps teachers understand what influences the brain's choice about what is kept in memory and what is discarded. Some key categories of neurotransmitters are indicated below.

Emotional States and Neurotransmitters

Studies on neurotransmitters seek to understand how the chemical (im)balances in the brain change behavior. For example, some studies have demonstrated the destructive

---

268. Some excellent studies in this area are found in Gazzaniga, (2005b) and Sakai (2005).
269. See Marian, Spivey, & Hirsch (2003) for more information on this topic.

effects of stress hormones, such as cortisol, on learning.[270] "Good" (moderate) stress (eustress)[271] heightens attention and helps learning, whereas "bad" stress detracts from learning potential by literally blocking the uptake of new information in the brain (Society for Neuroscience, 2007c). Moderate stress creates a heightened sense of awareness that is conducive to new learning and is typically seen in a class where students are "on their toes" (body language conveys an alertness that is made possible by a release of hormones). On the flip side, bad stress is both physiologically as well as psychologically damaging.

Unfortunately, many of us can testify first-hand to the insecurity and humiliation that riddle many classrooms, creating an inordinate level of stress in which learning is compromised. Great teachers know how to keep students on high alert by calling on them frequently without causing high-stress situations. We teachers should ask ourselves just what implications this finding has for the classroom and whether or not we manage to keep the level of stress in our classrooms at the right level. Teachers are responsible for classroom management and for creating high-alert states, but not stressful ones.

Other studies show how depression impacts memory.[272] Emotions are critical to decision-making, and depressive states can impede learning both for psychological as well as neurological reasons. The studies in this area are important for teachers to consider because students' (*and* teachers') frames of mind are influenced by class settings. Even if teachers don't cause a student's depression (though, in some cases, they may indeed do so), they need to be aware of the influence that such depression can have on student learning potential. Depression has a wide gamut of characteristics and a broad reach. Lethargy is one of many manifestations of depression and may be confused with lack of motivation by novices. Great teachers know their students well enough to be able to at least call attention to depressive states and help the student obtain the treatment he or she needs. Although teachers may not cause depressive states, we have a responsibility to help students understand that their learning is impacted by their mental state. All mental states are regulated by different balances of neurotransmitters.

Other studies of relevance to MBE science show how the neurotransmitter dopamine, often associated with happiness, has an impact on memory and learning;[273] it is no wonder that happy students are bright students. Happiness, often culminating in laughter, is linked to a release of dopamine and other endorphins that not only make you feel good, but which also enhance the probability of learning. We all enjoy a good laugh, and we

270. See research by Kalat (2004); Kotulak (2008).
271. Berk (2001).
272. See Sapolsky (2001) for an excellent understanding of this concept.
273. See El-Ghundi, O'Dowd, & George (2007).

now know why our brains appreciate such a moment: Laughter can enhance new information uptake. Laughter triggers the release of endorphins and enhances oxygenation in the brain, both of which aid in learning. Some studies on humor and learning show the impact of laughter on neural mechanisms related to memory and attention. Specifically, it is easier to remember concepts related to moments of laughter than those without. Some of these studies report changes in hormones during laughter, as demonstrated by Berk's work (2001) and the Society for Neuroscience (2007f). Many teacher practitioners have reported the results of using humor in classroom settings, including Bain (2004), Bonwell (1993), Filipowicz (2002), Garner (2006), and Littleton (1998). Given that humor is highly individualized, good teachers not only need to stimulate laughter in order to enjoy its learning benefits, but they also must understand what type of humor triggers this response for individual learners.

All of these studies remind us that how students feel (stressed, depressed, or happy) has an impact on how well they are able to learn.

Learning Circuits and Neurotransmitters

Other studies explain the neural circuitry between certain areas of the brain and attention functions during learning.[274] Once again, this type of research reminds us of the complexity of each learning task, all the different ways things can go wrong, and all of the different ways learning needs to be approached. Some studies in this group, concerned with the possible neural circuitry and neurobiology involved[275] in classical Pavlovian fear conditioning, have proven what psychology has known for decades. For over 100 years, for example, psychologists have studied human reactions to stimuli and subsequent conditioning; neuroscientists are now able to identify and track the changes in the brain that accompany this conditioning.

Some studies related to learning circuitry and neurotransmitters border on the fantastic. For example, there is research on neurotransmitters that shows how the brain changes when it conducts Internet searches,[276] goes through psychotherapy,[277] experiences meditation,[278] passes through pregnancy,[279] birth,[280] and adolescence.[281] It is important for

---

274. Posner, Rothbart, & Rueda (2008).
275. Maren & Quirk (2004).
276. Small, Moody, Siddarth, & Bookheimer (2009).
277. For examples, see Grosjean (2005); Oldham (2007); Paniagua (2004).
278. See Newberg & Iversen (2003) for a good review.
279. Work has been done in this area for decades (see Desan, Woodmansee, Ryan, Smock, & Maier, 1988).
280. For a good example of this type of research, see Herlenius & Lagercrantz (2001).
281. *The Journal of Adolescent Research* has good articles in this vein. See Males (2009) for an example.

teachers to know that such information corroborates the idea that the brain changes constantly with experience.

MBE science is helping teachers understand that learning is influenced by factors that are invisible to the naked eye. Chemicals play an important role in the learning process and have a direct impact on mental achievement and learning potential. An understanding of neurotransmitters and chemistry will probably play a greater role in teacher training in the near future as new drugs are marketed to enhance cognition, for example.

Now that we have reviewed who and what is studied, as well as why and how, we close this chapter with a consideration of the dimensions of teaching and learning that are of primary focus of MBE science.

Which Dimensions Are Studied

There are a myriad of ways to study the relationships among the mind, brain, and education. Two useful "lenses" are the theories of consciousness and neuroethics, each of which is explained below.

> *"Know thyself."*
> —Ancient Greek aphorism found at the Temple of Apollo at Delphi (2nd century B.C.E.)

Theories of Consciousness

Theories of human consciousness are important to MBE science because they explain core concepts about how individuals know themselves and others. The link between the mind and the brain remains a hotly debated topic. Are the mind and the brain separate entities? Is consciousness of one's own thought process enough to define oneself? Has "I think therefore I am" (Descartes, 1637) been replaced by "We feel, therefore we learn" (Immordino-Yang, 2008) or "I am not what I think. I am thinking what I think"?[282]

There is a developmental structure to studies related to theories of consciousness in the literature. Many studies, for example, begin with an explanation of how children begin to categorize their world.[283] After an understanding of categorization, children (as well as adults) then build concepts, and from these concepts,[284] we create the mental schemas that define our world. Mental schemas are the ways we organize our world into "normal" or

---

282. Butterworth (n.d.).
283. For example, see Keri (2003).
284. Some elegant examples of this are found in Markham & Gentner (2001); Martin & Caramazza (2003).

"average" category boxes.[285] For example, most Americans' mental schema of the concept "fruit" is an image of an apple. Why? Because we have been raised with the notion of an apple as being iconic of the concept of fruit since we were young (our alphabet songs begin with "Apple Apple *Ah Ah Ah*"; choices of fruit almost always include apples; every state in the union sells apples in their supermarkets; apple pie is synonymous with "American," etc.). The move from category learning to concepts to mental schema is fundamental to all future learning. Without these basic skills we would be inhibited in learning a language (verbs, nouns, pronouns, etc.), math (symbol concepts, values, etc.), or any other subject because they are all dependent on mental schemas.

Our mental schemas give us our first hints of how people know, and point to understandings about metacognitive processes. That is, once we can label our own mental schemas, we can begin to think about how we think and how others think similarly or differently from us. This is very important for teachers because it also explains why people who do not share the same mental schemas (e.g., do not relate "apple" to the concept of "fruit") have trouble understanding one another. For example, teachers whose school children come from different cultural backgrounds may not share the same mental schemas. Children from Ecuador think "banana" when asked about the concept of "fruit," meaning that they have to make a mental leap to conform to the mental schema of the U.S. majority (apple), adding an additional adaptive step to learning. How does this impact the way we teach? Well, first it means that we cannot anchor concepts to shared norms, because these norms vary greatly across cultures. This is important to teachers as most of our classrooms are filled with students from many cultures, as well as many different intellectual abilities, making our job more challenging. Being able to nurture the development of metacognitive skills (which can only come after developing mental schemas) is crucial to cultivating good learning experiences.

The literature is filled with studies that demonstrate how heightened consciousness through metacognition can improve learning.[286] Teachers are reminded that helping their students think about how they think (metacognition) improves children's overall quality of thinking. How does this occur in actual classrooms? By simply asking students how they reached their answers. Let's say Tommy gets the right answer on a math question, and Mary does not. If we ask Tommy to tell us how he got his answer, he gains (because the best way to learn is to teach), and Mary gains because she hears in peer-appropriate language a different explanation from the one the teacher might offer. Tommy also gains

285. Sternberg (2006).
286. Some very good examples can be found in Cromley (2000); Langer (1997).

because the simple act of having to articulate his own steps reinforces his metacognitive skills.

Many of the studies in this group explain the methods that can be used to understand consciousness from a neurological standpoint or explain the process of consciousness.[287] That is, how does the brain process conscious thought?[288] These studies seek to understand which parts of the brain are stimulated by what type of reflection in the hopes of being able to document actual thought processes. Other studies in this category seek to break down consciousness into neurological structures[289] and explain the complex neural pathways involved in becoming aware of oneself. Finally, other studies base the development of human consciousness in the historical query of how the brain stores the mind.[290] This is helpful to teachers because it reinforces what we see in behavior; different approaches resonate with varying levels of success for different students.

Some MBE studies on consciousness consider the "I" to "Other" clarification. This research considers questions such as "how do we know the minds of others?"[291], the answers to which are key to understanding the concept of empathy as well as understanding the motives of others. Theories of consciousness that are related to empathy help explain social cognition and interpersonal relationships. MBE science is concerned with these questions because human interaction plays a huge role in successful teaching and learning environments.

Neuroethics

A rich and controversial area of new reflection relevant to MBE science is neuroethics; this area of study contemplates right and wrong, or appropriate/inappropriate use of information about brains in social contexts, including children in schools. Neuroethics reflects upon what is known about the human biology of learning and how it can be manipulated through science. As MBE science standards are young, the parameters of neuroethics are often illusive. For the most part, literature on neuroethics is concerned with the application of ethical standards to potential moral challenges related to the brain and learning. For example, Sheridan and colleagues ask if being smarter on drugs is as legitimate as

---

287. See Bowden & Jung-Beeman (2007); Cohen (1996).
288. For example see Barsalou, Breazeal, & Smith (2007); Frith (2007).
289. Some good examples of this can be found in Berninger & Abbott (1992); Binder, Westbury, & McKiernan (2005); Dehaene (2002); Dietrich (2004a); Koch (2004); LeDoux (2003); Metzinger (2002).
290. This is a very complex area. For some intriguing ideas, see Pietsch (2001); Pinker (2003, 2009); Linden (2007a); Ornstein (1995); Restak (1991a); Steen (2007).
291. Some key studies in this area include Adolphs (2006b) and Muthukumaraswamy (2005).

without drugs?[292] This is a hotly debated concern. Neuroethical questions about drugs to enhance natural learning skills are like cosmetic surgery questions. Is it fair that some people can afford to enhance their looks through cosmetic surgery? Should a student who scores high on a test because he used memory-enhancing drugs be allowed to do so, even if others with less financial means are excluded from the same opportunity? Teachers, policy makers, and all of us who work with students need to be conscious of the potential dilemmas that will arise with the plethora of information about the brain becoming more commonly available. Other questions we must anticipate include such concerns as to whether children may soon begin their first days of school by bringing brain scans to their teachers, or in some cases, be denied entry to school because of some defects noted in their brains.[293] Is it possible that certain children will be given special treatment if they are born genetically inferior or superior?[294] Who is primarily responsible for the proper care of children's brains (teachers? parents? society at large? or only the student him- or herself?).[295] These dilemmas and many others do not yet have answers, but within the next decade, they will be discussed with vigor.[296]

Most of the literature about neuroethics is concerned with hypothetical situations that challenge the ethical and equal treatment of students.[297] Some studies in neuroethics ask readers to begin their own personal reflection about such issues[298] as they note the philosophical dilemmas. This adds to research processes relevant to MBE science[299] as well as to practical classroom application. It is heartening but worrisome in the same moment that writers in editorial capacities are currently making calls for *someone* to define neuroethics,[300] but only a few are stepping up to the plate. Although a small group of neuroscientists is actually taking a long and hard look at neuroethics as a new discipline of study,[301] the main issues and judgment processes are still ill-defined and concern us all. Individually and collectively, professionals in the discipline will have to reflect upon these issues.

292. For excellent reflections on this topic, see Sheridan et al. (2005); Gazzaniga (2005b); Turner & Sahakian (2006).
293. For a very good discussion on this, see Illes & Raffin (2005).
294. See Farah, Noble, & Hurt (2006).
295. See Sheridan et al. (2005); Illes (2005).
296. Highly recommended readings on neuroethics include Farah (2005) and Illes (2005).
297. Teachers will find discussions on this topic by Canli (2006); Coch (2007); Farah (2004); Farah & Wolfe (2004); Gray & Thompson (2004); and Sheridan et al. (2005) very useful.
298. See Caplan (2002); Farah (2002); Farah & Heberlein (2007).
299. Farah (2005).
300. Nature Editorial (2006); Farah & Herberlein (2007).
301. See very good discussions on this in Glannon (2006); Illes & Raffin (2002); Illes (2005, 2006a).

Suggested Reading

Plasticity

Cotman, C., & Berchtold, N. C. (2002). Exercise: A behavioral intervention to enhance brain health and plasticity. *Trends in Neuroscience, 25,* 295–301.

Doidge, N. (2007). *The brain that changes itself.* New York: Penguin.

Kalueff, A. (2007). Neurobiology of memory and anxiety: From genes to behavior. *Neural Plasticity,* 78171. doi:10.1155/2007/78171

Merzenich, M. (2008). *About brain plasticity.* Retrieved May 22, 2009, from *http://merzenich. positscience.com/?page_id=143.*

Nelson, C. (2000). Neural plasticity and human development: The role of early experience in sculpting memory teams. *Developmental Science, 3*(2), 115–136.

Biology, Genes and Neural Networks

Fossella, J., Sommer, T., Fan, J., Pfaff, D., & Posner, M. I. (2003). Synaptogenesis and heritable aspects of executive attention. *Mental Retardation and Developmental Disabilities Research Reviews, 9,* 78–183.

Reid, L., & Baylis, F. (2005, Mar./Apr.). Brains, genes, and the making of the self. *American Journal of Bioethics, 5*(2), 21–23.

Mind–Body Connection

Fonagy, P., & Target, M. (2007). The rooting of the mind in the body: New links between attachment theory and psychoanalytic thought. *Journal of the American Psychoanalytic Association, 55*(2), 411–456.

Sibley, B., & Etnier, J. L. (2003). The relationship between physical activity and cognition in children: A meta-analysis. *Pediatric Exercise Science, 15*(30), 243–256.

Stein, D., Collins, M., Daniels, W., Noakes T. D., & Zigmond, M. (2007). Mind and muscle: The cognitive–affective neuroscience of exercise. *CNS Spectrums, 12*(1), 19–22.

Sleep

Andrade, M., Benedito-Silva, A. A., Domenice, S., Arnhold, I. J., & Menna-Barreto, L. (1993). Sleep characteristics of adolescents: A longitudinal study. *Journal of Adolescent Health, 14,* 401–406.

Carskadon, M., Acebo, C., & Jenni, O. G. (2004). Regulation of adolescent sleep: Implications for behavior. *Annals of the New York Academy of Sciences, 1021,* 276–291.

Carskadon, M., Wolfson, A. R., Acebo, C., Tzischinsky, O., & Seifer, R. (1998). Adolescent sleep patterns, circadian timing, and sleepiness at a transition to early school days. *Sleep, 21,* 871–881.

Copinschi, G. (2005). Metabolic and endocrine effects of sleep deprivation. *Essential Psychopharmacology, 6,* 341–347.

Durmer, J., & Dinges, D. F. (2005). Neurocognitive consequences of sleep deprivation. *Seminars in Neurology, 25*(1),117–129.

Giannotti, F., Cortesi, F., Sebastiani, T., & Ottaviano, S. (2002). Circadian preference, sleep and daytime behaviour in adolescence. *Journal of Sleep Research, 11*(3), 191–199.

Hobson, A. J. (2004). *Dreaming: An introduction to the science of sleep.* New York: Oxford University Press.

Hobson, A. J., & Pace-Schott, E. F. (2002). The cognitive neuroscience of sleep: Neuronal systems, consciousness and learning. *Nature Reviews Neuroscience, 3*(9), 679–693.

Hobson, A. J., Pace-Schott, E. F., & Stickgold, R. (2000, Dec). Dreaming and the brain: Toward a cognitive neuroscience of conscious states. *Behavioral and Brain Sciences, 23*(6), 793.

Killgore, W., Blakin, T. J., & Wesensten, N. J. (2005, Mar). Impaired decision making following 49h of sleep deprivation. *Journal of Sleep Research, 15*(1), 7–13.

Mednick, S., Nakayama, K., & Stickgold, R. (2003). Sleep-dependent learning: A nap is as good as a night. *Nature Neuroscience, 6*(7), 697.

Pace-Schott, E., & Hobson, J. A. (2002). The neurobiology of sleep: Genetics, cellular physiology and subcortical networks. *Nature Reviews Neuroscience, 3*(8), 591–605.

Pérez-Chada, D., Pérez Lloret, S., Videla, A. J., Cardinali, D. P., Bergna, M. A., & Fernández-Acquier, M. (2007). Sleep disordered breathing and daytime sleepiness are associated with poor academic performance in teenagers: A study using the pediatric daytime sleepiness scale (PDSS). *Sleep, 30*(12), 1698–1703.

Stickgold, R. (2005). Sleep-dependent memory consolidation. *Nature, 437*(7063), 1272–1279.

Stickgold, R. (2006). Neuroscience: A memory boost while you sleep. *Nature, 444*(7119), 559–560.

Taylor, D., Jenni, O. G., Acebo, C., & Carskadon, M. A. (2005). Sleep tendency during extended wakefulness: Insights into adolescent sleep regulation and behavior. *Journal of Sleep Research, 14*(3), 239–244.

Yoo, S., Hu, P. T., Gujar, N., Jolesz, F. A., & Walker, M. P. (2007). A deficit in the ability to form new human memories without sleep. *Nature Neuroscience, 10*(3), 385–392.

Neurophysiological and Neuropharmacological Aspects of Learning
Atallah, H., Frank, M. J., & O'Reilly, R. C. (2004). Hippocampus, cortex, and basal ganglia: Insights from computational models of complementary learning systems. *Neurobiology of Learning and Memory, 82*(3), 253–267.

Bear, M., Connors, B. W., & Paradis, M. A. (2007). *Neuroscience: Exploring the brain* (3rd ed). Baltimore, MD: Lippincott, Williams & Wilkins.

Gazzaniga, M. (Ed.). (2005). *Cognitive neuroscience III.* Cambridge, MA: MIT Press.

Gibbs, A., Naudts, K. H., Spencer, E. P., & David, A. S. (2007). The role of dopamine in attentional and memory biases for emotional information. *American Journal of Psychiatry, 164*(10), 1603–1610.

Goswami, U. (2008). *Cognitive development: The learning brain.* London: Taylor & Francis.

Kitabatake, Y., Sailor, K. A., Ming, G. L., & Song, H. (2007). Adult neurogenesis and hippocampal memory function: New cells, more plasticity, new memories? *Neurosurgery Clinics of North America, 18*(1), 105–113.

Levy, R., & Goldman-Rakic, P. S. (2000). Segregation of working memory functions within the dorsolateral prefrontal cortex. *Experimental Brain Research, 133*, 23–32.

Sadato, N., Pascual-Leone, A., Rafman, J., Ibanez, V., Deiber, M. P., Dold, G., & Hallett, M. (1996). Activation of the primary visual cortex by Braille reading in blind subjects. *Nature, 380*, 526–528.

Schlaggar, B., & McCandliss, B. D. (2007). Development of neural systems for reading. *Annual Review of Neuroscience, 30*(1), 475.

Simos, P., Fletcher, J. M., Foorman, B. R., Francis, D. J., Castillo, E. M., Davis, R. N., et al. (2002). Brain activation profiles during the early stages of reading acquisition. *Journal of Child Neurology, 17*(3), 159–63.

Neuroimaging

Hitachi. (2008). *Optical Topography and Hideaki Koizumi.* Retrieved April 4, 2008, from *http://www.hitachi.com/New/cnews/040311b.html.*

Martin, A., & Caramazza, A. (2003). Neuropsychological and neuroimaging perspectives on conceptual knowledge: An introduction. *Cognitive Neuropsychology, 20*(3–6), 195–213.

Peretz, I., & Zatorre, R. J. (2005). Brain organization for music processing. *Annual Review of Psychology, 56*(1), 89–114.

Poldrack, R., & Wagner, A. D. (2004). What can neuroimaging tell us about the mind? Insights from prefrontal cortex. *Current Directions in Psychological Science, 13*(5), 177–181.

Shaywitz, S., Shaywitz, B. A., Fulbright, R. K., Skudlarski, P., Mencl, W. E., Constable, R. T., et al. (2003). Neural systems for compensation and persistence: Young adult outcome of childhood reading disability. *Biological Psychiatry, 54*(1), 25–33.

Stewart, L., Henson, R., Kampe, K., Walsh, V., Turner, R. & Frith, U. (2003). Brain changes after learning to read and play music. *NeuroImage, 20*(1), 71–83.

Tervaniemi, M., & Huotilainen, M. (2003). The promises of change-related brain potentials in cognitive neuroscience of music. *Annals of the New York Academy of Sciences, 999*, 29–39.

Neurogenesis

Bruel-Jungerman, E., Rampon, C., & Laroche, S. (2007). Adult hippocampal neurogenesis, synaptic plasticity and memory: Facts and hypotheses. *Reviews in the Neurosciences, 18*(2), 93–114.

Eriksson, P. (1998). Neurogenesis in the adult human hippocampus. *Nature Medicine, 4,* 1313–1317.

Ortega-Perez, I., Murray, K., & Lledo, P. M. (2007). The how and why of adult neurogenesis. *Journal of Molecular Histology, 38*(6), 555–562.

Thomas, R., Hotsenpiller, G., & Peterson, D. A. (2007). Acute psychosocial stress reduces cell survival in adult hippocampal neurogenesis without altering proliferation. *Journal of Neuroscience, 27*(11), 2734–2743.

Consciousness

Baars, B., & Gage, N. M. (2007). *Cognition, brain, and consciousness: Introduction to cognitive neuroscience.* New York: Academic Press.

Cohen, D. (1996). *The secret language of the mind: A visual inquiry into the mysteries of consciousness.* San Francisco: Chronicle Books.

Damasio, A. (2000). *The feeling of what happens: Body and emotion in the making of consciousness.* New York: Harvest Books.

Dehaene, S. (2002). *The cognitive neuroscience of consciousness.* Cambridge, MA: Bradford Books.

Dietrich, A. (2004). Neurocognitive mechanisms underlying the experience of flow. *Consciousness and Cognition, 13*(4), 746–761.

Douglas, H. (2007). *I am a strange loop.* New York: Basic Books.

Hobson, J., & Pace-Schott, E. F. (2002). The cognitive neuroscience of sleep: Neuronal systems, consciousness and learning. *Nature Reviews Neuroscience, 3*(9), 679–693.

Koch, C. (2004). *The quest for consciousness: A neurological approach.* Englewood, CO: Roberts.

Metzinger, T. (Ed.). (2002). *Neural correlates of consciousness: Empirical and conceptual questions.* Cambridge, MA: MIT Press.

Pinker, S. (2009). *How the mind works.* New York: Penguin Books.

Zeman, A. (2009). *The portrait of the brain.* New Haven: Yale University Press.

Neuroethics

Canli, T. (2006). When genes and brain unite: Ethical implications of genomic neuroimaging. In J. Iles (Ed.), *Neuroethics* (pp. 169–183). Oxford, UK: Oxford University Press.

Coch, D. (2007). Neuroimaging research with children: Ethical issues and case scenarios. *Journal of Moral Education, 36*(1), 1–18.

Farah, M. (2002). Emerging ethical issues in neuroscience. *Nature Neuroscience, 5*(11), 1123–1129.

Farah, M. (2004). Neurocognitive enhancement: What can we do and what should we do? *Nature Reviews Neuroscience, 5*(5), 421–425.

Farah, M. (2005). Neuroethics: The practical and the philosophical. *Trends in Cognitive Science, 9,* 34–40.

Farah, M. (2007). Social, legal, and ethical implications of cognitive neuroscience: "Neuroethics" for short. *Journal of Cognitive Neuroscience, 19*(3), 363–364.

Farah, M., Noble, K., & Hurt, H. (2006). Poverty, privilege, and brain development: Empirical findings and ethical implications. In J. Illes (Ed.), *Neuroethics* (pp. 277–289). Oxford, UK: Oxford University Press.

Farah, M., & Wolfe, P. (2004). Monitoring and manipulating brain function: New neuroscience technologies and their ethical implications. *Hastings Center Report, 34*, 34–45.

Glannon, W. (2006). Neuroethics. *Bioethics, 20*(1), 37–52.

Glannon, W. (Ed.). (2007). *Defining right and wrong in brain science: Essential readings in neuroethics.* New York: Dana Press.

Illes, J. (2005). *Neuroethics in the 21st century.* Oxford, UK: Oxford University Press.

Illes, J. (Ed.). (2006a). *Neuroethics.* Oxford, UK: Oxford University Press.

Illes, J. (2006b). *Neuroethics, neurochallenges: A needs-based research agenda.* Based on the David Kopf Annual Lecture on Neuroethics, Society for Neuroscience. Retrieved on May 10, 2007, from *http://neuroethics.stanford.edu/documents/Illes.NeuroethicsSFN2006.pdf.*

Illes, J., & Racine, E. (2005). Imaging or imagining? A neuroethics challenge informed by genetics. *American Journal of Bioethics 5*(2), 1–14.

Illes, J., & Raffin, T. (2002). Neuroethics: A new discipline is emerging in the study of brain and cognition. *Brain and Cognition, 50*(3), 341–344.

Illes, J., & Raffin, T. (2005). No child left without a brain scan? Toward a pediatric neuroethics. In C.A. Read (Ed.), *Cerebrum: Emerging ideas on brain science* (pp. 33–46). New York: Dana Foundation.

Marcus, S. (2004). *Neuroethics: Mapping the field.* New York: Dana Press.

Sheridan, K., Zinchenko, E., & Gardner, H. (2005). Neuroethics in education. In J. Illes (Ed.), *Neuroethics* (pp. 281–308). Oxford, UK: Oxford University Press. Retrieved on September 10, 2007, from *http://www.tc.umn.edu/~athe0007/BNEsig/papers/ NeuroethicsEducation.pdf.*

The Scientifically Substantiated Art of Teaching, Part 2

Human Survival and Life Skills

> *"All human actions have one or more of these seven causes: chance, nature, compulsions, habit, reason, passion, desire."*
> —Aristotle (c. 384–322 B.C.E.), as cited in Rosenberg (2006, p. 52)

In the previous chapter we looked at who, how, why, and which dimensions of research were considered in the new science of teaching and learning. In the next two chapters we consider major brain functions as they relate to human survival and life skills (Chapter 6) and to academic skills and school subjects (Chapter 7).

The main types of human survival and life skills can be grouped into eight broad categories: (1) affect, empathy, emotions, and motivation; (2) executive functions and/or decision-making; (3) facial recognition and interpretation; (4) memory; (5) attention; (6) social cognition; (7) spatial management; and (8) temporal management. While these skills are useful in academic settings, they contribute to survival and success in social situations even more so. MBE science studies brain functions as they relate to life skills with the goal of improving the quality of life in both academic and social settings. Each of these important areas of study is discussed briefly below in relation to both general and school contexts. However, before launching into the specific survival and life skills, it is important to remember two things that color all other findings: Learning occurs through sensory input, and culture can influence schematic interpretations. These two caveats are explained below.

• *Sensory input.* All learning requires some form of sensory input before it is converted into an experience of a human survival or life skill (or academic skill, for that matter). That is, one sees, feels, hears, tastes, or smells (or remembers seeing, feeling, hearing, tasting, or smelling) something, which in turn changes into one of the skills mentioned below. *Sensory input precedes all skill acquisition*: "Art works because it appeals to certain faculties of the mind. Music depends on details of the auditory system, painting and sculpture on the visual system. Poetry and literature depend on language."[302] Without proper sensory input, basic problems arise. If a person is incapable of perceiving another's face through the "normal" neural circuitry, it is probable that that person will misinterpret the intentions of the other as communicated via facial expression. Similarly, if one's sensory perception of one's body in space is misgauged, it is likely that overall spatial management will be slightly off. "Normal" neural circuitry for the complex array of sensory processing in the brain is vital for every survival or life skill listed below to function as expected. A thorough explanation of sensory processing has been clearly provided by others,[303] and all teachers are encouraged to be aware of the complexities of exactly how the brain sees, hears, feels, smells, and tastes to better appreciate the role sensory perception plays in learning.

• *Culture*. The second caveat of great importance relates to the influence of culture on MBE science findings, and specifically on human survival and life skills. All of the findings in this book apply to humans across all cultures, but it would be remiss to think that different cultural backgrounds do not shade teaching and learning practices as well as how we categorize if something is "threatening," "humorous," or "motivating," for example. In 1989, John Seely and Allan Collins published an article that drew attention to the importance of considering the influence of culture in learning situations. These authors argued that "many teaching practices implicitly assume that conceptual knowledge can be abstracted from the situations in which it is learned and used. [However, we] argue that knowledge is situated, being in part a product of the activity, context, and culture in which it is developed and used."[304] Though far more revolutionary in its time a few decades ago, the concept of situated learning remains preeminent today. The role of culture, in its many forms, is also of crucial importance when discussing the gamut of human survival and life skills, and readers should bear in mind how their own cultural lenses filter MBE science concepts.[305] These words of caution are meant to remind readers

302. Pinker (2002).
303. See Gazzaniga (2005a) for a thorough and detailed example.
304. Seely & Collins (1989, p. 32).
305. In MBE science there are challenges related to culture on at least two levels, as mentioned in the Introduction. First, there is the challenge of international interpretations of information, and second, there is the challenge of the interdisciplinary culture, which reminds us not to view the information as one profession or another (as teachers, neuroscientists, or psychologists), but rather to appreciate the unified cultural vision of MBE science. As an exhaustive review of the role of culture in MBE science is beyond the scope of this book, suggested readings are found at the end of this chapter.

to interpret the following findings on human survival and life skills with knowledge of sensory perception as well as a consciousness of the cultural lens that will color all of the information represented here.

Affect, Empathy, Emotions, and Motivation

• *Affect and empathy*. How students feel about a subject, such as math or reading, influences how they learn. Do we as teachers always consider the strong influence those responses have on our students' abilities to learn? The neurobiology of affect as it relates to specific academic skills, such as foreign language learning,[306] offers neuroscientific support for observable psychological traits (e.g., motivation) based on educational practices. Teachers who appreciate the value and importance of affect and empathy are more successful in their craft.

Teachers need to help students become aware of how they feel not only about their subjects but also about themselves and their classmates because affect and empathy are central to emotional intelligence (Goleman, 2006) and to the development of the individual.[307] "Empathy is also strongly related to effortful control, with children high in effortful control showing greater empathy," according to Rothbart, Posner, and Rueda[308] (2008). This means that students with effortful control, or self-management skills, are also able to learn empathy and how to interpret the feelings of others with more success. In some sense, one kind of success breeds another: Those who learn to recognize their own emotions and manage them well (emotional intelligence) demonstrate effortful control, and those with effortful control are more empathic. This finding also suggests a subtler link between emotional intelligence and metacognition. Many activities used to stimulate emotional intelligence in children ask them to reflect on what and why they felt the way they did in different emotional situations (e.g., anger or sadness). In many ways, the cultivation of emotional intelligence is directly related to metacognitive skills, or the *why* behind actions. All teachers should try to foster a triad of skills in their students: effortful control, empathy, and emotional intelligence (metacognition). Part of a teacher's role, especially in the early years, is to guide students as they learn to control their feelings.

---

306. See Schumann (1997) for one of the best works in this area.
307. To read more about this aspect of affect, see Blair (2007).
308. Posner, Rothbart, & Rueda (2008, p. 156).

> *"Men ought to know that from the brain, and from the brain only, arise our*
> *pleasures, joys, laughter, jests, as well as our sorrows, pains, griefs and tears. . . .*
> *These things that we suffer all come from the brain."*
> —Hippocrates, 5th B.C.E., as cited in Hergenhahn (2005, p. 451)

A great deal of research seeks to explain the development of affect regulation[309] and understanding the management of emotions that is so useful to teachers. School children need these skills as they develop social relationships that help them maneuver within their learning communities. Older students need these skills to become integrated members of social structures that support new learning.

Most teachers would probably agree that students with a sense of intellectual and social empathy are more successful because they get on better with their peers and can envision problems from different viewpoints. Some studies of interest to teachers in this category explain the neural mechanisms underlying empathy,[310] which might afford teachers clues about how to capitalize on this process. Are some children born more emotionally balanced than others? Can all students improve their level of emotional management, independent of where they start? Some researchers who study affect and empathy go so far as to suggest a new area called "implicit affect,"[311] which distinguishes affect that is inherent in a human being with affect that is learned through social conditioning. These studies distinguish types of social cognition that can be cultivated in school settings, as in the self-regulatory behavior we demonstrate in different social contexts. Teachers should also be aware of studies related to student feelings about different skills sets, such as math,[312] language acquisition,[313] or lexical improvements,[314] which indicate that how kids feel about the subject (or the teacher) influences their ability to learn. MBE science suggests that it is the job of teachers to stimulate as much growth as possible in this area.

Studies on affect and empathy are important for two reasons. First, these studies indicate how affect is cultivated and how empathy can be instilled in students to enhance their social cognition.[315] Empathy is a life skill that enables individuals to better understand their environments and negotiate their place in the world. While not crucial to intellec-

---

309. See Dahl (2003).
310. For example see Decety & Jackson (2004) and Singer (2007).
311. A term coined by Feit (2005).
312. See Ward (2008).
313. An excellent source of information on this topic is Schumann (1997).
314. For an example, see Frishkoff (2004).
315. See Levine (2000); Meltzoff & Decety (2003); Schmidt (2007).

tual growth, affect and empathy are useful in working with others, which is one of the ultimate goals of some education systems. The OECD countries, for example, noted that one of three key competencies for all basic education graduates is the ability to work with heterogeneous groups.[316] For this reason, researchers related to affect and empathy should be watched carefully in the coming years for continued evidence about how these can be cultivated within formal school learning environments.

• *Emotions.* Closely related but perhaps more complex than those on empathy and affect are studies in the realm of emotions. Emotions are the physiological reactions of a person to external stimuli, whereas affect is the conscious, subjective aspect of the inter-pretation of emotion. Emotions have been researched far more than any other aspects of brain skills relevant to MBE science research. Why? As the link between emotions and decision-making has grown clearer over recent years, the importance of understanding emotions has increased.

Perhaps the most well-respected researchers on emotions are Antonio Damasio (1994, 2000, 2003, 2004) and Joseph LeDoux (1996, 2000). Both authors have docu-mented how there is no decision-making without emotion. They also emphasize how our emotions become ourselves, not vice versa. Studies relevant to MBE science are concerned with several aspects of emotional functioning, such as how stress, anxiety,[317] and anger[318] can impact learning. These studies bridge observations of behavior with changes in brain processes, giving more credibility to claims that how a student feels about a teacher or subject can impact his or her actual performance in the class.

Research shows how excessive anxiety can negatively impact the state of the mind–body functions, and physical areas of the brain,[319] resulting in long-term learning prob-lems. For example, a vast number of articles report the way anxiety manifests during test situations, as in the work done by Hong,[320] in which he explains how students feel a sense of "blockage" when anxiety arises, and as a result, how their test scores are affected. Great teachers not only recognize the anxious states created by certain classroom situations, but they also teach students coping mechanisms. Coping mechanisms for dealing with subject-specific anxiety (e.g., math anxiety) as well as general test anxiety can (and, some would say, should) be explicitly taught in schools. Teaching such coping mechanisms is not as complicated as it sounds. Simply being aware of a test structure, for example,

---

316. For concrete examples, see PISA (2007); Sylwester (2003).
317. See Bryant (2005); Enck, Martens, & Klosterhalfen (2007).
318. See Sander, Grandjean, Pourtois, Schwartz, Seghier, Scherer, et al. (2005).
319. For some studies in this area, see Rauch, Shin, & Wright (2003); Walker, Toufexis, & Davis (2003).
320. Hong (1999).

reduces stress (e.g., how many questions, with what weight each; if they are presented in order of difficulty; how much time is available). Knowledge of the purpose of the test (i.e., to measure or to diagnose) also helps reduce stress, as does knowledge as to the importance of the test in relation to other evaluation measures. Great teachers do their best to reduce anxiety to a minimum because, unlike stress, there are no known benefits to anxious states related to learning. Anxiety is often confused for a subtype of stress; this is wrong for one basic reason. Anxiety is a feeling of fear or apprehension,[321] whereas stress can be caused by any number of situations, memories, or thoughts that cause a wide range of emotions, including anger, frustration, and anxiousness. That is, anxiety can be a cause of stress, but it is not a subcategory of stress.

Emotional memory, shown to be more permanent and influential than other types of memory,[322] is a vital area for teacher awareness. The earliest memories humans tend to have are emotionally tied (e.g., the birth of a younger sibling, being lost in the zoo, anxiety about being left at day care). When negative emotions are connected to certain learning experiences—for example, a math teacher who humiliates a student in front of his or her peers—then the emotional memory may block new learning in that subject area. This is not only a psychological phenomenon, it is a neurological fact, meaning that "getting over" this problem will require not only behavioral conditioning, but also neural changes.

Other studies that are of interest to teachers investigate the role of emotions and cognition[323] in decision-making[324] and learning processes.[325] Some studies explain the specific neural mechanisms of certain emotions without a direct link to academic learning, but with clear links to social situational learning. Some of these studies consider the neurobiology of positive emotions, as well as those related to fear and stressful situations.[326] The explanations of how emotions, both positive[327] and stressful, are processed in the brain help teachers understand how their actions might impact a student's ability to learn. Fear[328] and stress,[329] for example, cause or prevent the release of certain neurotransmitters that facilitate the consolidation of memories.

---

321. U.S. National Library of Medicine "Stress versus anxiety" (*http://www.nlm.nih.gov/medlineplus/ency/article/002140.htm*)
322. See Buchanan, Tranel, & Adolphs (2006); LaBar & Cabeza (2006).
323. See Bell & Wolfe (2004).
324. See Coricelli, Dolan, & Sirigu (2007).
325. See Sousa, (2000); Sylwester (1994).
326. See Bellace & Williams (2005); Damasio (2003); Panksepp (2003); Pert (1997); Phelps (2006).
327. See Burgdorf & Panksepp (2006).
328. See Helmuth (2003).
329. For examples, see Rauch, Shin & Wright (2003); Thomas, Hotsenpiller, & Peterson (2007).

Some studies are concerned with the link between emotions and sensory perceptions, such as how auditory stimuli are perceived and remembered in the brain[330]—that is, what types of sounds are remembered in what way. Some researchers consider how episodic memories are linked to certain sounds, such that individuals forever link certain tones to a specific moment and emotion. Other studies focus on visual stimuli. Can looks kill? Research concerned with how the brain reacts to emotionally charged facial expressions[331] would say yes, at least in the figurative sense related to learning. There appears to be a "fusiform face area" of the brain, which has the unique function of interpreting the intentions of other people's facial expressions (see the section below about facial interpretations). Other research demonstrates how positive emotions, such as those triggered by humor,[332] can enhance learning. These studies are contrasted with those that show how stress and adversity,[333] as well as disgust,[334] impede learning. These studies are relevant for teachers because they make clear the need for positive relations within the classroom setting in order to manage emotions for the betterment of learning. Finally, the importance of self-esteem and emotions as they impact learning in formal school settings has also been reviewed.[335] It is now clear that how students feel about themselves, not just the teacher or the subject matter, impacts their ability to learn. When a student feels (or has been told) that he or she is not good at a subject, the student simply stops trying to do well. The self-esteem of the professor impacts student learning as well. When a teacher doubts his or her own ability to instruct well, students perceive this lack of self-confidence, and this perception impacts their belief that they will learn from the teacher. This mistrust of the teacher's knowledge leads to student underachievement.

As we saw in an earlier section, there is no decision without emotions. As a consequence, emotions impact learning and influence life choices inside and out of school. Emotions as a field of study will also most likely grow in influence in the coming years, especially given that teachers rarely receive explicit instruction on how to manage emotions in the classroom setting.

• *Motivation.* It may seem obvious that people learn better when they are highly motivated than when they have little or no motivation.[336] Positive motivation and interest levels

330. See Ferbinteanu, Kennedy, & Shapiro (2006).
331. Ibid.
332. See Garner (2006); Littleton (1998).
333. See Lupien, Maheu, Tu, Fiocco, & Schramek (2007); Nelson (2000a); Samoilov (2000); Society for Neuroscience (2007j).
334. See Sprengelmeyer (2007).
335. See Sylwester (1997b); Vuilleumier, Armony, & Dolan (2003).
336. See Reeve (2004).

are linked. But where does motivation come from? No matter what the original level of motivation a student may have for a subject, it is impacted by the level of enthusiasm the teacher shows for that subject.[337] Motivation as a topic has generated thousands of studies, mainly in the psychological realm, but with more and more studies in neuroscience as well, all of which carry great weight in and out of the classroom. It should come as no surprise that positive motivation and interest levels are linked.[338] People with interest in a subject tend to devote more time to the pursuit of knowledge.[339] This is true for anyone who has ever had a hobby, for example; people spend more time doing what they like to do. As important a topic as motivation is, however, it is not known whether or not the motivation a person feels about the topic improves learning, or whether simply spending more time on task (due to being motivated) is what helps learning.

Motivation can be both positive and negative, as well as internally or externally driven.[340] People can be motivated by feel-good reasons or out of fear, for example. Learning can result from both positive and negative motivation; however, repetition of the learned skill may wane if the learning carries a negative valence. That is, if I learn to swim because I love the water and want to play with friends in the pool, I am more likely to use the skill on my own than if I am thrown in the pool and forced to learn to swim (literally sink or swim) to pass a test for school or summer camp.

Motivating factors are regulated in a highly individualized fashion; what is motivating to one individual may not be motivating to another. Some teachers use negative motivating practices such as threatening students with being thrown out of class if they act out or distract other students. Some students may react to this threat by behaving quietly from that point on. However, other students may view this punishment as a reward (they actually *want* to be thrown out of class). Good parents and teachers know that they should be the catalysts for self-motivating actions on the part of children; children have to want the same outcomes as parents and teachers—as in learning to swim—because it serves their own purposes. One of the best ways to achieve this concordance between adult and child is through positive modeling. Teachers are more likely to motivate students to learn by helping them articulate their own reasons for wanting to learn a skill. Passing algebra "because I say so" is not as motivating to a student as realizing the amount of real-world feats that can be achieved using the required formulas. Authentic learning is a key element

---

337. See Sass (1989).
338. For a classic example, see Halpern & Hakel (2002).
339. For examples, see McCann & Garcia (1999); Smith (2004).
340. See Berridge (2004).

in improving student motivation. We all should understand how motivation impacts learning and what we can do to improve it among the children in our lives.[341]

As mentioned, what motivates one student may not motivate another, however. Great teachers know that carrots and sticks differ tremendously, based on individual student backgrounds, experiences, and prior knowledge levels. In order to create highly motivating learning environments, great teachers concisely strategize, first, to help students find their own reason to feel motivated (intrinsic motivation), and second, to maintain their own high levels of enthusiasm and transmit their passion to the students.

Some of the studies of interest to teachers about motivation investigate the physical areas of the brain that are related to motivation itself,[342] or the neurotransmitters involved in mediating an experience of motivation.[343] Other educational studies make it clear that no matter what level of motivation the student comes to the class with, the teacher will impact it.[344] That is, both the highly motivated student and the student with low motivation will be influenced by what they think their teacher believes they will achieve, as well as what they think about the teacher himself. This finding has policy implications because it forces teachers to realize that motivation is not the sole responsibility of the students themselves, but rather that teachers are responsible, whether consciously or not, for student motivation. *Teacher self-efficacy*, or the teacher's belief in him- or herself to achieve the teaching task, is perceived, rightly or wrongly, and consciously or unconsciously, by students.[345] The students' judgments of how well they think the teacher thinks he or she can fulfill the teaching task impacts the students' motivation to learn.

The fact that students who believe in their teachers are more likely to trust them and learn from them has huge implications for teaching, as few teachers are taught about the importance of conveying confidence in their own abilities to their students. It is possible that simply by becoming aware of the importance of displaying a high level of self-esteem while in the classroom, teachers will actually become more confident; this is called a "virtuous circle." In a virtuous circle a positive action stimulates further positive action, which means that the teacher's high self-esteem causes students to feel confident that the teacher knows what he or she is doing, and, in turn, the teacher feels that he or she is reaching the students, and therefore feels more self-confident. Teacher self-efficacy normally comes with experience, but there is a spiral effect: The more confidence that a

341. Readers, especially those teaching at university level, are encouraged to read Fink (2003).
342. See Tracy, Jarrad, & Davidson (2001).
343. See Depue & Collins (1999).
344. Halpern & Hakel (2002).
345. Ibid.

teacher shows in his or her skills, the more confidence students have in the teacher—which in turn motivates the teacher to believe in him- or herself and inspires the students in both the teacher's ability to teach and their own ability to learn. This knowledge should be explicitly taught in teacher training programs.

Several psychological theories of motivation have been confirmed in neuroscience labs as well as observed in educational classroom settings. For example, Maslow's (1943) hierarchy of needs (see Figure 6.1), which has been a reference for nearly 70 years, is supported by studies in all three of the parent fields and is accepted as relevant to MBE science as well. There is evidence in neuroscience, psychology, and education that if basic physiological needs are not met (food, water), then humans cannot begin to consider safety needs (shelter, self-preservation). However, if one is able to achieve both physiological needs and safety needs, one is able to then move on toward securing social needs, such as friendship. If social needs can be met, then the individual can move "upwards" toward the fulfillment of esteem needs, or receiving respect from others. Only when this external approval has been reached then can an individual seek self-actualization, which is the pinnacle of human achievement, according to Maslow. Self-actualization involves fulfilling one's destiny, achieving what one was meant to do, and being completely satisfied with oneself. This is explained in more detail below based on each level in the hierarchy.

FIGURE 6.1
Maslow's Hierarchy of Needs

Source: Based on Maslow (1998).

1. *Physiological needs.* Humans have an evolutionary instinct to survive, and part of that survival is obtaining fundamental physiological basics like food, water, and shelter. Teachers need to be aware that some of their students may not have these basic physiological needs met. Some students arrive to class without having slept well, eaten enough, or even without having rested with a roof over their heads. All of these factors greatly impede learning.

2. *Safety needs.* Studies have illuminated how fear or anxiety (due to basic threats to safety), impedes learning. Students who feel threatened (e.g., due to bullying, gang activity, or the prevalence of firearms) are unable to perform well in school.[346] Safety needs include both psychological and physical forms of protection.

3. *Social needs.* There are also studies that show how humans are motivated by social needs. Many sociological, psychological, and educational studies attest to the social nature of human interaction and learning;[347] many students are motivated to do things because their peers do so.[348] Teachers need to be taught how to manage their classrooms in order to make the most of the personalities for group as well as individual benefits. This means that teachers need to be aware and take advantage of the social relationships that exist in their classroom. For example, by consciously mixing and matching students based on personalities and skill sets, teachers can use the heterogeneous makeup of their classroom to everyone's learning advantage.

4. *Esteem needs.* Studies have shown that humans are motivated by esteem needs, or the desire to be valued by others.[349] Everyone likes to be confirmed, get a pat on the back, and receive positive feedback about his or her work or progress. Teachers can take advantage of this need and provide the feedback that helps students feel good about themselves and to learn.[350]

5. *Self-actualization needs.* Finally, there are studies that relate to human motivation based on self-actualization needs or the development of a sense of self-fulfillment.[351] The human quest for self-understanding and eventual self-actualization is a lifelong pursuit, and not everyone will reach this level. Many motivational studies have demonstrated how humans are driven by inner forces to reach this highest tier on Maslow's pyramid. Maslow's theory is basically related to global incentive theories of motivation. Other moti-

---

346. For examples, see Close Conoley (2008); Hall (2006).
347. See Whitlow (2010).
348. See Wang, Peterson, & Morphey (2007).
349. A very interesting example of a meta-analysis of these needs can be found in Oishi, Diener, Lucas, & Suh (1999).
350. For interesting examples of this phenomenon, see Vázquez Recio & Ojeda Díaz (2010); Phuong Phan (2010).
351. See Maslow (1998) for a complete reflection on this topic.

vational theories—for example, cognitive dissonance theory, ERG theory (existence, relatedness, and growth), self-determination theory, and goal-setting theory—should also be studied to determine their relevance for MBE science.

Executive Functions and Decision-Making

The term *executive functions* refers to the ways in which the brain manages all higher-order cognitive processes, including decision-making and which sensory input should receive attention and which should be ignored. Some of the studies in this group describe the physiology (the neural mechanisms and biochemical processes) of executive functions and the parts of the brain that are most active during these types of thinking processes.[352] There are studies about the invisible aspects of decision-making, which relate to the neural mechanisms and bio-chemical processes involved in executive functions.[353] Teachers and parents can work better with the children in their lives if they understand how executive functions develop in childhood,[354] and, actually, throughout the lifespan on into old age.[355] Teachers know that central to good teaching are effective strategies. One of the best strategies for explaining complex concepts is the use of analogies, which feed into the natural way the brain prioritizes information[356] and receives reinforcement.[357] All good teachers know that some teaching methods work better than others when explaining new information to different students.[358] Analogies are one of the most elegant ways in which the mind transfers known concepts to new knowledge and are representative of the most difficult type of executive function.[359] One of the reasons analogies work so well is because they take advantage of the normal neural circuitry of the brain that "checks in" with the amygdala and hippocampus for points of reference before taking action.[360] Learning is facilitated by comparing new information with known contexts (*A* is to *B* as *X* is to *Y*).

Other research is more specifically related to certain problems of executive functions, such as those caused by ADD,[361] or how higher-order thinking skills may occur despite a

---

352. See Cole (2006); Holmboe & Johnson (2005).
353. For some examples, see Arnsten & Li (2005); Fellows (2004); Gilbert & Sigman (2007); Lee (2006); Luo & Knoblich (2007); McIntosh (1999); Miller & Cohen (2001); Opris & Bruce (2005).
354. See Espy (2004).
355. See Victor (2003).
356. See Bar (2007).
357. See Cohen & Ranganath (2007).
358. Wiggins & McTighe (2005).
359. Lipkens & Hayes (2009).
360. Leech, Mareschal, & Cooper (2008).
361. See Denckla (2005).

student's performance as a low achiever.[362] In order to meet the needs of diverse learners, teachers need to be aware that student achievement can be influenced by their ability to pay attention to the right stimuli at the right time. *Impulsivity* and its opposite, *self-control*,[363] are aspects of self-regulation that have a direct impact on learning within school contexts but also within society as a whole. Teachers have an obligation to help students become more conscientious about how the brain deals with conflicting stimuli[364] and to learn how to control and prioritize them.

Part of good teaching involves identifying what motivates students to make the correct decisions. Some of the relevant research relates to understanding how choices are triggered by different *reward systems* that are regulated, in part, by executive functions.[365] When teachers are in synch with which rewards system the student needs, then the teaching process is more effective. For example, if a teacher identifies that a student is most motivated by peer recognition (as opposed to good grades or teacher feedback, etc.), then that teacher can use the proper reward system for that particular student. Expectations are related to rewards systems. Students develop expectations based on past situations. This means that preparing students for learning experiences (prepping or priming) is just as important as the actual teaching of the new concept. Teachers should reflect on the process of modeling long-term repetition priming through practice[366] and recognize how certain expectations are created by certain habits of mind developed over time. Students develop individual reward systems based on their expectations. In home as well as in a classroom context, this simply looks like several "if–then" structures: If I do X, then I can expect Y to occur. An effective teacher knows how to use this practice to the advantage of the students' learning. For example, a student may become accustomed to having his effort recognized by a smiley face sticker on his homework, but he also accepts that his actual grade for the homework will be based on the quality/correctness of the answers he produces.

A novice is a first-time learner. An expert is someone who can synthesize past knowledge with speed and accuracy.[367] This means that novice learning is at the opposite extreme of expert learning. Some fascinating studies relate to intuition and decision-making, including the theory of "hyper" cognition,[368] in which the mind processes

362. See Zohar & Dori (2003).
363. See Kalenscher, Ohmann, & Gunturkun (2006).
364. See Matsumoto & Tanaka (2004).
365. See O'Doherty, Hampton, & Kim (2007).
366. See Colagrosso (2003).
367. See Griffin, Jee, & Wiley (2009).
368. For a beautiful explanation of this concept, see Gladwell (2005).

thoughts at a faster rate than normal due to an expert knowledge of the subject. Choices are always made based on past knowledge; the executive functions of people with expert status are quicker than those without expert status and lightning speed compared with novices. Studies of "hyper" cognition cases, similar to those of gifted individuals, help us understand "normal" cognition processes better.

Executive functions are a fascinating area of study in MBE science because they relate to choice, and making choices is an integral part of learning: Learners choose what to pay attention to, and what to ignore. The literature reviewed here explains how decision-making choices are made, through which neural mechanisms they are managed, and in some cases, instructional strategies as to how parents and teachers can maximize children's ability to focus.

Unlike executive functions, which involve choice making, the interpretation of facial expressions (e.g., the look on a teacher's face) can evoke strong emotional responses in students, often resulting in unconscious reactions. The next section considers how facial recognition is different from other visual memories, and how humans interpret each other's expressions.

Facial Recognition and Voice Interpretation

An intriguing area of research that is not known to most teachers but which has an impact on all students is that of facial recognition. In evolutionary terms facial recognition is a very basic ability; even monkeys are experts at interpreting each others' faces.[369] However, facial recognition is also one of the most complex mental functions, and one of the few human abilities that computers and artificial intelligence have not been able to duplicate.[370] Facial expressions are a basic means of communication. It appears that the brain's ability to "read faces" and the emotions they harbor is species-specific (humans can interpret each others' faces, as can chimpanzees interpret each others' facial expressions, but humans have trouble interpreting chimp faces). The interpretation of facial expressions has huge implications in the classroom and in life in general.

When a student feels that a teacher's facial expression conveys some sort of threatening message, then that student's brain goes into a panic mode and new learning is

---

369. Adachi, Chou, & Hampton (2009).
370. There has been great progress in this field, and a publication leader in this area has been the *International Journal of Pattern Recognition and Artificial Intelligence* (IJPRAI), which dedicated one of its 2009 issues to the topic of facial image processing and analysis. However, even this journal acknowledges that there is a long way to go before machines match humans in their abilities. See Grgic, Shan, Lukac, Wechsler, & Bartlett (eds.). (2009) for details.

impeded (this is independent of whether the teacher intends to make a threatening expression or not, or whether the student misinterpreted the teacher's expression). It has also been hypothesized that one of the key roles of mirror neurons, or neurons that fire both when they complete an action as well as when they imagine they are completing that act, is interpreting other people's facial expressions.[371] For example, mirror neurons in the brain for hitting a baseball are the same as those for actually hitting the baseball as well as watching someone else hit the baseball.[372] Related to faces, it is presumed that mirror neurons play a role in understanding the facial expressions of others as the person "wears" the other's face, so to speak, as he or she interprets the feelings and intentions behind the expression on the face[373] (see Figure 6.2).

FIGURE 6.2
Paul Eckman's Emotional Recognition

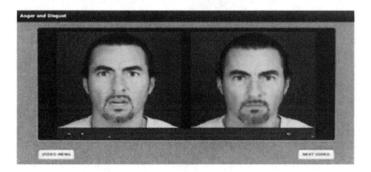

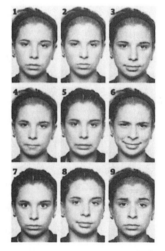

Source: Paul Ekman's Micro-Expressions
(http://www.paulekman.com/micro-expressions).

A remarkable study by Nalini Ambady and Robert Rosenthal (1993) demonstrated that students actually judged the quality of a teacher—his or her perceived knowledge of the subject and how to teach it—within seconds of viewing him or her on video (without sound), based on the instructor's body language, including facial expressions. The way in which teachers express themselves to their students (in part, through their facial expressions) influences learning. What students believe that their teachers think about them

371. See Rizzolatti, Fogassi, & Gallese (2008).
372. See Rizzolatti & Craighero (2004).
373. See Dapretto (2006).

impacts their learning; therefore, the way faces are perceived is important to learning. Because it is a fact that humans interpret each others' intentions through facial expressions, teachers need to understand how such expressions impact the classroom environment. Students and teachers interpret each others' motives through facial expressions all the time. Psychological studies have shown that student performance is influenced by what students think their teachers think about them.[374] Similarly, it is not uncommon to hear of teachers who feel a lack of motivation to work with certain groups because they "look so unmotivated" or "appear bored." Students base their perceptions of their teachers in part on their teachers' facial expressions, and vice versa. What is important for teachers to know is that the circle of interpretation is within their power to control. If a teacher enters the classroom apparently motivated and enthusiastic about his or her topic, then there is a greater likelihood that the students will be "infected" by the positive facial expressions accompanying this emotion and react positively to the class. In turn, the students will appear more engaged, which will give the teacher feedback to continue being enthusiastic. Unfortunately, the opposite is true as well: If a teacher begins to present a topic in a hesitant and unenthusiastic way, students are likely to react with bored looks. This serves to demotivate the teacher, who in turn acts even less excited about his or her subject and becomes unsure about the delivery, causing the students' opinion of the teacher to lower even further. In other influential studies it has been shown that smiling can actually make us feel happy even when we do not feel happy.[375] Neurotransmitters in the brain are apparently triggered by the physical changes in our facial muscles to occur when smiling, causing us to feel happy—or sad, depending on our expressions.[376]

Several researchers have studied how emotions are conveyed through facial expression.[377] Others are concerned with how the brain processes the emotions behind these expressions. These studies are complemented by research about how the brain "catches"

---

374. Mangels, Butterfield, & Lamb (2006).

375. The James–Lange theory of emotion states that changes in physical states can cause changes in emotional states (e.g., smiling to make yourself happy). In 1884 William James stated: "My theory . . . is that the bodily changes follow directly the perception of the exciting fact, and that our feeling of the same changes as they occur is the emotion. Common sense says, we lose our fortune, are sorry and weep; we meet a bear, are frightened and run; we are insulted by a rival, and angry and strike. The hypothesis here to be defended says that this order of sequence is incorrect . . . and that the more rational statement is that we feel sorry because we cry, angry because we strike, afraid because we tremble. . . . Without the bodily states following on the perception, the latter would be purely cognitive in form, pale, colorless, destitute of emotional warmth. We might then see the bear, and judge it best to run, receive the insult and deem it right to strike, but we should not actually feel afraid or angry" (p. 189). For an example of this phenomena in a social context, see Howard & Gengler (2001).

376. A review of this fascinating finding can be found in Kleinke, Peterson, & Rutledge (1998).

377. See Erikson & Schulkin (2003); Fitzgerald et al. (2006).

subtle changes in facial expressions,[378] including "overt and covert presentations of facial expressions of fear and disgust."[379] This is vital knowledge for teachers: Triggers for facial expression and selective attention are key in learning experiences.[380] Though much of the research on facial expressions has not yet been applied to classroom settings, it is without a doubt one of the most important new areas for teacher training.

Additionally, the human brain judges others' tones of voices for threat levels in a rapid and often unconscious way, influencing the way information from these sources is perceived (e.g., valid, invalid, trustworthy, untrustworthy). The fact that infants recognize their mother's voices from birth[381] indicates that vocal tones are probably an innate or early-learned perception of the brain. Some research in this area relates to how the brain processes emotional speech, specifically how the brain perceives anger via the sound of a particular vocal tone. All of these studies point to the fact that the brain perceives and judges vocal tones in an almost unconscious way.[382] Great teachers know how to use their voices to draw students into classroom discussions. This means that they manage their intonation levels consciously in order to not to repulse or bore students, but rather to convey a sense of excitement and intrigue about the topic.

Memory

The most popular brain ability studied over the past 30 years, memory[383] is vital to human survival: without it, the species would become extinct. If people did not remember what foods were poisonous or which predators were dangerous, then humankind would die out. There are many studies in this group, including those on short-term, working, long-term, and emotional memory, as well as others related to defining the terminology of memory in the cognitive neurosciences.[384] Memory is vital for learning in both formal and informal settings. Without long-term memory students are destined to fail in school and to be doomed to a nonfunctional existence in society. Perhaps the most important point for teachers to understand is the relationship between attention and memory, without which there would be no learning.[385] Teachers need to understand that if either memory or attention is missing, then there is no real learning.

378. See Smith, Gosselin, & Schyns (2007).
379. Phillips, Williams, Heining, Herba, Russell, Andrew, et al. (2004, p. 1484).
380. For exceptionally rich examples, see Vuilleumier (2002).
381. As shown by Purhonen et al. (2004).
382. For an example of this kind of study, see Sander et al. (2005).
383. Tokuhama-Espinosa (2008b).
384. See Glick & Budson (2005).
385. See Chun & Turk-Browne (2007) and Deco & Rolls (2005) for some examples.

Daniel Schacter, an expert on memory and forgetting, has identified seven "sins" of memory: transience, absent-mindedness, blocking, misattribution, suggestibility, bias, and persistence.[386] Studies have been conducted substantiating each of these "sins," and the findings have clear applications in everyday life as well as in successful classrooms.[387] If teachers knew, for example, that sometimes students "forget" because they have misattributed new information to an incorrect storage area in their brain, then they would be able to help students better. For example, a teacher may think that she taught the concept of "global warming," but the student may attribute the concept to "car pollution" and therefore log the information in the wrong category in his mind. This misattribution will mean that the concept of "global warming" cannot easily be retrieved. If the teacher understands how misattribution occurs, she might often be able to help the student improve his recollection.

Another expert in the area of memory is Eric Kandel (2007), who has spent several decades defining neuroscience[388] and the "biology of the mind."[389] Kandel is best known as the recipient of the 2000 Nobel prize in physiology or medicine for his explanation of the physiological basis of memory storage in neurons. Along with Daniel Schacter and Larry R. Squire, also known for studies on the neuronal basis of memory (1999), Kandel's understanding of memory has evolved with the growing body of research. However, perhaps the most applicable of memory research for the classroom teacher comes from Alan Baddeley, who has done tremendous research related to explaining the breakdowns that occur between the moment information is presented and put in temporary storage, and when it is either lost of moved into long-term memory.[390] Baddeley's Center for Working Memory and Learning at the University of York in the United Kingdom has done substantial research demonstrating the vital role of working memory training in enhancing learning in students.[391] Being able to maintain information in one's mind long enough to perform a task is the definition of good working memory. As all learning relies on good working memory, it seems logical that teachers should be better trained in extending the working memory parameters of their students. These researchers have produced valuable information that is useful in personal as well as academic realms.

386. Schacter (2001, p.4).
387. See Fitzpatrick (2007).
388. Kandel, Schwartz, & Jessell (2000).
389. Kandel (2005).
390. See Baddeley (2001, 2003).
391. For some examples of their work, see Holmes, Gathercole, Place, Dunning, Hilton, & Elliott (2009); Holmes, Gathercole, & Dunning (2009).

Other research on working memory directly relates to classroom methodologies and how memory can be improved to benefit students' learning.[392] Some researchers were ahead of their time, given the limited technology available, and considered how memory was affected by timing, that is, by how much time students are given to react when questioned.[393] In 1972 Thomas suggested that if teachers were to give students several seconds to reply to questions posed in class, rather than the 1-second average, they would generate better answers. Robert Sylwester[394] was also ahead of his time because few teachers in the 1980s considered the vital role of planning activities that enhanced memory. For example, by creating authentic learning experiences in which students related new information to something they had already experienced in real life, Sylwester found that students were able to recall that new information with greater ease than noncontetxualized information.

Other researchers consider the distinction of procedural versus declarative memory and the roles that each plays in different types of learning.[395] We normally think of procedural learning as including motoric processes that eventually become rote, such as learning how to walk or drive a car, and declarative knowledge to be explicitly taught content area, such as a math formula. Authors such as Baddeley have helped teachers understand how procedural versus declarative memories are processed in the brain, and they call attention to why teaching must adapt to the types of memory systems being used.

Several important studies can help teachers understand why certain emotionally linked memories, such as those involving fear, cause memory consolidation[396] and why this type of consolidation creates mental schemas that are hard to break. For example, students who are humiliated in classroom settings have a hard time disassociating new learning in the same subject from their negative memory. The product of this very strong and negative memory can be learning anxieties, such as fear of math, for example.[397] If teachers understand that emotional memories "override" memories of conceptual knowledge, they might be more careful in how they interact with students in class and the type of feedback used.

392. Examples can be found in Dretsch & Tipples (2007); Edin, Macoveanu, Olesen, Tegnér, & Klingberg (2007); Guo, Lawson, Zhang, & Jiang (2007); Linden (2007b); Meegan, Purc-Stephenson, Honsberger, & Topan (2004); Pickering & Phye (2006); Sprenger (1999).
393. Thomas (1972).
394. Sylwester (1985).
395. See Baddeley (2003); Hubert, Beaunieux, Chetelat, Platel, Landeau, Danion, et al. (2007).
396. See Monfils, Cowansage, & LeDoux (2007).
397. Studies by Legg & Locker (2009) and Ashcraft & Krause (2007) are useful in illustrating this point.

Yet other researchers investigate why there are different pathways for episodic memory (memory of autobiographical events), semantic memory (concept-based knowledge), spatial memory (of events that take place in a physical realm),[398] and sequence learning (related to the order of things).[399] This research reinforces the modern approach to teaching in which it is suggested that the same concept should be taught in several different ways, depending on the type of information and why different methods of teaching for different types of information produce storage in different memory neural pathways. This information, in turn, helps teachers understand why different types of knowledge need to be stored and retrieved through different types of stimuli.

Teachers who understand the complexities of memory storage are more efficient at their craft because they appreciate the need to present different types of concepts in different ways that facilitate optimal storage for ease and availability of later recall. Teachers who know that there are different neural mechanisms and physical areas of the brain concerned with different memory types[400] are able to appreciate students who can learn one type of knowledge or concept, but not another. If teachers know more about the biochemistry of memory,[401] they will be better prepared to diagnose some learning problems directly associated with poor diet, the influence of drugs, or sleep deprivation, for example.[402] Additionally, there are several studies related to memory chemical enhancers[403] that are pertinent to teachers. Should teachers encourage students who have access to drugs that can enhance their memory (as readily available as caffeine)[404] to use them? Without full knowledge of how memory is impacted, teachers are at a disadvantage. Studies that help teachers understand strategies to improve memory,[405] causes of memory loss, and problems that typically impede memory consolidation[406] should be considered basic knowledge in the modern teachers' studies.

All of this research can be viewed in terms of the following: Humans remember things that (1) have survival value, (2) are easy to associate with past experiences, or (3) have emotional value.[407] *Survival memories* are related to protecting the self from harm. For

398. See Moscovitch, Nadel, Winocur, Gilboa, & Rosenbaum (2006).
399. See Thomas, Hunt, Vizueta, Sommer, Durston, Yang, et al. (2004).
400. See Bussey & Saksida (2007); Jonasson (2003); Kalueff (2007); Levy & Goldman-Rakic (2000); Squire & Bayley (2007); Torriero, Oliveri, Koch, Caltagirone, & Petrosini (2004); Vallar (2006); Vuilleumier & Driver (2007).
401. See El-Ghundi, O'Dowd, & George (2007); Yamauchi & Yakugaku (2007).
402. For an example, see He (2010).
403. See Gazzaniga (2005b); Society for Neuroscience (2007g).
404. Addicott (2010).
405. See Banikowski & Mehring (1999).
406. See Hutterer & Liss (2006); Squire (2007).
407. Sousa (2000).

example, we remember that we should not cross the street on a red light because we might be hit by a vehicle. *Associative memories*—relating new things to already known things—are how students normally learn in school. This point deserves attention because associative memory is the type of memory that most teachers refer to when discussing student learning. This type of memory links past information of known concepts to new situations and novel information. For example, a child who knows how to add will find learning to subtract easier than a child who learns to subtract without first knowing how to add. Teachers can facilitate the retrieval of associative memories by asking students to develop metaphors, analogies, and similes,[408] which force learners to call upon the known before conquering the unknown. *Emotionally valuable memories* concern things about which students feel passionate and which they learn because they like them. Students who feel that the teacher cares about their learning learn better than students who think the teacher dislikes them. Other emotional links relate to personal enjoyment; people who see a connection between their own lives and what they are learning learn faster than those who ask themselves "when will I ever use that in real life?" Sousa (2000) has referred to the vital link of emotion in learning as providing "sense and meaning," such that lessons not only make sense (are logical) but have meaning in a learner's life.[409]

The closest bedfellow to memory is attention. Without the dynamic duo of memory and attention, there would be no learning.

Attention

> "Everyone knows what attention is. It is the taking possession by the mind, in
> clear and vivid form, of one out of what seem several simultaneously possible
> subjects or trains of thought. Focalization, concentration, of consciousness are
> of its essence. It implies withdrawal from some things in order to deal effectively
> with others."
>
> —William James, *The Principles of Psychology* (1981, pp. 381–382)

Attention is a cornerstone of learning—in fact, without attention there can be no learning.[410] Some educators have gone so far as to suggest that memory plus attention yields

408. For an excellent explanation of this core concept, see Schwartz & Fischer (2006); Wolfe (2008).
409. Sousa (2000).
410. Levine (2000).

learning; that is, without one or the other—without memory or without attention—learning is impossible.[411] It is for these reasons that attention is a major area of MBE science literature. The literature in this group falls into several categories. Perhaps the most important work related to attention from a neurological perspective comes from Michael Posner's work *Cognitive Neuroscience of Attention* (2004) and his many journal articles. In Posner and Rothbart's most recent work, *Educating the Human Brain* (2007), they describe "the anatomy, circuitry, development and genetics of three attention networks which are the alerting networks, orienting network and the executive network."[412] The key contribution to the MBE science literature that Posner and Rothbart make is that an understanding of the fact that different neural networks mediate attention may explain why some students learn better through one neural pathway or another. Teachers should be aware that by instructing information in different ways—through discussion, readings, videos, debates, projects, etc.—there is a greater possibility of student retention and learning because the information will be input in different (though sometimes overlapping) neural pathways.

Studies related to how attention networks develop in childhood[413] are very relevant to MBE science because they offer developmental indicators of when a child is prepared to exercise different types of attentional skills.[414] Attention problems can now be subdivided in terms of the different neural networks that underlie them. These range from the ability to manage attention, the way memory and attention are linked, self-regulation of attention, attention and performance, the link between emotion and attention, and the way we show we are paying attention in social settings. Each category offers a slightly different kind of insight about the role of attention in learning.

First, the research about managing attention[415] is closely related to the research investigating executive functions, as seen above. As noted earlier, if executive functions are not intact, and if an individual cannot effectively choose the right stimuli to pay attention to, then learning is jeopardized.

Second, the studies that document the interaction between attention and memory[416] have a direct connection from the laboratory to the classroom. While memory and attention are huge concepts individually, combined, they are decisive factors in learning. Without both memory and attention, there is no new learning.

---

411. See Levine (2000); Sousa (2000); Sylwester (1995).
412. Posner & Rothbart (2007a, pp. 60–61).
413. For examples, see Colombo (2002); Rueda, Fan, McCandliss, Halparin, Gruber, Lercari, et al. (2004).
414. See Raz & Buhle (2006).
415. For example, see Couperus (2004).
416. See Chun & Turk-Browne (2007) and Deco & Rolls (2005) for examples.

Third, the studies investigating the relationships between attention and self-regulation[417] show how easy (and how normal) it is for the brain to become distracted by stimuli if regulating mechanisms are not working well. In many educational circles, it is presumed that higher-order thinking relies, in part, on the brain's ability to self-regulate, which we now know is related to being able to pay attention.

Fourth, there are studies that consider the connections between attention and performance; that is, how does the ability to maintain attention impact one's ability to perform correctly (in social as well as academic settings)?[418] These studies are closely related to others concerned with attentional effort. It is easy to imagine how a trapeze artist might fall, for example, if she is not paying attention. What teachers must realize is that students are constantly conducting their own "balancing act" in class, and this effort impacts the level of "performance" they are able to produce.[419]

Fifth, research on emotion and attention studies what people choose to pay attention to and why. As mentioned in the previous section on emotions, how a person feels about stimuli (e.g., a new learning concept, a new contact, a new fact) can influence whether or not enough attention is paid to it to learn from it.[420] But in a twist, stimuli that demand attention are easier to remember. For example, an unexpected stimulus to the senses, such as a loud noise or the use of larger-than-normal text in a book, calls attention to itself and makes remembering easier.

Finally, there are studies about the importance of attention for good classroom performance,[421] as demonstrated by active listening, participating at an appropriate level, and knowing when to interject ideas into the classroom setting. In many ways these behaviors are related to social cognition (knowing how, when, and why to interact with others).

All of the studies concerned with attention in the MBE science literature contribute to a better understanding of teaching practices. Some studies explain how attention functions in the brain while learning is taking place, and others relate to aspects of attention and memory in the context of general learning. In summary, teachers should remember that attention is regulated by an individual's executive functions, but it is also highly influenced by his or her social cognition.

---

417. See Berger, Kofman, Livneh & Henik (2007) as an example.
418. See Pashler, Johnsyon, & Ruthruff (2001).
419. See Sarter, Gehring, & Kozak (2006).
420. See Sander, Grandjean, Pourtois, Schwartz, Seghier, Scherer, et al. (2005); Vuilleumier, Armony, & Dolan (2003).
421. See Smallwood, Fishman, & Schooler (2007).

Social Cognition

Social cognition refers to the ability to work well with others, understand others' perspectives, and comprehend how the self is perceived by others.[422] Several researchers in this subfield have worked to define the core concepts of social cognition.[423] In its earlier version, social cognition was deeply tied to the individual's emotional responses to others.[424] In its newer iteration, conceptualized as *social cognitive neuroscience*,[425] cognition is based on both its sociological as well as neurological correlates. An interesting theme in this new discipline is the *theory of mind* movement, in which there is reflection about how we perceive ourselves and others in social contexts.[426] This means that information is not only gathered from observable behavior in social situations, but it is compared with neuroscientific studies that allow us to "see" what is happening in the brain during these social interactions. Teachers can benefit from an understanding of how people perceive each other and which social settings are conducive to new experiences and learning. For example, the large number of studies explaining social interactions and human relationships can help teachers improve their classroom management techniques and understand the real motivations behind student behavior.[427] Others are more psychologically based and are concerned with the evaluation of attitudes in relation to consequential actions.[428] Combined, this new vision offers teachers a powerful theoretical base for explaining student classroom behavior.

Still other studies have laid the groundwork for understanding how social cognition influences a student's success in school by affecting the way in which an individual integrates within the group.[429] Humans are social creatures, and the brain is a social organ that thrives on interaction with others.[430] Research has shown, for example, that students learn best when they teach others; one of the best ways to learn is to teach.[431] Some educators argue that social interaction varies depending on individual learning styles,[432] while some neuroscientists make the case that shared information is reinforced in the brain. Learning

---

422. Levine (2000).
423. For example, see Beer & Ochsner (2006).
424. See Elias, Zins, Weissberg, Frey, Greenberg, Haynes, et al. (1997).
425. See Blakemore, Winston, & Frith (2004).
426. For a good review of the core context areas of social cognitive neuroscience, see Lieberman (2007).
427. For an excellent example, see Cozolino (2006).
428. See Cunningham & Zalazo (2007).
429. See Sylwester (1997a); Levine (2000).
430. Caine & Nummela Caine (1997).
431. See Sousa (2000).
432. In Wegerif (1998).

is solidified when we work with others to resolve problems. The role of social cognition relevant to MBE science is important and its role in the learning experience is clear. An area that is slightly less clear, but which does indeed play a role in learning is that of spatial management.

Spatial Sequential Management

Spatial sequential management is the ability to perceive and manage the position of one's self in space.[433] This extends to such practical skills such as map reading and getting from school back home on a bike. Spatial management includes managing one's physical possessions as well. There are many instances in which students are judged negatively by their teachers for their inability to manage school materials, as in appearing to have messy lockers or notebooks. Oftentimes, these students are underestimated by their peers because they don't carry themselves well; they stand and move in awkward ways. An ability, or lack thereof, in spatial management is also apparent in concepts of conceptual imagery,[434] as found in geometry, or in visually laying out a drawing or an essay before actually beginning. In early reading, for example, children with spatial management problems have difficulty forming letter parts in correct proportion. Some research in spatial management focuses on the visual word form area in the brain.[435] Other spatial studies related to reading measure the "spatio-temporal brain dynamics of saccade execution,"[436] or how the brain scans the words on a page as it reads (contrary to popular belief, only beginning readers consider every single letter; experienced readers "jump" around the sentence).[437] Similar studies have been conducted to investigate how children decipher math problems, which is very telling of what strategy they are using to solve the problem. A review of the precise mental functions employed to read or do math reminds teachers that each skill set (e.g., math or reading) is really a combination of several sub-skills, each of which can impact the quality with which we learn. For example, teachers who understand the way the brain reads are more likely to work with children by building each individual sub-skill and have better results than a teacher who thinks that reading is a single skill. More about this in Chapter 7.

433. Originally conceived by Levine (2000).
434. In Levine (2000).
435. See Cohen, Dehaene, Naccache, Lehericy, Dehaene-Lambertz, Henaff, et al. (2000).
436. Herdman & Ryan (2007, p. 420).
437. See Stanislas Dehaene's *Reading in the Brain* (2009) for a wonderfully entertaining and enlightening explanation of how the brain learns to read.

Navigational skills are also investigated by researchers in this area.[438] Maguire and colleagues offered empirical evidence for the belief that stimulation of spatial areas in the brain causes those areas to grow and strengthen.[439] By neuroimaging taxi drivers in a now-famous case, these researchers demonstrated that there is actually structural change in areas of the brain that are used for spatial orientation. In this case Maguire and colleagues[440] compared the brains of taxi drivers with navigational experience versus those without, and found that "the posterior hippocampi of taxi drivers were significantly larger relative to those of control subjects,"[441] meaning that long-term memory systems (the hippocampus) were changed by repeated physical maneuvering in space.

At first it may appear that research in spatial management is outside the realm of MBE science, however, after reviewing the literature it is evident that a better understanding of spatial management problems can lead to better teaching of math, reading, geography, and other topics requiring an understanding of objects outside of the person.

Time Management or Temporal Sequential Organization

Temporal sequential organization[442] is the ability to understand the concept of time. This ability becomes quite apparent in formal classroom settings in being able to manage the time allowed to complete a test, for example, or to plan for a long-term project. In many cases, time management is also related to spatial management.[443] Many human activities involve both temporal and spatial factors, such as music performances, dancing, playing sports, or even hearing the school bell and managing to get to the next class on time. Teachers need to be aware of the importance of timing in education and to help students develop temporal sequential organization.

Temporal sequential organization also relates to research on biological clocks.[444] Self-awareness of how and why we sense time in the way we do can be useful to students as they develop a better metacognitive awareness of themselves. An understanding of biological clocks is also useful to teachers who work with adolescents, because hormonal changes modify their normal sleep patterns. Studies like those produced by Carskadon

---

438. See Epstein, Higgins, & Thompson-Schill (2005); Mollison (2005).
439. Readers are encouraged to see the original study in Maguire, Gadian, Johnsrude, Good, Ashburner, Frackowiak, et al. (2000).
440. Ibid (p. 4298).
441. Ibid (p. 4398).
442. Levine (2000).
443. See Cohen, Dehaene, Naccache, Lehericy, Dehaene-Lambertz, Henaff, et al. (2000); Herdman & Ryan (2007).
444. See Society for Neuroscience (2007b).

and colleagues, which discuss "adolescent sleep patterns, circadian timing, and sleepiness at a transition to early school days,"[445] contribute to better teacher comprehension of classroom behavior and learning problems. For example, presuming a student doesn't pay attention in class because he doesn't get enough sleep might be only half the truth—the other half being that the student's brain didn't let him sleep any earlier (causing him to appear drowsy in class). Bodily functions, such as internal clocks, are not always (or ever) under conscious control of the individual.

Time management studies also investigate the neural mechanisms of timing in the brain,[446] and how misunderstandings of time might possibly be explained by problems in neural networks.[447] That is, many time management difficulties that students have may be due to miswirings with which they were born. Sometimes the normal network for concepts of time may be intact, but there may be an altered sense of time that can be elicited in the brain by chemicals.[448] This means that the physical mechanisms for processing time in the brain are normal, but that chemical imbalances can cause problems in the correct perception of time. This distinction is important because the perception of time is also linked to an understanding of memory formation,[449] and memories are vital to learning.

The wide repertoire of human skills needed for survival is vast and only a handful of topics have been discussed here. However, each of the skills mentioned in this chapter relates to vital aspects of learning and is crucial not only for the survival of the species, but extends to classroom concepts as well. Affect, empathy, emotions, and motivation are vital to human survival, as no decisions are made without them. An understanding of executive functions and/or decision-making is also important as all other cognitive processes are related. The new but fascinating area of facial recognition and interpretation has important implications for how we interact with students and should be taught in all teacher training institutions. The roles of memory and attention are vital to all learning processes, and they need to be understood by teachers at all levels. Social cognitive abilities play an important role in interactions, as humans are social creatures and rely on interactions for many types of new learning. Finally, both spatial and temporal management skills are useful and in some cases even vital for successful maneuvering of physical spaces and an understanding of timing. All eight of these human skills are crucial for survival and also have implications for school learning. Teachers concerned with best-practice activity in MBE science should stay abreast of developments in each of these areas.

445.   Carskadon, Wolfson, Acebo, Tzischinsky, & Seifer (1998).
446.   See Vibell, Klinge, Zampini, Spence, & Nobre (2007).
447.   See Vogeley & Kupke (2007).
448.   See Wittmann, Carter, Hasler, Rael Cahn, Grimberg, Spring et al. (2007).
449.   See Damasio (2002).

Suggested Reading

Affect, Emotions, and Motivation

Buchanan, T., Tranel, D., & Adolphs. R. (2006). Cognitive neuroscience of emotional memory. *Brain, 129*(1), 115.

Burgdorf, J., & J. Panksepp. (2006). The neurobiology of positive emotions. *Neuroscience and Biobehavioral Reviews, 30*(2), 173–187.

Damasio, A. (2000). *The feeling of what happens: Body and emotion in the making of consciousness.* New York: Harvest Books.

Damasio, A. (2003). *Looking for Spinoza: Joy, sorrow, and the feeling brain.* New York: Harvest Books.

Decety, J., & Jackson, P. L. (2004). The functional architecture of human empathy. *Behavioral and Cognitive Neuroscience Reviews, 3*(2), 71–100.

Immordino-Yang, M., & Damasio, A. (2007). We feel, therefore we learn: The relevance of affective and social neuroscience to education. *Mind, Brain, and Education, 1*(1), 3–10.

Junghofer, M., Schupp, H. T., Stark, R., & Vaitl, D. (2005). Neuroimaging of emotion: Empirical effects of proportional global signal scaling in fMRI data analysis. *NeuroImage, 25*(2), 520–526.

Kotulak, R. (2008). The effect of violence and stress in kids' brain. In *The Jossey-Bass reader on the brain and learning* (pp. 216–228). San Francisco: Wiley.

LaBar, K., & Cabeza, R. (2006). Cognitive neuroscience of emotional memory. *Nature Reviews Neuroscience, 7*(1), 54–66.

LeDoux, J. (1996). *The emotional brain: The mysterious underpinnings of emotional life.* New York: Simon & Schuster.

LeDoux, J. (2000). Emotion circuits in the brain. *Annual Review of Neuroscience, 23*(1), 155–184.

LeDoux, J. (2003). *Synaptic self: How our brains become who we are.* New York: Penguin Books.

LeDoux, J. (2008). Remembrance of emotions past. In *The Jossey-Bass reader on the brain and learning* (pp. 151–182). San Francisco: Wiley.

Lupien, S., Maheu, F., Tu, M., Fiocco, A., & Schramek, E. (2007). The effects of stress and stress hormones on human cognition: Implications for the field of brain and cognition. *Brain and Cognition, 65*(3), 209–237.

Panksepp, J. (2003). At the interface of the affective, behavioral, and cognitive neurosciences: Decoding the emotional feelings of the brain. *Brain and Cognition, 52*(1), 4–14.

Reeve, J. (2004). *Understanding motivation and emotion* (4th ed.). New York: Wiley.

Rosiek, J. (2003). Emotional scaffolding: An exploration of teacher knowledge at the intersection of student emotion and the subject matter. *Journal of Teacher Education, 54*(5), 399–412.

Sapolsky, R. (2003). Taming stress. *Scientific American, 289*(3), 86–95.

Schultz, D., Izard, C. E., & Bear, G. (2004). Children's emotion processing: Relations to emotionality and aggression. *Developmental Psychopathology, 16*, 371–387.

Wismer Fries, A., & Pollack, S. D. (2007). Emotion processing and the developing brain. In D. Coch, K.W. Fischer, & G. Dawson (Eds.), *Human behavior, learning, and the developing brain: Typical development* (pp. 329–361). New York: Guilford Press.

Executive Functions and Decision-Making

Byrne, B., Olson, R. K., Samuelsson, S., Wadsworth, S., Corley, R., DeFries, J. C., et al. (2006). Genetic and environmental influences on early literacy. *Journal of Research in Reading, 29*(1), 33–49.

Coltheart, M. (2006). The genetics of learning to read. *Journal of Research in Reading, 29*(1), 124–132.

Hayiou-Thomas, M., Harlaar, N., Dale, P. S., & Plomin, R. (2006). Genetic and environmental mediation of the prediction from preschool language and nonverbal ability to 7-year reading. *Journal of Research in Reading, 29*(1), 50–74.

Holtzer, R., Stern, Y., & Rakitin, B. C. (2004). Age-related differences in executive control of working memory. *Memory & Cognition, 32*(8), 1333–1346.

Kalenscher, T., Ohmann, T., & Gunturkun, O. (2006). The neuroscience of impulsive and self-controlled decisions. *International Journal of Psychophysiology, 62*(2), 203–211.

Mascolo, M., & Fischer, K. W. (2003). Beyond the nature–nurture divide in development and evolution. Review of Gilbert Gottlieb's "Individual development and evolution." *Contemporary Psychology, 48,* 842–847.

Nation, K. (2006). Reading and genetics: An introduction. *Journal of Research in Reading, 29*(1), 1–10.

O'Doherty, J., Hampton, A., & Kim, H. (2007). Model-based fMRI and its application to reward learning and decision making. *Annals of the New York Academy of Sciences, 1104,* 35–53.

Opris, I., & Bruce, C. J. (2005). Neural circuitry of judgment and decision mechanisms. *Brain Research Reviews, 48*(3), 509–526.

Facial Recognition

Gauthier, I., Tarr, M. J., Moylan, J., Skudlarski, P., Gore, J. C., & Anderson, A.W. (2000). The fusiform "face area" is part of a network that processes faces at the individual level. *Journal of Cognitive Neuroscience, 12*(3), 495–504.

Kanwisher, N., & Yovel, G. (2006). The fusiform face area: A cortical region specialized for the perception of faces. *Philosophical Transactions of the Royal Society of London Series B, Biological Sciences, 361*(1476), 2109–2128.

Levveroni, C., Seidenberg, M., Mayer, A. R., Mead, L. A., Binder, J. R., & Rao, S. M. (2000). Neural systems underlying the recognition of familiar and newly learned faces. *Journal of Neuroscience, 20*(2), 878–886.

Suslow, T., Ohrmann, P., Bauer, J., Rauch, A. V., Schwindt, W., Arolt, V., et al. (2006). Amygdala activation during masked presentation of emotional faces predicts conscious detection of threat-related faces. *Brain and Cognition, 61*(3), 243–248.

Memory
Achim, A., & Lepage, M. (2005). Neural correlates of memory for items and for associations: An event-related functional magnetic resonance imaging study. *Journal of Cognitive Neuroscience, 17*(4), 652–667.

Baddeley, A. (2001). Is working memory still working? *American Psychologist, 56*(11), 851–864.

Baddeley, A. (2003). Working memory and language: An overview. *Journal of Communication Disorders, 36*, 189–208.

Baddeley, A., & Andrade, J. (2000). Working memory and the vividness of imagery. *Journal of Experimental Psychology, General, 129*(1), 126–145.

Bauer, P. (2004). Getting explicit memory off the ground: Steps toward construction of a neuro-developmental account of changes in the first two years of life. *Developmental Review, 24*(4), 347–373.

Bauer, P. (2005). Developments in declarative memory. *Psychological Science, 16*(1), 41–47.

Benfenati, F. (2007). Synaptic plasticity and the neurobiology of learning and memory. *Acta Bio-Medica: Atenei Parmensis, 78*(Suppl. 1), 58–66.

Bright, P., & Kopelman, M. D. (2001). Learning and memory: Recent findings. *Current Opinion in Neurology, 14*(4), 449–455.

Jonides, J., & Nee, D. E. (2006). Brain mechanisms of proactive interference in working memory. *Neuroscience, 139*(1), 181–193.

Kandel, E. (2007). *In search of memory: The emergence of a new science of mind.* New York: Norton.

Linden, D. (2007). The working memory networks of the human brain. *The Neuroscientist, 13*(3), 257–267.

Liston, C., & Kagan, J. (2002). Brain development: Memory enhancement in early childhood. *Nature, 419*, 896.

Moscovitch, M., Nadel, L., Winocur, G., Gilboa, A., & Rosenbaum, R. S. (2006). The cognitive neuroscience of remote, episodic, semantic, and spatial memory. *Current Opinion in Neurobiology, 16*(2), 179–190.

Pickering, S., & Phye, G. D. (2006). *Working memory and education.* Burlington, MA: Academia Press.

Schacter, D. (2001). *The seven sins of memory: How the mind forgets and remembers.* New York: Houghton Mifflin.

Schacter, D., & Addis, D. R. (2007). The cognitive neuroscience of constructive memory: Remembering the past and imagining the future. *Philosophical Transactions of the Royal Society of London Series B, Biological Sciences, 362*(1481), 773–786.

Squire, L. (2007). Neuroscience: Rapid consolidation. *Science, 316*(5821), 57.

Squire, L., & Bayley, P. J. (2007). The neuroscience of remote memory. *Current Opinion in Neurobiology, 17*(2), 185–196.

Squire, L., & Schacter, D. L. (Eds.). (2002). *Neuropsychology of memory* (3rd ed.). New York: Guilford Press.

Vallar, G. (2006). Memory systems: The case of phonological short-term memory: A festschrift for cognitive neuropsychology. *Cognitive Neuropsychology, 23*(1), 135–155.

Attention

Fossella, J., Posner, M. I., Fan, J. Swanson, J. M., & Pfaff, D. M. (2002). Attentional phenotypes for the analysis of higher mental function. *Scientific World Journal, 2*, 217–223.

Hopfinger, J., Buonocore, M. H., & Mangun, G. R. (2000). The neural mechanisms of top-down attentional control. *Nature Neuroscience, 3*(3), 284–291.

Iidaka, T., Aderson, N., Kapur, S., Cabeza, R., & Craik, F. (2000). The effort of divided attention on encoding and retrieval in episodic memory revealed by positron emission tomography. *Journal of Cognitive Neuroscience, 12*(2), 267–280.

Kok, A., Ridderinkhof, K. R., & Ullsperger, M. (2006). The control of attention and actions: Current research and future developments. *Brain Research, 1105*(1), 1–6.

Lawrence, N., Ross, T. J., Hoffmann, R., Garavan, H., & Stein, E. A. (2003). Multiple neuronal networks mediate sustained attention. *Journal of Cognitive Neuroscience, 15*(7), 10281038.

Martens, S., Munneke, J., Smid, H., & Johnson, A. (2006). Quick minds don't blink: Electrophysiological correlates of individual differences in attentional selection. *Journal of Cognitive Neuroscience, 18*(9), 1423–1438.

Pashler, H., Johnsyon, J. C., & Ruthruff, E. (2001). Attention and performance. *Annual Review of Psychology, 52*(1), 629–651.

Posner M. (Ed). (2004). *Cognitive neuroscience of attention*. New York: Guilford Press.

Posner, M., & Rothbart, M. K. (1998). Developing attention skills. In J. Richards (Ed.), *Cognitive neuroscience of attention: A developmental perspective* (pp. 317–323). Hillsdale, NJ: Erlbaum.

Posner, M., & Rothbart, M. K. (2007). Research on attention networks as a model for the integration of psychological science. *Annual Review of Psychology, 58*(1), 1–23.

Raz, A., & Buhle, J. (2006). Typologies of attentional networks. *Nature Reviews Neuroscience, 7*(5), 367–379.

Rueda, M., Fan, J., McCandliss, B. D., Halparin, J. D., Gruber, D. B., Lercari, L. P., & Posner, M. I. (2004). Development of attentional networks in childhood. *Neuropsychologia, 42*(8), 1029–1040.

Sarter, M., Gehring, W. J., & Kozak, R. (2006). More attention must be paid: The neurobiology of attentional effort. *Brain Research Reviews, 51*(2), 145–160.

Vuilleumier, P., & Driver, J. (2007, May). Modulation of visual processing by attention and emotion: Windows on causal interactions between human brain regions. *Philosophical Transactions of the Royal Society of London Series B, Biological Sciences, 362*(1481), 837–855.

Vuilleumier, P., Harmony, J., & Dolan, R. (2003). Reciprocal links between emotion and attention. In R. S. J. Frackowiak (Ed.), *Human brain function* (pp. 419–444). San Diego: Academic Press.

Social Cognition

Adolphs, R. (2003a). Cognitive neuroscience of human social behaviour. *Nature Reviews Neuroscience, 4*(3), 165–178.

Adolphs, R. (2003b). Investigating the cognitive neuroscience of social behavior. *Neuropsychologia, 41*(2), 119–126.

Adolphs, R. (2006b). How do we know the minds of others? Domain-specificity, simulation, and enactive social cognition. *Brain Research, 1079*(1), 25–35.

Azar, B. (2002). At the frontier of science: Social cognitive neuroscience merges three distinct disciplines in hopes of deciphering the process behind social behavior. *APA Monitor, 33*(1), 40–43.

Beer, J., & Ochsner, K. N. (2006). Social cognition: A multi level analysis. *Brain Research, 1079*(1), 98–105.

Cozolino, L. (2006). *The neuroscience of human relationships: Attachment and the developing social brain.* New York: Norton.

Damasio, A. (1994). *Descartes' error: Emotion, reason and the human brain.* New York: Avon Books.

Lieberman, M. (2007). Social cognitive neuroscience: A review of core processes. *Annual Review of Psychology, 58*(1), 259.

Mangels, J., Butterfield, B., & Lamb, J. (2006). Why do beliefs about intelligence influence learning success? A social cognitive neuroscience model. *Social Cognitive and Affective Neuroscience, 2,* 75–86. Retrieved September 12, 2007, from *http://scan.oxfordjournals.org/cgi/content/abstract/1/2/75.*

Meltzoff, A. (2007). "Like Me": A foundation for social cognition. *Developmental Science, 10*(1), 126–134.

Meltzoff, A,. & Decety, J. (2003). What imitation tells us about social cognition: A rapprochement between developmental psychology and cognitive neuroscience. *Philosohpical Transactions of the Royal Society of London (B Biological Science), 358*(1431), 491–500. Retrieved September 14, 2007, from *http://home.uchicago.edu/~decety/publications/ Meltzoff_Decety_PTRS03.pdf.*

Sander, D., Grandjean, D., Pourtois, G., Schwartz, S., Seghier, M., Scherer, K. R., & Vuilleumier, P. (2005). Emotion and attention interactions in social cognition: Brain regions involved in processing anger prosody. *NeuroImage, 28,* 848–858.

Singer, T. (2007). The neuronal basis of empathy and fairness. *Novartis Foundation Symposium, 278,* 20–30.

Suslow, T., Ohrmann, P., Bauer, J., Rauch, A. V., Schwindt, W., Arolt, V., et al. (2006). Amygdala activation during masked presentation of emotional faces predicts conscious detection of threat-related faces. *Brain and Cognition, 61*(3), 243–248.

Mirror Neurons

Braten, S. (2007). *On being moved: From mirror neurons to empathy (Advances in Consciousness Research)*. Amsterdam: Benjamins.

Buccino, G., Binkofski, F., & Riggio, L. (2004, May). The mirror neuron system and action recognition. *Brain and Language, 89*(2), 370–376.

Iacoboni, M. (2008). *Mirroring people: The new science of how we connect with others*. New York: Farrar, Straus & Giroux.

Pineda, J. A. (2008). *Mirror neuron systems: The role of mirroring processes in social cognition*. New York: Humana Press.

Rizzolatti, G., & Craighero, L. (2004). The mirror-neuron system. *Annual Review of Neuroscience, 27*(1), 169–192.

Rizzolatti, G., Fogassi, L., & Gallese, V. (2008). Mirrors in the mind. In *The Jossey-Bass reader on the brain and learning* (pp. 12–19). San Francisco: Wiley.

Rizzolatti, G., Sinigaglia, C., & Anderson, F. (2008). *Mirrors in the brain: How our minds share actions, emotions, and experience*. New York: Oxford University Press.

Culture and Cognition

Ehrlich, P., & Feldman, M. (2007). Genes, environments, behaviors. *Daedalus, 136*(2), 5–12.

Posner, M., Rothbart, M. K., & Harman, C. (1994). Cognitive science contributions to culture and emotion. In S. Ktayma & H. Marcus (Eds.), *Culture and emotion* (pp. 197–216). Washington, DC: American Psychological Association.

Siok, W., Perfetti, C. A., Jin, Z., & Tan, L. H. (2004). Biological abnormality of impaired reading is constrained by culture. *Nature, 431*, 71–76.

Sylwester, R. (2003). *A biological brain in a cultural classroom: Enhancing cognitive and social development through collaborative classroom management*. Thousand Oaks, CA: Corwin Press.

Tomasello, M. (1999). *The cultural origins of human cognition*. Cambridge, MA: Harvard University Press.

Exercise, Nutrition and Learning

Cotman, C., & Berchtold, N. C. (2002). Exercise: A behavioral intervention to enhance brain health and plasticity. *Trends in Neuroscience, 25*, 295–301.

Etnier, J. L., Slazar, W., Landers, D. M., Petruzzello, S. J., Han, M., & Nowell, P. (1997). The influence of physical fitness and exercise upon cognitive functioning: A meta-analysis. *Journal of Sport and Exercise Psychology, 19*(2), 249–277.

Liu, J. (2004). Malnutrition at age 3 years and externalizing behavior problems at ages 8, 11, and 17 years. *American Journal of Psychiatry, 161*(11), 13.

Marcason, W. (2005). Can dietary intervention play a part in the treatment of attention deficit and hyperactivity disorder? *Journal of the American Dietetic Association, 105*(7), 1161–1161.

Reynolds, D., Nicolson, R. I., & Hambly, H. (2003). Evaluation of an exercise-based treatment for children with reading difficulties. *Dyslexia, 9*(2), 124–126.

Stein, D., Collins, M., Daniels, W., Noakes T. D., & Zigmond, M. (2007). Mind and muscle: The cognitive-affective neuroscience of exercise. *CNS Spectrums, 12*(1), 19–22.

Intelligence and Nature versus Nurture (Genetics, Environment)

Arnsten, A., & Li, B. M. (2005). Neurobiology of executive functions: Catecholamine influences on prefrontal cortical functions. *Biological Psychiatry, 57*(11), 1377–1384.

Espy, K. (2004). Using developmental, cognitive, and neuroscience approaches to understand executive control in young children. *Developmental Neuropsychology, 26*(1), 379–384.

Ridley, M. (2003). *Nature via nurture: Genes, experience and what makes us human.* New York: Harper Collins.

CHAPTER **7**

The Laboratory in the Classroom
The Most Studied Academic Fields

"Education is simply the soul of a society as it passes from one generation to another."
　　　　　—Gilbert K. Chesterton, *Illustrated London News* (July 5, 1924)

"Education is a social process. Education is growth. Education is not a preparation for life; education is life itself."
　　　　　—John Dewey, *Teachers College Record* (1938, as cited in 1991, p. 343)

No two brains are alike.[450] Brains may be thought of as analogous to faces; they have the same basic parts, but no two are exactly alike. Not even identical twins, whose faces do look alike, have identical brains because people's individual experiences change the brain. This fact explains why pure localizationalism is no longer accepted. Though it is possible to say that certain parts of the brain are in certain places, the actual functioning of each part may or may not be "textbook." For example, while it is possible to say that people's main language areas are usually in the left frontal and parietal lobes, this is not the case for 100% of humans. It is precisely because some brains are different, and because individual experiences change brains, that it can be risky to generalize findings about the brain.[451]

The Challenge: Diagnosis
Teaching is knowing what students already know, what they should know, and then bridging the gap between the two. What is clear is that being able to accurately *diagnose*

---

450. See Restak (2009); Sousa (2000); Wolfe (2001a).
451. Gazzaniga (2005b).

a child's level and learning problem are the first steps in helping that child maximize his or her potential within that subject area.

Because skills such as reading, writing, math, foreign language, science, art, and acting use vast mental systems that employ several different brain systems, diagnosing a child's weaknesses within a subject area is a complex but vital task. Pretending to box academic skills into specific brain areas is not only impossible, but also irresponsible. By reviewing the various sub-components of reading, writing, math, and other subjects, teachers become more aware of the array of problems that can occur, and they are better equipped to teach all children in a more differentiated fashion.

A myriad of courses is offered in educational settings. The most common in the Western world are language (communication, literature), math, social science (history, civics), and physical sciences (chemistry, biology, physics). In some schools students are also lucky enough to receive instruction in art, music, foreign languages, sports, computers, and philosophy (ethics). Of all of these academic fields, only a handful has been fully investigated by MBE science studies, though more are published each year. In the following section we review what is known about the most commonly taught academic subjects.

Language

As the most complex and uniquely human of mental tasks, language is managed by various interconnected parts of the brain. Written language, for example, uses more parts of the brain simultaneously than perhaps any other mental task.[452] Language skills in the brain are so complicated and overlap so many areas that Peter Indefrey and Marlene Gullenberg (2006) summarized their attempts to neatly separate them by asking rhetorically if it would not be more effective to ask which areas of the brain were *not* involved in language, as opposed to which were.

Some of the literature considers global theories to explain the neurological basis for language;[453] for example, how all of the sub-systems involved in language integrate so seamlessly to produce language. Other studies focus on language impairments[454] and, in doing so, help explain the "normal" workings of the brain when producing language. Yet other research considers the social, philosophical, as well as neurobiological bases of

---

452. See Gazzaniga (2005b); Pinker (1994).
453. See Brown & Hagoort (1999); Marantz, Miyashita, & O'Neil (2000); Winter (2003).
454. See Gauger, Lombardino, & Leonard (1997).

language[455] and investigates what brain changes occur during communication with others. Each one of these studies helps teachers decipher language problems in ways that break down the elements of language to create better interventions.

Impressive evolutionary theories for language development posit the idea that reading and writing are recent brain functions in evolutionary terms.[456] If these theorists are correct, there would be profound implications for teaching: Reading difficulties could potentially be explained by the "newness" of reading skills in the brain (would Johnny be able to read better if he were born a few more centuries down the line?). Maryanne Wolf (2007), one of the most articulate writers on this topic (see her exquisite treatise on this topic, *Proust and the Squid*), explains the profound implications that learning to read had not only on the brain, but on human development as a whole:

> We were never born to read. Human beings invented reading only a few thousand years ago. And with this invention, we rearranged the very organization of our brain, which in turn expanded the ways we were able to think, which altered the intellectual evolution of our species. Reading is one of the single most remarkable inventions in history. . . . (p. 3)

When viewed in this light, reading is elevated from a single academic subject to being the mechanism by which we know the world. But MBE science explains that there are so many ways for the reading process to go awry that it seems almost a miracle that children learn to read at all.

Some of the studies on reading demonstrate that distinct parts of the brain are involved in different aspects of language. For example, a student may be able to spell perfectly, but may have no memory of the meaning of the word he or she spells. This is because there are distinct neural mechanisms for metaphors[457] and spelling.[458] Other studies show how prosody is located in yet another area of the brain.[459] This means that a student may be good (or bad) in any combination of language traits, complicating a teacher's ability to accurately diagnose language problems. To make matters still more complex, the brain changes daily with experience.[460] There is fascinating research that

455. See Bennett, Dennett, Hacher, & Searle (2007).
456. See Calvin (1996); Calvin & Bickerton (2000); Dehaene (2009); Mehler, Nespor, Shukla, & Pena (2006); Pinker (1994); Wolf (2007).
457. See Argyris, Stringaris, Medford, Giampietro, Brammer, et al. (2007); Kacinik & Chiarello (2007).
458. See Henry, Beeson, Stark, & Rapcsa (2007).
459. See Friedrich (2003).
460. See Gazzaniga (2005b); Sakai (2005).

shows that the brain works differently when it is *learning* to read than when it already *knows* how to read.[461]

Reading

Reading is a sub-component of language and is treated separately in this literature review because of the quality and quantity of research available. Reading has been a favorite area of MBE science research primarily because it is one nonsensory aspect of learning that is unique to humans. (Whereas there are numerous neurological studies on how eyes react to light, or how startle reflexes are caused by loud noises, there are far fewer studies using human subjects that test uniquely human abilities such as reading.) Reading is also an element of language that is less "natural" than speaking. According to Stanislas Dehaene, some neurons have been "recycled" and adapted to culturally newer tasks, such as reading. Dehaene writes:

> I propose a novel theory of neurocultural interactions, radically opposed to cultural relativism, and capable of resolving the reading paradox. I call it the "neuronal recycling" hypothesis. According to this view, human brain architecture obeys strong genetic constraints, but some circuits have evolved to tolerate a fringe of variability. Part of our visual system, for instance, is not hardwired, but remains open to changes in the environment. Within an otherwise well-structured brain, visual plasticity gave the ancient scribes the opportunity to invent reading. (2009, p. 7)

Reading and writing require the brain to perform evolutionarily newer tasks than simple oral communication; all cultures around the world have oral communication,[462] whereas far fewer have a written language. Explanations of how the brain learns to read,[463] including the underlying neural networks,[464] are incredibly useful in generating strategies that improve reading.[465]

---

461. See Marian, Spivey, & Hirsch (2003).
462. See Dehaene (2009); Wolf (2007).
463. See Holden (2004); Poldrack & Sandak (2004); Simos, Fletcher, Foorman, Francis, Castillo, et al. (2002); Society for Neuroscience (2007h); Wolf (2007).
464. See Schlaggar & McCandliss (2007); Simos, Fletcher, Foorman, Francis, Castillo, et al. (2002); Wolf (2007).
465. See editorial in *Nature Neuroscience* (2004); Katzir & Paré-Blagoev (2006); Shaywitz & Shaywitz (2007); Shaywitz, Shaywitz, Blachman, Pugh, Fulbright, et al. (2004); Vellutino, Scanlon, & Tanzmanm (1991).

An interesting example of these types of studies considers the distinct sub-components of reading, such as orthographic versus spelling areas of the brain.[466] Though it might seem illogical at first sight, understanding a symbol-to-sound reference (orthography) does not involve the same processes as spelling (which often contradicts the logic of symbol-to-sound reference). These studies actually offer a neurological explanation for the confusion that teachers see on the faces of their students as they grapple with comparisons of *through*, *cough*, and *tough*. Research on the sub-components of language is useful to teachers because it provides empirical evidence that students may master one aspect of language without being able to master another. These studies show that the sub-components of language are mediated by different neural pathways in the brain and therefore can have distinct impacts on overall language ability. For example, as seen above, orthographic learning takes place in the brain in a different way from phonological processing,[467] but they are complementary mechanisms when it comes to reading. This explains the logic of newer theories of reading difficulties that suggest extended reading-aloud periods to develop greater fluency in linking auditory phonological and visual orthographic representations.

As mentioned earlier, studies related to how dyslexic brains learn to read have been useful in explaining normal reading mechanisms,[468] as have studies on nondyslexic reading impairments[469] (thanks to dyslexia, the reading brain has been mapped for all its stages of learning). Finally, other reading studies consider the cultural aspects of learning to read.[470] It is now known, for example, that there are distinct neural pathways for a new Chinese learner than for a new English learners.[471] This intriguing fact helps us think about the logic of certain instructional practices. For example, in the United States we teach children to print before they write in cursive, whereas it is the opposite in France and Germany. The logic of the Europeans is that the stroke order in cursive makes it nearly impossible to incorrectly write each letter, whereas the stroke order in printed form can be random. Similarly, the stroke order in Chinese (as well as Japanese, Korean, and Arabic) is vital to the correct formation of the world. How does a brain that has been trained to perform certain motor sequences in correct stroke order differ from a brain without this discipline? These and other questions remain unanswered, but they potentially hold the key to better reading instruction.

466. For an example, see Tainturier, Schiemenz, & Leek (2006).
467. See Booth, Burman, Meyer, Gitelman, Parrish, et al. (2004).
468. See Klein & McMullen (1999); Shaywitz & Shaywitz (2005); Shaywitz, Shaywitz, Pugh, Mencl, Fulbright, et al. (2002).
469. See McCandliss & Noble (2003); Shaywitz, Shaywitz, Fulbright, Skudlarski, Mencl, et al. (2003).
470. For example, see Siok, Perfetti, Jin, & Tan (2004).
471. Wolf (2007).

Reading Interventions

MBE science is young. Despite being one of the goals of MBE science research, there are few proven methods available to improve the teaching of reading. This is why teaching is as much an art as a science at this point in history: Evidence-based methods are few and far between.

Based on the information in the literature, Reading is a highly complex task and involves at least 12 competencies (a combination of knowledge, skills and attitudes):[472]

1. The use of executive functions to pay attention to what is being read
2. The physical ability to see a word
3. The ability to generalize conceptual understanding of different symbol representations of the same content (e.g., three, III, 3, ● ● ●)
4. The ability to mentally sound out the words in one's mind (verbal coding)
5. The ability to convert the phonemes into words
6. The ability to search one's memory for the word (vocabulary retrieval)
7. The ability to search one's memory for the meaning of the words (semantic understanding)
8. The ability to correctly order words and unify words into a coherent phrase (syntactic meaning)
9. The ability to associate context with appropriate prosody and intonation (mentally or out loud)
10. The ability to unite all these pieces into a coherent sentence
11. The ability to unify sentences into paragraphs of complex meaning
12. The ability to retain sentences and paragraphs in mind long enough to associate them with past experiences and give meaning to the concepts

Table 7.1 also provides a list of reading sub-skills. Problems can occur at any point along this process. In addition to these 12 competencies are four more social ones that can also impact a student's ability to read:

472. The following is compiled research from the following sources: Beaton (2004); Byrne, Olson, Samuelsson, Wadsworth, Corley, et al. (2006); Coltheart (2006); Dehaene (2009); Fischer, Bernstein, & Immordino-Yang (2007); Fowler & Swainson (2004); Hauser, Chomsky, & Fitch (2002); Johnston & Costello (2005); Joseph, Noble, & Eden (2001); Pare-Blagoev (2006); Poldrack & Sandak (2004); Schlaggar & McCandliss (2007); Simos, Fletcher, Foorman, Francis, Castillo, et al. (2002); Tainturier, Schiemenz, & Leek (2006); Wolf & Katzir-Cohen (2001); Wolf (2007); Wolfe & Nevills (2004); Ziegler & Goswami (2005).

13. The way the child feels about the learning process (self-esteem)
14. How it impacts his or her social standing in the group (social cognition)
15. His or her relationship with teachers
16. Motivational factors can also impact his or her ability to read well.

When considering "good" MBE scientific interventions to address problems related to reading (or any other subject matter) keep in mind the complex nature of learning and ask, does the intervention address all of these components, or just one or two? This does not mean that suggested interventions, methods, activities, or curriculum structures to remedy "reading problems" or "math problems" are not good approaches, but it does mean that they are often incomplete.

TABLE 7.1
Types of Reading Sub-Skills

READING	
Sub-skill	Example
Declarative knowledge	Link between sounds and phonemes (phonological and phonemic awareness)
Procedural knowledge	Each sentence has a subject, verb, and object; punctuation rules
Conceptual knowledge	Semantic and syntactic knowledge; word decoding skills and phonics
Estimation skills	Ability to judge quantities; prosody; fluency
Vocabulary	Ability to build and use age-appropriate vocabulary
Verbal coding skills	Mental language rehearsal of facts; naming skills
Spatial skills	Draw or visualize relationships
Higher-order thinking skills	Selectively choose what to pay attention to (i.e., while in working memory) and successfully relate new concepts with old (in long-term memory)
Difference between symbols and forms ("III," "3," & " ● ● ●," and "three")	Ability to conceptualize different forms and representations of numbers
Sensory pathways	Ability to see, hear, pronounce, write normally
Graphic skills	Orthographic skills (ability to write)
Visual phonemic coding and decoding skills	Reading comprehension

Sources: Based on the compilation of research by Beaton, 2004; Byrne et al., 2006; Coltheart, 2006; Dehaene (2009); Fischer, Bernstein, & Immordino-Yang, 2007; Fowler & Swainson, 2004; Hauser, Chomsky & Fitch, 2002; Johnston & Costello, 2005; Joseph, Noble, & Eden, 2001; Pare-Blagoev, 2006; Poldrack & Sandak, 2004; Schlaggar & McCandliss, 2007; Simos et al., 2002; Tainturier, Schiemenz, Leek, 2006; Wolf, 2007; Wolf & Katzir, 2001; Wolfe & Nevills, 2004; Ziegler & Goswami, 2005.

Reading interventions are not very common in MBE science at this point, but having said that, there are more in reading than in any other academic subject. The few quality interventions that are worthy of MBE science attention are considered below.

New Language Interventions

The main reason that there are so few evidence-based intervention tools available is due to the complexity of most human activities, especially academic skills. This complexity means that a variety of problems can occur in any learning process, and thus there is no single intervention that is sufficient for all children. That is, just as some people can beat a cold by taking *X* remedy, the same remedy might not have any effect at all on others. Students can have difficulties in one or more components of the learning process. This puts a heavy burden on teachers, whose job is equally dependent on a good diagnosis of the problem as on a good solution. To ensure that new tools stand up to the scrutiny of MBE standards, teachers should use the four categories of information on the OECD continuum explained in Table 4.1 (see p. 78) as well as the checklist in Figure 4.2 (see p. 101). Does the new teaching intervention adhere to what is well established in MBE science? (If concepts from other categories are included, can they be justified by the literature?) Is the new teaching tool free of neuromyths? If so, then it is considered a worthwhile tool. To put this into context, let's look at the specific case of reading interventions.

The ultimate utility of MBE science will be measured by its successful application in real classrooms with real students. Therefore, the immediate future of the discipline rests on an evaluation of programs that claim to adhere to principles and instructional guidelines established by the discipline. Specifically, reading programs such as Fast ForWord,[473] RAVE-O,[474] Thinking Reader™,[475] and WiggleWorks™,[476] which were developed by neuroscientists and have been applied in the classroom, should be judged against MBE standards. One possible tool to achieve this evaluation is presented in Table 7.2, which combines the OECD categories with the Best Evidence Encyclopedia[477] and the What Works Clearinghouse,[478] as suggested by Briggs (2008).

---

473. See Gillam (1999); Lavin (2005); Loeb, Store, & Fey (2001); Scientific Learning Corporation (n.d.).
474. Wolf (2008).
475. Dr. David Rose and Dr. Bridget Dalton, see *http://www.tomsnyder.com/products/product.asp?sku=THITHI*.
476. Dr. David Rose and Dr. Bridget Dalton, see *http://teacher.scholastic.com/products/wiggleworks/index.htm*.
477. Funded by the U.S. Department of Education and run by the Johns Hopkins University School of Education's Center for Data-Driven Reform in Education (CDDRE).
478. Founded in 2002, this is an initiative of the U.S. Department of Education's Institute of Education Sciences.

TABLE 7.2 How Curriculum Design in MBE Science Can Be Evidence-Based			
Curriculum Design	Four Categories of Information in the Emerging Field of Educational Neuroscience / Mind, Brain, and Education Science	Best Evidence Encyclopedia	What Works Clearinghouse
Fast ForWord	Well-established? Probably so? Intelligent speculation? Neuromyth?	Strong evidence of effectiveness? Moderate evidence of effectiveness? Limited evidence of effectiveness? Insufficient evidence (no qualifying studies)?	Positive effects? Potential positive effects? Mixed effects? No discernible effects? OR No qualifying studies? Potentially negative effects? Negative effects?
RAVE-O	Well-established? Probably so? Intelligent speculation? Neuromyth?	Strong evidence of effectiveness? Moderate evidence of effectiveness? Limited evidence of effectiveness? Insufficient evidence (no qualifying studies)?	Positive effects? Potential positive effects? Mixed effects? No discernible effects? OR No qualifying studies? Potentially negative effects? Negative effects?
Thinking Reader	Well-established? Probably so? Intelligent speculation? Neuromyth?	Strong evidence of effectiveness? Moderate evidence of effectiveness? Limited evidence of effectiveness? Insufficient evidence (no qualifying studies)?	Positive effects? Potential positive effects? Mixed effects? No discernible effects? OR No qualifying studies? Potentially negative effects? Negative effects?
WiggleWorks	Well-established? Probably so? Intelligent speculation? Neuromyth?	Strong evidence of effectiveness? Moderate evidence of effectiveness? Limited evidence of effectiveness? Insufficient evidence (no qualifying studies)?	Positive effects? Potential positive effects? Mixed effects? No discernible effects? OR No qualifying studies? Potentially negative effects? Negative effects?

Curriculum design is an especially intriguing and important area for future research. Two intervention designs, Fast ForWord and RAVE-O, are explained in brief below.

FAST FORWORD

Fast ForWord was developed in 1997 by Paula Tallal and Michael Merzenich to help remediate auditory processing deficits in children ages 4–14. The first decade of results has shown significant findings, though all through self-published reports based on field studies by the Scientific Learning Corporation.[479] These reports show gains of up to 1–2 years in language abilities within 4–8 weeks of training, though these numbers have not been independently confirmed.

Fast ForWord[480] is based on the belief that improving *phonemic temporal processing* has a direct and positive impact on language skills, one of the 16 sub-components of reading mentioned on pages 182–183. Fast ForWord is an Internet-based CD-ROM program divided into seven computer games that "use acoustically modified speech to help children learn to discriminate acoustic features of speech."[481] These programs train sound, word, and complex language processes in the brain through exercises in temporal processing and phoneme identification.[482] The ideal outcome of the program is enhanced phonological awareness and improvements in both expressive as well as receptive language skills—which in turn manifest as improved reading abilities. According to the Scientific Learning Corporation, ideally children should play five to seven games a day (each game lasting about 15–20 minutes), eventually spending 5 days a week for 6–8 weeks for about 100 minutes a day.[483] Children receive daily feedback on their results, and the Scientific Learning Corporation regulates their advances.

Fast ForWord is not a program to remediate all reading problems, but it does seem to demonstrate remarkable results with children who have auditory processing problems. According to Fischer, Bernstein, and Immordino-Yang (2007), "When marketed as a cure for reading difficulties, Fast ForWord will certainly disappoint many. When marketed as a important tool to address one of the root deficits in some students with learning disabilities, Fast ForWord may prove to be an excellent choice" (2007, p. 289). Others have come to similar conclusions. Rouse and Krueger (2004) suggest that Fast ForWord helps in some aspects of children's language abilities (auditory discrimination), but not neces-

---

479. Richard (2000).
480. See Scientific Learning Corp (n.d.).
481. Simpson, Smith-Myles, Griswold, Adams, de Boer-Ott, et al. (2004, p. 111).
482. See Simpson, Smith Myles, Griswold, Adams, de Boer-Ott, et al. (2004).
483. Scientific Learning (n.d.).

sarily with overall improvement in reading. Similarly, Pokorni, Worthington, and Jamison, (2004) and Hook, Macaruso, and Jones (2001) caution in overextending promises about a reading cure-all. Critics of Fast ForWord make it clear that if there is one cardinal intervention principle for students with learning difficulties, it is that training only in motor, visual, neural, or cognitive processes does not generalize to the academic arena. This means that Fast ForWord has the distinction of being one of the first reading tools accepted in MBE science, but only with reading problems that can be specifically linked to auditory processing difficulties.

RAVE-O

RAVE-O (retrieval, automaticity, vocabulary, engagement with language, orthography)[484] was developed at Tufts University's Center for Reading and Language Research. In 2003 this project received financing as a large 5-year, National Institute for Child Health and Human Development (NICHD) intervention project in three cities (Boston, Toronto, and Atlanta) aimed at first through fourth graders. The general idea of the RAVE-O program is to teach children carefully selected core words with the logic that "the more the child knows about a word, the faster and better the word is read and understood." The focus of the research project was to "investigate the efficacy of state-of-the-art reading intervention packages with discrete subtypes of reading-disabled children."[485] The structure of this program is "as a pull-out program for use with students one-on-one and in small groups."[486] RAVE-O uses knowledge about how the brain achieves phonological processing, decoding principles, vocabulary development, and lexical retrieval (four sub-components of reading) in order to read. The research at Tufts is convincing because it begins with the premise that reading is a highly complex process that involves a large number of sub-systems. For example, Norton, Kovelman, and Petitto (2007) showed that there are different neural pathways for spelling related to the role of rules and memory; Cirino et al. (2002) considered the role of decoding and reading disabilities; and Wolf and Bowers (2000) investigated naming speed processes. Each of these sub-components of the reading process is addressed in the RAVE-O program.

The RAVE-O program seeks to facilitate the retrieval of "words that include letter and letter-pattern knowledge, multiple meanings, grammar, and morphological endings."[487] Additionally, the Tufts program recognizes that reading is not just a neural process, but also involves sociolinguistic, cultural, and value elements as well. According to the RAVE-O

484. Wolf (2008).
485. Tufts University (2009).
486. SEDL (2009).
487. Ibid.

website: "Students who have completed the curriculum have shown significant gains in both specific and global reading skills."[488]

Language and other academic subjects and skills involve overlapping areas of the brain. A growing number of studies show, for example, how language and calculation share common areas in different neural systems of the brain.[489] To understand these areas better, we now turn to the academic subject of mathematics and the sub-elements of this academic skill set.

Math

Mathematic skills are highly prized in formal education. Two of the main researchers seeking to identify the neuroscientific bases for numeracy skills are Stanislas Dehaene and Daniel Ansari.[490] Dehaene's work is focused on explaining how the brain is capable of creating a conceptual understanding of numbers.[491] Other studies related to math are concerned with how numbers are learned.[492] These studies illustrate how the brain understands 3, *three*, *III*, or ● ● ● in different parts of the brain, influencing the conceptual processing of number systems. This phenomenal breakthrough should excite teachers because it indicates that a symbolic understanding of three (in written letters), as in 3 (in Arabic numerals), is treated differently in the brain from more concrete visual representations such as ● ● ●. Such information has an impact on instructional design and explains such things as why Montessori manipulatives work so well. In Montessori schools children interact with a variety of materials that offer concrete representations of symbolic concepts. For example, children play with bar or pie calculators and beads that allow a visual representation of often difficult fraction concepts. These types of manipulatives bridge the conceptual links between concrete number knowledge and the more abstract symbolic understanding of letters and numerals.

As mentioned, other studies identify how language and calculations share areas of the brain.[493] This research helps teachers understand why children often have both language and math problems together: They are due to the neural systems that overlap in the brain. Different but equally important is the acknowledgment that some children may appear to

488. SEDL (2009).
489. For example see Cohen, Dehaene, Chochon, Lehericy, & Naccache (2000).
490. See Ansari & Karmiloff-Smith (2002); Ansari, Donlan, Thomas, Ewing & Karmiloff-Smith (2003); Dehaene (1999a); Dehaene (1999b). Dehaene's *The Number Sense* is a classic in the math discipline (1999b).
491. Dehaene (1997, 2004).
492. See Ansari & Karmiloff-Smith (2002).
493. For example, see Cohen, Dehaene, Chochon, Lehericy, & Naccache (2000); Sigman (2004).

have math problems but, in reality, actually have language problems. That is, the brain is not deciphering the linguistic code of math, making it impossible for a child to understand the conceptual ideas behind the math (though this all occurs via language).

Still other research shows how the brain understands how to use numbers and calculate successfully[494]—that is, how the brain takes the symbolic understanding of the number and manipulates that symbol into a calculation that actually represents something else. There are several studies that attempt to explain exactly why there is a breakdown of certain neural mechanisms that cause individuals to do poorly at math[495] that teachers should use to their benefit. These explanations are not meant to excuse individuals for doing poorly in math, but rather to offer explanations for some children's poor math abilities. It passes to the realm of teachers, then, to use this information to better design course content and interventions to meet the needs of students who have breakdowns in their neural networking of math skills.

Finally, many studies in MBE science make the explicit link between logical and mathematical cognition. A person who is good at calculations is not necessarily one who is good at logic; however, a person who is good at logical inferences has a greater possibility of achieving success with math problems. The structure and design of math problems means that "if–then" scenarios, often called for in logic, are used frequently. Individuals are more likely to meet with success in math classes if they are able to manage these logic scenarios. Numerous studies in MBE science demonstrate how and where math and logic systems overlap in the brain—information that can be useful in enhancing teaching methods. All of these studies contribute to a more comprehensive understanding of how best to teach math.[496]

New Math Interventions

Similar to language, there are many sub-components to the processing of math in the brain. MBE science makes a clear link among math, language, logic skills, and critical thinking systems in the brain. Math is characterized by the same complexities as reading when it comes to determining good interventions. In order to assess what exactly is being "treated" in different interventions, it is first important to understand all of the different sub-components of "math." According to Coch, Fischer, and Dawson (2007):

---

494. See Gobel & Rushworth (2004); Nieder (2005).
495. For example, see Rourke & Conway (1997).
496. See Houde & Tzourio-Mazoyer (2003); Sigman (2004).

Mathematical competence is said to involve five component aspects: (1) *declarative knowledge*, or an extensive storehouse of math facts (e.g., that $15^2 = 225$); (2) *procedural knowledge*, or an extensive storehouse of goal-directed processes such as computational algorithms, strategies, and heuristics (e.g., the least common denominator method for adding fractions); (3) *conceptual knowledge*, or an extensive network of concepts (e.g., ordinality, cardinality) that help problem solvers understand the meaning of facts and procedures (e.g., why one must invert and multiply when dividing fractions); (4) *estimation skills*; and (5) the ability to *graphically depict and model mathematical relationships* and outcomes. (p. 41)

Additionally, math is hypothesized by some to incorporate a *"triple code model."*[497] First, a visual *Arabic code* helps us understand strings of digits as well as parity or the concept of even numbers. This math sub-skill appears to be "located in the left and right inferior occipital-temporal areas"[498] in most people. Second, there is an *analogical quantity* or *magnitude code* that relates to a type of *mental number line*. This mental number line helps us assess that one number is closer than another, or that one number is larger or smaller than another ("located in the left and right inferior parietal areas"[499]). And third, math involves a *verbal code* that is located in language areas of the brain, specifically Broca's and Wernicke's areas. This math sub-area is a verbal code that abbreviates "rote memories of arithmetical facts."[500] All of these sub-areas involved in math processing point to the need to design separate interventions, depending on student needs. The sub-skills needed for each sub-area are ordered in a typical developmental pattern. For example, if a child does not have a sense of ordinality, then it will be difficult, if not impossible, to understand higher-order math concepts.[501]

To make matters even more complex, math also involves other areas of the brain (though not the same areas that are used in spatial reasoning tasks)[502] as well as the frontal lobes during higher-order cognitive processes. Diagnosing individual math problems and helping students improve their math skills begins with a clear understanding of the

---

497. Dehaene & Cohen (1995).
498. Coch et al. (2007, p. 42).
499. Ibid.
500. Ibid.
501. See Byrnes & Wasik (1991); Case, R., Okamoto, Y., Griffin, S., McKeough, A., Bleiker, C., Henderson et al., (1996).
502. See Barnes, Wilkinson, Boudesquire et al. (2006), as cited in Coch, et al. (2007, p. 43).

various roots of potential problems. Combined, these studies make the case for the needed math sub-skills shown in Table 7.3.[503]

TABLE 7.3
Types of Math Sub-Skills

MATH	
Sub-Skill	Example
Declarative knowledge	$15^2 = 225$
Procedural knowledge	The least common denominator method for adding fractions
Conceptual knowledge	Ordinality, cardinality
Estimation skills	Ability to judge quantities
Graphic skills	Draw a graph; model mathematical relationships and outcomes
Visual Arabic coding skills	Understand strings of digits as well as parity or the concept of even numbers
Analogical quantity skills or magnitude code	Ability to use a mental number line
Verbal coding skills	Mental language rehearsal of arithmetical facts
Spatial skills	Draw or visualize relationships
Higher-order thinking skills	Selectively choose what to pay attention to and successfully relate new concepts with old
Difference between "three," "III," "3," and " ● ● ● "	Ability to conceptualize different forms and representations of numbers
Sensory pathways	Ability to see, hear, write, speak normally

Sources: Based on the compilation of research by Ansari, Donlan, & Karmiloff-Smith, 2007; Ansari & Karmiloff-Smith, 2002; Bisanz, Sherman, Rasmussen & Ho, 2005; Byrnes, 2008; Cohen, Dehaene, Chochon, Lehericy, & Naccache, 2000; Dehaene, 2008a; Dehaene, Moiko, Cohen, & Wilson, 2004; LeFevre et al., 2006; Sherman & Bisanz, 2007

To create efficient math interventions, one would first need to analyze what sub-component of math needs remediating for each child. This means that any remediation of mathematical skills should take into account at least one of the aspects noted in Table 7.3. The difficulty with many math intervention approaches is that they are often more focused on the way in which students are corrected (i.e., motivational factors) than on the math concepts themselves. For example, one way to categorize math interventions is by

503. Compilation of research by the following authors: Ansari & Karmiloff-Smith (2002); Ansari, Donlan, & Karmiloff-Smith (2007); Bisanz, Sherman, Rasmussen, & Ho (2005); Byrnes (2001b); Cohen, Dehaene, Chochon, Lehericy, & Naccache (2000); Dehaene (2008a); Dehaene, Moiko, Cohen, & Wilson (2004); LeFevre, Smith-Chant, Fast, Skwarchuk, Sargla, et al. (2006); Sherman & Bisanz (2007).

their focus on general metacognitive skills.[504] That is, do the interventions help students reflect on specific concepts in math, think about their use (or misuse), and "own" the new concepts? Other types of intervention emphasize comparison and contrast approaches (comparing good answers with bad). These help students consider model examples in math responses and then take note of how close their own answer is. In general, these interventions help students think about their strategy and approach.

Still other interventions do not address math per se, but rather focus on self-esteem (e.g., via praise or reward). Have students learned to reward themselves for successful work, or do they rely on the teacher to tell them if they are right, wrong, or somewhere in between?[505] The general goal of these interventions is to help children learn *why* they do *what* they do in a math sequence. The most effective models of intervention help children understand and develop different schematic representations of core mathematical concepts.[506] Authors in this area remind teachers that children construct their world through concepts that develop into mental schemas or ways to see or categorize their surroundings.

The Number Race

Based on state-of-the-art understanding of the brain circuits underlying numerical cognition, Anna Wilson and Stanislas Dehaene, both prominent scientists specializing in mathematics, developed *The Number Race*. According to their website, "The Number Race software is designed for remediation of dyscalculia [impaired ability to learn grade-appropriate mathematics] in children aged 4–8. It may also be useful for prevention of dyscalculia, or to teach number sense in kindergarten children without specific learning disabilities." Unlike other interventions, this software is available in open source and in both English and Spanish. The preliminary results, though conducted on a small population and reported in 2006, showed very positive results:

> The Number Race software trains children on an entertaining numerical comparison task, by presenting problems adapted to the performance level of the individual child. We report full mathematical specifications of the algorithm used, which relies on an internal model of the child's knowledge in a multidimensional "learning space" consisting of three difficulty dimensions: numerical

---

504. For an example of this concept, see Shapiro (2004).
505. Möller, Streblow, & Pohlmann (2009).
506. See Tanner & Jones (2000); Jitendra (2002).

distance, response deadline, and conceptual complexity (from non-symbolic numerosity processing to increasingly complex symbolic operations). (p. 1)

The program is based on four ideas that address the sub-components of math comprehension as a whole. First, the overall goal of the software is to enhance number sense—that is, help students understand quantity representation and develop a better mental schema of number relations. Second, the program is designed to "cement the links between representations of number" (p. 3); that is, help students clarify symbolic representations of numbers and quantities. Third, the design of The Number Race helps students conceptualize and improve "automatic arithmetic"; that is to become more fluent in basic addition and subtraction facts. In this way they consolidate their conceptual understanding of numerical values. Finally, the fourth key element to the program design is to maximize student motivation for use. The program was designed around a series of games to maintain student attention and motivation by providing constant positive reinforcement (this was achieved by an adaptive algorithm that continuously adapted task difficulty to maintain performance at 75% correct).

Perhaps one of the reasons The Number Race seems to enjoy so much success is due to the limited nature of the intervention. The Number Race does not try to be all things to all math learners; rather it is focused principally on helping young children overcome dyscalculia. The design of the software is based on the premise that "dyscalculia is due to a 'core deficit' in number sense or in the link between number sense and symbolic number representations," and the intervention design is limited to this deficit. It appears that "less is more" in the sense that the program does not try to be all things to all people, but rather, to serve a specific population, and this precision has yielded excellent results.

There are few interventions in MBE science, but the small number that do exist are proving to be superior to any other options available to parents and teachers. The development of new intervention programs will certainly be the focus of research and development in the coming years.

Other Subjects

As noted, the most studied academic area is reading, followed by math.[507] There are less frequent references to how the brain learns art, music, science, or social studies. This liter-

---

507. Tokuhama-Espinosa (2008b).

ature base is sure to grow, however. A brief description of these other subject areas is offered below.

Science

The MBE science literature offers a smattering of studies that point to brain-compatible teaching methods for science. Some studies provide general recommendations about how to teach science. These "brain-based methods" are useful, but as of yet, not fully substantiated with empirical evidence. There is some evidence of research that tries to offer a neurological explanation of how the brain learns science. Several of these studies focus on logical cognition, or the ability to maneuver "if–then" structures, as found in math problems (for example, if $x = 0$, then the solution will always be "less than zero"). There is also research suggesting that the best curriculum structures for teaching science include applying greater use of metaphors when teaching science concepts.[508] This research shows teachers how advantageous it is to use prior knowledge to construct metaphors that parallel new concept learning.

It could be hypothesized that one of the reasons research in science is so scarce in MBE science is that it is neurologically more complex than reading or math, though this is unlikely. It would be more logical to assume that there is little research in this area because the pedagogy of science is relatively young. It can also be speculated that science is a subject that can be "learned" through pure rote memorization, at least in the early years, by reproducing formulas, tables, and charts, but without necessarily a true understanding.[509] A more profound understanding of scientific concepts requires teaching methodologies that encourage deeper reflection on core concepts.[510] In the coming decades it is very likely that MBE science efforts to document science learning processes will increase as better research models are devised.

Art

The literature related to the brain's ability to perceive, produce, and appreciate art is relatively large, though there are fewer references on the most effective teaching methods. Some of this literature is concerned with the overall ability of the brain to fathom art. These studies seek to determine how art is processed in the brain,[511] how the brain then

---

508. Schwartz & Fischer (2006).
509. Soehner (2005).
510. See Volz & von Cramon (2006); Wyoming Clearinghouse for Mathematics and Science (WCMS; 2000).
511. For examples, see Gardner (1984); Goguen & Myin (2000); Sousa (2006).

makes sense of those images or sounds, and finally how the brain reaches value-laden assessments of whether the perceived art is "good" or not.[512]

Other literature in this group justifies the teaching of the arts as a means of stimulating other types of learning[513] (e.g., teaching math through architectural design or science through nature patterns). Studies have demonstrated the benefits of art as an aid for general cognition; this research suggests that overall learning benefits to thinking skills are cultivated through contact with art.[514] There is no conclusive evidence that use of the arts makes learning other subjects any easier, although "art for the brain's sake" has been argued very convincingly.[515] During a time in which funding for the arts and for formal school instruction has diminished, there appear to be several arguments in favor of maintaining, if not increasing, their instruction in schools.

Creativity

Closely related to research on the arts are studies about creativity. Creativity spans a large gamut of abilities, from painting to music to problem solving and beyond. There are at least 33 different ways to be creative,[516] among which are creative problem-solving skills. Some studies, which have gone undisputed for decades,[517] argue that intelligence and creativity go hand in hand. Most seem to think that creativity is, in the least, a good addition to formal education, and at its best, a sought-after skill. However, there is an ongoing debate in the literature as to whether or not one can teach people to be creative or if one is either born creative or not.[518] In some studies, MBE science attempts to document the neurobiology of creative activity and show how certain neurotransmitters are released during spells or "flow" of inspiration.[519] Many of these works suggest the need to establish a cognitive neuroscience of creativity[520] in an attempt to find some way to enhance creative experience in the average student. This literature seeks to document neuroscientific evidence for creativity by measuring performance on specific tasks,[521] with the thought that such evidence could benefit average students as well. Though it seems paradoxical,

512. For an example of this, see Eisner (2004); Csikszentmihalyi (1996).
513. For examples, see Eisner (2004); Jensen (2001a); Sylwester (1998); Ruppert (2006).
514. See Goguen & Myin (2000); Trimble (2007); Wright (2003a).
515. This is the title of an article by Sylwester (1998). Also see Etland (2002) and Sousa (2006).
516. Riccardelli (1992).
517. See Torrance (1974).
518. For a wonderful review of these types of studies, see Alexander & Winne (2006); Csikszentmihalyi (1996); Runco & Pritzker (1999); Sternberg (1998); Weisberg (1993).
519. See Boden (2004); Heilman, Nadeau, & Beversdorf (2003); Kaufman & Sternberg (2006); Csikszentmihalyi (1991).
520. See Abraham & Windmann (2007); Dietrich (2004a, 2004b); Wagmeister & Schifrin (2000).
521. For example, see Fink, Benedek, Grabner, Staudt, & Neubauer (2007).

these writers attempt to identify the "science" behind inspiration.[522] Yet other studies research how creativity is manifested in certain personality types,[523] as documented by the lives of inspirational artists.

Finally, several theorists have proposed that the brain's ability to learn is based, in part, on its ability to be creative. That is, the brain's search for patterns as well as its curiosity for novelty help people learn.[524] It could be speculated that, if this hypothesis could be proven, then it would show that creativity is actually more natural than the lack thereof.

Whether viewed as a reflection of intelligence or a natural brain function, creativity remains one of the most difficult aspects of human cognition to define. If creativity is, indeed, related to intelligence, should teachers consider ways of stimulating creative tendencies in children, not only for creativity itself, but also for tangential academic benefits? Likewise, if creativity is teachable, should it not be integrated into the human repertoire of formal schooling activities? A strong argument for including creativity in MBE science guidelines is grounded in the need to develop more divergent thinkers in society.

Music

Studies in MBE science that are concerned with music fall into a few basic categories: Those explaining the neural mechanisms of music processing in the brain, the relationship of music and emotions, and those that show the influence of music on other skills. (For a broader consideration of music and the brain, Oliver Sacks' book [2008], *Musicophilia: Tales of Music and the Brain*, is highly recommended.)

Related to music processing in the brain is research that attempts to link music neural networks with other networks, such as language and math. For example, there is strong evidence for an overlap in structural processing between language and music,[525] and some evidence that auditory memory processing for language is enhanced by music training. Related to math, written music is very similar to the structure of a math formula. While this is far less romantic than the concept of music as one of the most inspirational and least understood human skills, it does explain in part why people who excel in music at an early age tend to do well in math. Depending on the quality of the music program involved, better music training can lead to improved math test scores.[526] In addition, a

522. See Andreasen (2005); Sternberg & Lubart (1999).
523. For example, see Gardner (1994a, 1994b).
524. For example, see Gruber & Bödeker (2005).
525. In Fedorenko, Patel, Casasanto, Winawer, & Gibson (2009).
526. For example, see Johnson & Memmott (2006).

large number of studies claim that music aids general cognitive development.[527] Still other research links musical training to improvement in other skill areas; for example, some studies show that musical training helps with verbal memory,[528] spatial skills,[529] and math.[530]

Some of the most impressive studies show how musical training changes the physical structure of the brain.[531] Among the physical changes documented in these studies are changes in the motor cortex that occur with increased rehearsal of musical instruments. Additionally, there is increased use of spatial areas in the brains of musicians, presumably because rhythm is both temporally as well as spatially organized. This may be due in part to the way that music is perceived for tempo, texture, and mode.[532]

Finally, a large category of literature shows the way music impacts emotional states; studies in the area of *musical affect* show how music changes the way people feel.[533] Manipulating different tonal qualities, experimenters offer a "prediction of musical affect using a combination of acoustic structural cues,"[534] which, to some degree, show a nearly universal reaction toward different tonal combinations, which curiously points to music as being a universal language, or at a minimum, of universal tonal value. Other studies show how music enhances classroom environments (with a focus on the emotional value of music, but without empirical evidence).[535] There are also studies related to the use of music therapy to help individuals relax.[536] Other more neutral studies seek to explain exactly how an individual perceives music and receives his or her first "induction" to sound values.[537]

Many books in the popular press on brain-based teaching and learning recommend the use of music to improve classroom environments.[538] However, the evidence of the value of music in this context needs to be further validated before it is generally recommended for all classrooms. Furthermore, not all studies related to music show benefits. Several studies have debunked certain neuromyths, such as the belief that the "Mozart

---

527. See Koepke (2002).
528. See Chan, Ho, & Cheung (1998).
529. See Raucherm, Shaw, Levine, Wright, Dennis, et al. (1997).
530. See Hazlewood, Stouffer, & Warshauer (1989).
531. For example, see Pantev, Oostenvel, Engelien, Ross, Roberts, et al. (1998); Peretz & Zatorre (2005); Zatorre (2003).
532. Webster & Weir (2005).
533. Leman, Vermeulen, De Voogdt, Moelants, & Lesaffre (2005).
534. Leman et al. (2005, p. 39).
535. See Weinberger (1998).
536. For example, Feas, (2003); Menon & Levitin (2005).
537. Juslin & Laukka (2004).
538. See Jensen (1998b).

effect" aids memory and enhances testing skills.[539] Not even the original authors of the Mozart effect study believed that playing Mozart for brief periods before a test would help improve test scores.[540] Music is a fascinating domain of study, though its benefits are still not completely understood. More research in the area of music and the brain are sure to emerge in the coming years.

Suggested Reading

Language and Reading

Bennett, M., Dennett, H. D., Hacher, P., & Searle, J. (2007). *Neuroscience and philosophy: Brain, mind, and language.* New York: Columbia University Press.

Cohen, L., Dehaene, S., Naccache, L., Lehericy, S., Dehaene-Lambertz, G., Henaff, M., & Michel, F. (2000). The visual word form area: Spatial and temporal characterization of an initial stage of reading in normal subjects and posterior split-brain patients. *Brain, 123*(2), 291–307.

Corina, D., Richards, T. L., Serafín, S., Richards, A. L., Steury, K., Abbott, R. D., et al. (2001). fMRI auditory language differences between dyslexic and able reading children. *Neuroreport, 12*(6), 1195–1201.

Dehaene, S. (2009). *Reading in the brain.* New York: Penguin Viking.

Fischer, K. W., Bernstein, J., & Immordino-Yang, M. H. (2007). *Mind, brain, and education in reading disorders.* New York: Cambridge University Press.

Fowler, A., & Swainson, B. (2004). Relationships of naming skills to reading, memory, and receptive vocabulary: Evidence for imprecise phonological representations of words by poor readers. *Annals of Dyslexia, 54*(2), 247–281.

Johnston, P., & Costello, P. (2005). Principles for literacy assessment. *Reading Research Quarterly, 40*(2), 256–267.

Katzir, T., & Paré-Blagoev, J. (2006). Applying cognitive neuroscience research to education: The case of literacy. *Educational Psychologist, 41*(1), 53–74.

Mehler, J., Nespor, M., Shukla, M., & Pena, M. (2006). Why is language unique to humans? *Novartis Foundation Symposium, 270,* 251–291.

Nevills, P. A., & Wolfe, P. (2004). *Building the reading brain, pre-K–3.* Thousand Oaks, CA: Corwin Press.

Pare-Blagoev, E. (2006). *Connecting neuroscience and education: The neural correlates of phonemic awareness in normal reading children.* Doctoral dissertation, (Ed.D.), Harvard University, Cambridge, MA.

---

539. See Cassidy, Henly, & Markley (2007) and McKelvie & Low (2002).
540. In McKelvie & Low (2002).

Pugh, K., Shaywitz, B. A., Shaywitz, S. E., Shankweiler, D. P., Katz, L., & Fletcher, J. M. (1997). Predicting reading performance from neuroimaging profiles: The cerebral basis of phonological effects in printed word identification. *Journal of Experimental Psychology: Human Perception and Performance, 23*(2), 299–318.

Schlaggar, B., & McCandliss, B. D. (2007). Development of neural systems for reading. *Annual Review of Neuroscience, 30*(1), 475.

Shaywitz, B., & Shaywitz S. E. (2005, April). *The brain science of overcoming dyslexia.* Paper presented at the Learning and the Brain Conference, Cambridge, MA.

Shaywitz, B., Shaywitz S. E., Blachman, B. A., Pugh, K. R., Fulbright, R. K., Skudlarski, P., et al. (2004). Development of left occipitotemporal systems for skilled reading in children after a phonologically-based intervention. *Biological Psychiatry, 55,* 926–933.

Shaywitz, S., Shaywitz, B. A., Fulbright, R. K., Skudlarski, P., Mencl, W. E., Constable, R. T., et al. (2003). Neural systems for compensation and persistence: Young adult outcome of childhood reading disability. *Biological Psychiatry, 54*(1), 25–33.

Shaywitz, B., Shaywitz, S. E., Pugh, K. R., Mencl, W. E., Fulbright, R .K., Skudlarski, P., et al. (2002). Disruption of posterior brain systems for reading in children with developmental dyslexia. *Biological Psychiatry, 52*(2),101–110.

Wolf, M. (2007). *Proust and the squid: The story and science of the reading brain.* New York: Harper.

Ziegler, J., & Goswami, U. (2005). Reading acquisition, developmental dyslexia, and skilled reading across languages: A psycholinguistic grain size theory. *Psychological Bulletin, 131*(1), 3–29.

Fast ForWord

Hook, P., Macaruso, P., & Jones, S. (2001). Efficacy of Fast ForWord training on facilitating acquisition of reading skills by children with reading difficulties—a longitudinal study. *Annals of Dyslexia, 51,* 75–96.

RAVE-O

Wolf, M., Miller, L., & Donnelly, K. (2000). Retrieval, automaticity, vocabulary, elaboration, orthography (RAVE-O): A comprehensive, fluency-based reading intervention program. *Journal of Learning Disabilities, 33*(4), 375–386.

Neuronal Recycling

Anderson, M. (2007). Evolution of cognitive function via redeployment of brain areas. *The Neuroscientist, 13*(1), 13–21.

Dehaene, S. (2005). Evolution of human cortical circuits for reading and arithmetic: The neuronal recycling hypothesis. In S. Dehaene, J.-R. Duhamel, M. D. Hauser, & G. Rizzolatti (Eds.), *From monkey brain to human brain: A Fyssen Foundation Symposium* (pp. 133–157). Cambirdge, MA: MIT Press.

Dehaene, S. (2008). Cerebral constraints in reading and arithmetic: Education as a "neuronal recycling" process. In A. Battro, K. W. Fischer, & P. J. Léna (Eds.), *The educated brain* (pp. 232–247). Cambridge, UK: Cambridge University Press.

Dehaene, S., & Cohen, L. (2007). Cultural recycling of cortical maps. *Neuron, 56*(2), 384–398.

Math

Ansari, D., Donlan, C., & Karmiloff-Smith, A. (2007). Atypical and typical development of visual estimation abilities. *Cortex: Special Issues on Selective Developmental Disorders, 6,* 758–768.

Ansari, D., Donlan, C., Thomas, M., Ewing, S., & Karmiloff-Smith, A. (2003). What makes counting count? Verbal and visuo-spatial contributions to typical and atypical number development. *Journal of Experimental Child Psychology, 85,* 50–62.

Ansari, D., & Karmiloff-Smith, A. (2002). Atypical trajectories of number development: A neuro-constructivist perspective. *Trends in Cognitive Sciences, 6*(12), 511–516.

Bisanz, J., Sherman, J., Rasmussen, C., & Ho, E. (2005). Development of arithmetic skills and knowledge in preschool children. In J. I. D. Campbell (Ed.), *Handbook of mathematical cognition* (pp. 143–162). New York: Psychology Press.

Byrnes, J. (2008). Math skills. *In The Jossey-Bass reader on the brain and learning* (pp. 301–330). San Francisco: Wiley.

Dehaene, S. (1999a). Counting on our brains. *Nature, 401*(6749), 114.

Dehaene, S. (1999b). *The number sense: How the mind creates mathematics*. New York: Oxford University Press.

Dehaene, S. (2002). *The cognitive neuroscience of consciousness*. Cambridge, MA: Bradford Books.

Dehaene, S. (2008b). Small heads for big calculations. In *The Jossey-Bass reader on the brain and learning* (pp. 273–300). San Francisco: Wiley.

Dehaene, S., & Cohen, L. (1995). Towards an anatomical and functional model of number processing. *Mathematic Cognition, 1,* 83–120.

Dehaene, S., Moiko, N., Cohen, L., & Wilson, A. J. (2004). Arithmetic and the brain. *Current Opinion in Neurobiology, 14*(2), 218–224.

Desoete, A., & Grégoire, J. (2006). Numerical competence in young children and in children with mathematics learning disabilities. *Learning and Individual Differences, 16*(4), 351–367.

Gardner, R., Ansari, D., Reishofer, G., Stern, E., Ebner, F., & Neuper, C. (2007). Individual differences in mathematical competence predict parietal brain activation during mental calculation. *NeuroImage, 38,* 346–356.

Geake, J. (2003). Young mathematical brains. *Primary Mathematics, 7*(1), 14–18.

Hoek, D., Van Den Eeden, P., & Terwel, J. (1999, Oct.). The effects of integrated social and cognitive strategy instruction on the mathematics achievement in secondary education. *Learning and Instruction, 9*(5), 427–448.

Nieder, A. (2005). Counting on neurons: The neurobiology of numerical competence. *Nature Reviews Neuroscience, 6*(3), 177–190.

Rourke, B., & Conway, J. A. (1997). Disabilities of arithmetic and mathematical reasoning: Perspectives from neurology and neuropsychology. *Journal of Learning Disabilities, 30*(1), 34–46.

Schmithorst, V. J., & Douglas Brown, R. (2004). Empirical validation of the triple-code model of numerical processing for complex math operations using functional MRI and group independent component analysis of the mental addition and subtraction of fractions. *NeuroImage, 2*(3), 1414–1420.

Sherman, J., & Bisanz, J. (2007). Evidence for use of mathematical inversion by three-year-old children. *Journal of Cognition and Development, 8*, 333–344.

Tanner, H., & Jones, S. (2000). *Becoming a successful teacher of mathematics.* Oxford, UK: Routledge.

Wilson, A. J., & Dehaene, S. (2007). Number sense and developmental dyscalculia. In D. Coch, K. Fischer, & G. Dawson (Eds), *Human behavior and the developing brain* (2nd ed.). New York: Guilford Press.

Wilson, A. J., Dehaene, S., Pinel, P., Revkin, S. K., Cohen, L., & Cohen, D. (2006). Principles underlying the design of "The Number Race": An adaptive computer game for remediation of dyscalculia. *Behavioral and Brain Functions, 2*, 19.

Science

Carey, S. (2000 Jan). Science education as conceptual change. *Journal of Applied Developmental Psychology, 21*(1), 13–19.

Grotzer, T. A. (2003). Learning to understand the forms of causality implicit in scientific explanations. *Studies in Science Education, 39*, 1–74.

Grotzer, T. A. (2004). Putting everyday science within reach: Addressing patterns of thinking that limit science learning. *Principal Leadership*, October, 16–21.

Holloway, J. (2000). How does the brain learn science? *Educational Leadership, 58*(3), 85–86.

Schwartz, M., & Sadler, P. (2007). Empowerment in science curriculum development: A microdevelopmental approach. *International Journal of Science Education, 29*(8), 987–1017.

Zohar, A. (2004). *Higher order thinking in science classrooms: Students' learning and teachers' professional development.* New York: Springer.

Art and Creativity

Abraham, A., & Windmann, S. (2007). Creative cognition: The diverse operations and the prospect of applying a cognitive neuroscience perspective. *Methods, 42*(1), 38–48. Retrieved October 12, 2007, from *linkinghub.elsevier.com/retrieve/pii/ S10462023 06002994.*

Andreasen, N. (2005). *The creative brain: The science of genius.* New York: Plume, Penguin Group.

Carlsson, I., Wendt, P. E., & Risberg, J. (2000). On the neurobiology of creativity. Differences in frontal activity between high and low creative subjects. *Neuropsychologia, 38,* 873–885.

Csikszentmihalyi, M. (1991). *Flow: The psychology of optimal experience.* New York: Harper Perennial.

Csikszentmihalyi, M. (1996). *Creativity: Flow and the psychology of discovery and invention.* New York: Harper Perennial.

Diamond, M., & Hopson, J. (1998). *Magic trees of the mind: How to nurture your child's intelligence, creativity, and healthy emotions from birth through adolescence.* New York: Plume.

Dietrich, A. (2007). Who's afraid of a cognitive neuroscience of creativity? *Methods, 42*(1), 22–27.

Gardner, H. (1984). *Art, mind and brain.* New York: Basic Books.

Gardner, H. (1994). *Creating minds: An anatomy of creativity seen through the lives of Freud, Einstein, Picasso, Stravinsky, Eliot, Graham, and Gandhi.* New York: Basic Books.

Goguen, J. A., & Myin, E. (2000). *Art and the brain II: Investigations into the science of art.* Charlottesville, VA: Imprint Academic.

Gruber, H. E., & Bödeker, K. (2005). *Creativity, psychology, and the history of science.* New York: Springer.

Hass-Cohen, N., Carr, R., & Kaplan, F .F. (2008). *Art therapy and clinical neuroscience.* London: Jessica Kingsley.

Kaufman, J. C., & Sternberg, R. J. (2006). *The international handbook of creativity.* New York: Cambridge University Press.

Runco, M. A., & Pritzker, S. R. (1999). *Encyclopedia of creativity.* New York: Elsevier.

Sousa, D. (2008). The brain and the arts. In *The Jossey-Bass reader on the brain and learning* (pp. 331–358). San Francisco: Wiley.

Srinivasan, N. (2007). Cognitive neuroscience of creativity: EEG based approaches. *Methods, 42*(1), 109–116.

Sternberg, R. (1998). *Handbook of creativity.* Cambridge, UK: Cambridge University Press.

Sylwester, R. (1998). Art for the brain's sake. *Educational Leadership, 56*(3), 36–40.

Trimble, M. R. (2007). *The soul in the brain: The cerebral basis of language, art, and belief.* Baltimore, MD: Johns Hopkins University Press.

Music

Brown, S., Martinez, M., & Parson, L. (2006). Music and language side by side in the brain: A PET study of the generation of melodies and sentences. *European Journal of Neuroscience, 23*(10), 2791–2803.

Cassity, H., Henley, T. B., & Markley, R. P. (2007). The Mozart effect: Musical phenomenon or musical preference? A more ecologically valid reconsideration. *Journal of Instructional Psychology, 34*(1), 13–17.

Gaser, C., & Schlaug, G. (2003). Brain structures differ between musicians and non-musicians. *Journal of Neuroscience, 8*(27), 9240–9045.

Gruhn, W., Galley, N., & Kluth, C. (2003). Do mental speed and musical abilities interact? *Annals of the New York Academy of Sciences, 999*, 485–496.

Hepp, C. (2006). Intelligent music teaching: Essays on the core principles of effective instruction. *American Music Teacher, 55*(5), 93–94.

Immordino-Yang, M., & Fischer, K. W. (2007). Dynamic development of hemispheric biases in three cases: Cognitive/hemispheric cycles, music and hemispherectomy. In D. Coch, K. W. Fischer, & G. Dawson (Eds.), *Human behavior, learning, and the developing brain: Typical development* (pp. 74–114). New York: Guilford Press.

Ivanov, V., & Geake, J. G. (2003). The Mozart effect and primary school children. *Music Psychology, 31*(4), 405–413.

Janata, P., & Grafton, S. T. (2003). Swinging in the brain: Shared neural substrates for behaviors related to sequencing and music. *Nature Neuroscience, 6*(7), 682–687.

Koelsch, S. (2005). Neural substrates of processing syntax and semantics in music. *Current Opinion in Neurobiology, 15*(2), 207–212.

Korenman, L., & Peynircioglu, Z. F. (2007). Individual differences in learning and remembering music: Auditory versus visual presentation. *Journal of Research in Music Education, 55*(1), 48–55.

Levitin, D. J. (2006). *This is your brain on music*. New York: Plume.

Levitin, D. (2008). My favorite thing: Why do we like the music we like? In *The Jossey-Bass reader on the brain and learning* (pp. 370–384). San Francisco: Wiley.

Meister, I., Krings, T., Foltys, H., Boroojerdi, B., Miller, M., & Topper, R. (2004). Playing piano in the mind: An fMRI study on music imagery and performance in pianists. *Cognitive Brain Research, 19*(3), 219–228.

Menon, V., & Levitin, D. J. (2005). The rewards of music listening: Response and physiological connectivity of the mesolimbic system. *NeuroImage, 28*(1), 175–184.

O'Herron, P., & Siebenaler, D. (2005). The intersection between vocal music and language arts instruction. *A Review of the Literature Applications of Research in Music Education, 25*(2), 16–26.

Pantev, C., Oostenvel, R., Engelien, A., Ross, B., Roberts, L. E., & Hoke, M. (1998). Increased auditory cortical representation in musicians. *Nature, 392*, 811–814.

Peretz, I., & Zartorre, R. J. (2005). Brain organization for music processing. *Annual Review of Psychology, 56*(1), 89–114.

Sacks, O. (2008). *Musicophilia: Tales of music and the brain.* New York: Picador.

Stewart, L., von Kriegstein, K., Warren, J. D., & Griffiths, T. D. (2006 Oct.). Music and the brain: Disorders of musical listening. *Brain, 129*(10), 2533–2553.

Zatorre, R., Chen, J. L., & Penhune, V. B. (2007). When the brain plays music: Auditory–motor interactions in music perception and production. *Nature Reviews Neuroscience, 8*(7), 547–558.

CHAPTER **8**

Evidence-Based Solutions for the Classroom
How MBE Science Offers Useable Knowledge to Teachers

"He who dares to teach must never cease to learn."
—John Cotton Dana (1856–1929). *Respectfully Quoted:*
A Dictionary of Quotations (1989)[541]

Great teachers seem to know by instinct what approaches resonate best with which students. Some may reach this level of expertise instinctively, but most do so after the accumulation of years on the front line and by experiencing a variety of personalities, cognitive preferences, socioeconomic backgrounds, and value systems—and via experimentation with a myriad of activities, props, methods and materials. Using MBE science, we can now explain neurologically in many cases why the things great teachers do work.

What Great Teachers Do and Why It Works

The information in MBE science can be used to teach better. This useable knowledge is divided into basic principles and tenets that can be used to teach better.[542] The principles are based on universals of the brain and learning, which are similar for all people (discussed below), and the tenets go into more individualized aspects of human learning, which have already been considered in this book (these include such areas as how motivation and emotional states impact learning). Together the principles and tenets point to better ways to teach.

541. "In 1912 [John Cotton] Dana, a Newark, New Jersey, librarian was asked to supply a Latin quotation suitable for inscription on a new building at Newark State College (now Kean College of New Jersey), Union, New Jersey. Unable to find an appropriate quotation, Dana composed what became the college motto" according to The *New York Times* Book Review, March 5, 1967, p. 55 as cited by Bartleby.com (*http://www.bartleby.com/73/1799.html*).

542. An explanation of all of these elements is beyond the scope of this book. Readers are invited to see *Mind, Brain, and Education Science: The New Brain-Based Education* for a more detailed review of classroom application of MBE science (Tokuhama-Espinosa, 2010).

Principles

To synthesize the information of this book and to offer teachers some immediately useable knowledge for the classrooms, some of the main principles are summarized in the table below.

TABLE 8.1
Principles That Great Teachers Follow

1. Great teachers know that each brain is unique and uniquely organized.

2. Great teachers know that all brains are not equally good at everything.

3. Great teachers know that the brain is a complex, dynamic system and is changed daily by experiences.

4. Great teachers know that learning is a constructivist process, and that the ability to learn continues through developmental stages as an individual matures.

5. Great teachers know that the search for meaning is innate in human nature.

6. Great teachers know that brains have a high degree of plasticity and develop throughout the lifespan.

7. Great teachers know that MBE science principles apply to all ages.

8. Great teachers know that learning is based in part on the brain's ability to self-correct.

9. Great teachers know that the search for meaning occurs through pattern recognition.

10. Great teachers know that brains seek novelty.

11. Great teachers know that emotions are critical to detecting patterns, to decision-making, and to learning.

12. Great teachers know that learning is enhanced by challenge and inhibited by threat.

13. Great teachers know that human learning involves both focused attention and peripheral perception.

14. Great teachers know that the brain conceptually processes parts and wholes simultaneously.

15. Great teachers know that the brain depends on interactions with other people to make sense of social situations.

16. Great teachers know that feedback is important to learning.

17. Great teachers know that learning relies on memory and attention.

18. Great teachers know that memory systems differ in input and recall.

19. Great teachers know that the brain remembers best when facts and skills are embedded in natural contexts.

20. Great teachers know that learning involves conscious and unconscious processes.

21. Great teachers know that learning engages the entire physiology (the body influences the brain, and the brain controls the body).

Great Teachers Know That Each Brain Is Unique and Uniquely Organized
Human brains are as unique as faces; although the basic structure is the same, there are no two that are identical. This principle is perhaps the most important cornerstone of MBE science. Each brain is distinct based on its individual experience, despite the general patterns of organization in how different people learn and which brain areas are involved. For example, a 16-year-old left-handed multilingual girl will have a slightly different brain structure than a 50-year-old right-handed monolingual man, based on their life experiences (in this case, exposure age, gender, and use of languages). The way these two people approach language problems will be colored by the way their brains have come to be wired based on their past contact with languages. Great teachers know that in order to maximize both people's potential to learn a new language (or solve a math problem or learn a musical instrument), they will need an understanding of their past life experiences to help clarify the way they will choose to approach new learning challenges. Student success hinges on a teacher's ability to differentiate instructional and evaluation practices that value each student's past experiences.

It stands to reason that if each brain is as unique as each face, due to genetic makeup as well as individual experiences, then preferences for learning based on this uniqueness would also exist. However, there is not enough evidence at this point to say that some people are "kinesthetic learners" as opposed to "auditory" or "visual learners," because such preferences depend greatly on the subject being learned, the stage of learning (new concepts vs. rehearsal), and the intrinsic motivation of the learner for the topic at hand. Nevertheless, Pashler and colleagues' global overview, to determine whether or not learning styles should be considered when evaluating teaching methods, showed that "children and adults will, if asked, express preferences about how they prefer information to be presented to them" (Pashler, Daniela, Rohrer, & Bjork, 2008, p. 105).[543] Great teachers recognize that all people use kinesthetic, visual, and auditory pathways (assuming these pathways function without deficits) to take in new information, *and* that different people use different processing strategies at different times, depending on the context of the learning. At a minimum, teachers should recognize that information could be delivered in different forms—kinesthetic and visual and auditory—to maximize possible retention.

543. The same authors noted, however: "At present, there is no adequate evidence base to justify incorporating learning styles assessment into general educational practice. Thus, limited education resources would be better devoted to adopting other educational practices that have a strong evidence base" (p. 105). This perspective is a result of the belief that "any credible validation of learning-styles-based instructions requires robust documentation of a very particular type of experimental finding," not just anecdotal evidence available in classrooms. In short, although teachers may have access to evidence in classes, it is not documented, nor is there a scientific, experimental base for learning styles.

Great Teachers Know That All Brains Are Not Equally Good at Everything

Context as well as ability influences learning. The context within which learning takes place (the environment), the level of motivation one has for the topic, and prior knowledge about it all influence a person's ability to learn. This means that expecting the same results for all students is probably unreasonable. The idea that all brains are not equally good at everything goes against the optimistic ideals of the 1970s and 1980s, in which teachers were trained to believe that with the right instruction (behavioral guidance), all children could reach the same levels of achievement.[544] This principle means that each child is born with a certain learning potential, which he or she inherits genetically. This potential can be maximized by good teaching techniques (or stagnated by poor ones). In this sense, a teacher's role changes from that of a behavioral modifier to one of a professional analyst who must diagnose the potential of each student, then design an individualized learning program to help that student understand his or own strengths and weaknesses.[545]

Great Teachers Know That the Brain Is a Complex, Dynamic System and
Is Changed Daily by Experiences

The brain is constantly changed by experience, though most of this change is only evident at a microscopic level. The brain's complexity and the constant changes it experiences countermand beliefs from the 1970s that personality and intelligence were fixed by a certain age. This principle confirms the dictum "Use it or lose it," based on the knowledge that active synapses are strengthened, while relatively less active synapses are weakened. Over time, this pattern of strengthening some synapses while weakening others shapes brain organization.[546] This point is also important for learners of all ages because it serves as a reminder that if knowledge is left unused, it will be lost, and that learning can be, and should be, a lifelong process. Great teachers know that slowly but surely their well-thought-out methodologies are changing the brains of their students, little by little, even before actual changes in behavior can be observed. Teachers armed with this knowledge are less likely to become frustrated at the slow pace of learning (the external behavior) because they realize that students are building up, slowly but surely, towards the great "Eureka!" moments in which enough links have been made at the neuronal level to manifest themselves in observable learned behavior.

544. Skinner (1974).
545. Levine (2000).
546. An exemplary book is Joseph LeDoux's *Synaptic Self: How Our Brains Become Who We Are* (2003).

Great Teachers Know That Learning Is a Constructivist Process, and That the Ability to Learn Continues through Developmental Stages as an Individual Matures
Each day we learn; it is impossible not to do so given the survival processes that are hardwired in the brain. The learning process does not occur in a vacuum, however; rather, it is always grounded on past knowledge and is constructed by the learner him- or herself. Although basic patterns in human development can and should be used as guidelines for understanding milestones, they are not the whole story. For example, it is important and useful for teachers to understand that the average child will begin to approach problems from a variety of angles (not from a single egocentric perspective) some time between the ages of 7 and 12 years old;[547] if a child fails to do so by the time he or she enters the teen years, red flags should go up in our minds. But aside from the red flags, great teachers would look for the reasons for the delay based on the child's past building blocks in learning. Because our experiences are unique, the foundations of our constructed knowledge are also different. This means that some students may not be prepared to move into this decentralized thinking stage if they have not acquired the previous building blocks.

Humans construct meaning based on their existing knowledge structures and mental schemas, and such structures are individually defined. Great teachers not only accept that the experiential baggage one child brings with him or her to class will differ from what another child brings, they can also take advantage of this to help build better learning moments using the child's own initial constructs.

Great Teachers Know That the Search for Meaning Is Innate in Human Nature
Humans are born to learn. The search for meaning is an inborn human need, and learning occurs due to the brain's evolutionary processes that indicate that learning is an act of survival.[548] If humans did not learn, the species would not survive.[549] Learning is based on adaptation, and the human brain is naturally programmed to learn as a survival function.[550] This principle implies that teaching should actually be easier than it sometimes appears to be. Why do some subjects (or ages or income groups, etc.) seem easier to teach than others? Great teachers tell you it is because of the "disconnect" between traditional (passive, teacher-centered) classrooms and more modern pedagogical practices that celebrate active, student-centered learning. The natural curiosity of children should be nurtured in school contexts. This is often done using the Five E's of good teaching:

547. This is called "decentering," in Piaget's terms.
548. Lynch & Granger (2008).
549. For examples, see Linden (2007a); Maloney (2004).
550. Calvin (1996).

"Engage, Explore, Explain, Elaborate, Evaluate,"[551] to take advantage of the way the brain naturally considers new information. If the brain is engaged, it continues to explore. To build upon this learning moment, teachers should ask students to explain what they think is going on, then view the concept in more detail (elaborate), and finally they should evaluate their findings and their own thinking about the concept. Though simple, the Five E's take advantage of the brain's innate desire to search for meaning.

Great Teachers Know That Brains have a High Degree of Plasticity and Develop Throughout the Lifespan

Plasticity is the physical demonstration of the brain's flexibility. Plasticity in youth is the epitome of new learning—the malleable structure of the brain and the myriad of new connections made on a daily basis constitute plasticity. Most people associate plasticity, however, with the recuperation of damaged brain areas—the ability of the brain to recruit different areas for tasks not normally associated with the damaged area, as when a stroke destroys the area of the brain related to speech, but the person recuperates this skill by engaging other areas. It was once believed that stroke victims "maxed out" on their capacity for new learning after a certain amount of time. For example, the level of recuperation of a stroke victim after 6–8 weeks of acute care and intensive therapy was thought to yield the expected total recuperation possible. We now know that plasticity can continue to mold the brain after longer periods of time and that continued therapeutic incentives can be helpful.[552] It is important to remember that the degree of plasticity declines with age for many reasons, including hormonal changes as well as lack of use. Many researchers note that the brain can remain agile and learn into old age if it receives proper stimuli. For example, it was found that people between the ages of 60 and 74 who participated in mentally challenging activities (as opposed to caring for a plant or doing nothing), staved off the brain's normal decline, remained more alert, and reported a better sense of well-being, presumably because mentally challenging activities keep the mind fit in the same way that physical exercise can keep the body fit.[553] This is an important group of studies that reminds teachers that the brain is "up to" the challenge of new learning across the lifespan, even if damaged. The outer limits of plasticity have been shown to be far greater than once thought. Great teachers and therapists alike know that there is reason to have higher expectations of the brain than previously imagined.

---

551. See Jones (n.d.) as cited in *The Teachers Network*: *http://www.teachersnetwork.org/ntol/howto/science/fivees.htm*.
552. In Doidge (2007).
553. See Rivera, Estrada, & Estrada (2007); Schreiber & Schneider (2007).

Great Teachers Know That MBE Science Principles Apply to All Ages
Human brains have a high degree of plasticity and develop throughout the lifespan, though there are major limits on this plasticity, and these limits increase with age, as just mentioned. Nevertheless, MBE science principles apply to learners across the lifespan; they are not bound to the early years, or even to school-age learners.[554] While it is clear that all of the content of the principles are modified and/or have different limitations based on the age of the individual, in general learning should be viewed as a lifelong process. Great teachers recognize that while there may be *sensitive periods* for learning some skills, there are no *critical periods* that limit opportunities to do so; the order in which skills are learned is more important than the age at which they are learned. This is a challenge to educational policy and a boost for proponents of allowing students to learn at their own pace.

Great Teachers Know That Learning Is Based in Part on the Brain's Ability to Self-Correct
The brain learns from experience through the analysis of data, self-reflection, and eventual *self-correction*. Connecting new information to prior knowledge (either experiences or learning competencies) facilitates learning. The brain goes through this self-correction process in part in response to *self-preservation processes*,[555] and in part because of its ability to engage in *self-reflection*.[556] Self-preservation means that the brain corrects its actions when the results of the actions are undesirable. This includes protecting oneself not just from bodily harm, but also from humiliation, other bad feelings, or damage to self-esteem. Brains adjust behavior when well-being is challenged. Great teachers know that in the classroom setting, some changes in student behavior are based on self-correction due to the need (or perceived need) to protect the self, as in pressure from peers or threats from parents about losing privileges if grades aren't improved, for example.

The brain's need for self-reflection means that in the best of cases and on an individual level, it considers actions that are morally challenging given personal values —that is, what is right and wrong. Second, self-reflection means that it takes time to ponder new ideas in relation to existing mental schemas. Time to think about new concepts helps students see how easily (or not) they can be incorporated into existing schemas. In both self-preservation and self-reflection the brain learns as it corrects itself. Great teachers know that the brain's ability to self-correct has strong implications for instruction and

554. This is further supported by the refutation that everything important about the brain is determined by the age of 3.
555. See Calvin (1996).
556. Bransford, Brown, & Cocking (2003).

especially assessment practices. Students who are given the time to reflect make better choices. Well-designed feedback offers a path for better learning.

Great Teachers Know That the Search for Meaning Occurs through Pattern Recognition
The brain receives information though the senses, and this information is constantly compared with what it already knows. For example, I see a certain type of cloud pattern and I predict rain based on my past experiences with the same cloud formation; I smell a certain combination of odors and I think, chocolate chip cookie, etc. Human brains seek *patterns* upon which they predict outcomes, and neural systems form responses to repeated patterns of activation (patterns being individually defined). Pattern recognition is achieved by continually comparing new information with what the brain already knows. There are patterns in nature, social behavior, math problems, architectural design, clothing design, literary genres, and literally in all walks of life. The brain then makes predictions about what it expects based on past experiences. Great teachers know that if they help students identify their own relationships to new learning, they learn faster.

For this reason, analogies, metaphors, and similes are especially useful in helping students see the connections between concepts.[557] Students may not understand an idea, but once that idea is linked to a familiar pattern, they are able to comprehend at least the gist. For example, telling a kid that he is in danger of getting a "third strike" or a "yellow card" in class delivers the warning message without the humiliation. Likewise, providing analogies such as "Horses are to past societies as cars are to future societies" or "Eiffel Tower is to France as Great Pyramid is to Egypt" helps students relate to unfamiliar conceptual ideas in a way that makes new learning easier.

Great Teachers Know That Brains Seek Novelty
Human brains seek, and often quickly detect, novelty (which is individually defined). According to research by Calvin (1996), Siegel (1999), and others, brains have evolved to detect fluctuations and change. While the brain searches for patterns, it is alerted to change by its "thirst" for novelty. This is a complementary processes to the previous point in which the brain seeks patterns (your brain finds novelty based on the detection of broken patterns). Teachers who know that brains seek novelty can use this information to their advantage by varying classroom routines and creating significant learning experiences. Great teachers realize that training in pattern detection in the early years, for

---

557. The word metaphor comes from the Greek word *metapherin* (meaning "transfer"), which explains why they are so useful in teaching—they help students transfer conceptual understandings from one realm to another.

example, is key to developing the ability to identify novelty in later years. What seems "out of place" (novel) can be a catalyst for new learning if managed well by teachers. For example, asking questions such as, "What is different about this case as compared with the last one?" or "What part of the drawing/math problem/poem structure/experiment is different from the other?" develops students' metacognitive understanding and facilitates new learning by linking past knowledge to new ideas.

Great Teachers Know That Emotions Are Critical to Detecting Patterns, to Decision-Making, and to Learning

Emotions play a vital role in learning as a whole and are particularly related to decision-making and choice making. Great teachers realize that this principle challenges the belief that learning is primarily a rational and conscientious undertaking; they also realize that there is enormous value in creating emotional links to learning contexts. The impact of emotions on learning has only recently entered the evidence-based category of knowledge for teaching.[558] Goleman's work on *Emotional Intelligence* (1996) was one of the earlier invitations to parents and teachers alike to reflect on the role of affect in learning. The idea that what a student feels about what is being taught, by whom, how, when, and where all impact the quality and efficiency of learning has recently become more accepted in science. If teachers appreciate this principle more, the likelihood that students will find their classes more relevant to their personal lives also increases.

Great Teachers Know That Learning Is Enhanced by Challenge and Inhibited by Threat

Learning is enhanced by challenge and is typically inhibited by threat (in which threat is individually defined). Though this concept seems to be very logical—few people enjoy threatening situations or find them conducive to learning—what constitutes "threat" or "challenge" is relative to the individual. This means that what you and I find threatening can be very different things, making the principle difficult to apply. To use this principle we actually need to look not at what our individual views of threat are, but rather, we should look at the opposite: what is nonthreatening. The basic premise relates to the definition of "good" learning environments, which are presumed to be filled with personal challenges and low threat levels. One of the key elements in designing good learning environments is the teacher's ability to manage the class; great teachers know that teacher–student interactions impact learning. One of the newer taxonomies in education

---

558. Only recently LeDoux (2008), a long-time expert in the field on emotions and learning, acknowledged this.

is L. Dee Fink's creative vision of class design. In *Fink's Taxonomy* (2003), half of the elements relate to designing high expectations by creating challenging learning situations, and the other half to designing low-threat situations (1. Foundational Knowledge; 2. Application; 3. Learning How to Learn; 4. Integration; 5. Caring; 6. Human Dimension). Teachers need to reflect upon their exchanges with students and ensure that their perceived level of threat is low while maintaining a high level of challenge.

Great Teachers Know That Human Learning Involves Both Focused Attention and Peripheral Perception

We all know that there is no learning without attention, which is why teachers normally demand that their students stay on task (focused attention), but they rarely take into account how students' peripheral perception is also constantly in play, dividing the brain's attention. Attention can be defined as the appropriate allocation of processing resources, or being able to concentrate on one aspect of incoming stimuli while effectively ignoring others.[559] From the brain's perspective, what happens around a student is just as important as what is happening directly in front of the student, as in the friend at the desk next door, the siren outside the window, or the chatter in the hallway. In evolutionary terms, without peripheral perception (vision, sound, smell), human beings as a species would not have survived. When a child drifts off at the sound of voices behind him or her or an open window in the room, he or she is actually paying attention, just not the right kind for a classroom setting. As teachers we know that some students are better at self-regulating their attention than others. For those who need help, we should be willing and able to offer certain accommodations, such as in removing distractions, if possible. Simply switching a child's seating position in the classroom (away from the window and the chattering neighbor to the front of the class where he or she can focus better) can often remedy what seem like hopeless cases.

Great Teachers Know That the Brain Conceptually Processes Parts and Wholes Simultaneously

The mind does not process input linearly in an orderly, first-come, first-serve fashion; rather, it is capable of processing whole concepts simultaneously, depending on the level of familiarity one has with the information. This means that students do not necessarily learn concepts in a step-by-step fashion but rather via epiphanies of linked concepts, when all the pieces come together in their minds. Teachers should be aware that great

---

559. Anderson (2005).

insights, so-called "*aha!*" moments, occur most frequently when all the pieces fall into place as a whole, rather than as each individual step is completed. As teachers we know in practice that we normally teach the concepts of a new idea in logical stages. However, we also know that the true understanding of the concept does not become clear to the students as they process the steps individually (parts), but rather when the larger concept of what, for example, the math formula represents is revealed (whole). Teachers should always keep in mind that it takes time to process all of the pieces into a larger whole (true learning). This explains why some students "get it" faster than others; they have processed the links between the sub-concepts faster than others. *Faster* does not necessarily mean *smarter*, however; it could also mean that the "quick" student simply had more rehearsal with the subconcepts than the other students, and therefore could link them faster. Slower students could catch up with the faster ones if they would take the time to rehearse the sub-concepts (e.g., as in completing homework).

Great Teachers Know That the Brain Depends on Interactions with Other People to Make Sense of Social Situations
Support (academic, moral, or otherwise) from others (often teachers, peers, or parents) is critical for optimal academic performance. Humans are social creatures and, as such, learning *cannot* be isolated from social contexts. Even if we are alone in a room reading a book and a "new" idea comes to us as a result, the idea itself is anchored in either our past experiences or in interactions with others, albeit virtual or through other literature, who shared our thoughts. Great teachers know that this principle supports pedagogical concepts such as active, peer, or collaborative learning activities. When individuals share perceptions, they often change how or what they think—which is why the idea "1 + 1 = 3" has merit. Each person has his or her own ideas, but once shared, what is produced by the combined effort is greater than the sum of the parts. This principle has important implications for teaching because it encourages instructional practices that are adapted to integrate space for shared conceptual learning.

Great Teachers Know That Feedback Is Important to Learning
Feedback and *authentic assessment* are important to human learning, though the importance and role of feedback vary greatly across individuals, domains, and processes. In education, feedback is based on the premise that in order to improve learning, students

need to know what they do not yet know (where they erred). That is, when a student is guided toward recognition of his or her errors and is then given implicit or explicit direction as to how to correct these errors, the student then knows how to improve his or her performance the next time. Great teachers know that moments of evaluation can and should always become moments of teaching. Gone are the days of simply returning a test paper and moving on to the next topic. Teachers now know that these are some of the best teaching moments because students become (sometimes painfully) aware of where they went wrong, but they often don't know why. It is at those moments that the teacher needs to take the time to give feedback on how to improve. Feedback is important for all age groups, not just for small children; in order to motivate continued learning, adult learners need to hear how well they are doing just as much as kids. Although some teachers manage feedback well as a natural outcome of their personalities, most need to learn to do this tactfully to encourage rather than discourage students. This principle has implications for teacher training because the art of giving feedback is not normally taught in teacher development.

Great Teachers Know That Learning Relies on Memory and Attention
Memory + Attention = Learning. Though overly simple, this formula makes it clear that there is no learning without both memory and attention ("memory" and "attention" as defined in the glossary and in previous parts of this book). This principle means that learning will be inhibited if either memory system (e.g., long-term, short-term, emotional, social) or attentional systems (focused or peripheral) malfunctions. Great teachers know how to create classroom activities and assessment processes that enhance long-term memory of concepts and that maintain student attention. This principle also implies a shift in responsibilities; great teachers now accept their role in designing classroom activities that are engaging and capture student attention (no longer are passive lecture courses tolerated in great classrooms). While it is true that the students also bear the burden of paying attention, the teacher is responsible for designing engaging and memorable learning experiences. Great teachers know that one way to ensure student attention is to keep it focused on the students themselves; student-centered activities help maintain a higher level of alertness than teacher-focused activities.

Great Teachers Know That Memory Systems Differ in Input and Recall

The brain uses its different memory systems (e.g., short-term, working, long-term, emotional, spatial, rote) to receive and process information in slightly different ways. In practice, if teachers present learning challenges in ways that facilitate the input of information through several neural pathways, the likelihood of retrieval of that information is higher in the future. This means that varying classroom activities to stimulate different sensory modes (hearing, seeing, touching, smelling, tasting) allows for slightly different types of neural pathways to be formed in relation to the same concept.

A great deal of important research is currently focused on how the brain moves information from short-term storage to long-term memory, where it can be used to build learning.[560] We all have experienced cases where students appear to be satisfactorily completing classroom work, only to find that this was a demonstration of good working memory: keeping the information in mind just long enough to complete the task. When asked to do the same thing a day later, we see that students are unable to perform. Why? Because the memory system used on Day 1 was working memory and what was called upon on Day 2 was long-term memory. This means that the information on Day 1 did not make it from working to long-term memory. Teachers need to give students more time in class to reflect on new concepts to stimulate the move from working to long-term memory. Working memory studies explain the far-too-typical case where a student appears to "know" something in class, but cannot recall it after a few days (or cannot transfer that knowledge from one context—the classroom—to another—real life). To enhance the movement of concepts from working memory to long-term memory and to stimulate recall on demand, teachers must devise classroom practices and homework that contextualize learning. For example, *problem-based learning* (PBL) is an excellent means of helping students develop authentic links to learning concepts. A physics or math teacher can identify a real community problem, for example—one that all of the students have heard about or read about in the papers—and ask the students to design a solution. In doing so, the students take "loose" concepts (data, formulas, dates, names, etc.) and link them to their own realities. The practical link, extended rehearsal, and authentic nature of PBL leads to long-term understanding of the once loose (i.e., disconnected, free-floating) concept.

---

560. For some good examples, see Funahashi, Takeda, & Watanabe (2004); Jonides & Nee (2006).

Great Teachers Know That the Brain Remembers Best When Facts and Skills Are Embedded in Natural Contexts

The human brain learns best when facts and skills are embedded in natural contexts or concrete examples, in which the learner understands the problems he or she faces, and recognizes how the facts or skills might play roles in solving that problem. Memory is improved by proper learning contexts, or contexts that are closer to "real life," as suggested by Given (2002). Placing facts and skills in context facilitates memory processes as these memories are embedded within real-life experiences. Although this sounds like a logical supposition, many of us have experienced the need to learn certain concepts out of context. For example, certain micro and macro scientific concepts are difficult to teach in their natural context without specialized equipment. The division of cells or the order of the planets in the solar system, for example, are hard to explain without a microscope or telescope. Great teachers know that they have one of two options—either they can use existing tools (models, videos, Internet, virtual fieldtrips), or they can rely on students' use of sheer rote memorization—and these teachers opt for the latter, more often than not. Both options get information into the brain, but only the former allows the user to truly learn the content, whereas the latter results in a regurgitation of facts and formulas without necessarily understanding anything. We know that while brains may learn best when facts and skills are embedded in natural contexts, this is not imperative for learning to occur. This principle is logical to good teachers, and it should also be more widely taught in teacher training programs.

Great Teachers Know That Learning Involves Conscious and Unconscious Processes

Sometimes we are aware (conscious) of our learning, and other times we are unaware (unconscious) of our learning. This means that both novice as well as expert learners simply cannot always answer the question "How do you know that?" While all teachers are aware that learning involves conscious processes (including classroom learning), the mechanisms of unconscious learning are not so clear. There are two ways learning occurs unconsciously. First, there is the unconscious perception of voices and faces, which influences how we feel about the way information is delivered. The human brain judges others' faces and tones of voices for threat levels in a rapid and often unconscious way, influencing the way information from these sources is perceived, as explained in Chapter 6 of this book. Great teachers know how to manage their facial expressions and vocal tones to the benefit of a good learning environment.

Second, as an unconscious process sleep is important for declarative memory consolidation. This means that sleep deprivation also has a negative impact on memory. Studies in the literature related to sleep and different levels of consciousness and learning mechanisms, such as those by Hobson and colleagues,[561] show that learning does indeed occur at different levels of consciousness. Great teachers know that, because of the role that REM sleep plays in memory consolidation, students who "pull all-nighters" (stay up all night) to study are less likely to remember the information in the long term than those who study and have a good night's sleep.[562] Teachers need to help students become aware that they the "A" they received on the test after the all-nighter will be meaningless in the long term, because they really did not learn the information—they merely maintained it in working memory just long enough to put the answers on the paper. When it comes to the final cumulative exam, these students will have to study the information all over again as they really did not learn it (get it into long-term memory) in the first place.

Great Teachers Know That Learning Engages the Entire Physiology (the Body Influences the Brain, and the Brain Controls the Body)

The *mind–body connection* in learning means that nutrition,[563] sleep,[564] and exercise[565] all influence the brain's potential to learn. Though choices about nutrition, sleep, and exercise originate in the home, their impact is felt in the classroom. Great teachers need to help parents and students understand the devastating impact that poor nutrition, bad sleeping habits, or lack of exercise can have on learning potential. When students have poor eating habits, their classroom performance is compromised. If they do not sleep well enough, not only their body is tired, but their mind is also at a less-than-optimal state to learn, and what was taught the day before may not make it into long-term memory. "Couch potato" students who rarely exercise are not taking advantage of the fact that fit bodies, in which all organs are in good shape—including the brain—learn better. It behooves learning institutions and policy makers to ponder carefully what we know about the mind–body link and to incorporate guidance for parents into the overall scheme of student learning. After all, education is the responsibility of society as a whole; a concerted effort between schools and families is required to fully maximize the potential of all learners.

561. See Hobson's many books and articles on this important topic (2004); Hobson & Pace-Schott (2002); Hobson, Pace-Schott & Stickgold (2000).
562. For an excellent summary, see Pace-Schott & Hobson (2002).
563. See Liu (2004).
564. See Stickgold (2005).
565. See King (1999).

Useable Knowledge

Good Learning Environments Are Key

Balanced with high-content knowledge, the learning environment is one of the most important determinants of high quality teaching–learning exchanges. Broadly defined, good learning environments in education are those that provide physical and mental security, respect, intellectual freedom, self-direction, paced challenges, feedback, and active learning experiences.[566] Each of these elements of a good learning environment relates to different principles and tenets. For example, an environment that employs "respect" as its main rule responds to the general rule that emotional states influence the ability to learn. Good learning environments seek to develop a state of "relaxed alertness"[567] in which students are paying attention but do not feel anxiety.

Experienced teachers know that good learning environments are made, not found. Great teachers acknowledge the importance of creating good learning environments and thus design their classroom interactions around this knowledge. Starting in kindergarten and on through adult education, testimonies about how students feel (secure, challenged, etc.) show that these emotions impact learning.[568] Once teachers have designed good learning environments, they can turn their attention to designing course work that has both sense and meaning.

The Role of Sense, Meaning, and Transfer

Formal education has several goals, among them (a) to develop critical thinking abilities and (b) to impart knowledge in content areas such as math, language, science, and the arts. Neither of these goals is possible without an application of the concepts of sense, meaning, and transfer. Sousa (2000) describes sense and meaning as putting learning into context within the learner's world—a concept that others simply call "transfer." That is, students learn best when what they learn makes sense and has a logical order, as well as has some meaning in their lives. All great teachers know how difficult it is to convince students to learn things they feel are irrelevant to their lives. This relates to the idea that the brain remembers information best when facts and skills are embedded in authentic experiences (natural contexts).

Great teachers make the attempt to link school knowledge with life experiences, to contextualize knowledge in authentic situations, or at least to offer metaphorical refer-

---

566. For summary references to this concept, see Billington (1997); Kaufeldt (2010).
567. In Caine & Caine (2001).
568. See Jonassen & Land (2008).

ences. Teachers who try to link what is taught in class with applications in the students' lives are more successful. Making these linkages requires not only thorough knowledge of the subject matter, but also of the students. A clear assessment of prior knowledge and appreciation of the cultural-based neural networks of the knowledge students bring with them to class are both required.

Great Teachers Take Advantage of Different Types of Memory Pathways

Since learning is dependent on memory to a certain extent, it stands to reason that taking advantage of the brain's different memory systems will make teachers more effective. Teachers who design learning experiences that store memories in a variety of ways, in order to increase recall possibility, are more successful. One way to take advantage of the different memory systems is to vary classroom activities because different modes of instruction take advantage of different sensory pathways in the brain. Teachers should teach to auditory, visual, and kinesthetic pathways as well as allow for both individual and group work in order to improve the chances of recall and engage students in opportunities to discuss, debate, and question ideas.

Teachers can facilitate the development of long-term memory by instigating forced recall sessions that "jar" students' memories; in this way students begin to develop a "habit of mind" about how to store and retrieve important information. The development of memory in students relies heavily on the teacher's ability to (a) design memorable activities and (b) to help students develop their own system of recall (through individually chosen mnemonic devices).

As we have seen throughout this book, memory and attention are close allies in learning. The next instructional guideline relates to how teachers can help students pay better attention in class.

Know How To Take Advantage of Natural Attention Spans

The average student has an attention span that ranges between 10 and 20 minutes, depending on age and degree of maturity. Attention spans are short because vigilance takes a lot of energy.[569] No class is just 10–20 minutes long; therefore teachers need to learn how to divide up their class time into manageable chunks in which core concepts

---

569. Many teachers suspect that attention spans are actually getting even shorter due to the great number of stimuli in the environment that require faster and faster information exchanges, such as video games. This is a logical presumption if we accept that neural plasticity is based on what the brain does the most (e.g., if it spends more time on video games than on reading, the brain becomes primed for shorter attention spans).

can be taught and reinforced. In order to take advantage of this timeframe, great teachers recognize that students learn best when there is a change of person (e.g., from teacher to student), place (e.g., a change of seat), or topic (e.g., a conceptual refocus) at least every 20 minutes. It is difficult, if not impossible (unless a student is highly intrinsically motivated), for attention spans to last beyond this. Lecture format, which I like to compare with a delivery-room metaphor, is convenient for the presenter (the doctor), but it is not necessarily efficient for the receiver (as a patient, lying down when you give birth is not as efficient as other positions that take better advantage of gravity). In order to maintain attention, the protagonist of the class activity should be the learner, not the teacher, which explains why student-centered classrooms are so popular in modern pedagogy.

Great teachers also understand the need for "down time" during which students reflect upon new information in order to maximize memory consolidation. Because this down time is directly related to improved metacognitive abilities, it is imperative that moments of intense concentration be balanced with reflection time about the content knowledge. Such reflection time can take place through journal writing, group discussion, or explicit quiet time.

Interest impacts attention spans and, consequently, the motivation for learning. Teachers can improve attention spans by taking the time to get to know their students and by utilizing their interests. Another impact on attention is known as primacy-recency effect. Humans remember best what occurs first, second-best that which occurs last, and least what occurs in the middle. Great teachers begin their classes with engaging activities to reel in the interest levels (and avoid losing the greatest moments of attention by taking roll or talking individually to students). The midpoint of the class should involve some type of group activity in which each student can use/discuss or question the new knowledge. (It is impossible not to pay attention when the attention is on you.) The end of class should be used to summarize core concepts. To take advantage of attention spans, teachers can minimize passive activities, which can easily bore students.

The Social Nature of Learning

Most people choose to learn with others as opposed to alone. The brain is a social organ, and people learn best when they are able to "grow" ideas and "bounce" concepts off of others. There are hundreds of documents related to the social nature of learning. Great teachers understand that learning often occurs in social contexts, such as classrooms, and seek to enhance this reality through social interaction, as in student group work or discussions. Teaching activities that encourage active exchanges of perceptions and information are more efficient than individual work (e.g., reading quietly to oneself, which has other types of merits). Debates and small-group activities encourage social interactions, which are orchestrated in such a way as to encourage maximum participation in constructing student learning. Peer teaching is another format that encourages interaction. Conscientiously grouping different-level learners has a positive effect for both teacher and learner and capitalizes on the brain's social nature.

New Policies Based on the Mind–Body Connection

The brain chooses how to use the body, but the quality of the brain is impacted by the way we nurture the body: The body impacts the brain, and the brain controls the body. Students learn best when the needs of the body are met, as we saw in earlier sections. Teachers can implement this guideline by utilizing active learning techniques and reminding students about the importance of sleep, nutrition, and physical exercise.

Great teachers serve not only to model a balance between body and mind practices; they can also institute new school policies and explicitly teach students about how different food choice or bedtimes can give them an edge. Often students are unconscious of how their choice of beverage can lead to peaks and valleys in their attention spans, for example. And while many students might feel the effects of staying up late to study, few actually understand that they are not really doing themselves a favor, because the information is not being consolidated for long-term recall. Armed with this knowledge, many students self-correct damaging behaviors.

Orchestration and "Midwifing"

When using *orchestrated immersion*,[570] teachers immerse students in complex experiences that support learning by calling on individuals one by one to bring out their voices and then weaving them into a single class experience. For example, exercises that require higher-order thinking, such as debates, require refined classroom management skills that allow for maximum student participation that allows all voices to be heard. Teachers must integrate different gifts and help each player perform to his or her best ability for the good of the group. At the core of this guideline is the belief that each individual contributes not only to his or her own development, but to the overall learning of the group as well.

---

570. This term was first coined by Nummela-Caine and Caine in 1999.

Teachers who carefully plan the structure and form of each class in a way that takes advantage of each student's knowledge, and which compensates for student weaknesses, are more successful in their practice. Socrates suggested that teachers are like midwives whose job is essentially to help students give birth to their own understanding. Together the ideas of orchestration and midwifing consolidate the need for learning in social contexts, effective methodology, and excellent classroom management skills.

The teachers who accept that their classrooms will be filled with different types of students—with different brain content from different past experiences and different preferences of receiving new information—will not only be more productive, they will also be less frustrated. Successful teachers consider these differences to be an opportunity, and they create interactions that integrate the strengths and weaknesses of the learners.

Active Processes in Classroom Design

As we mentioned earlier, great teachers do not risk loss of comprehension to passive experiences; instead they design learning experiences that demand the active participation of the students. To be engaged, learners need to be involved. This means that teachers conscientiously plan learning experiences that use the talents of each member, give students active roles and responsibilities, and combine these with their knowledge of how to manage attention and memory systems to improve learning.

In active classrooms students are involved in more than passive listening; they display higher-order thinking skills, engage in activities that put less emphasis on the information transmission and greater emphasis on developing student skills, and they explore their attitudes and values, receiving immediate feedback from their instructors.[571] Teachers who apply active processes take the time to design significant learning experiences that require students to act on their own knowledge.

The Development of Metacognition and Self-Reflection Skills in Students

All learning relies, to some extent, on reflective thought processes—thinking about thinking, or metacognition. Teachers who incorporate activities that stimulate metacognition (e.g., asking, "How did you reach that answer?") enhance students' overall conceptual grasp of new ideas. Great teachers balance the need to be active with the need for "down time" to give space to metacognitive reflection. This means that teachers need to allow time during class and to assign homework outside of class that requires the use of

---

571. A classic example in this field comes from Bonwell & Eison (1991).

metacognitive skills. For example, great teachers often reserve the last minutes of class for a metacognitive activity that encourages higher-order thinking skills, such as journal writing, end-of-class reflections, or questions about the subject matter. Teachers can help students improve their metacognitive skills by guiding their development of habits of mind that encourage reflection.

Learning Occurs Throughout the Lifespan
All of the previous principles, tenets, and instructional guidelines apply to all ages. The general public tends to think that learning occurs solely in school-age populations, whereas great teachers know that people can and do learn throughout the lifespan. It is clear that quality learning is more dependent on the order in which a skill is learned than on the age of the student. That is, it is more important to teach letter recognition, for example, before spelling, whether the learner is 3, 13, or 30. Teachers need to learn that developmentally appropriate age-related activities should serve as milestones and benchmarks to guide practice, but they should not result in the creation of roadblocks for learners.

We also know that human learning is achieved through developmental processes that follow a universal pattern that characterizes most skill acquisition, including academic skills shared across literate cultures, such as reading, writing, and math. As mentioned previously, there are "sensitive periods" in human brain development in which certain skills are learned with greater ease than at other times. These sensitive periods are *not*, however, critical periods in which windows of opportunity close if they are missed.

Precisely because sensitive periods are not critical, great teachers resist the temptation to label students who do not meet the standard developmental milestones. Rather, these teachers provide remedial activities to help the students fill in whatever gaps in knowledge exist in order to advance their learning and fulfill their potential.

Learning throughout the lifespan also means that knowledge is acquired into old age. People can and do successfully return to school later in life. With aging populations on the rise around the world, it behooves us to encourage active, healthy mental pursuits into old age not only for the benefit of the individual, but for society as a whole.

This chapter placed the research of MBE science into the useable knowledge structure in hopes of contextualizing the sometimes overwhelming number of studies in MBE science. Teachers who can apply this knowledge in class will be more efficient, effective, and engaging.

Suggested Reading

Ansari, D., & Coch, D. (2006). Bridges over troubled waters: Education and cognitive neuroscience. *Trends in Cognitive Sciences, 10*(4), 146–151.

Armstrong, T. (2006). *The best schools: How human development research should inform educational practice.* Alexandria, VA: Association for Supervision and Curriculum Development.

Battro, A., Fischer, K. W., & Léna, P. J. (Eds). (2008). *The educated brain: Essays in neuroeducation.* Cambridge, UK: Cambridge University Press.

Blakemore, S., & Frith, U. (2007). *The learning brain: Lessons for education.* Malden, MA: Blackwell.

Borich, G. (2006). *Effective teaching methods: Research based practice* (6th ed.). New York: Prentice Hall.

Bransford, J., Brown, A. L., & Cocking, R. R. (Eds.). (2003). *How people learn: Brain, mind, experience and school.* Washington, DC: National Academy Press.

Bransford, J., Brown, A. L., & Cocking, R. R. (2008). Mind and brain. In *The Jossey-Bass reader on the brain and learning* (pp. 89–108). San Francisco: Wiley.

Bruer, J. (2008a). In search of . . . brain-based education. In *The Jossey-Bass reader on the brain and learning* (pp. 51–69). San Francisco: Wiley.

Bruer, J. (2008b). Building bridges in neuroscience. In A. M. Battro, K. W. Fischer ,& P. J. Léna (Eds.), *The educated brain* (pp. 43–58).Cambridge, UK: Cambridge University Press.

Byrnes, J. (2001). *Minds, brains, and learning: Understanding the psychological and educational relevance of neuroscientific research.* New York: Guilford Press.

Byrnes, J. P. (2007a). *Cognitive development and learning in instructional contexts* (3rd ed.). Boston: Allyn & Bacon.

Byrnes, J. (2007b). Some ways in which neuroscientific research can be relevant to education. In D. Coch, K. W. Fischer, & G. Dawson (Eds.), *Human behavior, learning, and the developing brain: Typical development* (pp. 30–49). New York: Guilford Press.

Chance, P. (2006). *Learning and behavior: Active learning edition,* (5th ed.). Belmont, CA: Wadswoth.

Coch, D., Dawson, G., & Fischer, K. W. (Eds.). (2007). *Human behavior, learning, and the developing brain: Atypical development.* New York: Guilford Press.

Coch, D., Fischer, K. W., & Dawson, G. (Eds.). (2007). *Human behavior, learning, and the developing brain: Typical development.* New York: Guilford Press.

Diamond, M. (1988). *Enriching heredity: The impact of the environment on the anatomy of the brain.* New York: Free Press.

Erlauer, L. (2003). *The brain-compatible classroom: Using what we know about learning to improve teaching.* Alexandria, VA: Association for Supervision and Curriculum Development. Retrieved August 20, 2007, from *http://www.ascd.org/portal/site/ ascd/ template.chapter/menuitem.b71d101 a2f7c208cdeb3ffdb62108a0c/?chapterMgmtId=88fbcba5ddcaff00VgnVCM1000003d01a8c0RCRD.*

Fink, L. (2003). *Creating significant learning experiences: An integrated approach to designing college courses*. San Francisco: Jossey-Bass Books.

Fischer, K. W. (2007a). Dynamic cycles of cognitive and brain development: Measuring growth in mind, brain, and education. In A. M. Battro & K. W. Fischer (Eds.), *The educated brain*. Cambridge UK: Cambridge University Press. Retrieved January 28, 2008, from *http://gseweb.harvard.edu/~ddl/publication.htm*.

Fischer, K. W. (2007b). *Mind, brain, and education: Analyzing human learning and development* [Podcast]. Inaugural launch of the journal *Mind, Brain, and Education*, April 2, 2007. Cambridge, MA: Harvard University.

Fischer, K. W., Daniel, D. B., Immordino-Yang, M. H., Stern, E., Battro, A., & Koizumi, H. (Eds.). (2007). Why mind, brain, and education? Why now? *Mind, Brain, and Education, 1*(1), 1–2.

Fischer, K. W. (2009). Mind, brain, and education: Building a scientific groundwork for learning and teaching. *Mind, Brain, and Education, 3*(1), 3–16.

Gardner, H. (2008). Who owns intelligence? In *The Jossey-Bass reader on the brain and learning* (pp. 120–132). San Francisco: Wiley.

Geake, J. (2000). Knock down the fences: Implications of brain science for education. *Principal Matters, April*, 41–43.

Geake, J. (2005). Educational neuroscience and neuroscientific education: In search of a mutual middle way. *Research Intelligence, 92*, 10–13.

Geake, J., & Cooper, P. (2003). Cognitive neuroscience: Implications for education? *Westminster Studies in Education, 26*(1), 7–20.

Goldberg, E. (2006). *The wisdom paradox: How your mind can grow stronger as your brain grows older*. New York: Gotham Books.

Goswami, U. (Ed.). (2002). *Blackwell's handbook of childhood cognitive development*. Oxford, UK: Blackwell.

Goswami, U. (2004). Neuroscience and education. *British Journal of Educational Psychology, 74*, 1–4.

Goswami, U. (2005a). The brain in the classroom? The state of the art. *Developmental Science, 8*(6), 468–469.

Goswami, U. (2005b). Neuroscience and education: The brain in the classroom [Target article with commentaries]. *Psychology of Education Review, 29*(2).

Goswami, U. (2006). Neuroscience and education: From research to practice. *Nature Reviews Neuroscience, 7*(5), 406–413.

Goswami, U. (2007). *Cognitive development: The learning brain*. London: Taylor & Francis.

Goswami, U. (2008). Neuroscience and education. In *The Jossey-Bass reader on the brain and learning* (pp. 33–50). San Francisco: Wiley.

Goswami, U., & Ziegler, J. C. (2005 Jul). A developmental perspective on the neural code for written words. *Trends in Cognitive Neuroscience, 9*(7), 335-341.

Hall, J. (2005). Neuroscience and education. *Education Journal, 84*, 27–29.

Hart, L. (1999). *Human brain and human learning* (5th ed.). Kent, WA: Books for Educators.

Howard-Jones, P. (2007). *Neuroscience and education: Issues and opportunities. Commentary by the Teacher and Learning Research programme.* London: TLRP. Retrieved January 14, 2008, from *http://www.tlrp.org/pub/commentaries.html.*

Howard-Jones, P., & Pickering, S. (2006). *Perception of the role of neuroscience in education: Summary report for the DFES Innovation Unit.* Retrieved January 14, 2008, from *http://www.bristol.ac.uk/education/research/networks/nenet.*

Levine, M. (2000). *A mind at a time.* New York: Simon & Schuster.

Muris, P., Merckelbach, H., & Damsma, E. (2000). Threat perception bias in nonreferreed, socially anxious children. *Journal of Clinical Child Psychology, 29*(3), 348–359.

Posner, M., & Rothbart, M. K. (2007). *Educating the human brain.* Washington, DC: American Psychological Association.

Tokuhama-Espinosa, T. (2009). *The new science of teaching and learning: Using the best of mind, brain, and education science in the classroom.* New York: Teachers College Press.

Warminster, J., & Schifrin, B. (2000). Thinking differently, learning differently. *Educational Leadership, 58*(3), 45–48.

Westwater, A., & Wolfe, P. (2000). The brain-compatible curriculum. *Educational Leadership, 58*(3), 49–52.

Wiley, John & Sons. (2008). *The Jossey-Bass Reader on the brain and learning.* San Francisco: Wiley.

Willis, J. (2007). *Brain-friendly strategies for the inclusion classroom.* Alexandria, VA: Association for Supervision and Curriculum Development.

Yan, Z., & Fischer, K. W. (2002). Always under construction: Dynamic variations in adult cognitive development. *Human Development, 45*(3), 141–160.

CHAPTER **9**

Conclusions

Education has never had so many tools at its disposal to improve the teaching and learning processes. These are exciting times for everyone in the discipline. Neuroscience and psychology nurture our understanding of how the brain learns and help us identify the best teaching practices possible. Although the tools of the trade are important, the greatest single change occurring, thanks to MBE science, is the transformation of the teacher role into a catalyst for societal change.

Development of the Teacher Practitioner

In a thoughtful letter to the editor of *Nature* in 2005, Daniel Ansari applauded the introduction of neuroscience into the classroom and made specific recommendations for how this should occur. I believe it is time to think about the interactions between education and cognitive neuroscience in broader terms than simple exchanges of information, and more in terms of a partnership. It is also now essential to begin integrating the teaching of scientific evidence from cognitive neuroscience into teacher training and further education programs to facilitate the creation of a "research-practitioner" model of the field of education (Ansari, 2005b, p. 26).

Such a model is beginning to emerge. There are now several undergraduate and graduate programs that are designed to form the new MBE research-practitioner of the future (see Appendix B for some of the better-known programs). The National Science Foundation has designed an initiative in which the application of neuroscience findings to classrooms is considered.[572] It is predicted that MBE will grow quickly to be incorporated

572. See the National Science Foundation's website on Science and Learning Centers: *http://www.nsf.gov/funding/pgm_ summ.jsp?pims_id=5567&WT.mc_id=USNSF_39.*

within teacher training around the world. Hopefully this will be a three-way street that will expand to educational psychology programs and educational neuroscience programs around the world as well.

It is hoped that a proliferation of "new and improved" teacher training programs based on MBE science concepts will emerge in the near future. Unlike many previous programs, however, these will be held to higher levels of scrutiny and be judged by the empirical evidence supporting their principles, tenets, and instructional guidelines. Training that is not backed by science[573] will fall into oblivion.[574] The discipline itself will begin to self-regulate and will haul in "false prophets," and the general level of common knowledge shared in the discipline will grow.

The discipline will continue to mature as better imaging techniques become available and methods for studying the brain improve. Currently the young discipline of MBE science has a limited number of studies on how the brain best learns to read, do math, conceive of music, and conduct higher-order thinking. These sparse sources of guidance will grow in number as well as quality as technology evolves and becomes less costly. Neuroimaging will become common in even low-budget universities, instead of being reserved for prestigious research institutions. As a result, graduate studies will proliferate, adding quantity to quality in MBE science studies. It is anticipated that better brain imaging techniques will allow for improvements in many areas. Some of these developments will likely include (1) reading and writing strategies that are more personalized as a larger number of studies document individual differences; (2) increased differentiated assessment in schools based on evidence that each child's brain is unique; (3) increased educational software production that takes advantage of knowledge related to attention spans; and (4) parent insistence on better teacher provision of positive learning environments and policy decisions that are more in line with the natural way the brain learns. Based on the direction the field is taking, it is presumed that the next decade will be a decisive one. The realization of these projections will be based, in part, on successful future research in the new discipline.

MBE science has evolved slowly but steadily as the new and improved model of brain-based learning. The rich and nurturing parent fields of neuroscience, psychology, and education have given birth to a new learning science that promises to change the way we conduct research and how we teach. By the grace of intellectual humility, people formed originally in psychology, education, or the neurosciences have reached compro-

---

573. As with Brain Gym® and the Mozart effect.
574. See Carroll (2006); Ellers (2004); Hyatt (2007).

mises that resulted in the development of a new academic discipline that is potentially more powerful in pedagogical terms than any other before. New researchers, practitioners, and policy makers in this discipline bear a particular responsibility for ensuring that the standards are respected and that the goals are met. If they do so, society will be the biggest beneficiary.

In this book we began by celebrating the new discipline of MBE science. We considered some of the more problematic conceptual debates that exist, but also identified the promise of how better communication between parent fields (if each acknowledges that it can both inform as well as learn from the others) could lead to a truly unique entity. In Chapter 3 we overviewed the history of MBE science to better understand that we are now at the moment of birthing a new learning science that employs better teaching methods. In Chapter 4 we considered the research, practices, and goals and standards of the new discipline. We learned why there are some concepts in education that are classified as neuromyths, or plain falsehoods, about the brain and learning. We also put the Socratic method to the test against MBE standards and found that this tried-and-true teaching instrument came through with shining colors and has survived for the past 2,500 years with good reason. We recommended that all "best-practice" methods in teaching be tested against MBE standards. In Chapter 5 we looked at who, what, how, and which dimensions of teaching and learning were considered in MBE science and explained why they were relevant to teachers. In Chapter 6 we shifted to the more practical application of MBE science in terms of understanding human survival skills. We reviewed eight domains: affect–empathy–emotions and motivation; executive functions and decision-making; facial recognition and interpretation; memory; attention; social cognition; spatial sequential management; and temporal sequential management. Each of these domains, in which humans develop important skill sets, was explained in terms of basic survival uses as well as how they relate to the classroom experience. In Chapter 7 we reviewed school subject areas and considered the science behind language (reading and writing), math, art, creativity, music, and science. We also considered state-of-the-art interventions that apply to MBE standards and which seem to have encouraging results. Finally in Chapter 8 we considered the ways in which this information translates into actual classroom practice.

This book comes at an exciting time for all of us in education. Great teachers are now able to understand the science behind their art, good teachers are now given tools that make them become better, and students are the overall beneficiaries. However, this is just the beginning. Each of us has a role to play in the continual development of this new discipline. As teachers in the classroom there are several things we can do: (1) We can begin to be more conscientious consumers of information about the brain and learning; (2) we can start to document our classroom interventions in order to reflect more on our practice; and (3) we can bring best-practice activities to the attention of neuroscientists in the lab to encourage them to research questions more authentically related to our real-life class situations.

Psychologists have special responsibilities in this change. In many ways psychology is the natural bridge between neuroscience and education. This pivotal position places an extremely important role on psychologists, who can perhaps more naturally extend invitations to the neuroscientist in the lab to work on collaborative ventures than can the teacher in the classroom. Psychologists are asked to be visionaries in this sense: where are the possible links between research ideas? How can already complementary findings be bridged into a more precise study? Who should be involved? Psychologists can link people in neuroscience with those in education and, in doing so, pave the way for grand new findings in MBE science.

Neuroscientists have different responsibilities than psychologists in this change. Neuroscientists can extend an invitation to teachers to recommend areas of research and develop partnerships with them to create better exchanges between colleagues. Publications should seek to find a more common vocabulary in order to reach the widest audience possible. Some neuroscientists, such as Stanislas Dehaene, Judy Willis, Usha Goswami, Michael Posner, and Michael Gazzaniga, and educators, such as David Sousa and Pat Wolfe, have been able to "find their voice" across disciplines and write eloquently to specialists as well as laypeople. However, the new genre of writing about MBE science is just beginning to emerge and needs more people who speak this common language.

Shared Vocabulary

In order for MBE science to continue to grow successfully, several challenges will have to be overcome. Among the most pressing challenges is that of developing a vocabulary that is common to all participants in the discipline and that includes a clear definition of all of the terms in the lexicon, with the goal of improving communication processes between the different parent disciplines.

An example of the difficulty in creating a unifying vocabulary was seen when the Delphi panel of experts was asked to select important words for the discipline, and to begin by defining the word *learning* (2008). The Delphi panel began by asking experts to modify a one-sentence definition of the word *learning*, which eventually grew into a 166-word treatise:

> Learning can be said to take place in the mind in a psychological sense, and in the brain in a neurological sense. Learning is instantiated in the brain and is prompted by internal thought processes, sensory input, motor training, or simulated perceptual input in the mind resulting in a physiological and measurable change in the neural networks, as well as changes in the muscles and other parts of the body. Human learning is complex and is intricately related to emotions, cognition, action, volition, and perception. Learning is always accompanied by brain changes, which in fact underlie learning itself as well as changes in behavior, including thought and feeling. Human learning can be achieved through active and constructive processes such as in formal school contexts. Much learning can be observed neurologically before being expressed in behavior, as in implicit learning, which results in subtle changes in behavior and is usually only noticeable when new learning is scaffolded upon it, as is much of the early childhood learning.[575]

It is clear that such a long and complex definition is unwieldy and requires continued honing and refinement. The differences of opinion in the exact definition of the word *learning* are primarily due to the different professional affiliations of the experts and the worldviews they embrace. This conflict was recognized in a recent article by Varma, McCandliss, and Schwartz (2008):

> The differences in the vocabularies of education and neuroscience might ultimately be too great to allow multidisciplinary theorizing. The vocabulary of education belongs to the social sciences and includes mental terms such as *understanding* and *identity*. It is tailored for the description of behavioral phenomena—both psychological and social. By contrast, the vocabulary of neuroscience belongs to the biological sciences. It includes material terms such

---

575. Tokuhama-Espinosa (2008b, p. 23).

as *hemodynamic response* and *white matter tract*. It is tailored for the description of physical phenomena. These differences are problematic. (p. 143)

In short, different types of professionals in the discipline consider different vocabulary fundamental. It should be noted, however, that other academic disciplines do expect certain core vocabulary knowledge of their professionals. For example, all psychologists are, at a minimum, familiar and most likely utilize certain terms within the execution of their profession, independent of their sub-specialization. Whatever the challenges, further development of a common vocabulary is needed. For a first attempt at a common vocabulary base, readers are invited to review and critique the Glossary.

To close, it is worth remembering that at the start of this book I mentioned the insightful work of Bruno della Chiesa, Vanessa Christoph, and Christina Hinton (2009). These researchers and pioneers in MBE science noted three main characteristics of those people who will move the discipline forward. First, we need people who are willing to share knowledge outside of their parent discipline. Second, we need people willing to adapt their language to a wider audience. And third, we need people who realize that connecting information across different fields and viewing problems with an interdisciplinary lens will end up not only nurturing their own perspectives, but those of others as well, for the overall benefit of all. These new roles for educators, psychologists, and neuroscientists require a level of initiative never requested before of anyone in the discipline. While everyone may want better communication, more collaborative research, shared language, etc., *someone* has to be the catalyst and get the ball rolling. This is an invitation to do so.

Glossary

"Every challenge is an opportunity."
—Anonymous

Shared terminology is imperative if the field is to develop in a coherent fashion with clear discussion and debate. Being able to speak the same language is necessary for neuroscientists, psychologists, and educators to be able to share their research and to continue to develop new and improved practices that benefit human learning. A first attempt by psychologist Sashank Varma, neuroscientist Daniel Ansari, and myself, an educator, resulted in a basic lexicon for MBE practitioners (2008). The 858 words found in this lexicon are the beginning of the first dictionary of MBE science terms. The glossary was compiled with data from the following sources:

Barker & Barasi (2008)
California State University at Chico (2009)
Carlson (2005)
Council of Chief State School Officers (2008)
Eggen & Kauchak (2001)
Johnson & Becker (2009)
Medline Plus (2009)
Merriam-Webster Online Dictionary (2009)
National Joint Committee on Learning Disabilities (2008)
North Central Regional Educational Laboratory (2002)

Ormrod (2000)
Ramachandran (2002)
School Wise Press (2008)
Serendip Brywn Mawr (2009)
Sullivan (1990)
Tzeng (2009)
Wojtczak (2006)

Readers are encouraged to critique this list and comment as to its usefulness in order to make shared vocabulary a reality in MBE science. Send comments to ttokuhama@ usfq.edu.cc.

ability — Skill, natural aptitude, or acquired proficiency.

abnormal — Deviating from the normal or average; unusual, exceptional.

acalculia — Difficulties with arithmetic. May be the result of damage to the angular gyrus in the hemisphere dominant for speech and language.

accommodations — Adaptations in assessment tools and standards to permit children to show what they know and can do. Adjustments may be made, for example, in the way a test is administered or presented, in the timing, in the language, or in how the child responds.

acetylcholine — A neurotransmitter for motor neurons that is involved in the inhibitory function (as is dopamine) of the basal ganglia and is a major neurotransmitter in the autonomic nervous system related to muscle function.

achievement gaps — A consistent difference in scores on student achievement tests between certain groups of children. For example, the data document a strong association between poverty and students' lack of academic success as measured by achievement tests.

action potential — An electrical signal that travels along the axon, away from the cell body to the axon terminal, where it triggers the release of neurotransmitters.

activation (neuroscience) — To make reactive or more reactive (as molecules) or to convert (as a provitamin) into a biologically active derivative.

active learning — A process whereby learners are actively engaged in the learning process, rather than passively absorbing lectures.

adaptation — Adjustment to environmental conditions; modification of an organism or its parts that makes it fitter for existence under the conditions of its current environment.

additive — A combination (as in drug responses or gene products) in which the causative factors, when they act together, are the sum of their individual effects.

affect (in a learning context) — The conscious, subjective aspect of an emotion (considered apart from bodily changes) that has an impact on the reception of new information.

affective filter (hypothesis) — Affective filter is a metaphor that conveys how a learner's attitudes affect the relative success of second-language acquisition; negative feelings such as lack of motivation, lack of self-confidence, and learning anxiety act as filters that hinder and obstruct language learning.

afferent neuron — See "sensory neuron."

afferent pathway — Bearing or conducting inward. In neuroscience, conveying impulses toward the central nervous system. Refers to a neuron or pathway that sends information into the central nervous system, typically sensory in nature.

age-equivalent score — In a norm-referenced assessment, individual student scores are reported relative to age and those of the normal population.

agnosia — An abnormal forgetting caused by various forms of brain disease resulting in severe memory loss. Lack of sensory recognition as the result of a lesion in the association pathways or sensory association areas of the brain.

agraphia — Acquired disturbance of writing due to brain injury.

alerting network (attention) — One of three networks underlying attention (the other two being orientation and selective attention networks).

alexia — Acquired disturbance of reading due to brain injury.

alignment (education) — The degree to which assessments, curriculum, instruction, textbooks and other instructional materials, teacher preparation and professional development, and systems of accountability all reflect and reinforce the educational program's objectives and standards.

alleles — Any of the alternative forms of a gene that may occur at a given locus.

alphanumeric learning — The ability to read words and to interpret digits (which have common and distinct neurological features).

alternative assessment — Ways other than standardized tests (e.g., oral reports, projects, performances, experiments, and class participation) to get information about what students know and where they need help.

amnesia — A condition in which memory is disturbed. Organic causes include damage to the brain through trauma or disease or use of certain (generally sedative) drugs. Functional causes are psychological factors, such as defense mechanisms.

amygdala — A brain structure that is attached to the tail of the caudate nucleus (one in each hemisphere), the amygdalae are considered to be a part of the limbic system and involved in emotion and memory.

analogical quantity of magnitude code (math) — Mental links between time, space, and quantity that are part of a generalized magnitude (proportional size) system.

analogy — A similarity between like features of two things, on which a comparison may be based.

anatomical — The art of separating the parts of an organism in order to ascertain their position, relations, structure, and function.

anatomy — The structure of an animal or plant, or of any of its parts.

anger — A strong feeling of displeasure and belligerence aroused by a wrong; wrath; ire.

angular gyrus — The gyrus that lies near the superior edge of the temporal lobe involved in the recognition of visual symbols and the most important cortical areas of speech and language.

anomia — Difficulty with word-finding or naming. May be the result of damage to the angular gyrus in the hemisphere dominant for speech and language; however, it should be noted that anomia can be localized with the least reliability of any of the aphasic syndromes.

anterior cingulate cortex (ACC) — The frontal part of the cingulate cortex that appears to play a role in a wide variety of autonomic functions, such as regulating blood pressure and heart rate, as well as rational cognitive functions, such as reward anticipation, decision-making, empathy, and emotion.

anterior position — Toward the front (opposed to posterior).

anxiety — An abnormal and overwhelming sense of apprehension and fear often marked by physiological signs (e.g., sweating, tension, increased pulse), by doubt concerning the reality and nature of the threat, and by self-doubt about one's capacity to cope with it.

aphasia — The loss of a previously held ability to speak or understand spoken or written language, due to disease or injury of the brain. Aphasia can affect auditory comprehension, oral expression, reading, and writing.

apraxia (of speech) — A disorder of the nervous system, characterized by an inability to perform purposeful movements, but not accompanied by a loss of sensory function or paralysis. Apraxia of speech is a disruption of the capacity to execute the skilled oral movements necessary for speech.

Arabic code (math) — Digits used in Western society (e.g., 1, 2, 3, 4, 5, 6, 7, 8, and 9).

architectonic structure — Having an organized and unified structure that suggests an architectural design.

arcuate fasciculus — The groups of fibers that connect Broca's area with Wernicke's area (these fibers connect to the angular gyrus) and are located below the supramarginal gyrus. Damage to this area results in conduction aphasia, or the inability to carry out normal language functions.

arousal — To rouse or stimulate to action or to physiological readiness for activity.

ascending pathway — A nerve pathway that goes upward from the spinal cord toward the brain carrying sensory information from the body to the brain.

Asperger's syndrome — An autism spectrum disorder in which people show significant difficulties in social interaction, and other restricted and repetitive patterns of behavior and interests. Differs from other autism spectrum disorders by its relative preservation of linguistic and cognitive development.

assay — A procedure in molecular biology for testing and/or measuring the activity of a drug or biochemical in an organism or organic sample.

assembly (cell; Hebb) — See "Hebbian synapse theory."

assessment (education) — Teacher-made tests, standardized tests, or tests from textbook companies that are used to evaluate student performance.

association area — The parietal, temporal, and occipital lobes organize sensory information into a coherent perceptual model of our environment, centered on our body image. The frontal lobe or prefrontal association complex is involved in planning actions and movement, as well as abstract thought. These areas function to produce a meaningful perceptual experience of the world, enable people to interact effectively, and support abstract thinking and language.

associative memory — See "memory (associative)."

asymmetry (brain) — Refers to at least two distinct findings: (1) neuroanatomical differences between the left and right sides of the brain; and (2) lateralized functional differences between the left and right hemispheres.

attention — The ability to concentrate on a particular stimulus, event, or thought while excluding competing stimuli. The brain processes meaning before details in a hierarchy of visual information-processing features: We pay attention to a rotating three-dimensional image more than just about anything else; second, we are built to detect two-dimensional visual motion; third, we pay attention to static three-dimensional objects; and fourth, we pay attention to static two-dimensional objects.

attention networks — Divisions of attention suggested by Posner and Rothbart: alerting, orienting, and executive attention.

attention deficit/hyperactivity disorder (ADHD) — Any of a range of behavioral disorders characterized by symptoms that include poor concentration, an inability to focus on tasks, difficulty in paying attention, and impulsivity.

attentional effort — Energy needed to stay on task (which can be inhibited by distractors, prolonged time-on-task, changing target stimulus characteristics and stimulus presentation parameters, circadian phase shifts, stress, or sickness).

atypical — Irregular or unusual way in which something functions or operates.

auditory association areas — Brodmann's areas 21 and 22; responsible for auditory memory and association.

auditory discrimination — Ability to detect differences in sounds; can involve a gross ability (e.g., detecting the differences between the noises made by a bird and cat) or fine ability (e.g., detecting the differences made by the sounds of the letters m and n).

auditory figure–ground — Ability to attend to one sound against a background of sound (e.g., hearing the teacher's voice against classroom noise).

auditory memory — Ability to retain information that has been presented orally. This can take place in short-term memory, such as recalling information presented several seconds before, or long-term memory, such as recalling information presented more than a minute before, or sequential memory, such as recalling a series of information in proper order.

auditory processing disorder (APD) — An inability to accurately process and interpret sound information. Students with APD often do not recognize subtle differences between sounds in words.

authentic assessment — An umbrella concept that refers to the measurement of worthwhile, significant, and meaningful accomplishment, as compared to what is measured by multiple-choice standardized tests. Authentic assessment can be devised by the teacher or in collaboration with the student. Authentic assessment uses multiple forms of evaluation that reflect student learning, achievement, motivation, and attitudes on classroom activi-ties. Examples of authentic assessment include performance assessment, portfolios, and student self-assessment. Also see "performance-based assessment."

autism — A developmental disability that affects social interaction, communication, and imaginative play. A person with autism has a mind that has trouble conceiving of other minds. Autism is categorized as a "pervasive developmental disorder" because so many aspects of development are disturbed: intelligence, perception, socializing skills, language, and emotion.

automaticity — A general term that refers to any skilled and complex behavior that can be performed easily, with little attention, effort, or conscious awareness. These skills become automatic after extended periods of training. With practice and good instruction, students become automatic at word recognition, that is, retrieving words from memory, and are able to focus attention on constructing meaning from the text, rather than on decoding.

autonomic nervous system (ANS) — One of the three main divisions of the nervous system. The ANS innervates the involuntary structures of the body (e.g., heart, smooth muscles, glands) and is involved in control of automatic and glandular functions. The ANS is divided into two parts, the sympathetic and parasympathetic.

autonomy — Independence or freedom, as of the will or one's actions.

axon — Extension from the cell that carries nerve impulses from the cell body to other neurons.

backward (curriculum) design (or understanding by design) — Backward design challenges the traditional methods of curriculum planning. In backward design, one starts with objectives or goals, then considers assessments or acceptable evidence, and finally chooses activities.

Baldwin effect — Theory by James Mark Baldwin (1896) that suggests a mechanism for selection of general learning ability (what is beneficial to the species will be remembered in the genes and passed on to subsequent generations).

basal ganglia — The basal ganglia is composed of the caudate nucleus and the lenticular nucleus and located at the level of the thalamus. This group of structures, located in the forebrain, coordinates movement. The basal ganglia is the largest subcortical structure of the brain.

baseline — A line serving as a basis or starting point, used in scientific studies as a point of comparison against which experiments can be measured.

behavioral neuroscience — A sub-discipline of both neuroscience and psychology. Neuroscience is the scientific study of the nervous system, while psychology is the study of behavior. Behavioral neuroscience is largely concerned with ascertaining the function of neural systems in generating behavior. The field is therefore closely allied with systems neuroscience, cognitive neuroscience, and biological psychology.

behaviorism — A theory suggesting that learning occurs when an environmental stimulus triggers a response or behavior. Based on classical conditioning theory, behaviorism applies to educational practices that reward performance behaviors to encourage repetition of those behaviors. This is a theoretical viewpoint that emphasizes the study of observable behaviors, especially as they pertain to learning processes.

benchmark (education) — Statement that provides a description of student knowledge expected at specific grades, ages, or developmental levels. Clear, specific descriptions of knowledge or skill that can be supported through observations, descriptions, and documentations of a child's performance or behavior and by samples of a child's work often used as points of reference in connection with more broadly stated content standards. Benchmarks often are used in conjunction with standards.

benchmark performances — Performance examples against which other performances may be judged.

Best Evidence Encyclopedia — A free website created by the Johns Hopkins University School of Education's Center for Data-Driven Reform in Education (CDDRE) with funding from the Institute of Education Sciences, U.S. Department of Education, which provides summaries of scientific reviews produced by many authors and organizations, as well as links to the full texts of each review.

best practice (teaching) — Referred to as teaching methodologies with certain characteristics said to include being student-centered, experiential, holistic, authentic, expressive, reflective, social, collaborative, democratic, cognitive, developmental, constructivist, and challenging (Zemelman, Daniels, & Hyde, 1998/2005).

bidirectional property — Anything that can move in two directions.

bilateral property — Having two sides, as in the right and left sides of the body or the right and left members of paired organs.

binding problem — Difficulty in binding or linking information relating to each object and distinguishing it from others.

biochemistry — The study of the chemical processes in living organisms that deals with the structure and function of cellular components such as proteins, carbohydrates, lipids, nucleic acids, and other biomolecules.

biofeedback — A nonmedical process that involves measuring a subject's specific and quantifiable bodily functions, such as blood pressure, heart rate, skin temperature, sweat gland activity, and muscle tension, conveying the information to the patient in real time to allow the patient to exert conscious control over those functions.

biological neuroscience — The application of the principles of biology, particularly neurobiology, to the study of mental processes and behavior in human and nonhuman animals.

biology — The science of studying living organisms that examines the structure, function, growth, origin, evolution, distribution, and classification of all living things. Five unifying principles form the foundation of modern biology: cell theory, evolution, gene theory, energy, and homeostasis.

biopsychology — A branch of psychology that analyzes how the brain and neurotransmitters influence our behaviors, thoughts, and feelings.

block design — In combinatorial mathematics, a particular kind of set system that has applications to experimental design, among other areas.

blood flow — The flow of blood in the cardiovascular system; can be calculated by dividing the vascular resistance into the pressure gradient.

Bloom's Taxonomy (taxonomy of learning objectives) — In 1956, Benjamin Bloom et al. sought to establish a taxonomy of learning objectives. Bloom's Taxonomy is divided into six hierarchical categories: knowledge, comprehension, application, analysis, synthesis, and evaluation.

BOLD contrast MRI imaging — Blood oxygenation level-dependent (BOLD) contrast MRI is an fMRI technique that tracks the coupling of cerebral blood flow, energy demand, and neural activity.

bottom-up processing — When information flows from the bottom of the system to the top of the system (e.g., as in taking recommendations from classrooms to decide lab experiments, or in studying neurons to explain behavior).

boundaries — Something that indicates or fixes a limit or extent.

brain — The portion of the vertebrate central nervous system enclosed in the skull and continuous with the spinal cord through the foramen magnum, which is composed of neurons and supporting and nutritive structures (e.g., glia). This organ integrates sensory information from inside and outside the body in controlling autonomic function (e.g., heartbeat and respiration), coordinates and directs correlated motor responses, and mediates the process of learning. This multilayered structure contains billions of neurons, countless numbers of neuronal connections, and thousands of specialized regions.

brain-based learning — Education that moves beyond pedagogy alone to include the use of information about how the brain learns to teach better.

brain development study — The study of neural development draws on both neuroscience and developmental biology to describe the cellular and molecular mechanisms by which complex nervous systems emerge during embryonic development and throughout life.

brain map (cortical map) — A set of neuroscience techniques predicated on the mapping of biological quantities or properties onto spatial representations of the brain. Cortical maps are areas of mini-columns in the cortex that have been identified as performing a specific information-processing function.

brainstem — A region of the brain that consists of the midbrain, pons, and medulla and is responsible for functions such as breathing, heart rate, and blood pressure. Also known as the hindbrain.

branch (neuroscience) — Projections of a neuron that conduct the electrochemical stimulation received from other neural cells to the cell body.

Broca's aphasia — Language impairment in which patient exhibits telegraphic speech, affected syntax, and/or labored and slow speech, flat melodic contour, and impaired articulatory agility. Repetition is typically impaired, as is word finding. Auditory comprehension tends to be superior to expressive language. Also known as expressive aphasia or motor aphasia.

Broca's area — The area of the brain involved in the programming of motor movements for the production of speech sounds; also involved in syntax. Broca's area is located on the inferior third frontal gyrus (Brodmann's area #44) in the hemisphere dominant for language; injuries here may result in apraxia or Broca's aphasia.

Brodmann areas or regions of the brain — A Brodmann area is a region of the cortex defined in terms of its cytoarchitecture, or organization of cells. Brodmann areas were originally defined and numbered by Korbinian Brodmann in 1909, based on the organization of neurons he observed in the cortex and published. Although the Brodmann areas have been discussed, debated, refined, and renamed exhaustively for nearly a century, they remain the most widely known and frequently cited cytoarchitectural organization of the human cortex.

Brodmann's classification system — A map of the cortex developed by neurologist Korbinian Brodmann that classifies the different areas of the brain by number.

Brodmann's areas —

Areas 3, 1, & 2: primary somatosensory cortex (frequently referred to as Areas 3, 1, 2 by convention)

Area 4: primary motor cortex

Area 5: somatosensory association cortex

Area 6: premotor cortex and supplementary motor cortex (secondary motor cortex; supplementary motor area)

Area 7: somatosensory association cortex

Area 8: includes frontal eye fields

Area 9: dorsolateral prefrontal cortex

Area 10: anterior prefrontal cortex (most rostral part of superior and middle frontal gyri)

Area 11: orbitofrontal area (orbital and rectus gyri, plus part of the rostral part of the superior frontal gyrus)

Area 12: orbitofrontal area (used to be part of BA11, refers to the area between the superior frontal gyrus and the inferior rostral sulcus)

Area 13 and Area 14: insular cortex

Area 15 and Area 16*: interior temporal lobe

Area 17: primary visual cortex (V1)

Area 18: secondary visual cortex (V2)

Area 19: associative visual cortex (V3)

Area 20: inferior temporal gyrus

Area 21: middle temporal gyrus

Area 22: superior temporal gyrus, of which the caudal part is usually considered to contain Wernicke's area

Area 23: ventral posterior cingulate cortex
Area 24: ventral anterior cingulate cortex
Area 25: subgenual cortex
Area 26: ectosplenial area
Area 27: piriform cortex
Area 28: posterior entorhinal cortex
Area 29: retrosplenial cingulate cortex
Area 30: part of cingulate cortex
Area 31: orsal posterior cingulate cortex
Area 32: dorsal anterior cingulate cortex
Area 33: part of anterior cingulate cortex
Area 34: anterior entorhinal cortex (on the parahippocampal gyrus)
Area 35: perirhinal cortex (on the parahippocampal gyrus)
Area 36: parahippocampal cortex (on the parahippocampal gyrus)
Area 37: fusiform gyrus
Area 38: temporopolar area (most rostral part of the superior and middle temporal gyri)
Area 39: angular gyrus, considered by some to be part of Wernicke's area
Area 40: supramarginal gyrus, considered by some to be part of Wernicke's area
Areas 41 & 42: primary and auditory association cortex
Area 43: subcentral area (between insula and post/precentral gyrus)
Area 44: pars opercularis, part of Broca's area
Area 45: pars triangularis, part of Broca's area
Area 46: dorsolateral prefrontal cortex
Area 47: inferior prefrontal gyrus
Area 48: retrosubicular area (a small part of the medial surface of the temporal lobe)
Area 52: parainsular area (at the junction of the temporal lobe and the insula)

CAT scan (computer axial tomography) — An imaging method in which a cross-sectional image of the structures in a body plane is reconstructed by a computer program from the X-ray absorption of beams projected through the body in the image plane.
caudal position — From the Latin cauda, "toward the tail"; often means the same as inferior.
caudate nucleus — One of the two structures that make up the basal ganglia, which is divided into a head, body, and tail and is bounded on one side by the lateral ventricle.

causality — Refers to the relationship between one event (the cause) and a second event (the effect), where the second, the event, is the direct consequence of the first.

cell (brain) — See "neuron."

central nervous system (CNS) — Portion of the nervous system that includes the brain and the spinal cord.

central sulcus (fissure of Rolando) — The deep sulcus (divide) that separates the frontal and parietal lobes in the brain.

cerebellar theory (dyslexia) — A biological theory that claims that the cerebellum of people with dyslexia is mildly dysfunctional.

cerebellum — Involved in the coordination and production of speech, the organization of muscle movement, the coordination of fine motor movement, and balance. The cerebellum is the center of a feedback loop involving motor and sensory information. Cerebellum is Latin for "little brain."

cerebral (part of the brain) — Refers to the cerebrum or telencephalon, together with the diencephalon, which constitute the forebrain.

cerebral cortex — The outer covering of the cerebral hemispheres consisting mostly of nerve cell bodies and branches. The cerebral cortex (often just called cortex) is involved in functions such as thought, voluntary movement, language, reasoning, and perception.

cerebral hemisphere — Defined as one of the two regions of the brain that are delineated by the body's median plane. The brain can thus be described as being divided into left and right cerebral hemispheres. Each of these hemispheres has an outer layer of gray matter, the cerebral cortex, which is supported by an inner layer of white matter. The hemispheres are linked by the corpus callosum, a very large bundle of nerve fibers, and also by other smaller commissures, which transfer information between the two hemispheres to coordinate localized functions. The architecture, types of cells, and types of neurotransmitters and receptor subtypes are all distributed between the two hemispheres in a markedly asymmetrical fashion. However, while some of these hemispheric distribution differences are consistent across human beings, or even across some species, many observable distribution differences vary from individual to individual within a given species.

challenge — A test of one's abilities or resources in a demanding but stimulating undertaking.

channel (ion) — Pore-forming proteins that help establish and control the small voltage gradient across the plasma membrane of all living cells by allowing the flow of ions down their electrochemical gradient.

chemistry — The science of the composition, structure, properties, and reactions of matter, especially of atomic and molecular systems.

cholinergic property — Related to the neurotransmitter acetylcholine; if a receptor uses acetylcholine as its neurotransmitter, it is cholinergic.

chunking of information (memory) — In cognitive psychology and mnemonics, chunking refers to a strategy for making more efficient use of short-term memory by recoding information and organizing items into familiar manageable units.

cingulate (gyrus) — A cortical area (a gyrus) considered to be part of the limbic system, which is located immediately superior to the corpus callosum.

circle of Willis (circulus arteriosus) — A point where the blood carried by the two internal carotids and the basilar system comes together and is subsequently redistributed by the anterior, middle, and posterior cerebral arteries, and is the main arterial anastomotic trunk of the brain.

circuit physiology — The study of how the circuits of the brain interact to guide behavior.

classical conditioning — A type of associative learning formed by pairing two stimuli in what is known as the learning of conditioned behavior. Also known as Pavlovian conditioning or respondent conditioning.

classification — The assignment to groups within a system of categories distinguished by structure, origin, etc.

coaching — An instructional method in which a teacher supports students as they perfect old skills and acquire new skills.

coactivation — A process by which proteins called coactivators are recruited to DNA-binding transcription factors through their activation domains. They increase transcription by relaxing the chromatin structure to allow greater access to a gene or by bringing in components of the basal transcription complex needed for transcription to occur.

coarse (coding) — Generalization from state X to state Y depends on the number of features in their receptive fields that overlap.

coding (observation) — The assignment of organisms to groups within a system of categories distinguished by structure, origin, etc.

cognition — The action or faculty of knowing, specifically including perceiving, conceiving, etc.; the acquisition and possession of empirical factual knowledge or a perception, a sensation, a notion, an intuition.

cognitive development — A field of study in neuroscience and psychology focusing on a child's development in terms of information processing, conceptual resources, perceptual skill, and other topics in cognitive psychology. A large amount of research has gone into understanding how a child conceptualizes the world. Jean Piaget was a major force in the founding of this field, forming his "theory of cognitive development."

cognitive dissonance theory (motivation) — Proposes that people have a motivational drive to reduce dissonance by changing or rationalizing their attitudes, beliefs, and behaviors.

cognitive maps — A type of mental processing, or cognition, composed of a series of psychological transformations by which an individual can acquire, code, store, recall, and decode information about the relative locations and attributes of phenomena in everyday or metaphorical spatial environments. (Also known as mental maps, mind maps, scripts, schemas, frames of reference, cognitive models, or mental models.)

cognitive neuroscience — A science investigating how people learn rather than what they learn. Prior knowledge and out-of-classroom experience help form the foundation on which teachers build effective instruction. Also referred to as MBE science, the study of the mind or brain studies in educational circles. In psychological circles, cognitive neuroscience is the fusion of psychology and brain science.

cognitive neuropsychology — Branch of study that aims to understand how the structure and function of the brain relates to specific psychological processes.

cognitive neuroscience — An academic field concerned with the scientific study of biological substrates underlying cognition.

cognitive preference — Learning style or choice of sensory pathway through which one elects to take in information.

cognitively guided instruction — An instructional strategy in which a teacher assesses what students already know about a subject and then builds on students' prior knowledge. Students typically are asked to suggest a way to represent a real problem posed by the teacher. Guided questions, encouragement, and suggestions further encourage students to devise solutions and share the outcome with the class. (Also known as constructivism.)

cognitivism — A theoretical approach that uses quantitative, positivist, and scientific methods and describes mental functions as information-processing models. Cognitivism adopts two assumptions: that psychology can be (in principle) fully explained by the use of experiment, measurement, and the scientific method; and that cognition consists of discrete, internal mental states (representations or symbols) whose manipulation can be described in terms of rules or algorithms.

collaborative learning or cooperative learning — An instructional approach in which students of varying abilities and interests work together in small groups to solve a problem, complete a project, or achieve a common goal, and in which each student has a specific responsibility within the group.

collocation — An example of lexical units; the relationship between two words or groups of words that often go together and form a common expression.

comparative methods/studies — The comparative method is often used in the early stages of the development of a branch of science. Comparison is one of the most efficient methods for explicating or utilizing tacit knowledge or attitudes. This can be done, for example, by showing in parallel two slightly different objects or situations and by asking people to explain verbally their differences.

compensatory action/property — To offset or counterbalance.

competence — The state or quality of being adequately or well qualified. Also known as an ability or a specific range of skill or knowledge.

competencies (education) — The combination of knowledge, skills, and attitudes. Possession of a satisfactory level of relevant knowledge and acquisition of a range of relevant skills that includes interpersonal and technical components at a certain point in the educational process. Such knowledge, skills, and attitudes are necessary to perform the tasks that reflect the scope of professional practices.

competition — A contest for resources that arises whenever two or more parties strive for a goal that cannot be shared. Competition occurs naturally between living organisms that coexist in the same environment. Competition may give incentives for self-improvement.

complementary learning systems — In neuroscience, related to the connectionist models of learning and memory in which benefits from one system (e.g., the hippocampus), lead to benefits in another (e.g., the neocortex).

complexity theory — The study of complex systems.

comprehension strategies (education) — Techniques to teach reading comprehension, including summarization, prediction, and inferring word meanings from context.

comprehension strategy instruction — The explicit teaching of techniques that are particularly effective for comprehending text. The steps of explicit instruction include direct explanation, teacher modeling ("think-alouds"), guided practice, and application.

computational theory of mind (CTM) — A philosophical concept that the mind functions as a computer or symbol manipulator.

conceptual imagery — Mental representation.

conceptual knowledge — A person's representation of the major concepts in a system.

conditioned learning — The process of learning associations between environmental events and behavioral responses; based on the idea that animals learn to respond to a neutral sensory input in the same way they would respond to an effective, threatening, or negative stimulus. They then form associations between the neutral stimulus and the negative stimulus. In this process, responses become linked to particular stimuli, and learning takes place.

confirmatory factor analysis (CFA; statistics) — A special form of factor analysis used to assess the number of factors and the loadings of variables. In contrast to exploratory factor analysis, where all loadings are free to vary, CFA allows for the explicit constraint of certain loadings to be zero.

conflict detection (databases) — In computers, an aspect of file syncronization. Conflict detection is found during file synchronization (or "syncing"), which is the process of making sure that files in two or more locations are updated according to certain rules.

congenital learning disabilities — Learning problems existing at or before birth, usually due to heredity factors.

connected instruction — A way of teaching systematically in which the teacher continually shows and discusses with the students the relationship between what has been learned, what is being learned, and what will be learned.

connectionism — A set of approaches in the fields of artificial intelligence, cognitive psychology, cognitive science, neuroscience, and philosophy of mind that models mental or behavioral phenomena as the emergent processes of interconnected networks of simple units. There are many forms of connectionism, but the most common forms use neural network models.

connectivist model — A model that links or networks previously unconnected areas.

connectivity (and white matter tracts) — In neuroscience, related to typical areas of white matter tracts that are connected during specific conditions.

consciousness — Subjective experience, awareness, wakefulness, or the executive control system of the mind. In psychology and philosophy consciousness has four characteristics: subjectivity, change, continuity, and selectivity. In biology, consciousness usually requires some form of selective attention and a short-term storage of information.

consolidation (memory) — The process of converting short-term memory traces to longer, sturdier forms, which can occur either through conscious learning activities or during certain stages of sleep.

constructivism — Theory suggesting that students learn by constructing their own knowledge, especially through hands-on exploration. It emphasizes that the context in which an idea is presented, as well as student attitude and behavior, affects learning. Students learn by incorporating new information into what they already know. Constructivism values developmentally appropriate, teacher-supported learning that is initiated and directed by the student.

content standards — Statements that provide a clear description of what a child should know and be able to do in a content area at a particular (grade or age) level.

continuous assessment — An element of responsive instruction in which the teacher regularly monitors student performance to determine how closely it matches the instructional goal over time.

contralateral takeover — When the functions of a damaged area of the brain are taken over by the corresponding area in the opposite hemisphere (e.g., from a damaged left temporal cortex to intact right temporal cortex). This is different from ipsilateral or interhemispheric transfer, in which the transfer is from the damaged area of the brain to an adjoining undamaged area of the same hemisphere.

control (cognitive) — Cognitive control is another term for executive functions, a supervisory attentional system theorized in psychology to control and manage other cognitive processes.

corpus callosum — The large bundle of axons that connects the two cerebral hemispheres and disseminates information from the cerebral cortex on one side of the brain to the same region on the other side.

"Corpus sanus in mente sana" — "Sound mind, sound body."

correlational relationship — Studies which look for a continuous relation between variables.

correspondence — The agreement of things with one another, which may or may not show a particular similarity. Also used to refer to a relation between sets in which each member of one set is associated with one or more members of the other.

cortical columns — A group of neurons in the cortex that can be successively penetrated by a probe inserted perpendicularly to the cortical surface, and which have nearly identical receptive fields.

cortices — Plural of cortex. (See "neocortex.")

cortisol — Usually referred to as the "stress hormone" because it is involved in responses to stress and anxiety. Cortisol is a corticosteroid hormone or glucocorticoid produced by the adrenal cortex, which is part of the adrenal gland. It increases blood pressure and blood sugar, and reduces immune responses.

cranial nerves (12) — The 12 sets of nerves that originate from the brainstem, retina, and nose and which mediate the senses and provide the motor and sensory innervation of the head and neck.

creativity — A human mental phenomenon based on the deployment of mental skills and/or conceptual tools, which, in turn, originate and develop innovation, inspiration, or insight. In some circles, correlated with overall, or even called, intelligence.

criterion-referenced assessment — An assessment that measures what a student understands, knows, or can accomplish in relation to specific performance objectives. It is used to identify a student's specific strengths and weaknesses in relation to skills defined as the goals of the instruction, but it does not compare students to other students.

critical pedagogy — A teaching approach that attempts to help students question and challenge the beliefs and practices that dominate in society. A theory and practice of helping students achieve critical consciousness. The teacher leads students to question ideologies and practices considered oppressive (including those at school) and encourages libratory collective and individual responses to the actual conditions of their own lives.

critical period — Referred to as that time in development when there is maximum plasticity in the evolving neural system, such that it can be modified by environmental inputs. (See "sensitive period.")

critical thinking (higher-order thinking skills) — Logical thinking that draws conclusions from facts and evidence and consists of a mental process of analyzing or evaluating information, particularly statements or propositions that people have offered as true. It forms a process of reflecting upon the meaning of statements, examining the offered evidence and reasoning, and forming judgments about the facts. Critical thinking has its basis in intellectual values that go beyond subject-matter divisions and which include clarity, accuracy, precision, evidence, thoroughness, and fairness.

crowding (neuroscience) — Related to the visual theory of the cause of dyslexia. Considers dyslexia to be a visual impairment that gives rise to difficulties with the processing of letters and words on a page of text, due to unstable binocular fixations, poor convergence, or increased visual crowding.

culture — The set of shared attitudes, values, goals, and practices that characterizes an institution, organization, or group, which can include an integrated pattern of human knowledge, belief, and behavior and that depends upon the capacity for symbolic thought and social learning.

cultural mediation (Vygotsky) — Vygotsky's belief that the role of culture and interpersonal communication is fundamental in the development of the individual, who improves higher mental functions via social interactions. Through these interactions, a child comes to learn the habits of mind of his or her culture.

curriculum/curricula — A plan of instruction that details what students need to know, how they are to learn it, what the teacher's role is, and the context in which learning and teaching will take place.

curriculum-based assessment — A type of informal assessment in which the procedures directly assess student performance in learning-targeted content in order to make decisions about how to better address a student's instructional needs.

cytoarchitectonics — The study of the cellular composition of the body's tissues under the microscope.

cytoarchitecture — The cellular composition of a bodily structure.

damage — Loss or harm resulting from injury.

data-driven decision-making (education) — A process of making decisions about curricula and instruction based on the analysis of classroom data and standardized test data. Data-driven decision-making utilizes data on function, quantity, and quality of inputs, and how students learn in the process of proposing educational solutions. It is based on the assumption that the scientific methods used to solve complex problems in industry can effectively evaluate educational policy, programs, and methods.

Decade of the Brain — 1990–2000.

decentering (Piaget) — A child's eventual relinquishment of a narrow ethnocentric position and the coordination of his or her views with those held by others.

declarative knowledge — Knowledge that is, by its very nature, expressed in declarative sentences or indicative propositions. This distinguishes descriptive knowledge from what is commonly known as "know-how" or procedural knowledge (the knowledge of how, and especially how best, to perform some task), and "knowing of," or knowledge by acquaintance (the knowledge of something's existence). (Also known as descriptive knowledge or propositional knowledge.)

declarative memory — The conscious recall of people, names, places, objects, facts, and events (e.g., knowledge that there are seven days in a week). Humans can hold about seven pieces of declarative information in mind for about 30 seconds. Without active rehearsal, the context in which the information was learned fades. If repeated, however, the information can go into a buffer, called "working memory," where it can be held for anywhere between 90 to approximately 120 minutes. If not repeated, the information is lost; however, if repeated, it can be recruited to long-term memory (also referred to as "explicit memory"), and learned. See also "memory (working)."

decoding (memory) — The reverse process of transforming information from one format into another.

deficit theorizing — Theory that deficits in neural networks cause certain problems, such as ADHD, autism, etc.

degenerate condition — Having declined or become less specialized (as in nature, character, structure, or function) from a former state.

degrade — To wear down by erosion or to reduce the complexity.

dementia — A usually progressive condition (e.g., Alzheimer's disease) marked by deteriorated cognitive functioning, often with emotional apathy and volatility.

dendrite — Extensions of the cell body that act as reception surfaces for the neuron. The part of the neuron that receives messages from the axons of other nerve cells; the two types of dendrites are apical dendrites and basilar dendrites.

deoxygenation — A reduction in hemoglobin.

deoxyhemoglobin — The form of hemoglobin without the bound oxygen.

depression — A condition of general emotional dejection and withdrawal; sadness greater and more prolonged than that warranted by any objective reason; involving complex brain mechanisms.

deprivation — Loss; a state of lacking provisions; an act or instance of depriving.

descending pathways — The nerve pathways that go down the spinal cord and allow the brain to control movement of the body below the head.

developmental aphasia — A severe language disorder that is presumed to be due to brain injury rather than to developmental delay in the normal acquisition of language.

developmental assessment — An ongoing process of observing a child's current competencies (including knowledge, skills, dispositions, and attitudes) and using the information to help the child develop further in the context of family/caregiving and learning environments.

developmental neuroscience — Study of the development of the nervous system in the broadest sense, including the brain.

developmental psychology — The study of human development, i.e., of systematic psychological changes that occur in human beings over the course of the lifespan.

diagnosis — The process of determining the existing status and the factors responsible for producing it. In medicine, the diagnosis should take into account etiology, pathology, and severity of the clinical state; in education, the identification of the nature or level of student ability or skill.

diagnostic test — Any kind of test performed to aid in the diagnosis or detection of a problem.

dichotomy — A division into two mutually exclusive or contradictory groups or entities; something with seemingly contradictory qualities.

differentiated instruction — An approach to teaching that includes planning and executing various approaches to content, process, and product; offers several different learning experiences within one lesson to meet students' varied needs, readiness, interestests, or learning styles, as in different teaching methods for students with learning disabilities.

differentiation — Varying instructional approaches to meet students' individual needs.

diffusion tensor imaging (DTI) — A magnetic resonance imaging (MRI) technique that enables the measurement of the restricted diffusion of water in tissue in order to produce neural tract images instead of using this data solely for the purpose of assigning contrast or colors to pixels in a cross-sectional image.

dipole (electric) — A separation of positive and negative charge. A magnetic dipole is a closed circulation of electric current.

direct instruction — An approach to academic subjects that emphasizes the use of carefully sequenced steps that include demonstration, modeling, guided practice, and independent application.

disaggregated data — The presentation of data broken into segments of the student population instead of the entire enrollment. Typical segments include students who are economically disadvantaged, from racial or ethnic minority groups, have disabilities, or have limited English fluency. Disaggregated data allow parents and teachers to see how each student group is performing in a school.

discharge — To release electrical energy.

discipline — An area of academic study.

disinhibition — The loss or reduction of a restraint.

disorder — The disturbance of regular or normal functions.

dispersion — The scattering of the values of a frequency distribution from an average.

dissociation — The process by which a chemical combination breaks up into simpler constituents; especially (1) one that results from the action of energy (as heat) on a gas or of a solvent on a dissolved substance; (2) the separation of whole segments of the personality (as in dissociative identity disorder) or of discrete mental processes (as in the schizophrenias) from the mainstream of consciousness or of behavior.

distance learning — Using technology such as two-way interactive television so that teacher and student(s) in different locations can communicate with one another, as in a regular classroom setting.

divergent thinking — Creative or novel approaches to information. A type of thinking used to rehabilitate certain types of language disorder. For example, a patient with aphasia is required to produce several creative responses to every stimulus; the patient might be asked to think of several unusual ways to make use of an everyday object.

dizygotic (DZ) twins — Commonly known as fraternal twins (also referred to as nonidentical twins or biovular twins); usually occur when two eggs are independently fertilized by two different sperm cells and are implanted in the uterine wall at the same time. The two eggs, or ova, form two zygotes; hence the terms dizygotic and biovular. Dizygotic twins, like any other siblings, have an extremely small chance of having the same chromosome profile.

documentation (education) — The process of keeping track of and preserving children's work as evidence of their progress or of a program's development.

domain — The knowledge, skills, attitudes (competencies), and professional characteristics that can be combined into one cluster and should be learned during post secondary studies.

dopamine — A pleasure-inducing neurotransmitter involved in the inhibitory function of the basal ganglia, it is produced by the substantia nigra.

dorsal position — Anatomical term referring to structures toward the back of the body or top of the brain.

dorsolateral prefrontal cortex — The last area (45th) to develop (myelinate) in the human cerebrum. A more restricted definition of this area describes it as roughly equivalent to Brodmann areas 9 and 46.

dual-code theory — A theory of cognition that was first advanced by Allan Paivio that postulates that visual and verbal forms of information are processed differently and along distinct channels, with the human mind creating separate representations for information processed in each channel. Both visual and verbal codes for representing information are used to organize incoming information into knowledge that can be acted upon, stored, and retrieved for subsequent use.

dualism — The idea that mind and body are separate entities that interact to produce sensations, emotions, and other conscious experiences. Division of human beings—distinguished by Descartes and earlier proposed by Aristotle and Thomas Aquinas—into physical substance and thinking substance. In particular, mind–body dualism claims that neither the mind nor matter can be reduced to each other in any way, and thus is opposed to materialism in general, and reductive materialism in particular.

dura mater — Latin for "*hard mother*," the dura mater is the most superior of the layers of the meninges; this tough, inflexible tissue forms several structures that separate the cranial cavity into compartments and protect the brain from displacement as well as forming several vein-like sinuses that carry blood back to the heart.

dynamic cycles (Fischer) — A means of explaining human cognitive and brain growth correlations in which dynamic systems analysis is combined with human growth cycles in cognitive and brain development to provide a foundation for moving beyond the difficulties of analyzing brain–behavior relations.

dyscalculia — Loss or absence of computational skills; also referred to as acalculia.

dysfunction — Impaired or abnormal behavior.

dysgraphia — A deficiency in the ability to write, regardless of the ability to read, not due to intellectual impairment; also known as agraphia.

dyslexia — A developmental disorder marked by difficulty in reading or in understanding written words; said to be a neurological disorder with biochemical and genetic markers.

dyspraxia (developmental) — One or all of a heterogeneous range of development disorders affecting the initiation, organization, and performance of action. It entails the partial loss of the ability to coordinate and perform certain purposeful movements and gestures, in the absence of other motor or sensory impairments (e.g., cerebral palsy, muscular dystrophy, multiple sclerosis, Parkinson's disease).

early childhood education — Education of a child from the period from birth to 8 years of age.

early (childhood) intervention — A support system for children with developmental disabilities or delays and their families.

early learning standards — Statements that describe expectations for the learning and development of young children across the domains of health and physical well-being; social and emotional well-being; approaches to learning; language development and symbol systems; and general knowledge about the world.

early stimulation — Belief in the value of providing language and other cognitive forms of stimulation, as well as sensory and motor stimulation, to enhance learning through whole-body experiences in very young children.

ecological (validity) — A form of validity in a research study in which the methods, materials, and setting of the study must approximate the real-life situation that is under investigation. Unlike internal and external validity, ecological validity is not necessary to the overall validity of a study.

education — A social science field that encompasses the teaching and learning of specific knowledge, beliefs, and skills. Licensed and practicing teachers in the field use a variety of methods and materials in order to impart a curriculum.

education for the masses — A historical national movement to provide free education for all citizens.

educational neuropsychology — Study of the relationship between brain function, behavior, and psychological processes in educational contexts.

educational neuroscience — A branch of neuroscience dedicated to the study of how humans learn in formal settings.

educational psychology — The study of how humans learn in educational settings, the effectiveness of educational treatments, the psychology of teaching, and the social psychology of schools as organizations. Concerned with the processes of educational attainment among the general population and sub-populations, such as gifted children and those subject to specific disabilities.

EEG (electroencephalography) — The recording of electrical activity along the scalp produced by the firing of neurons within the brain. In clinical contexts, EEG refers to the recording of the brain's spontaneous electrical activity over a short period of time, usually 20–40 minutes, as recorded from multiple electrodes placed on the scalp.

effectiveness — A measure of the extent to which a specific intervention, procedure, regimen, or service, when deployed in the field in routine circumstances, does what it is intended to do for a specified population. In the health field, it is a measure of output from those health services that contributes toward reducing the dimension of a problem or improving an unsatisfactory situation.

efferent pathway — To carry outward, from.

efficacy — The ability to produce the necessary or desired result.

efficiency — An ability to perform well or achieve a result without wasted energy, resources, effort, time, or money. Efficiency can be measured in physical terms (technical efficiency) or terms of cost (economic efficiency). Greater efficiency is achieved when (1) the same amount and standard of services are produced for a lower cost, (2) a more useful activity is substituted for a less useful one at the same cost, or (3) needless activities are eliminated.

effortful/effortless (or controlled) processing — Part of a dual-processing model in cognitive psychology dividing information processing into two systems. One system slowly learns general regularities (effortful), whereas the other can quickly form representations of unique or novel events (effortless).

egocentrism — The tendency to perceive, understand, and interpret the world in terms of the self.

elasticity — The ability of a material to recover its original shape or size once a deforming stress has been removed.

electrical synapse — An electrically conductive link between two neurons that is formed at a narrow gap between the pre- and postsynaptic cells known as a gap junction.

electrode — An electrical conductor used to make contact with a nonmetallic part of a circuit.

electromagnetic field — A physical field produced by electrically charged objects; it affects the behavior of charged objects in the vicinity of the field.

electrophysiology — The study of the electrical properties of biological cells and tissues.

eliminative position (reductionism) — Related to philosophy of mind, the belief that mental states can be reduced to brain states.

emergent property — In the process of coming out.

emotions — Intense feeling. Emotions tend to be labeled in opposing pairs: love–hate; lust–disgust; gratitude–resentment; self-confidence–embarrassment; trust–distrust; empathy–contempt; pride–humiliation; truthfulness–deceit; atonement–guilt; despair–elation.

empathy — The intellectual identification with, or vicarious experiencing of, the feelings, thoughts, or attitudes of another.

emotional intelligence (Goleman) — A focus on a crucial set of human capacities within individuals; the ability to manage one's emotions and inner potential for positive relationships.

emotionally competent stimulus (EMS) — A relevant "hook," used to gain attention in a lecture or presentation, which triggers an emotion.

emotionally valued memories — Memories that are characterized by their affective importance.

encoding — In the study of memory, encoding is the processing of physical sensory input into memory. It is considered the first of three steps in memory information processing; the remaining two steps are storage and retrieval. During memory encoding, information can be processed about space, time, and frequency through either automatic or effortful processing.

endorphins — Endogenous opioid polypeptide compounds produced by the pituitary gland and the hypothalamus in vertebrates during strenuous exercise, excitement, pain, and orgasm; they resemble the opiates in their abilities to produce analgesia and a sense of well-being. Endorphins work as "natural pain relievers," whose effects can be enhanced by other medications.

engagement (education) — The sense of participation and motivation a student feels or does not feel toward learning or the learning environment.

enriched environment — Surroundings that have greater value or significance to people relative to their understanding of "enriched" (i.e., enrichment is relative to the learner).

enrichment — To make rich by the addition or increase of some desirable quality, attribute, or ingredient.

environmental factors — Elements (circumstances, objects, or conditions) by which one is surrounded that actively contribute to the production of a result.

epigenesis (biology) — The unfolding development in an organism; in particular, the development of a plant or animal from an egg or spore through a sequence of steps in which cells differentiate and organs form. Also the theory that plants and animals develop in this way, in contrast to the theory of preformationism, which contends that an organism is fully formed at conception and that reproduction is thereafter simply a process of growth.

epilepsy — A common chronic neurological disorder characterized by recurrent, unprovoked seizures. These seizures are transient signs and/or symptoms of abnormal, excessive, or synchronous neuronal activity in the brain.

episodic buffer — Proposed by Baddeley, the episodic buffer is a function related to working memory that links input across domains to form integrated units of visual, spatial, and verbal information with time sequencing (or chronological ordering), such as the memory of a story or a movie scene. The episodic buffer is also assumed to have links to long-term memory and semantic meaning.

episodic memory — Memories of experienced events. Stored with memories of the context in which the event occurred. Also referred to as "flashbulb memory."

epistemology — The branch of philosophy that deals with the nature, origin, and scope of knowledge. Historically, it has been one of the most investigated and most debated of all philosophical subjects. Much of this debate has focused on analyzing the nature and variety of knowledge and how it relates to similar notions such as truth and belief. Much of this discussion concerns the justification of knowledge claims; that is, the grounds on which one can claim to know a particular fact.

epoch training — A mathematical or computational model that tries to simulate the structure and/or functional aspects of biological neural networks. It consists of an interconnected group of artificial neurons and processes information using a connectionist approach to computation.

equilibrium — The condition of a system in which competing influences are balanced.

equity (education) — The state of educational impartiality and fairness in which all children—minorities and nonminorities, males and females, successful students and those who fall behind, students with special needs and students who have been denied access in the past—receive a high-quality education and have equal access to the services they need in order to benefit from that education.

ERG theory (existence, relatedness, and growth) (psychology) — Clayton Alderfer's needs hierarchy based on Maslow's hierarchy of needs.

ERPs (event-related brain potentials) — Any measured brain response that is directly the result of a thought or perception. More formally, it is any stereotyped electrophysiological response to an internal or external stimulus. ERPs are measured with EEG.

estimation skills (math) — The ability to make an intelligent approximation of a degree of worth.

ethics — The branch of philosophy that deals with distinctions between right and wrong and with the moral consequences of human actions.

eugenics — The study of methods of improving genetic qualities by selective breeding (especially as applied to human mating).

eustress — Stress that is deemed healthful or that gives one the feeling of fulfillment.

evaluation — The measurement, comparison, and judgment of the value, quality, or worth of children's work and/or of their schools, teachers, or a specific educational program based upon valid evidence gathered through assessment.

evoked potential — An electrical potential recorded from the nervous system of a human or other animal following presentation of a stimulus, as distinct from spontaneous potentials detected by EEG or electromyography (EMG).

evolution (biology) — Change in the genetic material of a population of organisms from one generation to the next. The basis of evolution is the genes that are passed on from generation to generation, which produce an organism's inherited traits.

evolutionary psychology — A branch of psychology that attempts to explain psychological traits, memory, perception, and/or language as adaptations, or the functional products of natural selection.

excitatory (vs. inhibitory) quality — Indicates a neuron or synapse that depolarizes its target, increasing the chance that the neuron will fire.

executive functions — The complex cognitive processes (e.g., reasoning and judgment) that are mediated by the most anterior part of the frontal lobe. The ability to organize cognitive processes, including the ability to plan ahead, prioritize, stop and start activities, shift from one activity to another, and to monitor one's own behavior.

experiential learning (hands-on learning/discovery learning) — "Learning by doing." The process of actively engaging students in an authentic experience that will have benefits and consequences in which students make discoveries and experiment with knowledge themselves instead of hearing or reading about the experiences of others. Related to the constructivist learning theory.

explicit learning — Learning that is fully revealed or expressed without vagueness, implication, or ambiguity, leaving no question as to meaning or intent.

explicit memory — The conscious, and intentional recollection of previous experiences and information.

extinction — The gradual weakening and disappearance of conditioned behavior. In operant conditioning, extinction occurs when an emitted behavior is no long followed by a reinforcer.

extracellular position (biology) — "Outside the cell." This space is usually taken to be outside the plasma membranes, and it is occupied by fluid. The term is used in contrast to intracellular (inside the cell).

facial recognition and interpretation — Identification and deciphering of facial expressions.

facilitator — A role for classroom teachers that allows students to take a more active role in learning. Teachers assist students in making connections between classroom instruction and students' own knowledge and experiences by encouraging students to create new solutions, by challenging their assumptions, and by asking probing questions.

fear — A distressing emotion aroused by impending danger, evil, pain, etc., whether the threat is real or imagined; the feeling or condition of being afraid.

feedback (education) — The situation when output from (or information about the result of) an event or phenomenon in the past will influence the same event/phenomenon in the present or future. The transmission of evaluative or corrective information about an action, event, or process to the original or controlling source.

feedforward (neural) network — A feedforward neural network is an artificial neural network where connections between the units do not form a directed cycle. This is different from recurrent neural networks.

fibers — A class of materials composed of continuous filaments or discrete elongated pieces, similar to lengths of thread. They are very important for holding tissues together in the biology of both plants and animals.

Fink's taxonomy — L. Dee Fink's six points for significant learning: foundational learning, application, learning how to learn, integration, caring, and human dimension.

First do no harm — *Primum non nocere* is Latin for "First, do no harm." This is one of the principal precepts of medical ethics and a guiding principle in MBE.

fMRI (functional magnetic resonance imaging) — Imaging technique that tracks the flow of oxygenated blood by virtue of its magnetic properties, which differ from those of nonoxygenated blood. Because oxygenated blood preferentially flows to where it is in high demand, fMRI highlights brain areas that are most active when someone is thinking or doing something.

focal lesion — Any type of lesion of the central nervous system (e.g., stroke, brain tumor, multiple sclerosis) will cause a type of ataxia (incoordination and lack of balance) corresponding to the site of the lesion: cerebellar if in the cerebellum, sensory if in the dorsal spinal cord (and rarely in the thalamus or parietal lobe), vestibular if in the vestibular system (including the vestibular areas of the cerebral cortex).

forebrain — The frontal division of the brain that contains cerebral hemispheres, the thalamus, and the hypothalamus.

formal assessment — A procedure for obtaining information that can be used to make judgments about characteristics of children or programs using standardized instruments. The process of gathering information using standardized, published tests or instruments in conjunction with specific administration and interpretation procedures, and used to make general instructional decisions.

formative assessment — Any form of assessment used by an educator to evaluate students' knowledge and understanding of particular content and then to adjust instructional practices accordingly toward improving student achievement in that area. Formative assessments are designed to evaluate students on a frequent basis so that adjustments can be made in instruction to help them reach target achievement goals.

foundations of educational neuroscience theory (Connell) — A theory to connect neuroscience and education by using computational models to link neural mechanisms to behavioral patterns, and then using these causal neural–behavioral models to inform education.

frontal lobe — The most anterior lobe of the brain; it is bounded posteriorly by the central sulcus and inferiorly by the lateral fissure; this lobe is associated with higher cognitive functions and is involved in the control of voluntary muscle movement.

frontoparietal position — Relating to or characteristic of both frontal and parietal bones.

function — Any of a group of related actions contributing to a larger action.

functionalism — A doctrine or practice that emphasizes practical utility or functional relations. A late-19th to early 20th-century American school of psychology concerned especially with how the mind functions to adapt the individual to the environment. A theory that stresses the interdependence of the patterns and institutions of a society and their interaction in maintaining cultural and social unity.

fusiform face area — A part of the human visual system located in the ventral stream on the ventral surface of the temporal lobe on the fusiform gyrus, which might be specialized for facial recognition.

fusiform gyrus — Part of the temporal lobe.

GABA (gamma-aminobutyric acid) — A glutamate neurotransmitter that is involved in the inhibitory function of the basal ganglia.

gender — The range of differences between men and women, extending from the biological to the social.

gene — The basic unit of heredity in a living organism. Genes hold the information that builds and maintains their cells and passes genetic traits to offspring.

expression (gene) — The process by which information from a gene is used in the synthesis of a functional gene product. These products are often proteins, but in nonprotein coding genes such as rRNA or tRNA genes, the product is a functional RNA.

genetics — The science of heredity and variation in living organisms.

genome — A full set of chromosomes or genes in a gamete, which includes both the genes and the noncoding sequences of the DNA.

genotype — The genetic constitution of a cell, an organism, or an individual (i.e., the specific allele makeup of the individual), usually with reference to a specific character under consideration. It is a generally accepted theory that inherited genotype, transmitted epigenetic factors, and nonhereditary environmental variation contribute to the phenotype of an individual.

genotyping — The process of determining the genotype of an individual by the use of biological assays.

gifted ability (education) — An intellectual ability significantly higher than average. Gifted children develop asynchronously; their minds are often ahead of their physical growth, and specific cognitive and emotional functions often are at different stages of development within a single person. The concept of giftedness has historically been rife with controversy, some even denying that this group exists.

gifted and talented education — A program that offers supplemental, differentiated, challenging curriculum and instruction for students identified as being intellectually gifted or talented.

glial cells — Nonneuronal brain cells that provide structural, nutritional, and other forms of support to the brain. Glial cells are 10 times as common as neurons and make up two-thirds of all brain cells.

glucose — A simple sugar also known as grape sugar, blood sugar, or corn sugar, it is a very important carbohydrate in biology.

glutamate — An excitatory neurotransmitter that plays a critical role in the process of long-term potentiation. About 80% of the signaling in the brain is carried out by two neurotransmitters that balance each other's effect: the major excitatory neurotransmitter glutamate stirs up activity to begin the signaling cascade, and the major inhibitory neurotransmitter GABA clamps down on activity.

goal-setting theory (motivation) — The use of goals to narrow attention, encourage direct effort and persistence, and provide for tangible, measureable results.

good learning environments (Billington; Kaufeldt) — In education, good learning environments are those that provide security (physical and emotional); where there is intellectual freedom, respect, self-guided learning; and where there are paced challenges, active learning, and constant feedback.

graphic organizers — Text, diagram, or other pictorial devices that summarize and illustrate interrelationships among concepts. Graphic organizers are often known as maps, webs, graphs, charts, frames, or clusters.

graphically depicted and modeled mathematic relationships — Using a visual model to depict arithmetic associations.

graphomotor functions (Levine) — Motor skills related to writing; distinct from fine and gross motor skills.

gray matter — Areas of the brain that are dominated by cell bodies and have no myelin (in contrast to white matter).

gyrus/gyri — A ridge on the cerebral cortex, generally surrounded by one or more sulci.

habits of mind — A collection of 16 thinking dispositions designed to help people develop their critical and creative thinking skills developed by Professor Arthur L. Costa: (1) persisting—stick to it; (2) thinking and communicating with clarity and precision; (3) managing impulsivity; (4) gathering data through all senses; (5) listening with understanding and empathy; (6) creating, imagining, innovating; (7) thinking flexibly; (8) responding with wonderment and awe; (9) thinking about your thinking (metacognition); (10) taking responsible risks; (11) striving for accuracy and precision; (12) finding humor; (13) questioning and problem posing; (14) thinking interdependently; (15) applying past knowledge to new situations; and (16) remaining open to continuous learning.

habituation — The most widespread of all forms of learning, thought to be the first learning process to emerge in human infants. Through habituation animals, including human beings, learn to ignore stimuli that have lost novelty or meaning; habituation frees them to attend to stimuli that are rewarding or significant for survival.

hands-on/minds-on activities — Activities that engage students' physical as well as mental skills to solve problems. Students devise a solution strategy, predict outcomes, activate or perform the strategy, reflect on results, and compare end results with predictions.

head cap — Used in tomography scanning to attach electrode sensors to the scalp (looks like a swim cap).

Hebbian synapse theory — Describes a basic mechanism for synaptic plasticity wherein an increase in synaptic efficacy arises from the presynaptic cell's repeated and persistent stimulation of the postsynaptic cell. Introduced by Donald Hebb in 1949, it is also called Hebb's rule, Hebb's postulate, Hebbian synapse, and cell assembly theory; use it or lose it.

hemispatial neglect — A neuropsychological condition in which, after damage to one hemisphere of the brain, a deficit in attention to and awareness of one side of space is observed. Hemispatial neglect is very commonly contralateral to the damaged hemisphere, but instances of ipsilesional neglect (on the same side as the lesion) have been reported. Also called hemiagnosia, hemineglect, unilateral neglect, spatial neglect, or neglect syndrome.

hemisphere — If the brain is split down the middle between the eyes into two halves, each half is called a hemisphere and referred to as either the "right hemisphere" or the "left hemisphere." Each hemisphere is grouped into four different chunks or parts called "lobes." The four lobes are referred to as the frontal (front), temporal (side), parietal (top), and occipital (back). The two hemispheres are linked by the corpus callosum.

hemispherectomy — A surgical procedure where one cerebral hemisphere (half of the brain) is removed or disabled. This procedure is used to treat a variety of seizure disorders where the source of the epilepsy is localized to a broad area of a single hemisphere of the brain.

hemodynamics — A medical term for the dynamic regulation of the blood flow in the brain. It is the principle on which fMRI is based. Neurons, like all other cells, require energy to function. This energy is supplied in the form of glucose and oxygen (the oxygen being carried in hemoglobin). The blood supply of the brain is dynamically regulated to give active neural assemblies more energy while inactive assemblies receive less energy.

hemoglobin — The iron-containing oxygen-transport metalloprotein in the red blood cells. Hemoglobin transports oxygen from the lungs to the rest of the body, where it releases the oxygen for cell use.

heritability (genetics) — The proportion of phenotypic variation in a population that is attributable to genetic variation among individuals. Variation among individuals may be due to genetic and/or environmental factors. Heritability analyses estimate the relative contributions of differences in genetic and nongenetic factors to the total phenotypic variance in a population.

heterogeneous grouping — Grouping together students of varying abilities, interests, or ages.

higher-order questions — Questions that require thinking and reflection rather than single-solution responses.

higher-order thinking skills — Understanding complex concepts and applying sometimes conflicting information to solve a problem, which may have more than one correct answer.

hindbrain — The rear division of the brain, including the cerebellum, pons, and medulla (also called the rhombencephalon).

hippocampus — A cortical area classified as part of the limbic system; a gyrus located on the medial edge of the temporal lobe involved with long-term memory and important for converting short-term memory to more permanent memory.

histology — The study of the microscopic anatomy of cells and tissues of plants and animals performed by examining a thin slice (section) of tissue under a microscope; an essential tool of biology and medicine.

holistic scoring — Using a scoring guide or anchor papers to assign a single overall score to a performance.

homeschooling — A generic term for children schooled at home during the compulsory schooling ages (6–16). To home-school a child the parents/caregivers must satisfy the ministry (Department of Education) that the child will be taught at least as regularly and as well as in a registered school.

homunculus — Latin for *"little man"*; a pedagogical device that is used to explain and demonstrate the functioning of the motor strip of the human cortex.

hormone — A chemical released by one or more cells that affects cells in other parts of the organism. It is essentially a chemical messenger that transports a signal from one cell to another. Hormones in animals are often transported in the blood. Cells respond to a hormone when they express a specific receptor for that hormone. The hormone binds to the receptor protein, resulting in the activation of a signal transduction mechanism that ultimately leads to cell-type-specific responses.

hypothalamus — Part of the diencephalon, ventral to the thalamus. The structure is involved in functions including homeostasis, emotion, thirst, hunger, circadian rhythms, and control of the autonomic nervous system. In addition, it controls the pituitary, a subcortical structure located immediately below the thalamus; by controlling the functioning of the pituitary gland, it regulates basic biological functions (e.g., appetite, body temperature, sex drive).

iconic store — Human beings store a perfect image of the visual world for a brief moment, before it is discarded from memory.

image (mental) — Something one remembers or imagines. The subject of an image need not be real; it may be an abstract concept, such as a graph, function, or imaginary entity.

imagery — A collection of images that can have auditory, affective, metal, motor, as well as visual components.

imaging (neuro-) — See "neuroimaging."

imitation (psychology) — In psychology, cognitive imitation is a type of social learning. Like the imitation of motor rules (i.e., motor imitation), cognitive imitation involves learning and copying specific rules by observation. The principal difference between motor and cognitive imitation is the type of rule (and stimulus) that is learned and copied by the observer. Whereas in the typical imitation learning experiment subjects must copy novel actions on objects or novel sequences of specific actions (novel motor imitation), in a novel cognitive imitation paradigm subjects have to copy novel rules, independently of specific actions or movement patterns.

self-efficacy (and learning) — The impact on learning of the belief that one is capable of performing in a certain manner to attain certain goals.

impairment — Disability.

implicit memory — See "memory (implicit)."

impoverished condition — Lacking in provision of basic human needs such as nutrition, clean water, health care, clothing, and shelter because of the inability to afford them.

impoverished environment — Poor or reduced surroundings.

impulsivity — A type of human behavior characterized by the inclination of an individual to act on impulse rather than conscious thought.

inclusion — The practice of placing students with disabilities in regular classrooms; also known as mainstreaming.

independent value (math) — Not depending upon another for its value.

independent quality (social) — Not influenced or controlled by others in matters of opinion or conduct.

indicator — Various statistical values, data, or other reported information that, when aggregated, provide an indication of the condition or direction of movement relative to a standard or issue under study. A variable that helps to measure changes directly or indirectly and permits one to assess the extent to which objectives and targets of a goal are being attained.

individual differences — The ways individuals differ in their behavior (including learning).

individual education program (IEP) — A written plan created for a student with learning disabilities by the student's teachers, parents or guardians, the school administrator, and other interested parties. The plan is tailored to the student's specific needs and abilities, and outlines goals for the student to reach.

individualized education — A method of instruction in which content, instructional materials and media, and pace of learning are based upon the abilities and interests of each individual learner.

inferior location (anatomy) — Refers to the lower parts of the nervous system.

inferotemporal position — Situated or occurring in, on, or under the temporal lobe of the cerebral cortex.

informal assessment — A procedure for obtaining information that can be used to make judgments about characteristics of children or programs using means other than standardized instruments. The process of collecting information to make specific instructional decisions, using procedures largely designed by teachers and based on the current instructional situation.

informal knowledge — Knowledge about a topic that children learn through experience outside of the classroom.

inherit — To get from one's ancestors either through legal succession (e.g., "inherit the throne") or from genetic transmission (e.g., "inherited color-blindness from his father").

inhibition (physiology) — The process by which some nerve cells use their presynaptic terminals to stop the receiving cells from relaying information. An inhibitory neuron or inhibitory synapse is one that hyperpolarizes its target, decreasing the chance that the neuron will fire an action potential. Also referred to as suppression.

inhibitory neurotransmitter — A neurotransmitter released from the presynaptic neuron whose work increases the resting membrane potential (a value) of the postsynaptic neuron, making it much more difficult for the neuron to fire (i.e., inhibiting it).

innateness — Intrinsic; denoting a property of some thing or action that is essential and specific to that thing or action, and which is wholly independent of any other object, action, or consequence. A characteristic that is not essential or inherent is extrinsic.

inner voice (Vygotsky) — Thinking in words.

inquiry — A process in which students investigate a problem, devise and work through a plan to solve the problem, and propose a solution to the problem.

inquiry education — A student-centered method of education focused on asking questions. Students are encouraged to ask questions that are meaningful to them and that do not necessarily have easy answers; teachers are encouraged to avoid speaking at all when this is possible, and in any case to avoid giving answers in favor of asking more questions. Sometimes known as the inquiry method or Socratic questioning.

instinct — Any response that is natural (i.e., inborn and unlearned) and a characteristic of a given species.

instructional design — The analysis of learning needs and systematic development of instruction. Instructional designers often use instructional technology as a method for developing instruction. Instructional design models typically specify a method that, if followed, will facilitate the transfer of knowledge, skills, and attitudes to the recipient of the instruction. Also known as instructional systems design.

insular cortex — A cerebral cortex structure deep within the lateral sulcus between the temporal lobe and the parietal lobe. The insular is divided into two parts: the larger anterior insula and the smaller posterior insula, in which more than a dozen field areas have been identified. The insula plays a role in diverse functions usually linked to emotion or the regulation of the body's homeostasis, perception, motor control, self-awareness, cognitive functioning, and interpersonal experience.

insult (medicine) — An injury or trauma.

integrated curriculum — Refers to the practice of using a single theme to teach a variety of subjects. It also refers to an interdisciplinary curriculum that combines several school subjects into one project.

integrated learning — A learning theory describing a movement toward making lessons that help students form connections across curricula.

integrated teaching — A method of teaching that interrelates or unifies subjects frequently taught in separate academic courses or departments. In integrated teaching, subjects are presented together as a meaningful whole. Integration can be horizontal or vertical. Horizontal integration functions between parallel disciplines such as anatomy, histology, and biochemistry or medicine, surgery, and pharmacology. Vertical integration functions between disciplines traditionally taught in different phases of curriculum; it can occur throughout the curriculum with medical and basic sciences beginning together in the early years.

integrative neuroscience — Brings together biological, psychological, and clinical models of the human brain within neuroscience and focuses on the brain as an adaptive system. It is concerned with how all the components of the brain are coordinated, and aims for a unified understanding of brain function across timescales.

intellectual freedom — A human right defined as the freedom of opinion and expression; this right includes freedom to hold opinions without interference and to seek, receive, and impart information and ideas through any media and regardless of frontiers.

intelligence(s) — The mental capacity to reason, plan, solve problems, think abstractly, comprehend ideas and language, and learn. Although nonscientists generally regard the concept of intelligence as having much broader scope, in psychology, the study of intelligence generally regards this trait as distinct from creativity, personality, character, or wisdom.

interconnections — Links between different areas.

intercortical connections — Links within the cerebral cortex.

interdependence — Relying one upon the other.

interdisciplinary — Combining or involving two or more academic disciplines or fields of study.

interdisciplinary curriculum — A curriculum that consciously applies the methodology and language from more than one discipline to examine a central theme, issue, problem, topic, or experience.

interference (psychology) — The distorting or inhibiting effect of previously learned behavior on subsequent learning; the forgetting of information or an event due to inability to reconcile it with conflicting information obtained subsequently.

interference theory — The theory that forgetting is caused by one memory competing with or replacing another, which offers an explanation for why we forget. According to the theory there are three kinds of interference: proactive, retroactive, and output interference.

internalization — To incorporate the cultural values, mores, motives, etc., of another or of a group, as through learning, socialization, or identification.

intervention (education) — Funds that schools get for students who are not learning at grade level. They can be used to fund before-school or after-school programs or to pay for materials and instructors.

invariant representations (psychology) — The brain's internal pattern for representations. Learning sequences are the most basic ingredients for forming invariant representations of real-world objects. Objects can be "concrete" or "abstract"; they are treated the same way by the brain (as sequences of patterns that occur over time, in a predictable fashion).

ions (channel) — Pore-forming proteins that help establish and control the small voltage gradient across the plasma membrane of all living cells by allowing the flow of ions down their electrochemical gradient. Present in the membranes that surround all biological cells.

IPS (intraparietal sulcus) — Located on the lateral surface of the parietal lobe and consists of an oblique and a horizontal portion. Its principal functions are related to perceptual–motor coordination (for directing eye movements and reaching) and visual attention and may also be related to processing symbolic numerical information, visuospatial working memory, and interpreting the intent of others.

isomorphic relationship — A kind of mapping between objects, which shows a relationship between two properties or operations. If there exists an isomorphism between two structures, the two structures are isomorphic.

isotope (PET) — Any of the different types of atoms of the same chemical element, each having a different atomic mass (mass number). Isotopes of an element have nuclei with the same number of protons (the same atomic number) but different numbers of neutrons.

kinesthesia — Feedback from muscle spindles related to feeling.

knowledge (education) — The acquisition or awareness of facts, data, information, ideas, or principles to which one has access through formal or individual study, research, observation, experience or intuition. Information of which someone is aware. Knowledge is also used to mean the confident understanding of a subject, with the potential to use it for a specific purpose.

latency — Present but not visible, apparent, or actualized; existing as potential.

latent learning — Learning that occurs in the absence of reinforcement but is not behaviorally demonstrated until a reinforcer becomes available.

lateral position (anatomy) — Literally, toward the sides.

lateralization — Functional specialization of the brain, with some skills being more associated with one hemisphere than another. Researchers often criticize popular psychology books for misrepresenting lateralizations; often the functions are distributed across both hemispheres, although mental processing is divided between them.

layer (cortical) — The human cortex is a roughly 2.4 mm thick sheet of neuronal cell bodies that forms the external surface of the telencephalon. The human cerebral cortex is composed of six layers, each layer identified by the nerve cell type and the destination of these nerve cells' axons (within the brain).

layered curriculum design — Three layers of curriculum design that consider basic knowledge, application, and critical thinking skills; developed by Kathie Nunley.

learner-centered education — Classroom in which students are encouraged to choose their own learning goals and projects. This approach is based on the belief that students have a natural inclination to learn, learn better when they work on real or authentic tasks, benefit from interacting with diverse groups of people, and learn best when teachers understand and value the difference in how each student learns. Learners are responsible for identifying knowledge gaps, actively participating in filling them, and keeping track of their learning gains.

learning — Learning can be said to take place in the mind, in a psychological sense, and in the brain, in a neurological sense. Learning is instantiated in the brain and is prompted by internal thought processes, sensory input, motor training, or simulated perceptual input in the mind, resulting in a physiological and measurable change in the neural networks, as well as changes in the muscles and other parts of the body. Human learning is complex and is intricately related to emotions, cognition, action, volition, and perception. Learning is always accompanied by brain changes, which underlie learning itself, as well as changes in behavior, including thought and feeling. Human learning can be achieved through active and constructive processes such as those that occur in formal school contexts. Much learning can be observed neurologically before being expressed in behavior, as in implicit learning, which results in subtle changes in behavior and is usually noticeable only when new learning is "scaffolded" upon it, as is much of the early childhood learning.

learning environment — The surroundings in which successful teaching experiences take place.

learning by teaching — Designates a method that allows pupils and students to prepare and teach lessons or parts of lessons, or in which peers teach one another. Learning by teaching should not be confused with presentations or lectures by students; in teaching their classmates a certain area of the respective subject, students do not only convey a certain content, but choose their own methodological and didactical approach.

learning disability — Used to refer to sociobiological conditions that affect a person's communicative capacities and potential to learn. The term includes conditions such as perceptual disability, brain injury, minimal brain dysfunction, autism, dyslexia, and developmental aphasia; in general terms, a developmental disability.

learning styles — Approaches to learning, problem solving, and processing information.

lesion — Any abnormal tissue found on or in an organism, usually damaged by disease or trauma.

"less is more concept" (education) — A principle built on the idea that quality is more important than quantity. It is reflected in instruction that guides students to focus on fewer topics investigated in greater depth, with teachers performing the task of prioritizing subjects as well as specific skills within those subjects.

levels-of-processing effect — Describes memory recall of stimuli as a function of the depth of mental processing. The mental processing depth of a stimulus is determined by connections with preexisting memory, time spent processing the stimulus, cognitive effort, and sensory input mode. Depth of processing falls on a shallow to deep continuum. Shallow processing leads to a fragile memory trace that is susceptible to rapid decay. Conversely, deep processing results in a more durable memory trace.

lexical retrieval — Ability to search for and successfully find the correct word choice.

lifelong learning — Continuous training over the course of a professional career. The concept that "It's never too soon or too late for learning," a philosophy that has taken root in a whole host of different organizations, providing learning opportunities at all ages and in numerous contexts: at work, at home, and through leisure activities, not just through formal channels such as school and higher education.

lifespan development — Development over the average or maximum length of time an organism, material, or object can be expected to survive or last.

limbic system — The most ancient and primitive part of the brain composed of both cortical and subcortical structures located on the medial, inferior surfaces of the cerebral hemispheres. The limbic system is involved in the processing of olfactory stimuli, emotions, motivation, and memory, and may be involved in cortical speech and language behavior.

lobes (frontal, temporal, occipital, parietal) — The four main areas of the cerebral cortex.

localist — A range of philosophies or epistemologies that prioritize the local (or a single disciplinary) vision.

localization — A fading idea, being replaced by neuroplasticity, that the pathways in which experience gets into our minds are hardwired in very specific brain locations.

long-term habituation — Stage of habituation in which the number of presynaptic connections among sensory neurons and motor neurons decreases.

long-term memory — See "memory (long-term)."

long-term potentiation (LTP) — A chemical process that occurs at the neuronal level and that strengthens the connections between neurons (supporting the concept that "neurons that fire together, wire together"). A long-lasting increase in synaptic strength between two neurons.

macaques — A genus of Old World monkeys. Aside from humans, the macaques are the most widespread primate genus, ranging from northern Africa to Japan. In medical testing, most nonhuman primates used are macaques.

magnet — A force that pulls on other ferromagnetic materials and attracts or repels other magnets. A material or object that produces a magnetic field, which is invisible but is responsible for the most notable property of a magnet. Several imaging techniques use magnets, including the fMRI.

magnocellular theory (dyslexia) — Globally unifying theory about the origins of dyslexia in which the magnocellular dysfunction is not restricted to the visual pathways but is generalized to all modalities (visual and auditory as well as tactile).

manipulatives (education) — Three-dimensional teaching aids and visuals that teachers use to help students with math concepts. Any physical object (e.g., blocks, toothpicks, coins) that can be used to represent or model a problem situation or develop a mathematical concept. Typical tools include counting beads or bars, base 10 blocks, shapes, fraction parts, and rulers.

mapping (brain) — A set of neuroscience techniques predicated on the mapping of (biological) quantities or properties onto spatial representations of the human or nonhuman brain.

Maslow's hierarchy of needs — Motivational theory developed by Abraham Maslow in 1943, which considers five levels: physiological, safety, association, esteem, and self-actualization.

mathematical cognition — The psychology of numeracy.

mathematical theories — An analytical structure designed to explain a set of empirical observations. Roughly 70 mathematical theories exist in 2010.

matrix sampling — An assessment method in which no student completes the entire assessment but each completes a portion of it. Portions are allotted to representative samples of students. Group (rather than individual) scores are obtained for an analysis of school or district performance.

maturation — Pertaining to or characteristic of full development.

mechanism (psychology) — The habitual operation and interaction of psychological forces within an individual that assist in interpreting or dealing with the physical or psychological environment.

medial — Literally, toward the center.

medicine — The art and the science of healing. A branch of health care study that researches the preservation of the body and the treatment of illness.

medulla — Refers to the middle of something. In medicine it refers to either bone marrow, the spinal cord, or more generally, the middle part of a structure (as opposed to the cortex).

MEG (magnetocephalography) — Neuroimaging technique that relies on the principle that if you touch different body parts, the localized electrical activity that results can be measured as changes in magnetic fields on the scalp. The major advantage of the technique is that it is noninvasive; one does not have to open the patient's scalp to peer inside the brain. Used to measure the magnetic fields produced by electrical activity in the brain.

memory (cognitive neuropsychology) — The ability to acquire and store information. A set of distinct psychological processes that operates with different representations and physiological mechanisms to retain information over time. Memories are stored not in the cells themselves, but in the overall pattern of electrical signals firing between cells. The memory of something and the perception of the same something share the same network. When changes in the network become lasting, the information becomes firmly established in long-term storage. The links between individual neurons, which bind them into a single memory, are formed through a process called LTP (long-term potentiation). Memory is a persistent representation for a sequence of patterns.

memory (associative) — The brain's ability to store, retain, and recall information by relating it to other like memories.

memory (declarative) — The aspect of human memory that stores facts.

memory (emotional) — The brain's ability to store, retain, and recall information by relating it to emotions.

memory (episodic) — The memory of autobiographical events (times, places, associated emotions, and other contextual knowledge) that can be explicitly stated.

memory (implicit) — A type of memory in which previous experiences aid in the performance of a task without conscious awareness of these previous experiences. Evidence for implicit memory arises in priming, a process whereby subjects show improved performance on tasks for which they have been subconsciously prepared.

memory (long-term) — A set of processes that retains information over days, months, and years. Long-term memories include both implicit, sensory–motor skills and declarative memories for autobiographical details and facts. Long-term memory is not simply an extension of short-term memory; not only do the changes in synaptic strength last longer but the actual number of synapses in the "circuit" changes. Long-term memories are processed in part in the hippocampus.

memory (procedural) — Unconscious memory for skills (e.g., riding a bike, playing tennis, knotting a tie). Procedural memory underlies habituation, sensitization, and classical conditioning, as well as perceptual and motor skills. Sometimes referred to as implicit memory.

memory (rote) — A learning technique that emphasizes memorization rather than understanding of a subject. The major practice involved in rote learning is learning by repetition; the idea is that one will be able to quickly recall the meaning of the material the more one repeats it.

memory (semantic) — Refers to the memory of meanings, understandings, and other concept-based knowledge unrelated to specific experiences. The conscious recollection of factual information and general knowledge about the world, generally thought to be independent of context and personal relevance. Semantic and episodic memory together make up the category of declarative memory, which is one of the two major divisions in memory.

memory (short-term) — A catch-all term for the capacity to hold a small amount of information in mind in an active, readily available state for a short period of time. A commonly cited capacity is 7 ± 2 elements. Also referred to as immediate, working, primary, or active memory.

memory (spatial) — The part of memory responsible for recording information about one's environment and its spatial orientation.

memory (survival) — Memories on which one's personal survival is dependent.

memory (working) — A form of short-term memory that does not last. For example, remembering a formula just long enough to use it on a test. Characterized by a small storage capacity, semantic representation, and short duration.

memory consolidation (and learning) — A category of processes that stabilizes a memory trace after the initial acquisition.

mental models — An explanation of someone's thought process for how something works in the real world. It is a representation of the surrounding world, the relationships between its various parts, and a person's intuitive perception about his or her own acts and their consequences. Our mental models help shape our behavior and define our approach to solving problems and carrying out tasks. (Also see "mental schema.")

mental number line (math) — Mental system for representing and ordering numbers related to the angular gyrus area of the brain.

mental schema — Structures we use to order the world around us; a structured cluster of preconceived ideas; an organized pattern of thought or behavior.

mentoring — A developmental relationship between a more experienced person and a less experienced partner, referred to as a mentee or protégé.

mesolimbic dopaminergic reward system — The pathway that begins in the ventral tegmental area of the midbrain and connects to the limbic system via the nucleus accumbens, the amygdala, and the hippocampus; it also connects to the medial prefrontal cortex known to be involved in modulating behavioral responses to stimuli that activate feelings of reward (motivation) and reinforcement through the neurotransmitter dopamine.

metabolism — The set of chemical reactions that occurs in living organisms to maintain life. These processes allow organisms to grow and reproduce, maintain their structures, and respond to their environments. Metabolism is usually divided into two categories: catabolism breaks down organic matter and anabolism uses energy to construct components of cells such as proteins and nucleic acids.

metacognition — The process of considering and regulating one's own learning and thinking processes. Activities include assessing or reviewing one's current and previous knowledge, identifying gaps in that knowledge, planning gap-filling strategies, determining the relevance of new information, and potentially revising beliefs on the subject.

metaphor — A figure of speech concisely expressed by an implied analogy between two objects or ideas, conveyed by the use of one word instead of another word.

methodology — The study and knowledge of methods as well as the study of techniques for problem-solving and seeking answers, as opposed to the techniques themselves.

microbiology — The study of microorganisms, which are unicellular or cell-cluster microscopic organisms.

midbrain — The most superior part of the brainstem (mesencephalon).

midline (brain) — Normally related to suprachiasmatic nucleus or nuclei (SCN).

midwifing (education) — Practices that nurture the development and "birth" of ideas or students' thinking processes.

migration (cell) — A central process in the development and maintenance of multicellular organisms. Tissue formation during embryonic development, wound healing, and immune responses all require the orchestrated movement of cells in particular directions to specific locations. Errors during this process have serious consequences, including mental retardation. Cells often migrate in response to, and toward, specific external signals, a process called chemotaxis.

milestone (developmental) — Milestones are changes in specific physical and mental abilities (e.g., walking and understanding language) that mark the end of one developmental period and the beginning of another. For stage theories, milestones indicate a stage transition. Studies of the accomplishment of many developmental tasks have established typical chronological ages associated with developmental milestones. However, there is considerable variation in the achievement of milestones, even between children with developmental trajectories within the normal range. Some milestones are more variable than others; for example, receptive speech indicators do not show much variation among children with normal hearing, but expressive speech milestones can be quite variable.

millimeter — A unit of length equal to one-thousandth of a meter and equivalent to 0.03937 inch.

millisecond — One-thousandth of a second.

mind–body connection — A general model or approach that posits that biological, psychological (thoughts, emotions, and behaviors), and social factors all play a significant role in human functioning in the context of illness or in learning. Also known as the biopsychosocial model.

mindful learning — Mindfulness is calm awareness of one's body functions, feelings, content of consciousness, or consciousness itself.

mind mapping (teaching activity) — A diagram used to represent words, ideas, tasks, or other items linked to and arranged around a central key word or idea. Mind maps are used to generate, visualize, structure, and classify ideas, and as an aid in study, organization, problem solving, decision-making, and writing.

mirror neurons — Neurons that represent actions performed both by oneself and by others. First described by Giacomo Rizzolatti and his research team in 1994 and found in the premotor cortex, parietal cortex, insula, cingulate and the secondary touch cortex of monkey brains, mirror neurons are thought to be the key to many higher mental functions including imitation, empathy, and the ability to "read" others' intentions. Currently the prime suspect in the hunt for the roots of autism. Some argue that the evolution of mirror neurons was important in the human acquisition of complex skills such as language and that their discovery is a most important advance in neuroscience.

mnemonic devices — Learning aids that rely on associations between easy-to-remember constructs that can be related back to the data to be remembered. Commonly, mnemonics are verbal—such as a very short poem or a special word used to help a person remember something—but can be visual, kinesthetic, or auditory.

modality (cognitive neuroscience) — Any of the qualitatively distinct types of sensation, such as sight, hearing, smelling, taste, or touch.

modeling — Demonstrating to the learner how to do a task, with the expectation that the learner can copy the model. Modeling often involves thinking aloud or talking about how to work through a task.

models — Patterns, plans, representations (especially in miniature), or descriptions designed to show the main object or workings of an object, system, or concept.

modularity — A general systems concept, typically defined as a continuum describing the degree to which a system's components can be separated and recombined.

molecular genetics — The field of biology that studies the structure and function of genes at a molecular level and how genes are transferred from generation to generation.

molecular systems — Refers to theoretical methods and computational techniques that model or mimic the behavior of molecules.

monozygotic (twins) — Frequently referred to as identical twins; occur when a single egg is fertilized to form one zygote (monozygotic), which then divides into two separate embryos. Monozygotic twins are almost always the same sex and their traits and physical appearances are very similar, but not exactly the same, although they have nearly identical DNA.

morphology (biology) — The study of the form or shape of an organism or part thereof.

morphology (linguistics) — The study of the structure and content of word forms.

morphometry — A field concerned with studying variation and change in the form (size and shape) of organisms or objects.

motivation (psychology) — The internal condition that activates behavior and gives it direction; energizes and directs goal-oriented behavior. According to various theories, motivation may be rooted in the basic need to minimize physical pain and maximize pleasure; or it may include specific needs such as eating and resting, or a desired object, hobby, goal, state of being, or ideal; or it may be attributed to less-apparent sources such as altruism or morality.

motor cortex — In the frontal lobe of the cerebral cortex, a region that sends impulses to motor neurons and is involved in coordination of movement.

Mozart effect — Highly controversial set of research results that indicate that listening to Mozart's music may induce a short-term improvement in the performance of certain kinds of mental tasks involving spatial–temporal reasoning.

MRI (magnetic resonance imaging) — Noninvasive neuroimaging technique that uses magnetic energy to generate images that reveal some of the structural details in the living brain and throughout the body.

multidisciplinary approach — Composed of or combining several usually separate branches of learning or fields of expertise.

musical affect — Feelings aroused by exposure to music.

myelin (sheath) — A fatty insulating substance that covers, at regular intervals, many of the axons in the central and peripheral nervous system. Myelin serves to increase the speed of transmission of impulses.

myelinization — The formation of the myelin sheath around a nerve fiber.

nativist philosophy — The doctrine that the mind produces ideas that are not derived from external sources.

nature versus nurture — The debate that concerns the relative importance of an individual's innate versus personal experiences. This question was once considered to be an appropriate division of developmental influences, but since both types of factors are known to play such interacting roles in development, many modern psychologists consider the question obsolete, representing an outdated state of knowledge.

near infrared (NIR) device — Devices to detect infrared radiation variances (not temperature).

negative transfer (language) — When the relevant unit or structure of two different languages is the same, linguistic interference can result in correct language production, called positive transfer. Negative transfer occurs when speakers and writers transfer items and structures that are not the same in both languages.

negativity effect (psychology) — The tendency of people, when evaluating the causes of the behaviors of a person they dislike, to attribute positive behaviors to the situations surrounding the behaviors and negative behaviors to the inherent disposition of that person. The negativity effect is the inverse of the positivity effect, which is found when people evaluate the causes of the behaviors of a person they like. The negativity effect plays a role in producing the fundamental attribution error, a major contributor to prejudice.

neocortex — In evolutionary terms, the recently evolved six-layered portions of the cerebral cortex (found in mammals), sometimes referred to as the isocortex, the neocortex comprises the bulk of the cerebral hemispheres.

nervous system — A network of specialized cells that communicate information about an organism's surroundings and itself. The interaction of the different neurons form neural circuits that regulate an organism's perception of the world and what is going on with its body, thus regulating its behavior. It processes this information and causes reactions in other parts of the body. It is composed of neurons and glial cells that aid in the function of the neurons. The nervous system is divided broadly into two categories: the peripheral nervous system and the central nervous system. Neurons generate and conduct impulses between and within the two systems. The neurons of the nervous systems of animals are interconnected in complex arrangements and use electrochemical signals and neurotransmitters to transmit impulses from one neuron to the next.

neural connectivity — Links between neurons that are measured from length of dendritic "trees" of cortical neurons.

neural network pathway — A neural tract connecting one part of the nervous system with another, usually consisting of bundles of elongated, myelin-insulated neurons, known collectively as white matter. Neural pathways serve to connect relatively distant areas of the brain or nervous system, compared to the local communication of gray matter.

neuroanatomy — A branch of neuroscience that deals with the study of the gross structure of the brain and the nervous system.

neuroarchitecture — Brain structure.

neurobiology — Forerunner to neuroscience, when the study of the brain was considered to be solely a biological science.

neurochemistry — The study of neurochemicals, which includes neurotransmitters and other molecules (e.g., neuroactive drugs) that influence neuron function. Closely examines the manner in which these neurochemicals influence the network of neural operation. This evolving area of neuroscience offers a neurochemist a micro–macro connection between the analysis of organic compounds active in the nervous system and neural processes such as cortical plasticity, neurogenesis, and neural differentiation.

neurocognitive model (Atherton) — An educational design suggested by Michael Atherton, based on a model of cognition using a metaphor of neural activation and supported by findings in the neurosciences.

neurodevelopmental constructs (Levine) — A theory of intelligence assessment developed by Mel Levine that focuses of eight mental systems: attention, temporal sequential ordering, spatial ordering, memory, language, neuromotor functions, social cognition, and higher-order cognition.

neuro-educator — A term coined first by O'Dell in 1981 and later used by Gardner to describe a new type of teacher who would be knowledgeable about how the brain works.

neuroethics — Most commonly understood to be a subcategory of bioethics concerned with neuroscience and neurotechnology.

neurogenesis — The process by which neurons divide and propagate; the brain's manufacture of new neurons, which continues into old age, though at a slower rate than in earlier decades.

neuroimaging — Includes the use of various techniques that allow scientists to see the living brain at work, either directly or indirectly creating different types of images of the structure, function, and pharmacology of the brain. Types of imaging include positron emission tomography (PET), magnetic resonance imaging (MRI), functional magnetic resonance imaging (fMRI), computed axial tomography (CAT), diffuse optical imaging, single positron emission computer tomography (SPECT), and optical tomography (OT).

neurology — A medical specialty dealing with disorders of the nervous system. Specifically, it deals with the diagnosis and treatment of all categories of disease involving the central, peripheral, and autonomic nervous systems. A neurologist is a physician (not a surgeon) who specializes in neurology and is trained to investigate, or diagnose and treat, neurological disorders.

neuromapping — A term used to describe the location of certain skills, neural pathways, or systems of the brain.

neuromarketing — A new field of marketing that studies consumers' sensorimotor, cognitive, and affective responses to marketing stimuli.

neuromyth — Misconception, misunderstanding, or misuse of information about the brain, which leads to false conclusions.

neuronal recycling — A hypothesis proposed by Stanislas Dehaene that suggests that the human capacity for cultural learning relies on a process of preempting or recycling preexisting brain circuitry.

neurons — Nerve cells located in the brain, which are composed of a nucleus, an axon, and dendrites. At birth, the typical brain contains over 100 billion neurons, whose number slowly diminishes with age. Each neuron makes anywhere from 1,000 to 10,000 synapses (connections) with other neurons. The basic building blocks of the brain, these cells receive input from other nerve cells and distribute information to other neurons; the information integration underlies the simplest and most complex of our thoughts and behaviors.

neuropathology — The study of disease of nervous system tissue, usually in the form of either small surgical biopsies or whole autopsy brains. Neuropathology is a sub-specialty of anatomical pathology.

neurophysiology — Part of physiology; the study of nervous system function.

neuroplasticity — The changing of neurons and the organization of their networks, and thus their function, via experience. This idea was first proposed in 1892 by Santiago Ramón y Cajal. Plasticity relates to learning by adding or removing connections or adding cells. The brain consists of nerve cells or neurons (and glial cells) that are interconnected; learning may occur through changes in the strength of the connections between neurons, by adding or removing connections, or by adding new cells.

neuropsychiatry — The branch of medicine dealing with mental disorders attributable to diseases of the nervous system.

neuropsychology — The scientific discipline that studies the structure and function of the brain related to specific psychological processes and overt behaviors. Alexander Luria integrated aspects of the psychoanalytic method and of psychology into neurology, becoming the founder of neuropsychology. The science that examines alterations in mental processes produced by brain damage.

neuroreceptors (biochemistry) — A receptor is a protein molecule, embedded in either the plasma membrane or cytoplasm of a cell, to which a mobile signaling molecule may attach. A molecule that binds to a receptor is called a ligand and may be a peptide (e.g., a neurotransmitter), a hormone, a pharmaceutical drug, or a toxin. When such binding occurs, the receptor undergoes a change that ordinarily initiates a cellular response.

neuroscience — The scientific discipline that studies the structure, function, development, genetics, biochemistry, physiology, pharmacology, and pathology of the nervous system. Traditionally it is seen as a branch of the biological sciences. However, recently there has been a convergence of interest from many allied disciplines, including psychology, computer science, statistics, physics, philosophy, mathematics, and medicine. The scope of neuroscience has now broadened to include any systematic scientific experimental and theoretical investigation of the central and peripheral nervous system of biological organisms. Furthermore, neuroscience is at the frontier of investigation of the brain and mind. The study of the brain is becoming the cornerstone in understanding how we perceive and interact with the external world and, in particular, how human experience and human biology influence each other.

neurotoxins — A toxin that acts specifically on nerve cells (neurons), usually by interacting with membrane proteins such as ion channels.

neurotransmitter — A brain chemical (molecule) that facilitates the communication between cells by binding to a receptor on the receiving (postsynaptic) neuron surface and activating a chemical (the second messenger) inside the cell. (Also referred to as a chemical transmitter.)

neurotrophic proteins — A family of proteins that induces the survival, development, and function of neurons.

NIH (National Institutes of Health, Bethesda, MD) — An agency of the United States Department of Health and Human Services primarily responsible for biomedical and health-related research.

NIRS (near infrared spectroscopy) — A spectroscopic method that uses the near infrared region of the electromagnetic spectrum. Typical applications include pharmaceutical, medical diagnostics, food and agrochemical quality control, as well as combustion research.

noise (language) — Unwanted sound; "noise pollution."

noninvasive medicine — A medical procedure in which there is no contact with the mucosa, or skin break, or internal body cavity beyond a natural or artificial body orifice. Also related to an abnormal tissue growth that doesn't spread (invade) to the surrounding healthy tissue.

nonlinear system — Any sytem wherein the variable(s) to be solved for cannot be written as a linear combination of independent components.

nonparametric statistics — Distribution free methods that do not rely on assumptions that the data are drawn from a given probability distribution.

norepinephrine — The first neurotransmitter scientists studied to try to understand mood. Norepinephrine often amplifies signals that influence attention, perception, motivation, and arousal.

normalization — Any process that makes something more normal, which typically means conforming to some regularity or rule, or returning from some state of abnormality.

norm-referenced assessment — Designed to discover how an individual student's performance or test result compares to that of an appropriate peer group. Also known as a standardized testing instrument by which the test-taker's performance is interpreted in relation to the performance of a group of peers who have previously taken the same test.

novelty — Newness.

nucleus accumbens — A collection of neurons within the striatum thought to play an important role in reward, laughter, pleasure, addiction, fear, and the placebo effect.

nucleus basalis — The gray matter of the substantia innominata (Latin for "unnamed substance") of the forebrain that consists mostly of cholinergic neurons and is related to focused attention.

numeracy — A contraction of "numerical literacy," also known as "quantitative literacy."

nutrition — The provision, to cells and organisms, of the materials necessary (in the form of food) to support life.

observational assessment — A process in which the teacher systematically observes and records information about students' level of development and/or knowledge, skills, and attitudes in order to (1) make a determination about what has been learned, (2) improve teaching, and (3) support students' progress. A checklist or notes are often used to record what has been observed.

observational learning — Learning that takes place through observing the actions of others.

occipital lobe — The most posterior lobe of the brain, associated with vision; also referred to as the visual cortex.

occipital position — Of, pertaining to, or situated near the occiput or the occipital bone.

occipitotemporal — Of, relating to, or distributed throughout the occipital and temporal lobes of a cerebral hemisphere.

olfactory — Sense of smell.

ontogeny — Describes the origin and development of an organism from the fertilized egg to its mature form.

open-ended question — A question that has many avenues of access and allows students to respond in a variety of ways. Such questions have more than one correct answer.

open-ended task — A performance task in which students are required to generate a solution or response to a problem when there is no single correct answer.

open-response task — A performance task in which students are required to generate an answer rather than select an answer from among several possible answers, but there is a single correct response.

operant conditioning — The modification of behavior brought about over time by the consequences of said behavior. Operant conditioning is distinguished from Pavlovian conditioning in that operant conditioning deals with voluntary behavior explained by its consequences, whereas Pavlovian conditioning deals with involuntary behavior triggered by its antecedents.

ophthalmology — The branch of medical science dealing with the anatomy, functions, and diseases of the eye.

optical topography (OT) — Real-time observation of brain functions using the better penetrating near infrared light, rather than visible light, to measure changes in blood hemoglobin concentrations in the brain. Infrared light is a type of radio wave that has a longer wavelength than that of visible light.

orbitofrontal position — Region of association cortex of the human brain involved in cognitive processes such as decision-making.

orchestrated immersion — One of three instructional techniques espoused by Renate and Geoffrey Caine in 1994 to provide learners with rich, complex educational experiences that include options and promote a sense of wholeness.

orienting network (attention) — One of three networks underlying attention (the other two being alerting and selective attention networks).

orthography — The correct way of using a specific writing system to write the language.

outcome-based education — An integrated system of educational programs that aligns specific student outcomes, instructional methods, and assessment. This approach emphasizes educational outcomes rather than the educational process and focuses on the product of education (such as what kind of professionals will be produced, and with what professional knowledge, skills, abilities, values, and attitudes in X field).

outcomes — Changes in behavior, knowledge, understanding, ability, skills, or attitudes that occur as a result of participating in a program or course of study, receiving services, or using a product. All possible demonstrable results that stem from causal factors or activities.

overlearning — A pedagogical concept according to which newly acquired skills should be practiced well beyond the point of initial mastery, leading to automaticity.

oxygen — The third most abundant element in the universe by mass after hydrogen and helium and the most abundant element by mass in the Earth's crust; vital for human life.

oxygenation — The process by which concentrations of oxygen increase within a tissue.

P600 — A language-relevant event-related potential (ERP), or peak in electrical brain activity, measured by electroencephalography (EEG). Because it is thought to be elicited by hearing or reading grammatical errors and other syntactic anomalies, it is a common topic of study in neurolinguistic experiments.

paced challenges — Tests of learning conducted in incrementally difficult stages.

parahippocampal gyrus — Also known as the hippocampal gyrus; a gray matter cortical region of the brain that surrounds the hippocampus and plays an important role in memory encoding and retrieval.

parallel distributed processing (PDP) — Original approach of the prevailing connectionist model; a neural network approach that stresses the parallel nature of neural processing and the distributed nature of neural representations.

parallel processing — The ability of the brain to simultaneously process incoming stimuli from several sources.

parasympathetic nervous system — One of the two systems that comprise the autonomic nervous system; a parasympathetic response constricts pupils, stimulates salivation, constricts airways, slows the heartbeat, stimulates digestion, etc.

(pars) opercularis — Literally, "the part that covers." This brain structure is the part of the inferior frontal gyrus that lies between the inferior precentral sulcus and the ascending ramus of the lateral sulcus. Called opercularis because it covers part of the insula.

parietal lobes — Located behind the frontal cortex and involved in perception of stimuli related to touch, pressure, temperature, and pain; and combines information from many sources: muscles, joints, eyes, and motor command centers. Associated with sensation (touch, kinesthesia, perception of temperature, vibration), writing, and some aspects of reading.

parietal position — Of or relating to the walls of a part, or forming the upper posterior wall of the head (as in parietal lobes of the brain).

pathway (neural) — A neural tract connecting one part of the nervous system with another, usually consisting of bundles of elongated, myelin-insulated neurons, known collectively as white matter. Neural pathways serve to connect relatively distant areas of the brain or nervous system, compared to the local communication of gray matter.

pattern (neuroscience) — In common usage, a pattern is a succession of repeating events: to follow a pattern is to do as was formerly done. Patterns of this type are governed by a generative rule: Repeat the last n events. The pattern can be continued when the rule has been discovered.

pattern recognition — The organism's ability to recognize a new object or a new problem as a member of an already familiar class of objects or problems. The pattern recognition capability of the association cortex and other advanced regions of the cortex is called emergent because it truly emerges in the brain. Pattern recognition is not unique to humans; it is shared by every other species capable of learning.

Pavlovian conditioning — A form of associative learning that was first demonstrated by Ivan Pavlov. The typical procedure for inducing classical conditioning involves presentations of a neutral unconditioned stimulus (US) along with a stimulus of some significance, the conditioned stimulus (CS). If the CS and the US are repeatedly paired, eventually the two stimuli become associated, and the organism begins to produce a behavioral response to the CS. Pavlov called this the conditioned response (CR). Also known as classical conditioning.

pedagogy — The art or science of teaching.

pediatrics — The branch of medicine that deals with the medical care of infants, children, and adolescents.

peer review or peer evaluation — Method for evaluating professional attitudes and behavior; used by trainees to assess each other and also used by supervisors, nurses, and patients to assess trainees. Typical measurement tools for this form of testing are checklists and questionnaires.

peptides — Any of various amides that are derived from two or more amino acids by combination of the amino group of one acid with the carboxyl group of another and are usually obtained by partial hydrolysis of proteins.

perception — Reports of sensory input. Perceptions emerge as a result of reverberations of signals between different levels of the sensory hierarchy, even across different senses. Many neuroscientists have suggested that perception arises not simply by building up bits of data through a hierarchy, but rather by matching incoming sensory data.

perceptual visual-noise exclusion hypothesis (dyslexia) — A hypothesis for the cause of dyslexia, related to the concept of a perceptual noise exclusion failure (impaired filtering of behaviorally irrelevant visual information in dyslexia).

performance assessment — Systematic and direct observation of a student performance or examples of student performances and ranking according to preestablished performance criteria. Students are assessed on the result as well as the process in which they engaged in completing a complex task or creating a product.

performance-based assessment — Any assessment strategy designed to estimate a child's knowledge, understanding, ability, skill, or attitudes in a consistent fashion and across individuals; emphasizes methods other than standardized achievement tests, particularly those using multiple-choice formats. Typically includes exhibitions, investigations, demonstrations, written or oral responses, journals, and portfolios.

performance criteria — The characteristics to be assessed for a given task. Performance criteria can be general, specific, analytical, trait, or holistic, and they can be expressed as a scoring rubric or scoring guide.

performance task — An assessment exercise that is goal- directed. The exercise is developed to elicit students' application of a wide range of skills and knowledge in solving a complex problem.

peripheral nervous system (PNS) — Portion of the nervous system that includes all the nerves and neurons outside the brain and spinal cord; collection of nerves throughout the body. The PNS brings messages from the sense receptors to the spinal cord and brain and carries messages from the brain and spinal cord to the muscles and glands. This system has two subdivisions: the autonomic nervous system and the somatic nervous system.

perisylvian fissure — One of the most prominent structures of the human brain, which divides the frontal lobe and parietal lobe above, from the temporal lobe below (also called lateral sulcus).

PET (positron emission tomography) scan — A nuclear medicine imaging technique that produces a three-dimensional image or picture of functional processes in the body. The system detects pairs of gamma rays emitted indirectly by a nuclear tracer, which is introduced into the body on a biologically active molecule. Images of tracer concentration in three-dimensional space within the body are then reconstructed by computer analysis.

pharmacology — The study of drug action; more specifically, the study of the interactions that occur between a living organism and exogenous chemicals that alter normal biochemical function.

phase — A stage in a process of change or development.

philosophy — The study of general and fundamental problems concerning subjects such as existence, knowledge, values, reason, mind, and language.

phenotype — An observable characteristic of an organism.

phoneme — In human phonology, the smallest segmental unit of sound employed to form meaningful contrasts between utterances.

phonemic temporal processing — The relationship between auditory temporal processing, phonemic awareness, and possible reading disability roots.

phonological deficit theory (dyslexia) — A theory about the cause of dyslexia that postulates a specific impairment in the representation, storage, or retrieval of speech sounds.

phonological processing — The study of the distribution and patterning of speech sounds in a language and of the tacit rules governing pronunciation.

phrenology — An outdated hypothesis stating that the personality traits of a person can be deduced from the shape of the skull; popularized by Franz Joseph Gall in 1796.

phylogeny — The development or evolution of a particular group of organisms.

physiology — The branch of biology dealing with the functions and activities of living organisms and their parts, including all physical and chemical processes.

Piaget's stages of cognitive development — Piaget's four levels of development are (1) infancy, (2) preschool, (3) childhood, and (4) adolescence. Each stage is characterized by a general cognitive structure that affects all of the child's thinking.

planum temporale — The cortical area just posterior to the auditory cortex within the Sylvian fissure. It is a triangular region and forms the heart of Wernicke's area, one of the most important functional areas for language.

plasticity — Refers to the ability to change the efficacy of synaptic transmission and neuronal connections in the face of altered afferent activity. Can occur at the level of synapses as well as within neural systems (e.g., visual cortex).

pole (temporal) — The anterior end of the temporal lobe in the brain is the temporal pole.

portfolio (education) — A collection of various samples of a student's work throughout the school year that can include writing samples, examples of math problems, and results of science experiments.

portfolio assessment — An assessment process based on the collection of student work (e.g., written assignments, drafts, artwork, and presentations) that represents competencies, exemplary work, or the student's developmental progress. A collection of work, usually drawn from children's classroom work, which, when subjected to objective analysis, becomes an assessment tool.

Anderson, M. (2004). *Ontogenetic forgetting of contextual attributes*. Doctoral dissertation, Kent State University, Kent, OH. AAT 3133658.

Anderson, M. (2007). Evolution of cognitive function via redeployment of brain areas. *The Neuroscientist, 13*(1), 13–21.

Anderson, S. (2007). *The effect of music on the reading comprehension of junior high school students*. Doctoral dissertation, Walden University, Baltimore, MD. AAT 3245966.

Andrade, M., Benedito-Silva, A. A., Domenice, S., Arnhold, I. J., & Menna-Barreto, L. (1993). Sleep characteristics of adolescents: A longitudinal study. *Journal of Adolescent Health, 14*, 401–406.

Andreasen, N. (2005). *The creative brain: The science of genius*. New York: Plume, Penguin Group.

Anonymous. (2008). Behavior. New findings in behavior described from University of Leeds. *Psychology & Psychiatry Journal, 87*. Retrieved October 27, 2009, from *proquest.umi.com/pqdweb?index=21&did=1539769891&SrchMode=1&sid=11&Fmt=3&VInst=PROD&VType=PQD&RQT=309&VName=PQD&TS=1256639984&clientId=86884*.

Ansari, D. (2005a, Nov). Paving the way towards meaningful interactions between neuroscience and education. *Developmental Science, 8*(6), 466–467.

Ansari, D. (2005b). Time to use neuroscience findings in teacher training. *Nature (Scientific Correspondence), 437*(7055), 26.

Ansari, D., & Coch, D. (2006). Bridges over troubled waters: Education and cognitive neuroscience. *Trends in Cognitive Sciences, 10*(4), 146–151.

Ansari, D., Donlan, C., & Karmiloff-Smith, A. (2007). Atypical and typical development of visual estimation abilities. *Cortex: Special Issues on Selective Developmental Disorders, 6*, 758–768.

Ansari, D., Donlan, C., Thomas, M., Ewing, S., & Karmiloff-Smith. (2003). What makes counting count? Verbal and visuo-spatial contributions to typical and atypical number development. *Journal of Experimental Child Psychology, 85*, 50–62.

Ansari, D., & Karmiloff-Smith, A. (2002). Atypical trajectories of number development: A neuroconstructivist perspective. *Trends in Cognitive Sciences, 6*(12), 511–516.

Argyris, K., Stringaris, N. C., Medford, V., Giampietro, M. J., Brammer, M., & David, A. S. (2007). Deriving meaning: Distinct neural mechanisms for metaphoric, literal, and non-meaningful sentences. *Brain and Language, 100*(2), 150–162.

Armstrong, T. (1998). *Awakening genius in the classroom*. Alexandria, VA: Association for Supervision and Curriculum Development.

Armstrong, T. (2006). *The best schools: How human development research should inform educational practice*. Alexandria, VA: Association for Supervision and Curriculum Development.

Arnsten, A., & Li, B. M. (2005). Neurobiology of executive functions: Catecholamine influences on prefrontal cortical functions. *Biological Psychiatry, 57*(11), 1377–1384.

Ashby, F., Isen, A. M., & Turken, U. (1999). A neuropsychological theory of positive affect and its influence on cognition. *Psychological Review, 106*(3), 529–550.

Ashby, W. R. (1960). *Design for a brain*. London: Chapman & Hall. (Original work published 1952)

Ashcraft, M. H. & Krause, J. A. (2007). Working memory, math performance, and math anxiety. *Psychonomic Bulletin & Review, 14*(2), 243–248.

Association for Supervision and Curriculum Development. (2002a). *The brain and learning, constructivism, and performance assessments.* Retrieved June 12, 2007, from *www.ascd.org/portal/site/ascd/menuitem.62bf453ae2bc40a98d7ea23161a001ca/*.

Association for Supervision and Curriculum Development. (2002b). *Professional development online: The brain and memory and learning strategies.* Retrieved August 10, 2007, from *www.ascd.org/framepdonline.html*.

Association for Supervision and Curriculum Development. (2007). *Standards.* Retrieved October 14, 2007, from *www.ascd.org/portal/site/ascd/menuitem.2a5fd0d221f7fffddeb3ffdb62108a0c/;jsessionid=D2aB8DEwHtjxIoyNsrEq116FHrJ25oEUNuB69jXM25PqfnXKjnM4!258856059*.

Atallah, H., Frank, M. J. & O'Reilly, R. C. (2004). Hippocampus, cortex, and basal ganglia: Insights from computational models of complementary learning systems. *Neurobiology of Learning and Memory, 82*(3), 253–267.

Atherton, M. (2002). *A neurocognitive model for student and educators.* Paper presented at the annual meeting of the Cognitive Science Society, Fairfax, VA.

Atherton, M. (2005). *Applying the neurosciences to educational research: Can cognitive neuroscience bridge the gap?* Part I. Retrieved May 5, 2007, from *www.tc.umn.edu/athe0007/BNEsig/papers/Educationand Neuroscience.pdf*.

Atherton, M., & Bart, W. M. (2002). *What the neurosciences can tell educators about reading and arithmetic: A review of current research.* Paper presented at the annual meeting of the American Educational Research Association, New Orleans, LA.

Awai, A. (2005). *A functional MRI study of the distributed neural circuitry of learning and reward.* Thesis (S.M. and S.B.), Massachusetts Institute of Technology, Cambridge, MA.

Aylward, E., Richards, T. L., Berninger, V. W., Nagy, W. E., Field, K. M., Grimme, A. C., et al. (2003). Instructional treatment associated with changes in brain activation in children with dyslexia. *Neurology, 61*(2), 212–219.

Azar, B. (2002). At the frontier of science: Social cognitive neuroscience merges three distinct disciplines in hopes of deciphering the process behind social behavior. *APA Monitor, 33*(1), 40–43.

Baars, B., & Gage, N. M. (2007). *Cognition, brain, and consciousness: Introduction to cognitive neuroscience.* New York: Academic Press.

Baddeley, A. (2001). Is working memory still working? *American Psychologist, 56*(11), 851–864.

Baddeley, A. (2003). Working memory and language: An overview. *Journal of Communication Disorders, 36*, 189–208.

Baddeley, A., & Andrade, J. (2000). Working memory and the vividness of imagery. *Journal of Experimental Psychology, General, 129*(1), 126–145.

Bain, K. (2004). *What the best college teachers do*. Cambridge, MA: Harvard University Press.

Baldwin, M. (1896). A new factor in evolution. *The American Naturalist, 30*(354), 441–451.

Baluch, F. (2006). *Human learning and the neural correlates of strategy formulation*. Thesis (M.S.), University of Houston, TX.

Banich, M. (2004). Cognitive neuroscience and neuropsychology. Boston: Houghton Mifflin.

Banikowski, A., & Mehring, T. A. (1999). Strategies to enhance memory based on brain-research. *Focus on Exceptional Children, 32*(2), 1–16.

Bar, M. (2007). The proactive brain: Using analogies and associations to generate predictions. *Trends in Cognitive Sciences, 11*(7), 280–289.

Barbiere, M. (2003). *What are the implications for lesson design using Dewey's mode of inquiry discovery and Sousa's brain based research?* Doctoral dissertation, Seton Hall University, South Orange, NJ. AAT 3190174.

Barbro, B., Johansson, B. B., & Belichenko, P. V. (2001). Neuronal plasticity and dendritic spines: Effect of environmental enrichment on intact and postischemic rat brain. *Journal of Cerebral Blood Flow and Metabolism, 22*, 89–96.

Barinaga, M. (1995). Dendrites shed their dull image. *Science, 268*(5208), 200–201.

Barker, R. A., & Barasi, S. (2008). *Neuroscience at a glance* (3rd ed.) [electronic version] Available on *www.medicalneuroscience.com*. Hoboken, NJ: Blackwell.

Barnes, A. (2005). A passion for languages: Motivation and preparation to teach modern foreign languages in eight cohorts of beginning teachers. *Research Papers in Education, 20*(4), 349–369.

Barnes, M., Wilkinson, M., Boudesquie, A., Khemani, E., Dennis, M., & Fletcher, J. M. (2006). Arithmetic processing in children with spina bifida: Calculation accuracy, strategy use, and fact retrieval fluency. *Journal of Learning Disabilities, 39*, 174–187.

Bartleby.com (2010). Citation of Dana, John Cotton from the *New York Times Book Review*, March 5, 1967, p. 55.

Barsalou, L., Breazeal, C., & Smith, L. B. (2007). Cognition as coordinated non-cognition. *Cognitive Processing, 8*(2), 79–91.

Bartzokis, G. (2004). Age-related myelin breakdown: A developmental model of cognitive decline and Alzheimer's disease. *Neurobiology of Aging, 25*(1), 5–18; author reply, 49–62.

Bartzokis, G., Beckson, M., Lu, P H., Neuchterlein, K. H., Edwards, N., & Mintz, J. (2001). Age-related changes in frontal and temporal lobe volumes in men: A magnetic resonance imaging study. *Archives of General Psychiatry, 58*(5), 461–465.

Bates, D. (2006). *The cognitive and affective repercussions of thought suppression following negative personal feedback*. Doctoral dissertation, University of Texas, Austin, TX. AAT 3246891.

Battro, A. M. (2000). *Half a brain is enough: The story of Nico*. Cambridge, UK: Cambridge University Press.

Battro, A. M., & Percival J. Denham. (2003). *Pensamiento crítico*. Argentina. Retrieved October 2004 from *www.byd.com.ar/ed6www4.htm*.

Battro, A. M., & Denham, P. J. (2007). *La inteligencia digital.* Buenos Aires: Academia Nacional de Educación. Available online at *www.byd.com.ar.*

Battro, A. M., Fischer, K. W., & Léna, P. J. (Eds). (2008). *The educated brain: Essays in neuroeducation.* Cambridge, UK: Cambridge University Press.

Bauer, P. (2004). Getting explicit memory off the ground: Steps forward in the construction of a neuro-developmental account of changes in the first two years of life. *Developmental Review, 24*(4), 347–373.

Bauer, P. (2005). Developments in declarative memory. *Psychological Science, 16*(1), 41–47.

Bear, M., Connors, B. W., & Paradis, M. A. (2007). *Neuroscience: Exploring the brain* (3rd ed.). Baltimore, MD: Lippincott Williams & Wilkins.

Beaton, A. (2004). *Dyslexia, reading and the brain: A sourcebook of psychological and biological research.* New York: Psychology Press.

Becker, B. (2006). *Nature and artifice lecture: History 135E Lecture 12,* University of California, Irvine. Retrieved June 2, 2007, from *https://eee.uci.edu/clients/bjbecker/NatureandArtifice/lecture12.html.*

Becker, R. (2005). *The effectiveness of follow-through staff development programs on brain-based research and its instructional implications.* Doctoral dissertation, Temple University, Philadelphia. AAT 3202988.

Becker, S. (2005). A computational principle for hippocampal learning and neurogenesis. *Hippocampus, 15*(6), 722–738.

Beer, J., & Ochsner, K. N. (2006). Social cognition: A multi level analysis. *Brain research, 1079*(1), 98–105.

Begley, S. (1996). Your child's brain. *Newsweek, 19,* 57–61.

Begley, S. (2001). Religion and the brain. *Newsweek, 7,* 50–61.

Begley, S. (2005, March 18). Beware of the cognitive brain paparazzi lurking in brain science labs. *Wall Street Journal* (science section). Retrieved September 14, 2007, from *ageless marketing.typepad.com/ageless_marketing/2005/03/beware_of_cogni.html.*

Begley, S. (2007). *Train your mind, change your brain: How a new science reveals our extraordinary potential to transform ourselves.* New York: Ballantine Books.

Bell, M., & Wolfe, C.D. (2004). Emotion and cognition: An intricately bound developmental process. *Child Development, 75*(2), 366–370.

Bellace, M., & Williams, J. M. (2005). *Activation of the hippocampus during emotional learning.* Doctoral dissertation, Drexel University, Philadelphia, PA. Retrieved from *dspace.library.drexel.edu/handle/1860/480.*

Bell-McGinty, S., Habeck, C., Hilton, H. J., Rakitin, B., Scarmeas, N., Zarahn, E., & (2004). Identification and differential vulnerability of a neural network in sleep deprivation. *Cerebral Cortex, 14*(5), 496.

Benar, J., & Miikkulainen, R. (2003). Learning innate face preferences. *Neural Computation, 15,* 1525–1557.

Bender, W. (2002). *Differentiation instruction for students with learning disabilities*. Thousand Oaks, CA: Corwin Press.

Benesh, B., Arbuckle, M., Robbins, P., & D'Arcangelo, M. (1998). *The brain and learning: New knowledge and understanding*. Alexandria, VA: Association for Supervision and Curriculum Development.

Benfenati, F. (2007). Synaptic plasticity and the neurobiology of learning and memory. *Acta Bio-Medica: Atenei Parmensis, 78*(Suppl. 1), 58–66.

Bennett, M., Dennett, H.D., Hacher, P., & Searle, J. (2007). *Neuroscience and philosophy: Brain, mind, and language*. New York: Columbia University Press.

Berger, A., Kofman, O., Livneh, U., & Henik, A. (2007). Multidisciplinary perspectives on attention and the development of self-regulation. *Progress in Neurobiology, 82*(5), 256–286.

Berk, L. (2001). Modulation of neuroimmune parameters during the eustress of humor-associated mirthful laughter. *Alternative Therapies in Health and Medicine, 7*(2), 62–72, 74–76.

Berninger, V., & Abbott, R. D. (1992). The unit of analysis and the constructive processes of the learner: Key concepts for educational neuropsychology. *Educational Psychology, 27*(2), 223–242.

Berninger, V., & Corina, D. (1998). Making cognitive neuroscience educationally relevant: Creating bidirectional collaborations between educational psychology and cognitive neuroscience. *Educational Psychology Review, 10*(3), 343–354.

Berninger, V., & Richards, T. L. (2002). *Brain literacy for educators and psychologists*. San Diego, CA: Academic Press.

Bernstein, J. (2000). Developmental neuropsychological assessment. In K. O. Yeates & M. D. Ris (Eds.), *Pediatric neuropsychology: Research, theory, and practice* (pp. 405–438). New York: Guilford Press.

Berridge, K. (2004). Motivation concepts in behavioral neuroscience. *Physiology and Behavior, 81*(2), 179–209.

Berridge, K., & Robinson, T. E. (2003). Parsing reward. *Trends in Neurosciences, 26*(9), 507–513.

Berthoud, H., & Morrison, C. (2008). The brain, appetite, and obesity. *Annual Review of Psychology, 59*, 55. Retrieved August 1, 2009, from Alumni—ProQuest Psychology Journals. doi: 1407590851.

Bertucci, P. (2006). *A mixed-method study of a brain-compatible education program of grades K–5 in a mid-Atlantic inner-city public elementary/middle school*. Doctoral dissertation, Johnson & Wales University, Providence, RI. AAT 3234449.

Best, J., Diniz Behn, C., Poe, G. R., & Booth, V. (2007). Neuronal models for sleep–wake regulation and synaptic reorganization in the sleeping hippocampus. *Journal of Biological Rhythms, 22*(3), 220–232.

Bialystok E., Fergus, C. & Freedman Morris, I. M. (2007). Bilingualism as a protection against the onset of symptoms of dementia. *Neuropsychologia, 45*(2), 459–464.

Bidell, T. R., & Fischer, K. W. (1992). Beyond the stage debate: Action, structure, and variability in Piagetian theory and research. In R. Sternberg & C. Berg (Eds.), *Intellectual development* (pp. 100–140). New York: Cambridge University Press.

Biederman, J., Petty, C. R., Dolan, C., Hughes, S., Mick, E., Monuteaux, M. C., et al. (2008). The long-term longitudinal course of oppositional defiant disorder and conduct disorder in ADHD boys: Findings from a controlled 10-year prospective longitudinal follow-up study. *Psychological Medicine, 38*(7), 1027–1036.

Billington, D. (1997). *Seven characteristics of highly effective adult learning environments.* Retrieved January 4, 2005, from *www.newhorizons.com.*

Binder, J., Westbury, C. F., & McKiernan, K. A. (2005). Distinct brain systems for processing concrete and abstract concepts. *Journal of Cognitive Neuroscience, 17*(6), 905–917.

Birsh, J. R. (2005). Research and reading disability. In J. R. Birsh, *Multisensory teaching of basic language skills.* Baltimore: Paul H. Brookes.

Bisanz, J., Sherman, J., Rasmussen, C., & Ho, E. (2005). Development of arithmetic skills and knowledge in preschool children. In J. I. D. Campbell (Ed.), *Handbook of mathematical cognition* (pp. 143–162). New York: Psychology Press.

Bjorkman, S. (2007). *Relationships among academic stress, social support, and internalizing and externalizing behavior in adolescence.* Doctoral dissertation, Northern Illinois University, DeKalb, IL. AAT 3279173.

Blair, C. (2006). How similar are fluid cognition and general intelligence? A developmental neuroscience perspective on fluid cognition as an aspect of human cognitive ability. *Behavioral and Brain Sciences, 29*(2), 109–125.

Blair, R. (2007). Dissociable systems for empathy. *Novartis Foundation Symposium, 278,* 134–141.

Blakemore, C. (2004). Brain research strategies for physical educators. *Journal of Physical Education, Recreation and Dance, 75*(1), 31–37.

Blakemore, S., & Frith, U. (2005). The learning brain: Lessons for education: A précis. *Developmental Science, 8*(6), 459–465.

Blakemore, S., & Frith, U. (2007). *The learning brain: Lessons for education.* Malden, MA: Blackwell.

Blakemore, S., & Frith, U. (2008a). Learning and remembering. In *The Jossey-Bass reader on the brain and learning* (pp. 109–119). San Francisco: Wiley.

Blakemore, S., & Frith, U. (2008b). The literate brain. In *The Jossey-Bass reader on the brain and learning* (pp. 229–241). San Francisco: Wiley.

Blakemore, S., Winston, J., & Frith, U. (2004). Social cognitive neuroscience: Where are we heading? *Trends in Cognitive Sciences, 8*(5), 216–222.

Blank, R. (2007). Policy implications of the new neuroscience. *Cambridge Quarterly of Healthcare Ethics, 16*(2), 169–180.

Blankertz, B., Dornhege, G., Krauledat, M. Schröder, J., Williamson, R., Murray-Smith, K. R., et al. (2006). *The Berlin Brain–Computer Interface presents the novel mental typewriter Hex-o-Spell*, 3rd International BCI Workshop and Training Course, Graz. Retrieved July 22, 2009, from *eprints.pascal-network.org/archive/00002463/*.

Blankertz, B., Krauledat, M., Dornhege, G., Williamson, J., Murray-Smith, R. & Müller, K.-R. (2007). *A note on brain actuated spelling with the Berlin brain-computer interface*. Lecture Notes in Computer Science, 4557, 759–768.

Blazevski, J. (2006). *Teacher efficacy for supporting student motivation*. Doctoral dissertation, University of Michigan, Ann Arbor, MI. AAT 3224822.

Bloom, B. (1956). *Taxonomy of educational objectives, handbook I: Cognitive domain*. New York: Longman.

Bloom, M. (2005). *Linking the processes of literacy with brain research to suggest possibilities for integrating movement activities into the classroom: A critical review of literature*. Master's thesis (M.S. Ed.), Bank Street College of Education, New York, NY.

Bluestone, A., Abdoulaev, G., Schmitz, C. H., Barbour, R. L., & Hielscher, A. H. (2001). Three-dimensional optical tomography of hemodynamics in the human head. *Optics Express, 9*, 272–286.

Bo, J. (2006). *Continuous versus discontinuous drawing: Possible cerebrellar involvement in the development of temporal consistency*. Doctoral dissertation, University of Maryland, College Park, MD. AAT 3212590.

Boden, M. (2004). *The creative mind: Myths and mechanisms*. New York: Routledge.

Bolivar, B. (2005). *Motivation des élèves au secondaire et pratiques d'enseignement: Recherche descriptive guidée par les théories du cerveau et de l'apprentissage dans un environnement technologique* [Secondary student motivation and teaching practices: Descriptive research guide on brain-based theories of learning with technology]. Doctoral dissertation, University of Manitoba, Winnipeg, Canada. AAT MR12285.

Bonwell, C. (1993). *Active learning: Creating excitement in the classroom*. Retrieved August 20, 2007, from *www.Active-Learning-Site.Com*.

Bonwell, C., & Eison, J. (1991). *Active learning: Creating excitement in the classroom*. Washington, DC: Jossey-Bass.

Booker, K., Invernizzi, M. A. & McCormick, M. (2007). Kiss your brain: A closer look at flourishing literacy gains in impoverished elementary schools. *Reading Research and Instruction, 46*(4), 315–340.

Boon, S. (2002). *The brain and learning*. Berglund Center for Internet Studies. Retrieved September 9, 2007, from *education.ed.pacificu.edu/aacu/workshop/ brainbased.html*.

Booth, J., Burman, D. D., Meyer, J. R., Gitelman, D. R., Parrish, T. B., & Marsel M. M. (2004). Development of brain mechanisms for processing orthographic and phonologic representations. *Journal of Cognitive Neuroscience, 16*(7), 1234–1249.

Borich, G. (2006). *Effective teaching methods: Research-based practice* (6th ed.). New York: Prentice-Hall.

Bourgeois, J. (2001). Synaptogenesis in the neocortex of the newborn: The ultimate frontier for individuation? In C. A. Nelson & M. Luciana (Eds.), *Handbook for developmental cognitive neuroscience* (pp. 23–34). Cambridge, MA: MIT Press.

Bowden, E., & Jung-Beeman, M. (2007). Methods for investigating the neural components of insight. *Methods, 42*(1), 87–99.

Bowell, T., & Kemp, G. (2002). *Critical thinking*. England, UK: International L.T.D.

Boylan, H., (2002). *What works: Research-based best practices in developmental education*. Boone, NC: Continuous Quality Improvement Network and National Center for Developmental Education, Appalachian State University.

Bradford-Meyer, C. (2003). *Follow-up of brain conference attendees and their application of brain research: A questionnaire approach*. Doctoral dissertation, Boise State University, Boise, ID. AAT DP13574.

Bragdon, A., & Gamon, D. (2000). *Brains that work a little bit differently: Recent discoveries about common brain diversities*. Cape Cod, MA: Brainwaves Center.

Brain Gym®. (2007). *The official Brain Gym® web site*. Retrieved September 3, 2007, from *www.braingym.org/*.

Brandt, R. (1997, Mar). On using knowledge about our brain: A conversation with Bob Sylwester. *Educational Leadership, 54*(6), 16–19.

Brandt, R. (1998). *Powerful learning*. Alexandria, VA: Association for Supervision and Curriculum Development.

Brandt, R. (1999, Nov). Educators need to know about the human brain. *Phi Delta Kappan, 81*(3), 235–238.

Bransford, J., Brown, A. L., & Cocking, R. R. (Eds.). (2003). *How people learn: Brain, mind, experience and school*. Washington, DC: National Academy Press.

Bransford, J., Brown, A. L., & Cocking, R. R. (2008). Mind and brain. In *The Jossey-Bass reader on the brain and learning* (pp. 89–108). San Francisco: Wiley.

Bransford, J., Brown, A. L., Cocking, R. R., Donovan, M. S., Pellegrino, J. W. & National Research Council. (Eds.). (1999). *How people learn: Bridging research and practice*. Washington, DC: National Academy Press.

Braten, S. (2007). *On being moved: From mirror neurons to empathy (Advances in Consciousness Research)*. Amsterdam: Benjamins.

Bray, S, Shimojo, S., & O'Doherty, J. P. (2007). Direct instrumental conditioning of neural activity using functional magnetic resonance imaging-derived reward feedback. *Journal of Neuroscience, 27*(28), 7498–7507.

Brier, M., Maguire, M., Tillman, G., Hart, J., & Kraut, M. (2008). Event-related potentials in semantic memory retrieval. *Journal of the International Neuropsychological Society, 14*(5), 815–822.

Briggs, D. (2008). Synthesizing casual inferences. *Educational Researcher Journal 37*(1), 15–22.

Bright, P., & Kopelman, M. D. (2001). Learning and memory: Recent findings. *Current Opinion in Neurology, 14*(4), 449–455.

British Psychological Association. (2006). *Quality standards for educational psychology services.* Retrieved October 14, 2007, from *www3.bps.org.uk/down loadfile.cfm?file_uuid=D2F2BF1F-1143-DFD0-7EDB-9FF1F6E9E755&ext=pdf.*

Broca, P. P. (1862). Loss of speech, chronic softening and partial destruction of the anterior left lobe of the brain. First published in *Bulletin de la Société Anthropologique, 2*, 235–238. Translation by Christopher D. Green. Retrieved on July 21, 2010, from *http://psychclassics.asu.edu /Broca/perte-e.htm#f1*

Brodmann, K. (1999). *Vergleichende Lokalisationslehre der Grosshirnrinde [Localisation in the cerebral cortex]* (L. J. Garey, Trans.). Leipzig, Germany: Smith-Gordon, Imperial College Press. (Original work published 1909)

Brodnax, R. (2004). *Brain compatible teaching for learning.* Doctoral dissertation, Indiana University, Bloomington, IN. AAT 3173526.

Brookes, S. (2008). *Science/Innovation: Research capability directory.* Flinders University Web site. Retrieved from *www.flinders.edu.au/.*

Brothers, L. (1997). *Friday's footprint: How society shapes the human mind.* New York: Oxford University Press.

Brown Foundation for Educational Equity, Excellence, and Research. (2009). Retrieved from *www.enotes.com/scholarships-loans/brown-foundation-educational-equity-excellence.*

Brown, C., & Hagoort, P. (Eds.). (1999). *The neurocognition of language.* Oxford, UK: Oxford University Press.

Brown, J. (2006). *The teacher-self: The role of identity in teaching.* Doctoral dissertation, University of Massachusetts, Lowell, MA. AAT 3217234.

Brown, R., & Bjorklund, D. F. (1998). The biologizing of cognition, development, and education: Approach with cautious enthusiasm. *Educational Psychology Review, 10*(3), 355–374.

Brown, S., Martinez, M., & Parson, L. (2006). Music and language side by side in the brain: A PET study of the generation of melodies and sentences. *European Journal of Neuroscience, 23*(10), 2791–2803.

Bruel-Jungerman, E., Davis, S., Rampon, C., & Laroche, S. (2006). Long-term potentiation enhances neurogenesis in the adult dentate gyrus. *Journal of Neuroscience, 26*(22), 5888–5893.

Bruel-Jungerman, E., Rampon, C., & Laroche, S. (2007). Adult hippocampal neurogenesis, synaptic plasticity and memory: Facts and hypotheses. *Reviews in the Neurosciences, 18*(2), 93–114.

Bruer, J. (1995). Penicillin for education: How cognitive science can contribute to education. *NASSP Bulletin, 79*(571), 68–81.

Bruer, J. (1997). Education and the brain: A bridge too far. *Educational Researcher, 26*(8), 4–16.

Bruer, J. (1998a). Brain science, brain fiction. *Educational Leadership, 56*(3), 14–19.

Bruer, J. (1998b). Let's put brain science on the back burner. *NASSP Bulletin, 82*(598), 9–20.

Bruer, J. (1999a). *The myth of the first three years: A new understanding of early brain development and lifelong learning.* Detroit: Free Press.

Bruer, J. (1999b). Neural connections: Some you use, some you lose. *Phi Delta Kappan, 81*(4), 264–277.

Bruer, J. (1999c). In search of . . . brain-based education. *Phi Delta Kappan, 80*(9), 648–657. Retrieved July 20, 2007, from *www.pdkintl.org/kappan/kbru9905.htm*.

Bruer, J. (2002a). Avoiding the pediatrician's error: How neuroscientists can help educators (and themselves). *Nature Neuroscience, 5*(11), 1031–1033.

Bruer, J. (2002b). *A rational approach to education: Integrating behavioral, cognitive, and brain science.* Herbert Spencer Lecture, Oxford University, Oxford, UK.

Bruer, J. (2008a). Building bridges in neuroscience. In A. M. Battro, K. W. Fischer, & P. J. Léna (Eds.), *The educated brain* (pp. 43–58).Cambridge, UK: Cambridge University Press.

Bruer, J. (2008b). In search of . . . brain-based education. In *The Jossey-Bass reader on the brain and learning* (pp. 51–69). San Francisco: Wiley.

Bruner, J. (1966). *Toward a theory of instruction.* Cambridge, MA: Harvard University Press.

Bruner, J. (1971). The course of cognitive growth. In P. S. Sears (Ed.), *Intellectual development* (pp. 255–282). New York: Wiley.

Bruner, J. (1997). *The culture of education* (2nd ed.). Cambridge, MA: Harvard University Press.

Bruning, R., Schraw, G. J., & Ronning, R. R. (1995). *Cognitive psychology and instruction.* Upper Saddle River, NJ: Prentice-Hall.

Bryant, R. (2005). Psychosocial approaches of acute stress reactions. *CNS spectrums, 10*(2), 116–122.

Buccino, G., Binkofski, F. & Riggio, L. (2004). The mirror neuron system and action recognition. *Brain and Language, 89*(2), 370–376.

Buchanan, T., Tranel, D., & Adolphs. R. (2006). Cognitive neuroscience of emotional memory. *Brain, 129*(1), 115.

Bulmer, M. (2003). *Francis Galton: Pioneer of heredity and biometry.* Baltimore, MD: Johns Hopkins University Press.

Burgdorf, J., & Panksepp, J. (2006). The neurobiology of positive emotions. *Neuroscience and Biobehavioral Reviews, 30*(2), 173–187.

Bussey, T., & Saksida, L. M. (2007). Memory, perception, and the ventral visua–perihinal–hippocampal stream: Thinking outside of the boxes. *Hippocampus, Jul 17.* Retrieved September 14, 2007, from *www.medworm.com/rss/search.php?qu=Hippocampus&t= Hippocampus&s=Search&f=source.*

Butler, A., & Wolf, S. L. (2007). Putting the brain on the map: Use of transcranial magnetic stimulation to assess and induce cortical plasticity of upper-extremity movement. *Physical Therapy, 87*(6), 719–736.

Butler-Bowdon, T. (2007). *50 psychology classics.* London: Nicholas Brealey.

Butterworth, E. (n.d.) *Eric Butterworth quotations.* Retrieved November 14, 2007, from *www.ericbutterworth.com/html/radio_transcirpts/truth.php.*

Buzsaki, G. (2006). *Rhythms of the brain.* New York: Oxford University Press.

Byrne, B., Olson, R. K., Samuelsson, S., Wadsworth, S., Corley, R., DeFries, J. C., et al. (2006). Genetic and environmental influences on early literacy. *Journal of Research in Reading, 29*(1), 33–49.

Byrnes, J. (2001a). *Cognitive development and learning in instructional contexts* (2nd ed.). Needham, MA: Allyn & Bacon.

Byrnes, J. (2001b). *Minds, brains, and learning: Understanding the psychological and educational relevance of neuroscientific research.* New York: Guilford Press.

Byrnes, J. (2007). Some ways in which neuroscientific research can be relevant to education. In D. Coch, K.W. Fischer, & G. Dawson (Eds.), *Human behavior, learning, and the developing brain: Typical development* (pp. 30–49). New York: Guilford Press.

Byrnes, J. (2008). Math skills. In *The Jossey-Bass reader on the brain and learning* (pp. 301–330). San Francisco: Wiley.

Byrnes, J., & Fox, N. A. (1998a). The educational relevance of research in cognitive neuroscience. *Educational Psychology Review, 10,* 297–342.

Byrnes, J., & Fox, N. A. (1998b). Minds, brains, and education: Part II. Responding to the commentaries. *Educational Psychology Review, 10,* 431–439.

Byrnes, J. (2007). *Cognitive development and learning in instructional contexts* (3rd Edition). Needham, MA: Allyn & Bacon.

Cabeza, R., & Kingstone, A. (2001). *Handbook of functional neuroimaging of cognition.* Cambridge, MA: MIT Press.

Cabeza, R., & Nyberg, L. (2000). Imaging cognition II: An empirical review of 275 PET and fMRI studies. *Journal of Cognitive Neuroscience, 12*(1), 1–47.

Cacioppo, J., Berntson, G. G., Lorig, T. S., Norris, C. J., Rickett, E., & Nusbaum, H. (2003). Just because you're imaging the brain doesn't mean you can stop using your head: A primer and set of first principles. *Journal of Personality and Social Psychology, 85*(4), 650–661.

Caine, G., & Caine, R. N. (1997). *Unleashing the power of perceptual change: The potential of brain-based teaching.* San Diego: Brain Store.

Caine, G., & Caine, R. N. (2001). *The brain, education and the competitive edge.* Lanham, MD: Scarecrow Press.

Caine, G., & Nummela-Caine, R. (1997). *Education on the edge of possibility.* Alexandria, VA: Association for Supervision and Curriculum Development.

Caine, G., Nummela-Caine, R., & Crowell, S. (1999). *Mindshifts: A brain-based process for restructuring schools and renewing education* (2nd ed). Tucson, AZ: Zephyr Press.

Caine Learning Institute. (2007). *Web site of the Caine Learning Corporation and Caine Learning Lab.* Retrieved November 10, 2007, from *www.cainelearning.com/index.html.*

Caine Learning Institute. (n.d.). *Home of brain/mind learning.* Retrieved September 14, 2007, from *www.cainelearning.com/index.html.*

Caine, R., & Caine, G. (1990). Understanding a brain-based approach to learning and teaching. *Educational Leadership, 48*(2), 66–70.

Caine, R., & Caine, G. (1994). *Making connections: Teaching and the human brain.* Menlo Park, CA: Addison-Wesley.

Caine, R., & Caine, G. (1995). Reinventing schools through brain-based learning. *Educational Leadership, 52*(7), 43.

Caine, R., & Caine, G. (1997a). *Education on the edge of possibility.* Alexandria, VA: Association for Supervision and Curriculum Development.

Caine, R., & Caine, G. (1997b). *Unleashing the power of perceptual change: The potential of brain-based teaching.* Alexandria, VA: Association for Supervision and Curriculum Development.

Caine, R., & Caine, G. (1998a). Building a bridge between the neurosciences and education: Cautions and possibilities. *NASSP Bulletin, 82*(598), 1–8.

Caine, R., & Caine, G. (1998b). *How to think about the brain.* School Administrator Web Edition, January 1998. Retrieved September 10, 2007, from *www.aasa.org/publications/sa/1998_01/caine.htm.*

Cajal, S. (1911). *Histologie du système nerveux de l'homme et des vertébrés* [History of the human nervous system]. Paris: Maloine.

California Department of Education. (2005). *A study of the relationship between physical fitness and academic achievement in California using 2004 test results.* Retrieved January 23, 2008, from *www.cde.ca.gov/ta/tg/pf/documents/2004pftresults. doc.*

California State University at Chico. (2009). *The neuroscience on the Web series.* Retrieved August 22, 2009, from *www.csuchico.edu/pmccaffrey//syllabi/glossaryce.htm#e.*

Calvin, W. (1996). *How brains think: Evolving intelligence, then and now.* New York: Basic Books.

Calvin, W., & Bickerton, D. (2000). *Lingua ex machina: Reconciling Darwin and Chomsky with the human brain.* Cambridge, MA: MIT Press.

Cameron, W., & Chudler, E. (2003). A role for neuroscientists in engaging young minds. *Nature Reviews Neuroscience, 4*(9), 763–768.

Campbell, D. (1997). *The Mozart effect: Tapping the power of music to heal the body, strengthen the mind, and unlock the creative spirit.* New York: Avon Books.

Campbell, L. (2002). *Mindful learning: 101 proven strategies for student and teacher success.* Thousand Oaks, CA: Corwin Press.

Canli, T. (2006). When genes and brain unite: Ethical implications of genomic neuroimaging. In J. Iles (Ed.), *Neuroethics* (pp. 169–183). Oxford, UK: Oxford University Press.

Caplan, A. (2002). No brainer: Can we cope with the ethical ramifications of new knowledge of the brain? In S. Marcus (Ed.), *Neuroethics: Mapping the field* (pp. 95–106). New York: Dana Press.

Caplan, D. (1987). The discoveries of Paul Broca: Localization of the faculty for articulate language, and classical connectionist models. In D. Caplan (Ed.), *Neurolinguistics and linguistic aphasiology: An introduction* (pp. 43–64). Cambridge, UK: Cambridge University Press.

Caplan, D. (2004). The neuro in cognitive neuropsychology. *Cognitive Neuropsychology, 21*(1), 17–20.

Capra, F. (1996). *The web of life: A new understanding of living systems.* New York: Doubleday.

Caprara, G. V., Fagnani, C., Alessandri, G., Steca, P., Gigantesco, A., Cavalli Sforza, L. L. & Stazi, M. A. (2009). Human optimal functioning: The genetics of positive orientation towards self, life, and the future. *Behavioral Genetics, 39,* 277–284.

Caramazza, A., & Coltheart, M. (2006). Cognitive neuropsychology twenty years on. *Cognitive Neuropsychology, 23*(1), 3–12.

Cardell, A. (2007). *Language development and verbal encoding implications for individual differences in short-term memory in 3-year-olds.* Master's thesis (M.A.), Virginia Polytechnic Institute and State University, Blacksburg, VA. Retrieved August 13, 2007, from *scholar.lib.vt.edu/theses/available/etd-05182007-180630.*

Cardellicho, T., & Field, W. (1997). Seven strategies that encourage neural branching. *Educational Leadership, 54*(6), 33–36.

Carey, S. (2000). Science education as conceptual change. *Journal of Applied Developmental Psychology, 21*(1), 13–19.

Carey, S., & Spelke, E. (1994). Domain-specific knowledge and conceptual change. In L. A. Hirschfeld & S. A. Gelman (Eds.), *Mapping the mind: Domain specificity in cognition and culture* (pp. 169–200). Cambridge, UK: Cambridge University Press.

Carlson, N. (2004). *Physiology of behavior* (8th ed.). Boston: Pearson.

Carlson, N. (2005). *Psychology: The science of behaviour* (3rd ed). Canada: Pearson Education.

Carlsson, I., Wendt, P. E., & Risberg, J. (2000). On the neurobiology of creativity: Differences in frontal activity between high and low creative subjects. *Neuropsychologia, 38,* 873–885.

Carroll, R. T. (2006). *The Mozart effect: The skeptic's dictionary.* Retrieved September 3, 2007, from *skepdic.com/Mozart.html.*

Carroll, R. T. (2009). *Placebo effect: The skeptic's dictionary.* Retrieved August 4, 2009, from *www.skepdic.com/placebo.html.*

Carskadon, M., Acebo, C., & Jenni, O. G. (2004). Regulation of adolescent sleep: Implications for behavior. *Annals of the New York Academy of Sciences, 1021,* 276–291.

Carskadon, M., Wolfson, A. R., Acebo, C., Tzischinsky, O., & Seifer, R. (1998). Adolescent sleep patterns, circadian timing, and sleepiness at a transition to early school days. *Sleep, 21,* 871–881.

Carter, R. (1998). *Mapping the mind.* Berkeley: University of California Press.

Case, R., Okamoto, Y., Griffin, S., McKeough, A., Bleiker, C., Henderson, B., Stephenson, K. M., Siegler, R. S. & Keating, D. P. (1996). The role of central conceptual structures in the development of children's thought. *Monographs of the Society for Research in Child Development, 61*(1-2 serial 246), i, iii–vi, 1–295.

Casey, B. (Ed.). (2004). *Developmental psychobiology*. Washington, DC: American Psychological Association.

Cassity, H., Henley, T. B., & Markley, R. P. (2007). The Mozart effect: Musical phenomenon or musical preference? A more ecologically valid reconsideration. *Journal of Instructional Psychology, 34*(1), 13–17.

Caulfield, J., Kidd, S., & Kocher, T. (2000). Brain-based instruction in action. *Educational Leadership, 58*(3), 62–65.

Chall, J., & Mirsky, A. (Eds.) (1978). *Education and the brain*. Chicago: University of Chicago Press.

Chan, A., Ho, Y. C., & Cheung, M. C. (1998). Music training improves verbal memory. *Nature, 396*(6707), 128.

Chan, T., & Petrie, G. F. (1998). The brain learns better in a well-designed school environment. *Classroom Leadership Online, 2*(3). Retrieved September 7, 2007, from *www.ascd.org/readingroom/classlead/9811/2nov98.html*.

Chance, P. (2006). *Learning and behavior: Active learning edition* (5th ed.). Belmont, CA: Thomson Wadsworth.

Chang, K. (2006). *Can we teach emotional intelligence?* Doctoral dissertation. University of Hawai'i, Manoa, HI. AAT 3244709.

Chang, S. (2005). *Brain research and its implications for providing optimal education for diverse learners in the classroom: A literature review*. Master's thesis (M.A. Ed.), Biola University, La Mirada, CA.

Chatham, C. (2004). *Recall deficits in infants born preterm: Sources of individual differences*. Doctoral dissertation, University of Minnesota, Minneapolis, MN.

Chatterjee, A. (2004). Cosmetic neurology: The controversy over enhancing movement, mentation, and mood. *Neurology, 63*(6), 968–974.

Chatterton, J. (2005). *Effects of individuals' learning-style strengths on reading recall and attitudes with and without pictures*. Doctoral dissertation, St. John's University School of Education and Human Services, Queens, NY. AAT 3189163.

Cheng, D. (2005). *Neural correlates of response expression during fear learning: Conditioning and awareness*. Doctoral dissertation, University of Wisconsin, Milwaukee, WI. AAT 3185606.

Chenhappa, S., Bhat, S., & Padakannaya, P. (2004). Reading and writing skills in multilingual/multiliterate aphasics: Two case studies. *Reading and Writing: An Interdisciplinary Journal 17*(1–2), 121–135.

Chesterton, G. K. (1924, July 5). *Selected quotes from G. K. Chesterton*. Illustrated London News. Retrieved March 13, 2010, from *www.river.org/dhawk/gkc-quotes.html*.

Chevreau, L. (2005). *Neurofeedback and childhood ADHD*. Doctoral dissertation, Saybrook Graduate School and Research Center, San Francisco, CA. AAT 3174284.

Chiles, O. (2006). *Test taking time and quality of high school education*. Master's thesis, University of South Alabama, Mobile, AL. AAT 1433221.

Chilson, F. (2002). *The effects of Brain Gym, a whole brain learning activity, on the Idaho Reading Indicator (IRI) scores of kindergarten students*. Master's thesis (M. Ed.), Idaho State University, Pocatello, ID.

Chin, A. (2007). *The authentic Confucius: A life of thought and politics*. New York: Scribner.

Choi, C. (2003). *A process of demystification: A curriculum on the brain and memory strategies for third and fourth grade students with learning disabilities*. Dissertation (M.S. Ed.), Bank Street College of Education, New York, NY.

Chow, K., & Stewart, D. L. (1972). Reversal of structural and functional effects of long-term visual deprivation in cats. *Experimental Neurology, 34*, 409–433.

Christoff, K. (2008). Applying neuroscientific findings to education: The good, the tough and the hopeful. *Mind, Brain, and Education, 2*, 55–58.

Chun, M., & Turk-Browne, N. B. (2007). Interactions between attention and memory. *Current Opinion in Neurobiology, 17*(2), 177–184.

Chungani, D. (2005, April). *The adaptability of the developing brain: Plasticity, experiences, critical learning periods and autism*. Paper presented at the Learning and the Brain Conference, Harvard University, Cambridge, MA.

Cirino, P. T., Rashid, F. L., Sevcik, R. A., Lovett, M. W., Frijters, J. C., Wolf, M., et al. (2002). Psychometric stability of nationally normed and experimental decoding and related measures in children with reading disability. *Journal of Learning Disabilities, 35*(6), 535–538.

Clary, J. (2003). *Executive functioning in adults with attention deficit-hyperactivity disorder: A thesis*. Master's thesis, Appalachian State University, Boone, NC.

Clements, S. D. (1966). Minimal brain dysfunction, terminology and identification. *NINDB Monograph, 3*(1415). Washington, DC: U.S. Department of Health, Education and Welfare.

Close Conoley, J. (2008). Sticks and stones can break my bones and words can really hurt me. *School Psychology Review, 37*(2), 217–220.

Coch, D. (2007). Neuroimaging research with children: Ethical issues and case scenarios. *Journal of Moral Education, 36*(1), 1–18.

Coch, D., Dawson, G., & Fischer, K. W. (Eds.). (2007). *Human behavior, learning, and the developing brain: Atypical development*. New York: Guilford Press.

Coch, D., Fischer, K. W. & Dawson, G. (Eds.). (2007). *Human behavior, learning, and the developing brain: Typical development*. New York: Guilford Press.

Cocker, C. (2002). *Reaching more students using a layered curriculum approach in a fifth grade social studies unit which integrates brain based research and multiple intelligences*. Master's thesis, Hamline University, St. Paul, MN.

Cohen, D. (1996). *The secret language of the mind: A visual inquiry into the mysteries of consciousness*. San Francisco: Chronicle Books.

Cohen Kadosh, R., & Walsh, V. (2006). Cognitive neuroscience: Rewired or crosswired brains? *Current Biology, 16*(22), R962–R963.

Cohen, L., Dehaene, S., Chochon, F., Lehericy, S., & Naccache, L. (2000). Language and calculation within the parietal lobe: A combined cognitive, anatomical, and fMRI study. *Neuropsychologia, 38*, 1426–1440.

Cohen, L., Dehaene, S., Naccache, L., Lehericy, S., Dehaene-Lambertz, G., Henaff, M., et al. (2000). The visual word form area: Spatial and temporal characterization of an initial stage of reading in normal subjects and posterior split-brain patients. *Brain, 123*(2), 291–307.

Cohen, L., Wilson, A. J., Izard, V., & Dehaene, S. (2007). Acalculia and Gerstmann's syndrome. In O. Godefroy & J. Bogousslavsky (Eds.), *Cognitive and behavioral neurology of stroke*. New York: Cambridge University Press.

Cohen, M. & Ranganath, C. (2007). Reinforcement learning signals predict future decisions. *Journal of Neuroscience, 27*(2), 371–378.

Cohen, P. (1995). Understanding the brain: Educators seek to apply brain based research. *Education Update, 18*(16), 35.

Colagrosso, M. D. (2003). *A rational theory of skilled performance and practice: Modeling long-term repetition priming*. Doctoral dissertation, University of Colorado, Boulder, CO. AAT 3113076.

Cole, T. (2006). *The way we think: A primer of education and psychotherapy by reeducation*. Whitefish, MT: Kessinger.

Coles, G. (2004). Danger in the classroom: "Brain glitch" research and learning to read. *Phi Delta Kappan, 85*(5), 344.

Colombo, J. (2002). Infant attention grows up: The emergence of a developmental cognitive neuroscience perspective. *Current Directions in Psychological Science, 11*(6), 196–200.

Coltheart, M. (2004). Brain imaging, connectionism, and cognitive neuropsychology. *Cognitive Neuropsychology, 21*(1), 21–25.

Coltheart, M. (2006). The genetics of learning to read. *Journal of Research in Reading, 29*(1), 124–132.

Columbia University. (1991). *Teachers College record, Volume 93*. New York, NY: Teachers College Press.

Comia, A. (2006). *Creative movement: A powerful strategy to teach science*. Master's thesis, University of Toronto, Canada. AAT MR21076

Compton, R., Heller, W., Banich, M. T., Palmieri, P. A., & Miller, G. A. (2000). Responding to threat: Hemispheric asymmetries and interhemispheric division of input. *Neuropsychology, 14*(2), 254–264.

Conant, B. (2002). *Early childhood educator's and family web corner: Brain research*. Retrieved July 10, 2007, from *users.stargate.net/ cokids/teacher10.html*.

Connell, D. (2005). *Brain-based strategies to reach every learner: Surveys, questionnaires, and checklists that help you identify students' strengths—plus engaging brain-based lessons and activities teaching strategies*. Washington, DC: Teaching Strategies.

Connell, M. (2005). *Foundations of educational neuroscience integrating theory, experiment, and design*. Doctoral dissertation, Harvard Graduate School of Education, Cambridge, MA. AAT 3207712.

Conner, K. (2003). *Mindmapping: A graphic means of addressing differing learning styles in the ESL classroom.* Master's thesis, Arizona State University, Tempe, AZ.

Cooper, A. & Holmes, L. (2006). *Lunch lessons: Changing the way we feed our children.* New York: Harper.

Copinschi, G. (2005). Metabolic and endocrine effects of sleep deprivation. *Essential Psychopharmacology, 6,* 341–347.

Córdova, C. (2005). *Attention, prediction, and sequence learning roles of the cholinergic basal forebrain and the retrosplenial cortex.* Doctoral dissertation, University of California, San Diego. AAT 3190141.

Coren, S. (1993). *The left-hander syndrome: The causes and consequences of left-handedness.* New York: Vintage Books.

Coricelli, G., Dolan, R. J., & Sirigu, A. (2007). Brain, emotion and decision making: The paradigmatic example of regret. *Trends in Cognitive Sciences, 11*(6), 258–265.

Corina, D., Richards, T. L., Serafín, S., Richards, A. L., Steury, K., Abbott, R. D., et al. (2001). fMRI auditory language differences between dyslexic and able reading children. *NeuroReport, 12*(6), 1195–1201.

Cotman, C., & Berchtold, N. C. (2002). Exercise: A behavioral intervention to enhance brain health and plasticity. *Trends in Neuroscience, 25,* 295–301.

Council of Chief State School Officers. (2008). *The words we use: A glossary of terms for early childhood education standards and assessment.* Retrieved August 20, 2009, from *www.ccsso.org/projects/SCASS/projects/early_childhood_education_assessment_consortium/publications_and_products/2840.cfm.*

Couperus, J. (2004). *The role of the development of selective attention in implicit learning.* Doctoral dissertation, University of Minnesota, Minneapolis, MN. AAT 3137160.

Cox, R. (1999). Representation construction, externalised cognition and individual differences. *Learning and Instruction, 9*(4), 343–363.

Cozolino, L. (2006). *The neuroscience of human relationships: Attachment and the developing social brain.* New York: Norton.

Crawford, M., & White, M. (1999). Strategies for mathematics: Teaching in context. *Educational Leadership, 57*(3), 34–39.

Creswell, J. (2003). *Research designs: Qualitative, quantitative, and mixed methods approaches* (2nd ed.). Thousand Oaks, CA: Sage.

Crivellato, E., & Ribatti, D. (2007). Soul, mind, brain: Greek philosophy and the birth of neuroscience. *Brain Research Bulletin, 71*(4), 327–336.

Cromie, W. J. (1999). Mozart effect hits sour notes. *Harvard Gazette Archives.* Retrieved August 4, 2009, from *www.news.harvard.edu/gazette/1999/09.16/mozart.html.*

Cromley, J. (2000). *Learning to think, learning to learn: What the science of thinking and learning has to offer adult education.* Washington, DC: National Institute for Literacy.

Csikszentmihalyi, M. (1991). *Flow: The psychology of optimal experience.* New York: Harper Perennial.

Csikszentmihalyi, M. (1996). *Creativity: Flow and the psychology of discovery and invention*. New York: Harper Perennial.

Cunningham, W., & Zelazo, P. D. (2007). Attitudes and evaluations: A social cognitive neuroscience perspective. *Trends in Cognitive Sciences, 11*(3), 97–104.

Cupo, P. (2005). *The effect of using brain-based learning strategies in an elementary level autistic*. Master's thesis, Gratz College, Melrose Park, PA.

Dahl, R. (2003). The development of affect regulation: Bringing together basic and clinical perspectives. *Annals of the New York Academy of Sciences, 1008*, 183–188.

Dalkey, N. (1969). *The Delphi method: An experimental study of group opinion*. Santa Monica, CA: Project RAND. Retrieved December 12, 2007, from *www.rand.org/pubs/research_memoranda/2005/RM5888.pdf*.

Damasio, A. (1994). *Descartes' error: Emotion, reason and the human brain*. New York: Avon Books.

Damasio, A. (2000). *The feeling of what happens: Body and emotion in the making of consciousness*. New York: Harvest Books.

Damasio, A. (2002). Remembering when. *Scientific American, 287*(3), 66.

Damasio, A. (2003). *Looking for Spinoza: Joy, sorrow, and the feeling brain*. New York: Harcourt.

Damasio, A. (2004). The neural basis of social behaviour. In S. Marcus (Ed.), *Neuroethics: Mapping the field* (pp. 100–107). New York: Dana Press.

Dana Foundation. (1998–2002). *The brainweb and brain information*. Retrieved September 10, 2007, from *www.dana.org/brainweb/fulllist.cfm*.

Dana Foundation. (n.d.). *Brain center*. Retrieved April 13, 2007, from *www.dana.org/braincenter.cfm*.

Danesi, M. (2003). *Second language teaching: A view from the right side of the brain (topics in language and linguistics)*. Berlin: Springer Press.

Dang-vu, T., Desseilles, M., Peigneux, P., & Maquet, P. (2006). A role for sleep in brain plasticity. *Pediatric Rehabilitation, 9*(2), 98–118.

Daniel, D. B. & Poole, D. A. (2009). Learning for life: An ecological approach to pedagogical research. *Perspectives on Psychological Science, 4*(1), 91–96.

Dapretto, M. (2006). Understanding emotions in others: Mirror neuron dysfunction in children with autism spectrum disorders. *Nature Neuroscience, 9*(1), 28–30.

D'Arcangelo, M. (2000). The scientist in the crib: A conversation with Andrew Meltzoff. *Educational Leadership, 58*(3), 8–13.

Dartmouth. (2008). *University degree programs*. Retrieved April 2, 2008, from *www.dartmouth.edu/psych/graduate/description.html*.

Davidson, R. (2001). The neural circuitry of emotion and affective style: Prefrontal cortex and amygdala. *Social Science Information, 40*(1), 11–37.

Davidson, R. (2003). Affective neuroscience and psychophysiology. *Psychophysiology, 40*, 655–665.

Davis, B., & Sumara, D. (2006). *Complexity and education: Inquiries into learning, teaching, and research*. Mahwah, NJ: Erlbaum.

Davis, S. (2000). Look before you leap: Concerns about "brain-based" products and approaches. *Childhood Education, 77*(2), 100–101.

Dawda, D. (2006). *The literacy hypothesis and cognitive development*. Doctoral dissertation, Simon Fraser University, Burnaby, B.C., Canada. AAT NR23882.

Dawson, M. (2003). *The effects of educational kinesiology: On the reading skills of elementary school children*. Master's thesis, Regis University, Denver, CO.

Deacon, T. (1998). *The symbolic species: The co-evolution of language and the brain*. New York: Norton.

Deacon, T. W. (2000). Evolutionary perspectives on language and brain plasticity. *Journal of Communication Disorders, 33*(4), 273–291.

Deacon, T. W. (2003). Universal grammar and semiotic constraints. In M. Christiansen & S. Kirby (Eds.), *Language evolution: The state of the art* (pp. 111–139). Oxford, UK: Oxford University Press.

Dean, S. (2006). *Understanding an achievement gap: Exploring the relationship between attention, working memory, and academic achievement*. Doctoral dissertation, University of Pennsylvania, Philadelphia, PA. AAT 3209993.

Debener, S., Ullsperger, M., Siegel, M., & Engel, A. K. (2006). Single-trial EEG–fMRI reveals the dynamics of cognitive function. *Trends in Cognitive Sciences, 10*(12), 558–563.

Decety, J., & Jackson, P. L. (2004). The functional architecture of human empathy. *Behavioral and Cognitive Neuroscience Reviews, 3*(2), 71–100.

Decker, L. (2004). *Brain-compatible classroom effects on college students in a public speaking class*. Doctoral dissertation, Regent University, Virginia Beach, VA. AAT 3127293.

Deco, G., & Rolls, E. T. (2005). Attention, short-term memory, and action selection: A unifying theory. *Progress in Neurobiology, 76*(4), 236–256.

Deeney, T., Wolf, M., & Goldberg O'Rourke, A. (2001). I like to take my own sweet time: Case study of a child with naming-speed deficits and reading disabilities. *Journal of Special Education, 35*(3), 145–155.

Dehaene, S. (1997). *The number sense*. Oxford Univeristy Press.

Dehaene, S. (1999a). Counting on our brains. *Nature, 401*(6749), 114.

Dehaene, S. (1999b). *The number sense: How the mind creates mathematics*. New York: Oxford University Press.

Dehaene, S. (2002). *The cognitive neuroscience of consciousness*. Cambridge, MA: MIT Press.

Dehaene, S. (2004). Evolution of human cortical circuits for reading and arithmetic: The "neuronal recycling" hypothesis. In S. Dehaene, J. R. Duhamel, M. Hauser, & G. Rizzolatti (Eds.), *From monkey brain to human brain* (pp. 133–158). Cambridge, MA: MIT Press.

Dehaene, S. (2008a). Cerebral constraints in reading and arithmetic: Education as a "neuronal recycling" process. In A. Battro, K. W. Fischer, & P. J. Léna (Eds.), *The educated brain* (pp. 232–247). Cambridge, UK: Cambridge University Press.

Dehaene, S. (2008b). Small heads for big calculations. In *The Jossey-Bass reader on the brain and learning* (pp. 273–300). San Francisco: Wiley.

Dehaene, S. (2008c). *Les neurones de la lecture* [The neurons of reading]. Paris: Odile Jacob.

Dehaene, S. (2009). *Reading in the brain*. New York: Penguin Viking.

Dehaene, S., & Cohen, L. (1995). Towards an anatomical and functional model of number processing. *Mathematic Cognition, 1*, 83–120.

Dehaene, S., & Cohen, L. (2007). Cultural recycling of cortical maps. *Neuron, 56*(2), 384–398.

Dehaene, S., Moiko, N., Cohen, L., & Wilson, A. J. (2004). Arithmetic and the brain. *Current Opinion in Neurobiology, 14*(2), 218–224.

deHann, M., Pascalis, O., & Johnson, M. H. (2002). Specializations of neural mechanisms underlying face recognition in human infants. *Journal of Cognitive Neuroscience, 14*(2), 199–209.

De Jager, M. (2005). *An evaluation of Brain Gym as a technique to promote whole brain learning: A personal and professional perspective*. Doctoral dissertation, University of Johannesburg, South Africa.

della Chiesa, B., Christoph, V., & Hinton, C. (2009). How many brains does it take to build a new light: Knowledge management challenges of a transdisciplinary project. *Mind, Brain, and Education, 3*(1), 17–26.

Denckla, M. (2005, April). *Paying attention to the brain and executive function: How learning and memory are impaired by the syndrome called ADHD*. Paper presented at the Learning and the Brain Conference, Harvard University, Cambridge, MA.

Dennis, M., Landry, S. H., Barnes, M., & Fletcher, J. M. (2006). A model of neurocognitive function in spina bifida over the lifespan. *Journal of the International Neuropsychological Society, 12*(2), 285–296.

Depue, R., & Collins, P. F. (1999). Neurobiology of the structure of personality: Dopamine facilitation of incentive, motivation, and extraversion. *Behavioral and Brain Science, 22*(3), 491–517.

De Raedt, R. (2006). Does neuroscience hold promise for the further development of behavior therapy? The case of emotional change after exposure in anxiety and depression. *Scandinavian Journal of Psychology, 47*(3), 225–236.

Derrida, J. (1988). *Limited Inc*. Evanston, IL: Northwestern University Press.

Desan, P., Woodmansee, W., Ryan, S., Smock, T. & Maier, S. (1988). Monoamine neurotransmitters and metabolites during the estrous cycle, pregnancy and the postpartum period in the rat. *Pharmacology, Biochemistry and Behavior, 30*, 563–568.

Descartes, R. (1965). *Discours de la méthode pour bien conduire sa raison, et chercher la vérité dans les sciences* [Discourse on the method of rightly conducting the reason, and searching for truth in the sciences]. In R. Descartes & L. Lafleur (Trans.), *Discourse on method and mediations* (p. 309). New York: The Liberal Arts Press. (Original work published 1637)

Desoete, A., & Grégoire, J. (2006). Numerical competence in young children and in children with mathematics learning disabilities. *Learning and Individual Differences, 16*(4), 351–367.

Devinsky, O., & D'Esposito, M. (2003). *Neurology of cognitive and behavioral disorders*. Oxford, UK: Oxford University Press.

Dewey, J. (1909). *How we think*. Boston: DC Heath.

Dewey, J. (1991). *Experience and education*. Toronto, Ontario, Canada: Collier. (Original work published 1938)

Diamond, M. (1988). *Enriching heredity: The impact of the environment on the anatomy of the brain*. New York: Free Press.

Diamond, M. (1997). *Significance of enrichment*. Retrieved July 23, 2007, from *www.newhorizons.org/neuro/diamond_enrich.htm*.

Diamond, M. (1999, February). *What are the determinants of children's academic successes and difficulties?* Excerpted from a presentation at an invitational conference, Harvard University, Cambridge, MA.

Diamond, M. (2001a). *My search for love and wisdom in the brain*. Retrieved September 9, 2007, from *www.newhorizons.org/neuro/diamond_wisdom.htm*.

Diamond, M. (2001b). *Response of the brain to enrichment*. Retrieved September 16, 2007, from *www.newhorizons.org/neuro/diamond_brain_response.htm*.

Diamond, M. (2001c). *Successful aging of the healthy brain*. Retrieved September 26, 2007, from *www.newhorizons.org/neuro/diamond_aging.htm*.

Diamond M., Connor, J. R., Orenberg, E. K., Bissell, M., Yost, M., & Krueger, A. (1980). Environmental influences on serotonin and cyclic nucleotides in rat cerebral cortex. *Science, 210*, 652–654.

Diamond, M., Greer, E. R., York, A., Lewis, D., Battro, T., & Lin, J. (1987). Rat cortical morphology following crowded-enriched living conditions. *Experimental Neurology, 96*, 241–247.

Diamond, M., & Hopson, J. (1998). *Magic trees of the mind: How to nurture your child's intelligence, creativity, and healthy emotions from birth through adolescence*. New York: Plume Press.

Diamond, M., & Hopson, J. (2008). Learning not by chance: Enrichment in the classroom. In *The Jossey-Bass reader on the brain and learning* (pp. 70–88). San Francisco: Wiley.

Diamond, M., Krech, D., & Rosenzweig, M. R. (1964). The effects of an enriched environment on the rat cerebral cortex. *Journal of Comparative Neurology, 123*, 111–119.

Diamond, M., & Scheibel, A. B. (1986). *The brain coloring book*. New York: Macmillan.

Dietrich, A. (2004a). The cognitive neuroscience of creativity. *Psychonomic Bulletin and Review, 11*(6), 1011.

Dietrich, A. (2004b). Neurocognitive mechanisms underlying the experience of flow. *Consciousness and Cognition, 13*(4), 746–761.

Dietrich, A. (2007). Who's afraid of a cognitive neuroscience of creativity? *Methods, 42*(1), 22–27.

Diket, R. (2005, Mar). *Applying the neurosciences to educational research: Can cognitive neuroscience bridge the gap? Part II*. Paper presented at the annual meeting of the American Educational Research Association, Montreal, Canada.

Dillon, S. (2009, January 22). Study see an Obama effect as listing black test-takers. *New York Times*, Retrieved from *www.nytimes.com/2009/01/23/education/23gap.html*.

Doidge, N. (2007). *The brain that changes itself*. New York: Penguin.

Donovan, M., Bransford, J. D., & Pellegrino, J.W. (Eds.). (1999). *How people learn: Bridging research and practice*. Washington, DC: National Academy Press.

Douglas, H. (2007). *I am a strange loop*. New York: Basic Books.

Dretsch, M. & Tipples, J. (2007). *Working memory involved in predicting future outcomes based on past experiences. Brain and Cognition Online*. Retrieved September 14, 2007, from *dionysus.psych.wisc.edu/ Lit/Articles/Dretsch2007.pdf*

Drew, A. (2006). *The brain, attention, and eye movements*. Doctoral dissertation, University of Oregon, Eugene, OR. AAT 3224083.

Dronen, M. (2005). *Best teaching practices grounded in brain research*. Master's thesis, Minnesota State University, Moorhead, MN.

du Bois, S. (2005). *The role of adults in altering the child's reading and learning brain*. Master's thesis, Alaska Pacific University, Anchorage, AK.

Dulay, H., & Burt, M. (1977). Remarks on creativity in language acquisition. In M. Burt, H. Dulay, & M. Finocchiaro (Eds.), *Viewpoints on English as a second language* (pp. 65–89). New York: Regents.

Durmer, J., & Dinges, D. F. (2005). Neurocognitive consequences of sleep deprivation. *Seminars in Neurology, 25*(1),117–129.

Dwyer, T., Sallis, J. F., Blizzard, L., Lazzarus, R., & Dean, K. (2001). Relation of academic performance to physical activity and fitness in children. *Pediatric Exercise Science, 13*(3), 225–237.

Dyslexic Research Institute. (2009). *Mission statement*. Retrieved July 20, 2009, from *www.dyslexia-add.org/*.

Economic and Social Research Council Teaching and Learning Research Programmes (ESRC TLRP) seminar series. (2005, July). *Collaborative frameworks for neuroscience and education*. Paper presented at the Teaching and Learning Conference, Cambridge University, Cambridge. Retrieved January 28, 2008, from *www.tlrp.org*.

Edin, F., Macoveanu, J., Olesen, P., Tegnér, J., & Klingberg, T. (2007). Stronger synaptic connectivity as a mechanism behind development of working memory-related brain activity during childhood. *Journal of Cognitive Neuroscience, 19*(5), 750–760.

Education Commission of the States. (1998). *Bridging the gap between neuroscience and education*. Denver, CO: Education Commission of the States.

Eggen, P. & Kauchak, D. (2001). *Educational psychology: Windows on classrooms* (5th ed.). Columbus, OH: Merrill, Prentice-Hall.

Ehrlich, P., & Feldman, M. (2007). Genes, environments, behaviors. *Daedalus, 136*(2), 5–12.

Eichenbaum, H. (2000). A cortical–hippocampal system for declarative memory. *Nature Reviews Neuroscience, 1*(1), 41.

Eimer, J., Salazar, W., Landers, D. M., Petruzzello, S. J., Jan, M., & Nowell, P. (1997). The influence of physical fitness and exercise upon cognitive functioning: A meta-analysis. *Journal of Sport and Exercise Psychology, 19*(3), 249–277.

Eisenberg, N., Valiente, C., Morris, A. S., Fabes, R. A., Cumberland, A., & Reiser, M. (2003). Longitudinal relations among parental emotional expressivity, children's regulations, and quality of socioemtoional functioning. *Developmental Psychology, 39*(2), 3–19.

Eisenhart, M., & DeHaan, R. L. (2005). Doctoral preparation of scientifically based education researchers. *Educational Researcher, 34*(4), 3–14.

Eisenhart, M., & Towne, L. (2003). Contestation and change in national policy on "scientifically based" education research. *Educational Researcher, 32*(7), 31.

Eisner, E.W. (2004). *The arts and the creation of the mind.* New Haven, CT: Yale University Press.

Eisner, E.W. (2008). The role of the arts in transforming consciousness: Education is the process of learning how to invent yourself. In *The Jossey-Bass reader on the brain and learning* (pp. 359–369). San Francisco: Wiley.

El-Ghundi, M., O'Dowd, B. F., & George, S. R. (2007). Insights into the role of dopamine receptor systems in learning and memory. *Reviews in the Neurosciences, 18*(1), 37–66.

Elias, M., Zins, J. E., Weissberg, R. P., Frey, K. S., Greenberg, M. T., Haynes, N. M., et al. (1997). *Promoting social and emotional learning: Guidelines for educators.* Alexandria, VA: Association for Supervision and Curriculum Development.

Eliot, L. (1999). *What's going on in there? How the brain and mind develop in the first five years of life.* New York, NY: Bantam Books.

Ellers, F. (2004). *New research spurs debate on early brain development.* Retrieved August 20, 2007, from *www.courier-journal.com/cjextra/ childcare /day1_brain. html.*

Elman, J., Bates, E., Johnson, M., Karmiloff-Smith, A., Parisi, D., & Plunkett, K. (1996). *Rethinking innateness: A connectionist perspective on development.* Cambridge, MA: MIT Press.

Elst, W., van der Boxtel, M., van Breukeln, G. J., & Jolles, J. (2007). Assessment of information processing in working memory in applied settings: The paper and pencil memory scanning test. *Psychological Medicine, 37*(9), 1335–1344.

Eluvathingal, T., Chungani, H. T., Behen, M. E., Juhász, C., Muzik, O., Maqbool, M., et al. (2006). Abnormal brain connectivity in children after early severe socioemotional deprivation: A diffusion tensor imaging study. *Pediatrics, 117*(6), 2093–2100.

Enck, P., Martens, U., & Klosterhalfen, S. (2007). The psyche and the gut. *World Journal of Gastroenterology, 13*(25), 3405–3408.

Endo, T., Roth, C., Landolt, H. P., Werth, E., Aeschbach, D., & Borbély, A. (1998). Selective REM sleep deprivation in humans: Effects on sleep and sleep EEG. *American Journal of Physiology, 274* [electronic version].

Engel, M. (1994). *With good reason.* New York: St. Martins Press.

Ennis, R. H. (1996). *Critical thinking.* Upper Saddle River, NJ: Prentice-Hall.

Enotes.com. (2009). *American education 1980s.* Retrieved December 13, 2009, from *www.enotes.com/1980-education-american-decades.*

Epstein, R., Higgins, J. S., & Thompson-Schill, S. L. (2005). Learning places from views: Variation in scene processing as a function of experience and navigational ability. *Journal of Cognitive Neuroscience, 17*(1), 73–83.

Erickson, K., & Schulkin, J. (2003). Facial expressions of emotion: A cognitive neuroscience perspective. *Brain and Cognition, 52*(1), 52–60.

Erikson, E. H. (1950). *Childhood and society.* New York: Norton.

Erikson, E. H. (1959). *Identity and the life cycle.* New York: International Universities Press.

Erikson Institute and Boston University School of Medicine, Zero to Three. (2001). *BrainWonders: Helping babies and toddlers grow and develop.* Retrieved September 26, 2007, from *www.zerotothree.org/ brainwonders/index.html.*

Eriksson, P. (1998). Neurogenesis in the adult human hippocampus. *Nature Medicine, 4,* 1313–1317.

Eriksson, P. S., Perfilieva, E., Njork-Eriksson, T., Alborn, A. M., Nordborg, C., Peterson, D. A., et al. (1998). Neurogenesis in the adult human hippocampus. *Nature Medicine, 4*(11), 1313–1317.

Erkens-Trutwin, A. (2004). *Findings revealed from research into the brain as related to meaningful learning and educational practices.* Master's thesis, St. Cloud State University, St. Cloud, MN.

Erlauer, L. (2003). *The brain-compatible classroom: Using what we know about learning to improve teaching.* Alexandria, VA: Association for Supervision and Curriculum Development.

Erlauer-Myrah, L. (2006). Applying brain-friendly instructional practices. *School Administrator, 63*(11), 16–18.

Eslinger, P., & Tranel, D. (2005). Integrative study of cognitive, social, and emotional processes in clinical neuroscience. *Cognitive and Behavioral Neurology, 18*(1), 1–4.

Espy, K. (2004). Using developmental, cognitive, and neuroscience approaches to understand executive control in young children. *Developmental Neuropsychology, 26*(1), 379–384.

ESRC Society Today. (2009). *Economic & Social Research Council.* Retrieved from *www.esrcsocietytoday.ac.uk/ESRCInfoCentre/ about/CI/CP/Social_Sciences/issue63/neuroscience.aspx.*

Etland, A. (2002). *Art and cognition: Integrating the visual arts in the curriculum.* New York: Teachers College Press.

Etnier, J. L., Slazar, W., Landers, D. M., Petruzzello, S. J., Han, M., & Nowell, P. (1997). The influence of physical fitness and exercise upon cognitive functioning: A meta-analysis. *Journal of Sport and Exercise Psychology, 19*(2), 249–277.

Evans, J. (2006). *The impact of brain-based teaching strategies on the retention and application of family and consumer sciences skills.* Master's thesis, Gratz College, Melrose Park, PA.

Evers, E., Cools, R., Clark, L., Veen, F. M. van der Jolles, J., Sahakian, B. J., et al. (2005). Serotonergic modulation of prefrontal cortex during negative feedback in probabilistic reversal learning. *Neuropsychopharmacology, 30*(6), 1138–1147.

Facione, P. (2007). *Critical thinking: What it is and why it counts.* Retrieved May 5, 2007, from *www.austhink.org/critical.*

Fallon, T. (2002). *Developing brain-based vocabulary and concept acquisition strategies for the secondary English classroom.* Master's thesis, Hollins University, Roanoke, VA.

Fancher, R. (1985). *The intelligence men: Makers of the IQ controversy.* New York: Norton.

Farah, M. (2002). Emerging ethical issues in neuroscience. *Nature Neuroscience, 5*(11), 1123–1129.

Farah, M. (2004). Neurocognitive enhancement: What can we do and what should we do? *Nature Reviews Neuroscience 5*(5), 421–425.

Farah, M. (2005). Neuroethics: The practical and the philosophical. *Trends in Cognitive Science 9*, 34–40.

Farah, M. (2007). Social, legal, and ethical implications of cognitive neuroscience: "Neuroethics" for short. *Journal of Cognitive Neuroscience, 19*(3), 363–364.

Farah, M., & Heberlein, A.S. (2007). Personhood and neuroscience: Naturalizing or nihilating? *American Journal of Bioethics, 7*(1), 37–48.

Farah, M., Noble, K., & Hurt, H. (2006). Poverty, privilege, and brain development: Empirical findings and ethical implications. In J. Illes (Ed.), *Neuroethics* (pp. 227–289). Oxford, UK: Oxford University Press.

Farah, M., & Wolfe, P. (2004). Monitoring and manipulating brain function: New neuroscience technologies and their ethical implications. *Hastings Center Report, 34*, 34–45.

Farley, B. (2002). *Brain research: How does movement enhance learning?* Master's thesis, Hamline University, St. Paul, MN.

Feas, A. (2003). *The neuropsychology of music processes and implications for treatment.* Doctoral dissertation, Carlos Albizu University, Miami, FL. AAT 3100820.

Fedorenko, E., Patel, A., Casasanto, D., Winawer, J., & Gibson, E. (2009). Structural integration in language and music: Evidence for a shared system. *Memory and Cognition, 37*(1), 1–9.

Feigenson, L., Dehaene, S., & Spelke, E. (2004). Core systems of number. *Trends in Cognitive Sciences, 8*(7), 307–314.

Feit, A. (2005). *Implicit affect: Affective neuroscience, cognitive psychology, and psychopathology and the emergence of a new discipline.* Doctoral dissertation, Adelphi University, New York, NY. AAT 3158457.

Fellows, L. (2004). The cognitive neuroscience of human decision making: A review and conceptual framework. *Behavioral and Cognitive Neuroscience Reviews, 3*(3), 159–172.

Fellows, L., Heberlein, A. S., Morales, D. A., Shivde, G., Waller, S., & Wu, D. H. (2005). Method matters: An empirical study of impact in cognitive neuroscience. *Journal of Cognitive Neuroscience, 17*(6), 850–858.

Ferbinteanu, J., Kennedy, P. J., & Shapiro, M. L. (2006). Effect of emotional context in auditory-cortex processing episodic memory: From brain to mind. *Hippocampus, 9*, 691–703.

Ferguson, S. (2007). *Effect of a cognitive neurodevelopmental program on learnings of number and operations for elementary students.* Doctoral dissertation, Walden University, Baltimore, MD. AAT 3249929.

Fernandes, M., & Moscovitch, M. (2000). Divided attention and memory: Evidence of substantial interference effects at encoding and retrieval. *Journal of Experimental Psychology: General, 129*(1), 155–176.

Ferrari, M., & Vuletic, L. (2010). *The developmental relations between mind, brain and education: Essays in honor of Robbie Case*. New York: Springer.

Filipowicz, A. (2002). *The influence of humor on performance in task-based interactions*. Doctoral dissertation, Harvard University, Cambridge, MA. AAT 3051159.

Fink, A., Benedek, M., Grabner, R. H., Staudt, B., & Neubauer, A. C. (2007). Creativity meets neuroscience: Experimental tasks for the neuroscientific study of creative thinking. *Methods, 42*(1), 68–76.

Fink, L. (2003). *Creating significant learning experiences: An integrated approach to designing college courses*. San Francisco: Jossey-Bass.

Fiorello, C., Hale, J. B., Holdnack, J. A., Kavanagh, J. A., Terrell, J., & Long, L. (2007). Interpreting intelligence test results for children with disabilities: Is global intelligence relevant? *Applied Neuropsychology, 14*(1), 2–12; discussion, 13–51.

Fischer, K. W. (1980). A cognitive theory of development: The control and construction of hierarchies of skills. *Psychological Reviews, 87*(6), 477–531.

Fischer, K. W. (2004). *The myths and promises of the learning brain*. Cambridge, MA: Harvard Graduate School of Education. Retrieved September 9, 2007, from *gseweb.harvard.edu/news/features /fischer12012004.html*.

Fischer, K. W. (2007a). Dynamic cycles of cognitive and brain development: Measuring growth in mind, brain, and education. In A. M. Battro & K. W. Fischer (Eds.), *The educated brain* (pp. 127-153). Cambridge, UK: Cambridge University Press. Retrieved January 28, 2008, from *gseweb.harvard.edu/ddl/publication.htm*.

Fischer, K. W. (2007b). *Mind, brain, and education: Analyzing human learning and development* [Podcast]. Inaugural launch of the journal *Mind, Brain, and Education*, April 2, 2007. Cambridge, MA: Harvard University.

Fischer, K. W. (2009). Mind, brain, and education: Building a scientific groundwork for learning and teaching. *Mind, Brain, and Education, 3*(1), 3–16.

Fischer, K. W., Bernstein, J., & Immordino-Yang, M. H. (2007). *Mind, brain, and education in reading disorders*. New York: Cambridge University Press.

Fischer, K. W., Daniel, D. B., Immordino-Yang, M. H., Stern, E., Battro, A., & Koizumi, H. (Eds.). (2007). Why mind, brain, and education? Why now? *Mind, Brain, and Education, 1*(1), 1–2.

Fischer, K. W., & Fusaro, M. (2006). From the president's desk: Building Mind, Brain, and Education. *MBE.PONS, 1*(2), 1.

Fischer, K. W., & Paré-Blagoev, J. (2000). From individual differences to dynamic pathways of development. *Child Development, 71*, 849–852.

Fischer, K. W., & Rose, L. T. (2001). Webs of skills: How students learn. *Educational Leadership, 59*(3), 6–12.

Fischer, K. W., & Rose, S. P. (1998). Growth cycles of brain and mind. *Educational Leadership, 56*(3), 56–60.

Fisher, J. (2005). *The development of perceptual expertise in the visual categorization of complex patterns.* Doctoral dissertation, Northwestern University, Evanston, IL. AAT 3200931.

Fitzgerald, D., Angstadt, M., Jelsone, L. M., Nathan, P. J., & Phan, K. L. (2006). Beyond threat: Amygdala reactivity across multiple expressions of facial affect. *NeuroImage, 30*(4), 1441–1448.

Fitzpatrick, S. (2007). Remember the future. In H. L. Roediger, Y. Dudai, & S. M. Fitzpatrick (Eds.), *Science of memory: Concepts* (pp. 1–9). New York: Oxford University Press.

Fogarty, R. (1997). *Brain compatible classrooms.* Arlington Heights, IL: Skylight Training.

Fogel, S. (2005). *The effects of simple procedural, cognitive procedural, and declarative learning on sleep.* Master's thesis, Brock University, Ontario, Canada. AAT MR00693.

Fogel, S., Smith, C. T., & Cote, K. A. (2007). Dissociable learning-dependent changes in REM and non-REM sleep in declarative and procedural memory systems. *Behavioural Brain Research, 180*(1), 48–61.

Fonagy, P., & Target, M. (2007). The rooting of the mind in the body: New links between attachment theory and psychoanalytic thought. *Journal of the American Psychoanalytic Association, 55*(2), 411–456.

Forbes, T., Buckland, H. T., Cunningham, S., Kunselman, M. M., Wilkinson, J., & Williamson, J. L. (2001). *Teaching study skills with brain sciences.* Retrieved September 10, 2007, from *www.newhorizons.org/neuro/forbes.htm*

Forester, A., & Reinhard, M. (2000). *The learner's way: Brain-based learning in action.* Canada: Portage & Main Press.

Fortner, S. (2004). *Examining pedagogical practices through brain-based learning in multiple intelligences theory.* Doctoral dissertation, Regent University, Virginia Beach, VA. AAT 3142354.

Fossella, J., & Posner, M. I. (2004). Genes and the development of neural networks underlying cognitive processes. In M. S. Gazzaniga (Ed.), *The cognitive neurosciences* (3rd ed., pp. 1255–1266). Cambridge, MA: MIT Press.

Fossella, J., Posner, M. I., Fan, J. Swanson, J. M., & Pfaff, D. M. (2002). Attentional phenotypes for the analysis of higher mental function. *Scientific World Journal, 2,* 217–223.

Fossella, J., Sommer, T., Fan, J., Pfaff, D., & Posner, M. I. (2003). Synaptogenesis and heritable aspects of executive attention. *Mental Retardation and Developmental Disabilities Research Reviews, 9,* 78–183.

Fossella, J., Sommer, T., Fan, J., Wu, Y., Swanson, J. M., Pfaff, D. W., et al. (2002). Assessing the molecular genetics of attention networks. *BMC Neuroscience, 3,* 14.

Foster-Deffenbaugh, L. (1996). *Brain research and its implications for educational practice.* Doctoral dissertation, Brigham Young University, Laie, Hawaii. AAT 9708861.

Fowler, A., & Swainson, B. (2004). Relationships of naming skills to reading, memory, and receptive vocabulary: Evidence for imprecise phonological representations of words by poor readers. *Annals of Dyslexia, 54*(2), 247–281.

Freed, J., & Parsons, L. (1998). *Right-brained children in a left-brained world: Unlocking the potential of your ADD child.* New York: Simon & Schuster.

Friederici, A. (2003, September). *The brain basis of language learning: Insights from natural and artificial grammar acquisition.* Paper presented at the Language Learning Roundtable: The Cognitive Neuroscience of Second Language Acquisition, University of Edinburgh, Scotland.

Friederici, A., & Ungerleider, L. G. (2005). Cognitive neuroscience. *Current Opinion in Neurobiology, 15*(2), 131–134.

Friedrich, C. (2003). *Prosody and spoken word recognition: Behavioral and ERP correlates.* Doctoral dissertation, Max Planck Institute of Cognitive Neuroscience, Leipzig Universitat, Leipzig, Germany.

Friedman, R. A. Marx, D. M., & Ko, S. J. (2009). The "Obama Effect": How a salient role model reduces race-based performance differences. *Journal of Experimental Social Psychology, 45,* 953–956.

Frishkoff, G. (2004). *Brain electrical correlates of emotion and attention in lexical semantic processing.* Doctoral dissertation, University of Oregon, Eugene, OR. AAT 3147820.

Friston, K. (2005). Models of brain function in neuroimaging. *Annual Review of Psychology, 56*(1), 57.

Frith, C. (2007). *Making up the mind: How the brain creates our mental world.* Boston: Blackwell.

Fritz, J., Elhilali, M., David, S. V., & Shamma, S. A. (2007). Does attention play a role in dynamic receptive field adaptation to changing acoustic salience in A1? *Hearing Research, 229*(1–2), 186–203.

Fuglestad, J. (2003). *Building connections: Improving memory and recall using strategies supported by brain research.* Master's thesis, Hamline University, St. Paul, MN.

Funahashi, S., Takeda, K., & Watanabe, Y. (2004). Neural mechanisms of spatial working memory: Contributions of the dorsolateral prefrontal cortex and the thalamic mediodorsal nucleus. *Cognitive, Affective, and Behavioral Neuroscience, 4*(4), 409–421.

Furnham, A., Christopher, A., Garwood, J., & Martin, N. (2008). Ability, demography, learning style, and personality trait correlates of student preference for assessment method. *Educational Psychology, 28*(1), 15.

Gabriel, A. (1999). Brain-based learning: The scent of the trail. *Clearing House, 72*(5), 288–290.

Gabriel, J. (2001). *Will the real brain-based learning please stand up?* Retrieved September 7, 2007, from *www.brainconnection.com/content/159_1.*

Gaddes, W. (1983). Applied educational neuropsychology: Theories and problems. *Journal of Learning Disabilities, 16,* 511–515.

Gall, F. (1810). Anatomie et physiologie du système nerveux en général, et du cerveau en paiticulier, avec des observations sur la possibilité de reconnaître plusieurs dispositions intellectuelles et morales de l'homme et des animaux par la configuration de leurs têtes. [Anatomy and physiology of the nervous system in general, and the brain in particular, with observations about the possibility of finding new support for the moral and intellectual disposition of men based on head configuration.] Paris: Institute of France.

Galton, F. (1869). *Hereditary genius: An inquiry into its laws and consequences.* London: Macmillan.

Gardner, H. (1974). *The shattered mind.* New York: Knopf.

Gardner, H. (1981). *The quest for mind: Piaget, Levi-Strauss, and the structuralist movement.* New York: Knopf.

Gardner, H. (1984). *Art, mind and brain.* New York: Basic Books.

Gardner, H. (1987). *The mind's new science: A history of the cognitive revolution.* New York: Basic Books.

Gardner, H. (1991). *The unschooled mind.* New York: Basic Books.

Gardner, H. (1993a). *Frames of mind: The theory of multiple intelligences.* New York: Basic Books. (Original work published 1983)

Gardner, H. (1993b). *Multiple intelligences: The theory in practice.* New York: Basic Books.

Gardner, H. (1994a). *The arts and the human development: A psycological study of the artistic process.* New York: Basic Books.

Gardner, H. (1994b). *Creating minds: An anatomy of creativity seen through the lives of Freud, Einstein, Picasso, Stravinsky, Eliot, Graham, and Gandhi.* New York: Basic Books.

Gardner, H. (1996). *Leading minds: An anatomy of leadership.* New York: HarperCollins.

Gardner, H. (1998). A multiplicity of intelligences. *Scientific American Presents: Exploring Intelligence, 9*(4), 6–11.

Gardner, H. (1999). *The disciplined mind.* New York: Penguin Books.

Gardner, H. (2000). *Mind and brain: Only the right connections review of What makes us think?* Jean-Pierre Changeux and Paul Ricoeur, Princeton University Press, 2000. Retrieved November 6, 2007, from *www.pz.harvard.edu/PIs/HG_Changeux.htm.*

Gardner, H. (2001). *Intelligence reframed.* New York: Basic Books.

Gardner, H. (2005). *Development and education of mind: The selected works of Howard Gardner* (World Library of Educationalists Series). New York: Routledge Press.

Gardner, H. (2006). *Multiple intelligences: New horizons.* New York: Perseus Books.

Gardner, H. (2007). *Five minds for the future.* Cambridge, MA: Harvard Business School Press.

Gardner, H. (2008). Who owns intelligence? In *The Jossey-Bass reader on the brain and learning* (pp. 120–132). San Francisco: Wiley.

Gardner, J. (1990). *On leadership.* New York: Free Press.

Garner, R. (2006). Humor in pedagogy: How ha-ha can lead to aha! *College Teaching, 54*(1), 177–180.

Gardner, R., Ansari, D., Reishofer, G., Stern, E., Ebner, F., & Neuper, C. (2007). Individual differences in mathematical competence predict parietal brain activation during mental calculation. *NeuroImage, 38,* 346–356.

Gaser, C., & Schlaug, G. (2003). Brain structures differ between musicians and non-musicians. *Journal of Neuroscience, 8*(27), 9240–9045.

Gauger, L., Lombardino, L. J., & Leonard, C. M. (1997). Brain morphology in children with specific language impairment. *Journal of Speech, Language, and Hearing Research, 40,* 1272–1284.

Gauthier, I., Tarr, M. J., Moylan, J., Skudlarski, P., Gore, J. C., & Anderson, A. W. (2000). The fusiform "face area" is part of a network that processes faces at the individual level. *Journal of Cognitive Neuroscience, 12*(3), 495–504.

Gazzaley, A., Rissman, J., & D'Esposito, M. (2004). Functional connectivity during working memory maintenance. *Cognitive, Affective, and Behavioral Neuroscience, 4*(4), 580–600.

Gazzaniga, M. (Ed.). (1979). *Neuropsychology: Handbook of behavioral neurobiology* (Vol. 2). New York: Plenum Press.

Gazzaniga, M. (Ed.). (1984). *Handbook of cognitive neuroscience.* New York: Plenum Press.

Gazzaniga, M. (1997). *Conversations in the neurosciences.* Cambridge, MA: MIT Press.

Gazzaniga, M. (2000). *The new cognitive neurosciences.* Cambridge, MA: MIT Press.

Gazzaniga, M. (Ed.). (2005a). *The cognitive neuroscience, III.* Cambridge, MA: MIT Press.

Gazzaniga, M. (Ed.). (2005b). Smarter on drugs. *Scientific American Mind, 11,* 32–37.

Gazzaniga, M. (2005c). *The ethical brain.* New York: Dana Press.

Gazzaniga, M. (2008). *Human: The science behind what makes your brain unique.* New York: Harper Perennial.

Gazzaniga, M., Ivry, R. B., & Mangun, G. R. (Eds.). (2002). *Cognitive neuroscience: The biology of the mind.* New York: Norton.

Gazzaniga, M., Steen, D., & Volpe, B. T. (1979). *Functional neuroscience.* New York: Harper & Row.

Geake, J. (2000). Knock down the fences: Implications of brain science for education. *Principal Matters, April,* 41–43.

Geake, J. (2003a). Adapting middle level educational practices to current research on brain functioning. *Journal of the New England League of Middle Schools, 15,* 6–12.

Geake, J. (2003b). Young mathematical brains. *Primary Mathematics, 7*(1), 14–18.

Geake, J. (2004a). Cognitive neuroscience and education: Two-way traffic or one-way street? *Westminster Studies in Education, 27*(1), 87–98.

Geake, J. (2004b). How children's brains think: Not left or right but both together. *Education, 32*(3), 65–72.

Geake, J. (2005a). Educational neuroscience and neuroscientific education: In search of a mutual middle way. *Research Intelligence, 92,* 10–13.

Geake, J. (2005b). The neurological basis of intelligence: Implications for education: An abstract. *Gifted and Talented, 9*(1), 8.

Geake, J. (2006a). The neurological basis of intelligence: A contrast with "brain-based" education. *Education-Line.* Retrieved January 28, 2008, from *www.leeds.ac.uk/educol/documents/156074.htm.*

Geake, J. (2006b). Review of David Sousa: How the brain learns to read. *Journal of Research in Reading, 29*(1), 135–138.

Geake, J. (2009). *The brain at school.* Berkshire, UK: Open University Press.

Geake, J., & Cooper, P. (2003). Cognitive neuroscience: implications for education? *Westminster Studies in Education, 26*(1), 7–20.

Geary, D. (1998). What is the function of the mind and brain? *Educational Psychology Review, 10*(4), 377–388.

Geisler, W., & Murray, R. (2003). Cognitive neuroscience: Practice doesn't make perfect. *Nature, 423*(6941), 696–697.

Genesee, F. (2000). *Brain research: Implications for second language learning.* ERIC Digest ED447727. Washington, DC: ERIC Clearinghouse on Languages and Linguistics.

George Mason University Graduate School of Education. (2007). *Brain and learning program.* Retrieved June 20, 2007, from *gse.gmu.edu/research/*.

Getz, C. (2003). *Application of brain-based learning theory for community college developmental English students: A case study.* Doctoral dissertation, Colorado State University, Fort Collins, CO. AAT 3107079.

Giannotti, F., Cortesi, F., Sebastiani, T., & Ottaviano, S. (2002). Circadian preference, sleep, and daytime behaviour in adolescence. *Journal of Sleep Research, 11*(3), 191–199.

Gibb, B. (2007). *The rough guide to the brain.* New York: Rough Guidelines.

Gibbs, A., Naudts, K. H., Spencer, E. P., & David, A. S. (2007). The role of dopamine in attentional and memory biases for emotional information. *American Journal of Psychiatry, 164*(10), 1603–1610.

Gibbs, K. (2007). *Study regarding the effects of Brain Gym on student learning.* Master's thesis, State University of New York, Brockport.

Gibson, J. J. (1982). More on Affordances. Online memo taken from E. S. Reed & R. Jones (Eds.), *Reasons for realism* (pp. 406–408). Hillsdale, NJ: Erlbaum. Available online at *www.computerusability.com/Gibson/files/moreaff.html*

Giedd, J. (2004). Structural magnetic resonance imaging of the adolescent brains. *Annals of the New York Academy of Sciences, 1021*, 77–85.

Giedd, J., Blumenthal, J., Jeffries, N. O., Castellanos, F. X., Liu, H., Zijdenbos, A., et al. (1999). Brain development during childhood and adolescence: A longitudinal MRI study. *Nature Neuroscience, 2*(10), 861–863.

Giedd, J., Snell, J. W., Lange, N., Rajapakse, J. C., Casey, B. J., & Kozuch, P. L. (1996). Quantitative MRI of the temporal lobe, amygdala, and hippocampus in normal human development: Ages 4–18. *Journal of Comparative Neurology, 366*(2), 223–230.

Gilbert, C., & Sigman, M. (2007). Brain states: Top-down influences in sensory processing. *Neuron, 54*(5), 677–696.

Gillam, R. (1999). Computer-assisted language intervention using Fast ForWord: Theoretical and empirical considerations for clinical decision-making. *Language, Speech and Hearing Services in Schools, 30*(4), 363–370.

Given, B. (2002). *Teaching to the brain's natural learning systems.* Alexandria, VA: Association for Supervision and Curriculum Development.

Givón, T., & Malle, B. F. (2002). *The evolution of language out of pre-language.* Amsterdam: Benjamins.

Gladwell, M. (2005). *Blink: The power of thinking without thinking.* New York: Little, Brown.

Glannon, W. (2006). Neuroethics. *Bioethics, 20*(1), 37–52.

Glannon, W. (Ed.). (2007). *Defining right and wrong in brain science: Essential readings in neuroethics.* New York: Dana Press.

Glasgow University and the Hamilton Institute, NUI Maynooth (2009). *Institute profile.* Retrieved July 27, 2010, from *www.hamilton.ie/.*

Glick, T., & Budson, A. E. (2005). Education and communication about memory: Using the terminology of cognitive neuroscience. *American Journal of Alzheimer's Disease and Other Dementias, 20*(3), 141–143.

Gobel, S., & Rushworth, M. F. (2004). Cognitive neuroscience: Acting on numbers. *Current Biology, 14*(13), R517–R519.

Gogtay, N., Giedd, J. N., Lusk, L., Hayashi, K. M., Greenstein, D., Vaituzis, A. C., et al. (2004). Dynamic mapping of human cortical development during childhood through early adulthood. *Proceedings of the National Academy of Sciences, 101*(21), 8174–8179.

Goguen, J. A., & Myin, E. (2000). *Art and the brain: II. Investigations into the science of art.* Ciudad, Mexico: Imprint Academic.

Goldberg, E. (2006). *The wisdom paradox: How your mind can grow stronger as your brain grows older.* New York: Gotham Books.

Goldsmith, H., & Davidson, R. J. (2004). Disambiguating the components of emotion regulation. *Child Development, 75*(2), 361–365.

Goleman, D. (2006). *Emotional intelligence: Why it can matter more than IQ* (10th ed.). New York: Bantam. (Original work published 1996)

Good Works Project. (2008). *Howard Gardner's good works project.* Retrieved May 7, 2008, from *www.goodworkproject.org.*

Goodenough, O. (2004). Responsibility and punishment: Whose mind? A response. Philosophical Transactions of the Royal Society of London, Series B, *Biological Sciences, 359*(1451), 805.

Goos, L. (2002). *The influence of genomic imprinting on brain development and behavior.* Doctoral dissertation, York University, Toronto, Canada. AAT NQ99177.

Gopnik, A., & Meltzoff, A. N. (1997). *Words, thoughts and theories.* Cambridge: MIT Press.

Gopnik, A., Meltzoff, A., & Kuhl, P. (1999). *The scientist in the crib.* New York: Morrow.

Gordon, E., Cooper, N., Rennie, C., Hermens, D., & Williams, L. M. (2005). Integrative neuroscience: The role of a standardized database. *Clinical EEG and Neuroscience, 36*(2), 64–75.

Gordon, N. (1995). *The magical classroom: Creating effective, brain-friendly environments for learning.* Tucson, AZ: Zephyr Press.

Goswami, U. (Ed.). (2002). *Blackwell's handbook of childhood cognitive development.* Oxford, UK: Blackwell.

Goswami, U. (2004). Neuroscience and education. *British Journal of Educational Psychology, 74,* 1–14.

Goswami, U. (2005a). The brain in the classroom? The state of the art. *Developmental Science, 8*(6), 468–469.

Goswami, U. (2005b). Neuroscience and education: The brain in the classroom. Target article with commentaries. *Psychology of Education Review, 29*(2), 17–18.

Goswami, U. (2006). Neuroscience and education: From research to practice. *Nature Reviews Neuroscience 7*(5), 406–413.

Goswami, U. (2008a). Cognitive development: The learning brain. London: Taylor & Francis.

Goswami, U. (2008b). Neuroscience and education. In *The Jossey-Bass reader on the brain and learning*, (pp. 33–50). San Francisco: Wiley.

Goswami, U., & Ziegler, J. C. (2007). A developmental perspective on the neural code for written words. *Trends in Cognitive Neuroscience 10*(4), 142–143.

Gould, S. J., (1995). *Dinosaur in a haystack: Reflections in natural history*. New York: Harmony Books.

Grahn, J., & Brett, M. (2007). Rhythm and beat perception in motor areas of the brain. *Journal of Cognitive Neuroscience, 19*(5), 893–906.

Gratton, G., & Fabiani, M. (2003). The event-related optical signal (EROS) in visual cortex: Replicability, consistency, localization, and resolution. *Psychophysiology, 40*, 561–571.

Graves, A. (2003). *Using brain-based teaching, multiple intelligence theory, and learning styles theory to teach students with learning disabilities in the general education classroom*. Master's thesis, Bethel College, Mishawaka, IN.

Graves, A., & Akar, N. Z. (2001). *Brain based learning: Another passing fad?* Retrieved September 11, 2007, from *www.angelfire.com/ok2/metu/brainbased.html*.

Gray, J., & Thompson, P. (2004). Neurobiology of intelligence: Science and ethics. *Nature Reviews Neuroscience, 5*(6), 471–482.

Gray Smith, F. (2008). *Perceptions of universal design for learning (UDL) in college classrooms*. Doctoral dissertation, George Washington University, Washington, DC. AAT 3296852.

Greenawalt, D. (2002). *Employing brain-compatible learning principles to enhance the teaching of the alphabet in a preschool classroom*. Master's thesis, Gratz College, Melrose Park, PA.

Greenberg, D. (2004). *An investigation of autobiographical memory using multiple methods*. Doctoral dissertation, Duke University, Durham, NC. AAT 3177873.

Greene, J. (2005). Emotion and cognition in moral judgment: Evidence from neuroimaging. In J. P. Changeux, A. R. Damasio, W. Singer, & Y. Christen (Eds.), *Neurobiology of human values* (pp. 57–66). Berlin: Springer-Verlag.

Greenfield, S. (1996). *The human mind explained: An owner's guide to the mysteries of the mind*. New York: Holt.

Greenleaf, R. (2003). Motion and emotion in student learning. *Education Digest, 69*(1), 37–42.

Greenleaf, R. (2005). *Brain based teaching: Making connections for long-term memory and recall*. Newfield, MN: Greenleaf & Papanek.

Greenough, W. (1987). In N. A. Krasnegor, E. M. Blass, M. A. Hofer, & W. P. Smotherman (Eds.), *Perinatal development: A psychobiological perspective* (pp. 195–221). London: Academic Press.

Greenough, W. (n.d). Faculty Profile. University of Illinois, Urbana-Champaign, Psychology Department. Retrieved March 12, 2010, from *www.psych.uiuc.edu/people/showprofile.php?id=61.*

Greenwalt, D. (2002). *Employing brain-compatible learning principles to enhance the teaching of the alphabet in a preschool classroom.* Master's thesis, Gratz College, Melrose Park, PA.

Greenwood, J. (2006). *Differentiation for student independence.* Master's thesis, Hamline University, St. Paul, MN.

Greenwood, R. (2006). *Educator acquisition and application of recent neurological and cognitive research.* Doctoral dissertation, University of Toronto, Canada. AAT NR21817.

Gregory, G., & Parry, T. (2006). *Designing brain-compatible learning.* Thousand Oaks, CA: Corwin Press.

Gregson, R. (1997). Nonlinear computation and dynamic cognitive generalities. *Behavioral and Brain Sciences, 20*(4), 688.

Grence-Leggett, L. (2005). *High school students' comparisons of newer versus traditional learning methods.* Doctoral dissertation, Walden University, Baltimore, MD. AAT 3162024.

Grgic, M., Shan, S., Lukac, R., Wechsler, H., & Bartlett M. S. (eds.). (2009). Special issue: Facial image processing and analysis. *International Journal of Pattern Recognition and Artifitial Intelligence, 23*(3), 355–657.

Griffin, T., Jee, B., & Wiley, J. (2009). The effects of domain knowledge on metacomprehension accuracy. *Memory & Cognition, 37*(7), 1001–1013.

Griggs, D. (2006). *A comparison between traditional instruction and brain-based instruction in seventh grade math.* Master's thesis, Troy University, Dothan, AL.

Grosjean, B. (2005). From synapse to psychotherapy: The fascinating evolution of neuroscience. *American Jounral of Psychotherapy, 59*(3), 181–197.

Gross, M. U. M. (2004). *Exceptionally gifted children.* New York: RoutledgeFalmer.

Grossman, A., Churchill, J. D., Bates, K. E., Klein, J. A., & Greenough, W. T. (2002). A brain adaptation view of plasticity: Is synaptic plasticity an overly limited concept? *Progress in Brain Research, 138,* 91–108.

Grossman, M., Koenig, P., Kounios, J., McMillan, C., Work, M., & Moore, P. (2006). Category-specific effects in semantic memory: Category–task interactions suggested by fMRI. *NeuroImage, 30*(3), 1003–1009.

Grotzer, T. (2003). Learning to understand the forms of causality implicit in scientific explanations. *Studies in Science Education, 39,* 1–74.

Grotzer, T. (2004). Putting science within reach: Addressing patterns of thinking that limit science learning. *Principal Leadership, 5*(2), 17–21.

Gruber, A. (2004). *Salience-based gating of information into working memory: An integrated model of dopamine-mediated effects in the basal ganglia and cortex.* Doctoral dissertation, Northwestern University, Evanston, IL. Dissertation Abstracts International 65-05B.

Gruber, H. E., & Bödeker, K. (2005). *Creativity, psychology, and the history of science.* New York: Springer.

Gruhn, W., Galley, N., & Kluth, C. (2003). Do mental speed and musical abilities interact? *Annals of the New York Academy of Sciences, 999*, 485–496.

Guild, P. (1997). Where do the learning theories overlap? *Educational Leadership, 55*(1), 30–31.

Guild, P., & Chock-Eng, S. (1998). Multiple intelligence, learning styles, brain-based education: Where do the messages overlap? *Schools in the Middle, 7*(4), 38–40.

Gullenberg, M., & Indefrey, P. (Eds.). (2006). *The cognitive neuroscience of second language acquisition*. Malden, MA: Blackwell.

Gülpinar, M., & Yegen, B. Ç. (2004). The physiology of learning and memory: Role of peptides and stress. *Current Protein and Peptide Science, 5*(6), 457–473.

Gunn, A., Richburg, R. W., & Smilkstein, R. (2006). *Igniting student potential: Teaching with the brain's natural learning process*. Thousand, Oaks, CA: Corwin Press.

Guo, C., Lawson, A. L., Zhang, Q., & Jiang, Y. (2007). *Brain potentials distinguish new and studied objects during working memory. Human Brain Mapping*. Retrieved September 12, 2007, from *www.mc.uky.edu/behavioral science/faculty/jiang.asp*.

Gutek, G. (2004). *Educational philosophy and changes*. Boston: Allyn & Bacon.

Gutierrez, R. (2005). *The effects of Brain Gym exercises on motor, communication and cognitive development in the kindergarten classroom*. Master's thesis, California State Polytechnic University, Pomona.

Hadj-Bouziane, F., Meunier, M., & Boussaoud, D. (2003). Conditional visuo-motor learning in primates: A key role for the basal ganglia. *Journal of Physiology, 97*(4–6), 567–579.

Hadjikhani, N., Joseph, R. M., Snyder, J., & Tager-Flusberg, H. (2006). Anatomical differences in the mirror neuron system and social cognition network in autism. *Cerebral Cortex, 16*, 1276–1282.

Hagen, M. (2004). *Neuroimaging of higher somaosensory processing in humans: Attention, space, and motion*. Doctoral dissertation, University of Minnesota, Minneapolis. AAT 3129216.

Haier, R., & Jung, R. E. (2007). Beautiful minds (i.e., brains) and the neural basis of intelligence. *Behavioral and Brain Sciences*. Retrieved September 14, 2007, from *www.journals.cambridge.org/production/action/cjoGetFulltext?fulltextid=1231212*.

Halary, K., & Weintrayub, P. (1991). *Right-brain learning in 30 days*. New York: St. Martin's Press.

Hale, T. (2004). *Brain laterality in adults with attention deficit hyperactivity disorder*. Doctoral dissertation, University of California, Los Angeles. AAT 3142513.

Halford, J. (1998). Brain-based policies for young children. *Educational Leadership, 56*(3), 85.

Halit, H., De Han, M., & Johnson, M. H. (2003). Cortical specialization for face processing: Face-sensitive event-related potential components in 3- and 12-month-old infants. *NeuroImage, 19*, 1180–1193.

Hall, J. (2005). Neuroscience and education. *Education Journal, 84*, 27–29.

Hall, K. R. (2006). Using problem-based learning with victims of bullying behavior. *Professional School Counseling, 9*(2), 231–238.

Halpern, D., & Hakel, M. D. (2002). *Applying the science of learning to university teaching and beyond*. San Francisco: Jossey-Bass.

Hansen, L., & Monk, M. (2002). Brain development, structuring of learning, and science education: Where are we now? A review of some recent research. *International Journal of Science Education, 24*(4), 343–356.

Harley, T. (2004a). Does cognitive neuropsychology have a future? *Cognitive Neuropsychology, 21*(1), 3–16.

Harley, T. (2004b). Promises, promises. *Cognitive Neuropsychology, 21*(1), 51–56.

Hart, L. (1999). *Human brain and human learning* (5th ed.). Kent, WA: Books for Educators. (Original published in 1983)

Hartnett-Edwards, K. (2006). *The social psychology and physiology of reading/language arts achievement*. Doctoral dissertation, Claremont Graduate University, Claremont, CA. AAT 3224953.

Hartwell, D. (2006). *Effects of a brain-based performance task on middle school students' joy of learning*. Master's thesis, Gratz College, Melrose Park, PA.

Harvard University Graduate School of Education. (2007a). *Brain and Learning Program*. Retrieved June 20, 2007, from *www.hgse.edu*.

Harvard University Graduate School of Education. (2007b). *Mind, Brain, and Education Program*. Retrieved October 21, 2007, from *www.gse.harvard.edu/academics /masters/mbe/*.

Harvey, S., & Goudvis, A. (2007). *Strategies that work: Teaching comprehension for understanding and engagement* (2nd ed.). Portland, ME: Stenhouse.

Hass-Cohen, N., Carr, R., & Kaplan, F. F. (2008). *Art therapy and clinical neuroscience*. Philadelphia: Jessica Kingsley.

Hastings, N. (2005). *The effects of learner age, gender, and visual complexity on visual learning*. Doctoral dissertation, Wayne State University, Detroit, MI. AAT 3196202.

Hauser, M. D., Chomsky, N., & Fitch, W. T. (2002). The faculty of language: What is it, who has it, and how did it evolve? *Science, 298*, 1569–1579.

Hawkins, J. (2004). *On intelligence: How new understanding of the brain will lead to the creation of truly intelligent machines*. New York: Owl Books.

Hay, C. (2008). *The theory of knowledge: A coursebook*. Cambridge, UK: Lutterworth Press.

Hayes, E. (2006). *Neural encoding of audiovisual speech: Relationships to literacy and cognitive ability*. Doctoral dissertation, Northwestern University, Evanston, IL. AAT 3213003.

Hayiou-Thomas, M., Harlaar, N., Dale, P. S., & Plomin, R. (2006). Genetic and environmental mediation of the prediction from preschool language and nonverbal ability to 7-year reading. *Journal of Research in Reading, 29*(1), 50–74.

Hayne, H., Boniface, J., & Barr, R. (2000). The development of declarative memory in human infants: Age-related changes in deferred imitation. *Behavioural Neuroscience, 114*(1), 77, 83.

Hazlewood, D., Stouffer, S., & Warshauer, M. (1989). Suzuki meets Polya: Teaching mathematics to young pupils. *The Arithmetic Teacher, 37*(3), 8–11.

He, K. (2010). *AMPA receptor and synaptic plasticity*. Dissertation (Ph.D.), University of Maryland, College Park, MD. AAT 3359277.

Healey, J. (1994). *Your child's growing mind: A guide to learning and brain development from birth to adolescence*. New York: Bantam Doubleday Dell.

Hebb, D. (1949). *The organization of behavior*. New York: Wiley.

Heeger, D., & Ress, D. (2002). What does fMRI tell us about neuronal activity? *Nature Reviews Neuroscience, 3*(2), 142–151.

Hergenhahn, B. R. (2005). *An introduction to the history of psychology*. Florence, KY: Cengage Learning.

Heilman, K. M., Nadeau, S. E. & Beversdorf, D. O. (2003). Creative innovation: possible brain mechanisms. *Neurocase, 9*, 369–379.

Heinze, T. (2003). *Kommunikationsmanagement* [Communication management]. Hagen, Germany: FernUniversität Hagen.

Helmuth, L. (2003). Cognitive neuroscience: Fear and trembling in the amygdala. *Science, 300*(5619), 568.

Henderson, L., & Buising, C. (2000, Oct). A peer-reviewed research assignment for large classes. *Journal of College Science Teaching, 30*(2), 109–113.

Hennevin, E., Huetz, C., & Edeline, J. M. (2007). Neural representations during sleep: From sensory processing to memory traces. *Neurobiology of Learning and Memory, 87*(3), 416–440.

Henry, M., Beeson, P. M., Stark, A. J., & Rapcsa, S. Z. (2007). The role of left perisylvian cortical regions in spelling. *Brain and Language, 100*(1), 44–52.

Henry, N. B. (Ed.). (1960). *Rethinking science education: The fifty-ninth yearbook of the National Society for the Study of Education*. Chicago: University of Chicago Press.

Henson, R. (2005). What can functional neuroimaging tell the experimental psychologist? *Quarterly Journal of Experimental Psychology Section A—Human Experimental Psychology, 58*(2), 193–233.

Hepp, C. (2006). Intelligent music teaching: Essays on the core principles of effective instruction. *American Music Teacher, 55*(5), 93–94.

Herdman, A., & Ryan, J. D. (2007). Spatio-temporal brain dynamics underlying saccade execution, suppression, and error-related feedback. *Journal of Cognitive Neuroscience, 19*(3), 420–432.

Hergenhahn, B. R. & Olson, M. H. (2004). *An introduction to theories of learning*. (7th ed.). New York: Prentice Hall.

Herlenius, E. & Lagercrantz, H. (2001). Neurotransmitters and neuromodulators during early development. *Early Human Development, 65*(18), 21–37.

Hersh, J. (2005). *The effect of relationship goals on visual attention in young adults*. Senior honors thesis, Brandeis University, Waltham, MA.

Hill, J. (2004). *The impact of learning styles and high school learning environments on students' decisions regarding higher education*. Doctoral dissertation, University of Central Florida, Orlando, FL. AAT 3144887.

Hillman, C., Castelli, D. M., & Buck, S. (2005). *Physical fitness and cognitive function in healthy preadolescent children.* Paper presented at the American Alliance for the Health, Physical Education, Recreation, and Dance annual convention and exposition, Chicago.

Hirschfeld, L. & Gelman, S. (1994). Toward a topography of mind: An introduction to domain specificity. In L. Hirschfeld & S. Gelman (Eds.), *Mapping the mind: Domain specificity in cognition and culture* (pp. 3–35). Cambridge, UK: Cambridge University Press.

Hitachi. (2008). *Optical topography and Hideaki Koizumi.* Retrieved April 4, 2008, from *www.hitachi.com/New/cnews/040311b.html.*

Ho, S. H. (2007). *Functional and neural mechanisms underlying cognition emotion interaction in incentive learning and decision making.* Doctoral dissertation, University of Michigan, Ann Arbor, MI. AAT 3253290.

Hobson, A. J. (2004). *Dreaming: An introduction to the science of sleep.* New York: Oxford University Press.

Hobson, A. J., & Pace-Schott, E. F. (2002). The cognitive neuroscience of sleep: Neuronal systems, consciousness, and learning. *Nature Reviews Neuroscience, 3*(9), 679–693.

Hobson, A. J., Pace-Schott, E. F., & Stickgold, R. (2000). Dreaming and the brain: Toward a cognitive neuroscience of conscious states. *Behavioral and Brain Sciences, 23*(6), 793.

Hodge, S. (2006). *The effects of a summer preschool literacy program on the development of early literacy skills.* Master's thesis, Idaho State University, Pocatello, ID. AAT MR22513.

Hoeft, E. (2002). *Using a brain-based pedagogy to enhance learning and retention of medical concepts: The case of a secondary school in southeast Wisconsin.* Master's thesis, Carroll College, Waukesha, WI.

Hoek, D., Van Den Eeden, P., & Terwel, J. (1999). The effects of integrated social and cognitive strategy instruction on the mathematics achievement in secondary education. *Learning and Instruction, 9*(5), 427–448.

Hoernemann, W. (2004). *Using brain based elements in the classroom.* Master's thesis, Bethel College, Mishawaka, IN. AAT 9939358.

Hoge, P. (2002). *The integration of brain-based learning and literacy acquisition.* Doctoral dissertation, Georgia State University, Atlanta, GA. AAT 3069680.

Hoiland, E. (2005). *Teacher and principal perceptions of use of brain research findings in reading instruction.* Doctoral dissertation, Seattle University, Seattle, WA. AAT 3181290.

Holden, C. (2004). Training the brain to read. *Science, 304*(5671), 677.

Holloway, J. (2000). How does the brain learn science? *Educational Leadership, 58*(3), 85–86.

Holmboe, K., & Johnson, M. H. (2005). Educating executive attention. *Proceedings of the National Academy of Sciences of the United States of America, 102*(41), 14479–14480.

Holmes, J., Gathercole, S. E., & Dunning, D. L. (2009). Adaptive training leads to sustained enhancement of poor working memory in children. *Developmental Science, 10*(4), F9–F15.

Holmes, J., Gathercole, S. E., Place, M., Dunning, D. L., Hilton, K. A., & Elliott, J. G. (2009). Working memory deficits can be overcome: Impacts of training and medication on working memory in children with ADHD. *Applied Cognitive Psychology.* doi: 10.1002/acp.1589.

Holtzer, R., Stern, Y., & Rakitin, B.C. (2004). Age-related differences in executive control of working memory. *Memory and Cognition, 32*(8), 1333–1346.

Hong, E. (1999). Test anxiety, perceived test difficulty, and test performance: Temporal patterns of their effects. *Learning and Individual Differences, 11*(4), 431–448.

Hong, S. (2005). *Cognitive effects of chess instruction on students at risk for academic failure.* Doctoral dissertation, University of Minnesota, Minneapolis, MN. AAT 3198098.

Hook, P., Macaruso, P., & Jones, S. (2001). Efficacy of Fast ForWord training on facilitating acquisition of reading skills by children with reading difficulties: A longitudinal study. *Annals of Dyslexia, 51*, 75–96.

Hopfinger, J., Buonocore, M. H., & Mangun, G. R. (2000). The neural mechanisms of top-down attentional control. *Nature Neuroscience, 3*(3), 284–291.

Houde, O., & Tzourio-Mazoyer, N. (2003). Neural foundations of logical and mathematical cognition. *Nature Reviews Neuroscience, 4*(6), 507–514.

Howard, D. J. & Gengler, C. (2001). Emotional contagion effects on product attitudes. *Journal of Consumer Research, 28*(2), 189–201.

Howard, P. (2000). *The owner's manual for the brain: Everyday applications from mind-brain research* (2nd ed.). Austin, TX: Bard Press.

Howard-Jones, P. (2005). An invaluable foundation for better bridges. *Developmental Science, 8*(6), 470–471.

Howard-Jones, P. (2007). *Neuroscience and education: Issues and opportunities. Commentary by the Teacher and Learning Research Programme.* London: TLRP. Retrieved January 14, 2008, from *www.tlrp.org/pub/commentaries.html.*

Howard-Jones, P., & Pickering, S. (2006). *Perception of the role of neuroscience in education: Summary report for the DfES Innovation Unit.* Retrieved January 14, 2008, from *www.bristol.ac.uk/education/research/networks/nenet.*

Howdy, R. (2005). *Diagnostics for neuro-ophthalmologic lesions: The eyes are the door to your brain—an interactive web-delivered training guide.* Master's thesis, University of Texas Southwestern Medical Center at Dallas, TX. Retrieved February 2008 from *edissertations.library.swmed.edu/pdf/HowdyR122005/HowdyRichard.pdf.*

Hsieh, H. C. (2003). *The effect of whole-brain instruction on student achievement, learning, motivation, and teamwork at a vocational high school in Taiwan.* Doctoral dissertation, Idaho State University, Pocatello, ID. AAT 3094891.

Huang, R. (2006). *Multisensory representations of space: Multimodal brain imaging approaches.* Doctoral dissertation, University of California, San Diego.

Hubert, V., Beaunieux, H., Chetelat, G., Platel, H., Landeau, B., Danion, J. M., et al. (2007). *The dynamic network subserving the three phases of cognitive procedural learning: Human brain mapping.* Retrieved September 14, 2007, from *www.galenicom.com/en/medline/article/17450582/The+dynamic+network+subserving+the+three+phases+of+cognitive+procedural+learning.*

Huitt, W., & Hummel, J. (2003). Piaget's theory of cognitive development. *Educational Psychology Interactive*. Valdosta, GA: Valdosta State University. Retrieved April 1, 2008, from *chiron.valdosta.edu/whuitt/col/cogsys/piaget.html*.

Hull, G., Rose, M., Fraser, K. C., & Castellano, M. (1991). Remediation as social construct: Perspectives from an analysis of classroom discourse. *College Composition and Communication, 42*, 299–329.

Hurby, G., & Hynd, G. (2006). Decoding Shaywitz: The modular brain and its discontents. *Reading Research Quarterly, 41*(4), 544–556.

Huttenlocher, P. R. (1979). Synaptic density in human frontal cortex: Developmental changes and effects of aging. *Brain Research, 163*, 195–205.

Huttlocher, P. R. (2002). *Neural plasticity: The effects of environment on the development of the cerebral cortex*. Cambridge, MA: Harvard University Press.

Huttenlocher, P. R. (2003). Basic neuroscience research has important implications for child development. *Nature Neuroscience, 6*(6), 541.

Huttenlocher, P. R., & Dabholkar, A.S. (1997). Regional differences in synaptogenesis in human cerebral cortex. *Journal of Comparative Neurology, 387*, 167–178.

Hutterer, J., & Liss, M. (2006). Cognitive development, memory, trauma, treatment: An integration of psychoanalytic and behavioral concepts in light of current neuroscience research. *Journal of the American Academy of Psychoanalysis and Dynamic Psychiatry, 34*(2), 287–302.

Hyatt, K. (2007). Brain Gym® building stronger brains or wishful thinking? *Remedial and Special Education 28*(2), 117–124.

Iaria, G., Petrides, M., Dagher, A., Pike, B., & Bohbot, V. D. (2003). Cognitive strategies dependent on the hippocampus and caudate nucleus in human navigation: Variability and change with practice. *Journal of Neuroscience, 23*(13), 5945–5952.

Iidaka, T., Aderson, N., Kapur, S., Cabeza, R., & Craik, F. (2000). The effort of divided attention on encoding and retrieval in episodic memory revealed by positron emission tomography. *Journal of Cognitive Neuroscience, 12*(2), 267–280.

Iacoboni, M. (2008). *Mirroring people: The new science of how we connect with others*. New York: Farrar, Straus & Giroux.

Iidaka, T., Aderson, N., Kapur, S., Cabeza, R., & Craik, F. (2000). The effort of divided attention on encoding and retrieval in episodic memory revealed by positron emission tomography. *Journal of Cognitive Neuroscience, 12*(2), 267–280

Illes, J. (2005). *Neuroethics in the 21st century*. Oxford, UK: Oxford University Press.

Illes, J. (Ed.). (2006a). *Neuroethics*. Oxford, UK: Oxford University Press.

Illes, J. (2006b). *Neuroethics, neurochallenges: A needs-based research agenda*. Based on the David Kopf Annual Lecture on Neuroethics, Society for Neuroscience. Retrieved May 10, 2007, from *http://neuroethics.stanford.edu/documents/Illes.NeuroethicsSFN2006.pdf*.

Illes, J., & Racine, E. (2005). Imaging or imagining? A neuroethics challenge informed by genetics. *American Journal of Bioethics, 5*(2), 1–14.

Illes, J., & Raffin, T. (2002). Neuroethics: A new discipline is emerging in the study of brain and cognition. *Brain and Cognition, 50*(3), 341–344.

Illes, J., & Raffin, T. (2005). No child left without a brain scan? Toward a pediatric neuroethics. In C.A. Read (Ed.), *Cerebrum: Emerging ideas on brain science* (pp. 33–46). New York: Dana Foundation.

Immordino-Yang, M. (2004). *A tale of two cases: Emotion and prosody after hemispherectomy.* Published online by the American Educational Research Association, Brain and Neurosciences Special Interest Group: *www.tc.umn.edu/athe0007/BNEsig/papers/Immordino-Yang.pdf.*

Immordino-Yang, M. (2007a). An evolutionary perspective on reading and reading disorders? In K.W. Fischer, J. H. Bernstein, & M. H. Immordino-Yang (Eds.), *Mind, brain and education in reading disorders* (pp. 16–29). Cambridge, UK: Cambridge University Press.

Immordino-Yang, M. (2007b). A tale of two cases: Lessons for education from the study of two boys living with half their brains. *Mind, Brain, and Education, 1*(2), 66–83.

Immordino-Yang, M., & Damasio, A. (2007). We feel, therefore we learn: The relevance of affective and social neuroscience to education. *Mind, Brain, and Education, 1*(1), 3–10.

Immordino-Yang, M., & Damasio, A. (2008). We feel, therefore we learn: The relevance of affective and social neuroscience to education. In *The Jossey-Bass Reader on the brain and learning* (pp. 183–198). San Francisco: Wiley.

Immordino-Yang, M., & Fischer, K. W. (2007). Dynamic development of hemispheric biases in three cases: Cognitive/hemispheric cycles, music, and hemispherectomy. In D. Coch, K.W. Fischer, & G. Dawson (Eds.), *Human behavior, learning, and the developing brain: Typical development* (pp. 74–114). New York: Guilford Press.

International Brain Research Association. (2002). *Welcome to the website of the International Brain Research Association—IBRO.* Retrieved September 4, 2007, from *www.ibro.org.*

International Mind, Brain, and Education Society. (2007). *Mission statement of IMBES.* Retrieved August 20, 2007, from *www.imbes.org.*

Iran-Nejad, A., Hindi, S., & Wittrock, M. C. (1992). Reconceptualizing relevance in education from a biological perspective. *Educational Psychology, 27*, 407–414.

Israely, I. (2004). *A critical role for the neuron specific protein delta-catenin in brain function: Implications for adhesion complexes in synaptic plasticity, learning and memory, and cognitive disorders.* Doctoral dissertation, University of California. AAT 3142464.

Ivanov, V., & Geake, J. G. (2003). The Mozart effect and primary school children. *Music Psychology, 31*(4), 405–413.

Jackendoff, R. (2003a). *Foundations of language: Brain, meaning, grammar, evolution.* New York: Oxford University Press.

Jackendoff, R. (2003b). Precis of foundations of language: Brain, meaning, grammar, evolution. *Behavioral and Brain Sciences, 26*(6), 651–665; discussion, 666–707.

Jackson, R. (2006). *A study of brain-based learning strategies and the outcomes on first grade reading achievement scores.* Ed.S. thesis, Alabama A&M University, Normal, AL.

Jacobs, M. (2003). *Brain-compatible mathematics strategies.* Doctoral dissertation, Saint Mary's University of Minnesota, Twin Cities, MN.

Jacobson, L. (2000a). Demand grows to link neuroscience with education. *Education Week, 19*(28), 5. Retrieved September 9, 2007, from *www.edweek.org/ew/ewstory.cfm?slug=28brain.h19.*

Jacobson, L. (2000b). *Study suggests that brain growth continues into adolescence.* Retrieved September 9, 2007, from *www.edweek.org/ew/ewstory.cfm?slug=28brains1.h19& keywords=brain.*

James, W. (1981). What is emotion? *Mind,* ix. (Original work published 1884)

James, W. (2007). *The principles of psychology.* New York: Cosimo. (Original work published in 1890)

Janata, P., & Grafton, S. T. (2003). Swinging in the brain: Shared neural substrates for behaviors related to sequencing and music. *Nature Neuroscience, 6*(7), 682–687.

Jantzen, M. (2004). *Specific and non-specific cognitive operations as language options for memory questions: An fMRI study.* Doctoral dissertation, Florida Atlantic University, Boca Raton, FL. AAT 3151194.

Japikse, K. (2002). *Interference in procedural learning: Effects of exposure to intermittent patterns.* Doctoral dissertation, Georgetown University, Washington, DC. AAT 3046279.

Jeffrey, J. (2004). *Brain-based learning and industrial technology education practice: Implications for consideration.* Doctoral dissertation, Central Michigan University, Mt. Pleasant, MI. AAT 3130140.

Jehee, J., Rothkopf, C., Beck, J. M. & Ballard, D. H. (2006). Learning receptive fields using predictive feedback. *Journal of Physiology—Paris, 100*(1–3), 125–132.

Jensen, E. (1995). *The learning brain.* San Diego, CA: Turning Point.

Jensen, E. (1996). *Brain-based learning.* San Diego, CA: Turning Point.

Jensen, E. (1997a). *Completing the puzzle: The brain compatible approach to learning.* Arlington Heights, IL: Skylight Training.

Jensen, E. (1997b). *Introduction to brain-compatible learning.* San Diego: Brain Store.

Jensen, E. (1998a). How Julie's brain learns. *Educational Leadership, 56*(3), 41–45.

Jensen, E. (1998b). *Teaching with the brain in mind.* Alexandria, VA: Association for Supervision and Curriculum Development.

Jensen, E. (2000a). *Brain-based learning.* San Diego: Brain Store.

Jensen, E. (2000b). Brain-based learning: A reality check. *Educational Leadership, 57*(7), 76–80.

Jensen, E. (2000c). *Learning with the body in mind.* Thousand Oaks, CA: Corwin Press.

Jensen, E. (2000d). Moving with the brain in mind. *Educational Leadership, 58*(3), 34–37.

Jensen, E. (2001a). *Arts with the brain in mind.* Alexandria, VA: Association for Supervision and Curriculum Development.

Jensen, E. (2001b). Fragile brains. *Educational Leadership, 59*(3), 32–37.

Jensen, E. (2002a). *Brain-based learning: Truth or deception? Brain research applied learning.* Retrieved September 8, 2007, from *www.jlcbrain.com/truth.html.*

Jensen, E. (2002b). Teach the arts for reasons beyond the research. *Education Digest, 67*(6), 47.

Jensen, E. (2006a). *Enriching the brain: How to maximize every learner's potential.* San Francisco: Wiley.

Jensen, E. (2006b). The social context of learning. In S. Feinstein (Ed.), *The Praeger Handbook of learning and the brain* (pp. 452–456), Westport, CT: Praeger Press.

Jensen, E. (2007). *Learning and brain expo.* Retrieved June 20, 2007, from *www.brainexpo.com/.*

Jensen, E. (2008). Exploring exceptional brains. In *The Jossey-Bass Reader on the brain and learning* (pp. 385–404). San Francisco: Wiley.

Jensen, E., & Johnson, G. (1994). *The learning brain.* San Diego: Brain Store.

Jernigan, T., Trauner, D. A., Hesselink, J. R., & Tallal, P. A. (1991). Maturation of human cerebrum observed in vivo during adolescence. *Brain, 114,* 2037–2049.

Johnson, C.M., & Memmott, J.E. (2006). Examination of relationships between participation in school music programs of differing quality and standardized test results. *Journal of Research in Music Education, 54*(4), 293.

Johnson, G. (2007). *On the relationship between psychology and neurobiology: Levels in cognitive and biological sciences.* Doctoral dissertation, University of Cincinnati, Cincinnati, OH AAT 3264438.

Johnson, J., & Becker, J. A. (1999). *The whole brain atlas.* Retrieved September 8, 2007, from *www.med.harvard.edu/AANLIB/home.html.*

Johnson, K. A., & Becker, J. A. (2009). *Harvard whole brain atlas.* Retrived August 23, 2009 from *www.med.harvard.edu/AANLIB/home.html.*

Johnson, K. & Maus, S. K. (2004). *What are some brain-based movement activities that contribute to learning in a kindergarten classroom?* Master's thesis, Hamline University, St. Paul, MN.

Johnson, M. (1997). *Developmental cognitive neuroscience.* Oxford, UK: Blackwell.

Johnson, M. (2007). The social brain in infancy: A developmental cognitive neuroscience approach. In D. Coch, K. W. Fischer, & G. Dawson (Eds.), *Human behavior, learning, and the developing brain: Typical development* (pp. 115–137). New York: Guilford Press.

Johnson, R., Chang, C. H., & Lord, R. G. (2006). Moving from cognition to behavior: What the research says. *Psychological Bulletin, 132*(3), 381–415.

Johnson, S. (2004). *Mind wide open: Your brain and the neuroscience of everyday life.* New York: Scribner.

Johnston, A. (2007). *The role of attentional control in reading comprehension.* Master's thesis, University of Guelph, Ontario, Canada. AAT MR25434.

Johnston, P., & Costello, P. (2005). Principles for literacy assessment. *Reading Research Quarterly, 40*(2), 256–267.

Jolles, J. (2007). *"Brain, learning and education" and the development of a large program for research and implementation in the Netherlands.* Maastrict, The Netherlands: Institute of Brain and Behavior.

Jonassen, D. H., & Land, S. (2008). *Theoretical foundations of learning environments.* Mahwah, NJ: Erlbaum.

Jonasson, Z. (2003). *Learning and memory in the hippocampal system: New evidence and theoretical perspectives*. Doctoral dissertation, Harvard University, Cambridge, MA. AAT 3106654.

Jones, C. (2006). *Exploring the practications [sic] of brain-based instruction in higher education*. Master's thesis, University of Colorado and Health Sciences Center, Denver, CO.

Jones, J. (n.d.). *How to teach science: Planning science lessons using the Five E's*. Teachers Network. Retrieved June 10, 2010, from *http://teachersnetwork.org/ntol/howto/science/fivees.htm*

Jones, J. (2004). *Influences and indicators of success for young children in the early childhood classroom according to educational and neuroscientific research*. Master's thesis, Cardinal Stritch University, Milwaukee, WI.

Jones, R. (2006). *What do educators know about executive dysfunction and recognizing students with this deficit?* Master's thesis, Governors State University, University Park, IL.

Jonides, J., & Nee, D. E. (2006). Brain mechanisms of proactive interference in working memory. *Neuroscience, 139*(1), 181–193.

Joseph, J., Noble, K., & Eden, G. (2001). The neurobiological basis of reading. *Journal of Learning Disabilities, 34*, 566–579.

Joseph, R. (1993). *The naked neuron: Evolution and the languages of the body and brain*. New York: Plenum Press.

Juan, S. (2006). *The odd brain: Mysteries of our weird and wonderful brains explained*. Kansas City, MO: Andrews McMeel.

Junghofer, M., Schupp, H. T., Stark, R., & Vaitl, D. (2005). Neuroimaging of emotion: Empirical effects of proportional global signal scaling in fMRI data analysis. *NeuroImage, 25*(2), 520–526.

Juslin, P. J., & Laukka, P. (2004). Expression, perception, and induction of musical emotions: A review and a questionnaire study of everyday listening. *Journal of New Music Research, 33*(3), 217–238.

Kacelnik, O. (2002). *Perceptual learning in sound location*. Doctoral dissertation, University of Oxford, UK. AAT 3181786.

Kacinik, N., & Chiarello, C. (2007). Understanding metaphors: Is the right hemisphere uniquely involved? *Brain and Language, 100*(2), 188–207.

Kalat, J. (2004). *Biological psychology* (8th ed.). Belmont, CA: Wadsworth/Thompson Learning.

Kalenscher, T., Ohmann, T., & Gunturkun, O. (2006). The neuroscience of impulsive and self-controlled decisions. *International Journal of Psychophysiology, 62*(2), 203–211.

Kalueff, A. (2007). Neurobiology of memory and anxiety: From genes to behavior. *Neural Plasticity*. doi: 10.1155/2007/78171

Kandel, E. (2005). *Psychiatry, psychoanalysis, and the new biology of mind*. Arlington, VA: American Psychiatric Publishing.

Kandel, E. (2007). *In search of memory: The emergence of a new science of mind*. New York: Norton.

Kandel, E., & Squire, L. R. (2000). Neuroscience: Breaking down scientific barriers to the study of brain and mind. *Science, 290*, 1113–1120.

Kandel, E., Schwartz, J. H., & Jessell, T. M. (2000). *Principles of neural science* (4th ed.). New York: McGraw-Hill.

Kanwisher, N., & Yovel, G. (2006). The fusiform face area: A cortical region specialized for the perception of faces. *Philosophical Transactions of the Royal Society of London Series B, Biological Sciences, 361*(1476), 2109–2128.

Kapelari, S. (2002). *Networks: An application of brain research to learning.* Master's thesis, City College of New York, New York City.

Karakas, S., & Basar, E. (2006). Quiet revolutions in neuroscience. *International Journal of Psychophysiology, 60*(2), 98–100.

Karmiloff-Smith, A. (1992). *Beyond modularity.* Cambridge, MA: MIT Press.

Karmiloff-Smith, A. (1994). Precis of beyond modularity: A developmental perspective on cognitive science. *Behavioral and Brain Sciences, 17*(4), 693–745.

Karten-Gary, L. (2006). *The role of the school environment in shaping adolescent attitudes towards academic brilliance, athleticism, and studiousness.* Doctoral dissertation, Hofstra University, Hempstead, New York. AAT 3239798.

Kashuba, D. (2003). *Brain-based teaching strategies: The influence of movement on student success and emotion in an elementary classroom.* Master's thesis, Pacific Lutheran University, Tacoma, WA.

Katzir, T., & Paré-Blagoev, J. (2006). Applying cognitive neuroscience research to education: The case of literacy. *Educational Psychologist, 41*(1), 53–74.

Kaufeldt, M. (2010). *Begin with the brain* (2nd edition). Thousand Oaks, CA: Corwin.

Kaufman, J. C., & Sternberg, R. J. (2006). *The international handbook of creativity.* New York: Cambridge University Press.

Keinath, K. (2005). *The effects of Brain Gym activities on second-grade students' academic performance and handwriting skills.* Master's thesis, Western Michigan University, Kalamazoo, MI.

Keri, S. (2003). The cognitive neuroscience of category learning. *Brain Research Reviews, 43*(1), 85–109.

Kerka, S. (1999). *New directions for cooperative education.* Retrieved August 21, 2007, from *www.ericdigests.org/2000-2/new.htm.*

Kessler, S. (2005). *Preschool educational growth using brain research and the multiple intelligences.* Master's thesis, Georgian Court University, Lakewood, NJ.

Keto, A. (2005). *Integrating brain-based learning into the college composition classroom.* Master's thesis, North Carolina State University, Raleigh, NC. Available online at *www.lib.ncsu.edu/theses/available/etd-11162005-133904/unrestricted/etd.pdf.*

Keuler, D., & Safer, M. A. (1998a). Memory bias in the assessment and recall of pre-exam anxiety: How anxious was I? *Applied Cognitive Psychology, 12*(7), S127–137.

Keuler, D., & Safer, M. A. (1998b). Movement opens pathways to learning. *Strategies, 19*(2), 11–16.

Keuper, C. (2007). *Understanding the figurative language of tropes in natural language processing using a brain-based organization for ontologies.* Doctoral dissertation, Nova Southeastern University, Fort Lauderdale-Davie, FL. AAT 3244325.

Kiley-Brabeck, K. (2003). *Social skills of children with 22q11 deletion syndrome: A social cognitive neuroscience approach.* Doctoral dissertation, Fordham University, New York, NY. AAT 3116864.

Killgore, W., Blakin, T. J., & Wesensten, N. J. (2005). Impaired decision making following 49 h of sleep deprivation. *Journal of Sleep Research, 15*(1), 7–13.

Kilts, C., Kelsey, J. E., Knight, B., & Ely, T. D. (2006). The neural correlates of social anxiety disorder and response to pharmacotherapy. *Neuropsychopharmacology, 31*(10), 2243.

Kim, E., Shirvalkar, P., & Herrera, D. G. (2003). Regulation of neurogenesis in the aging vertibrate brain: Role of oxidative stress and neuropsychiatric factors. *Clinical Neuroscience Research, 2*(5–6), 285–293.

Kimura, A., Donishi, T., Okamoto, K., Imbe, H., & Tamai, Y. (2007). Efferent connections of the ventral auditory area in the rat cortex: Implications for auditory processing related to emotion. *European Journal of Neuroscience, 25*(9), 2819–2834.

King, A. (1993). From sage on the stage to guide on the side. *Questia, 41,* 1. Retrieved August 4, 2009, from *www.questia.com/googleScholar.qst;jsessionid=K2zJ2Bn9J6hkGw1GsbGTsHHnM-zLhLgmdChqqbh194rZQrydp2wrh!675269528!676352415?docId=94305197.*

King, D. (1999). *Exercise seen boosting children's brain function.* Retrieved January 23, 2008, from *www.pelinks4u.org/news/bg brain.htm.*

Kinsella, H. (2005). *Successful teaching to right brain dominant learners.* Master's thesis, Regis University, Denver, CO.

Kirby, L. (2006). *The impact of a brain research course on knowledge of the brain and teacher efficacy.* Doctoral dissertation, George Mason University, Fairfax, VA. AAT 3239087.

Kitabatake, Y., Sailor, K. A., Ming, G. L., & Song, H. (2007). Adult neurogenesis and hippocampal memory function: New cells, more plasticity, new memories? *Neurosurgery Clinics of North America, 18*(1), 105–113.

Klein, R., & McMullen, P. (Eds.). (1999). *Converging methods for understanding reading and dyslexia.* Cambridge, MA: MIT Press.

Kleinke, C. L., Peterson, T. R., & Rutledge, T. R. (1998). Effects of self-generated facial expressions on mood. *Journal of Personality and Social Psychology, 74,* 272–279.

Kline, F., Silver, L. R., & Russell, S. C. (2001). *The educator's guide to medical issues in the classroom.* Baltimore: Brookes.

Knight, B. (2000). Inside the brain-based learning classroom. *BSMP Quarterly, 4*(3). Retrieved September 9, 2007, from *www.smp.gseis.ucla.edu/smp/publications/quarterly/quarterlyframes.html.*

Knutson, B., & Wimmer, G. E. (2007). Splitting the difference: How does the brain code reward episodes? *Annals of the New York Academy of Sciences, 1104,* 54–69.

Koch, C. (2004). *The quest for consciousness: A neurological approach.* Englewood, CO: Roberts.

Koelsch, S. (2005). Neural substrates of processing syntax and semantics in music. *Current Opinion in Neurobiology, 15*(2), 207–212.

Koepke, T. (2002). *The relationship of music and brain development on young children.* Master's thesis, Cardinal Stritch University, Milwaukee, WI.

Kohn, A. (1999). *The schools our children deserve: Moving beyond traditional classrooms and tougher standards.* Boston: Houghton Mifflin.

Koizumi, H. (1999). A practical approach to trans-disciplinary studies for the 21st century. *Journal of Seizon and Life Sciences, 9,* 5–24.

Kok, A., Ridderinkhof, K. R., & Ullsperger, M. (2006). The control of attention and actions: Current research and future developments. *Brain Research, 1105*(1), 1–6.

Korenman, L., & Peynircioglu, Z. F. (2007). Individual differences in learning and remembering music: Auditory versus visual presentation. *Journal of Research in Music Education, 55*(1), 48–55.

Kornack, D. R., & Rakic, P. (1999). Continuation of neurogenesis in the hippocampus of the adult macaque monkey. *Proceedings of the National Academy of Sciences, 96,* 5768–5773.

Kotulak, R. (2008). The effect of violence and stress in kids' brain. In *The Jossey-Bass reader on the brain and learning* (pp. 216–228). San Francisco: Wiley.

Kovalev, V., Kruggel, F., & von Cramon, D. Y. (2003). Gender and age effects in structural brain asymmetry as measured by MRI texture analysis. *NeuroImage, 19*(3), 895–905.

Kovalik, S., & Olsen, K. (1997). *Integrated thematic instruction: The model* (3rd ed.). Covington, WA: Books for Education.

Kovalik, S., & Olsen, K. (1998). How emotions run us, our students, and our classrooms. *NASSP Bulletin, 82*(598), 29–37.

Kral, V., & Maclean, P. D. (1973). *A triune concept of the brain and behaviour: The Hincks Memorial Lectures.* Toronto: University of Toronto Press.

Krasny, K. (2006). *Imagery, affect, and the embodied mind: Implications for reading and responding to literature.* Doctoral dissertation, Texas A&M University, College Station, TX. AAT 3202251.

Kravitz, D. (2002). *How can brain-based learning theory be applied to music education?* Master's thesis, California Pacific University, San Diego, CA.

Krehbiel, M. (2002). *The structure of intellectual functioning and its relationship to perceived control in a clinical sample of adults with cognitive impairments.* Doctoral dissertation, University of Maryland, College Park, MD. AAT 3094507.

Kucia-Stauder, K. (2006). *Stimulating intrinsic motivation: Brain-based pedagogy for the second-language writing classroom.* Master's thesis, California State University, San Bernardino, CA.

LaBar, K., & Cabeza, R. (2006). Cognitive neuroscience of emotional memory. *Nature Reviews Neuroscience 7*(1), 54–66.

LaBar, K., Gatenby, C., Gore, J. C., LeDoux, J. E., & Phelps, E. A. (1998). Human amygdala activation during conditioned fear acquisition and extinction. *Neuron, 29,* 937–945.

Lackney, J. (1998). *Brain-based principles for educational design.* Retrieved September 9, 2007, from *http://schoolstudio.engr.wisc.edu/brainbased.html.*

Lackney, J. (2004). *12 design principles based on brain-based learning research.* DesignShare: The International Forum for Innovative Schools. Retrieved November 4, 2004, from *www.designshare.com/Research/BrainBased Learn98.htm*

LaFrinier, J. (2004). *How does the curriculum of local childcare centers reflect what current brain research says about learning?* Master's thesis, Hamline University, St. Paul, MN.

Lakoff, G. (1987). *Women, fire, and dangerous things: What categories reveal about the mind.* Chicago: University of Chicago Press.

Lakoff, G., & Johnson, M. (1980). *Metaphors we live by.* Chicago: University of Chicago Press.

Lakoff, G., & Johnson, M. (1999). *Philosophy in the flesh: The embodied mind and its challenge to western thought.* New York: Basic Books.

Lang, S. (1997). *Challenges.* New York: Springer.

Lang, T. (n/d). *An overview of four future methodologies (Delphi, Environmental Scanning, Issues Management and Emerging Issue Analysis).* Retrieved October 31, 2006, from *www.soc. hawaii.edu/future/j7/LANG.htmlon31.*

Langer, E. (1997). *The power of mindful learning.* Cambridge, MA: Perseus Books Group.

Langhoff, B. (2006). *How does participating in a brain-based classroom impact students' attitudes when learning another language?* Master's thesis, Hamline University, St. Paul, MN.

Langley, S. (2007). *Identifying self-regulatory factors that influence the academic achievement motivation of underprepared college students.* Doctoral dissertation, University of Minnesota, Minneapolis, MN. AAT 3273170.

Languis, M. (1998). Using knowledge of the brain in educational practice. *NASSP Bulletin, 82*(598), 38–47.

Lavin, E. (2005). *Using technology to develop phonemic awareness and auditory processing skills to enhance academic performance: A qualitative analysis of the Fast ForWord language product.* Master's thesis, Bank Street College of Education, New York, NY.

Lawrence, N., Ross, T. J., Hoffmann, R., Garavan, H., & Stein, E. A. (2003). Multiple neuronal networks mediate sustained attention. *Journal of Cognitive Neuroscience, 15*(7), 1028–1038.

Lawton, M. (1999). The "brain-based" ballyhoo. *Harvard Education Letter, 15*(4), 5–7.

LeDoux, J. (1996). *The emotional brain: The mysterious underpinnings of emotional life.* New York: Simon & Schuster.

LeDoux, J. (2000). Emotion circuits in the brain. *Annual Review of Neuroscience, 23*(1), 155–184.

LeDoux, J. (2003). *Synaptic self: How our brains become who we are.* New York: Penguin Books.

LeDoux, J. (2008). Remembrance of emotions past. In *The Jossey-Bass reader on the brain and learning* (pp. 151–182). San Francisco: Wiley.

Lee, D. (2006). Neural basis of quasi-rational decision making. *Current Opinion in Neurobiology, 16*(2), 191–198.

Lee, L. (2005). *Academic achievement, attitudes, and retention: Application of whole brain instruction in the Principles of Accounting course in central Taiwan.* Doctoral dissertation, Idaho State University, Pocatello, ID. AAT 3172905.

Leech, R., Mareschal, D., & Cooper, R. (2008). Analogy as relational priming: A developmental and computational perspective on the origins of a complex cognitive skill. *Behavioral and Brain Sciences, 31*(4), 357–78; discussion, 378–414.

Leelawong, K. (2005). *Using the learning-by-teaching paradigm to design intelligent learning environments*. Doctoral dissertation, Vanderbilt University, Nashville, TN. AAT 3188042.

LeFevre, J., Smith-Chant, B. L., Fast, L., Skwarchuk, S. L., Sargla, E., Arnup, J. S., et al. (2006). What counts as knowing? The development of conceptual and procedural knowledge of counting from kindergarten through Grade 2. *Journal of Experimental Child Psychology, 93*, 285–303.

Legg, A., & Locker, L. (2009). Math performance and its relationship to math anxiety and metacognition. *North American Journal of Psychology, 11*(3), 471–485.

Leman, M., Vermeulen, V., De Voogdt, L., Moelants, D., & Lesaffre, M. (2005). Prediction of musical affect using a combination of acoustic structural cues. *Journal of New Music Research, 34*(1), 39–67.

Leppo, M., & Davis, D. (2005). Movement opens pathways to learning. *Strategies, 19*(2), 11–16.

Lesser, M. (2003). *The brain chemistry plan: The personalized nutritional prescription for balancing mood, relieving stress, conquering depression*. New York: Berkeley Publishing.

Levine, M. (2000). *A mind at a time*. New York: Simon & Schuster.

Levitin, D. (2008). My favorite thing: Why do we like the music we like? In *The Jossey-Bass reader on the brain and learning* (pp. 370–384). San Francisco: Wiley.

Levveroni, C., Seidenberg, M., Mayer, A. R., Mead, L. A., Binder, J. R., & Rao, S. M. (2000). Neural systems underlying the recognition of familiar and newly learned faces. *Journal of Neuroscience, 20*(2), 878–886.

Levy, R., & Goldman-Rakic, P. S. (2000). Segregation of working memory functions within the dorsolateral prefrontal cortex. *Experimental Brain Research, 133*, 23–32.

Lewis, A. (1997). Learning our lessons about early learning. *Phi Delta Kappan, 78*(8), 591–592.

Lieberman, M. (1962). *The future of public education*. Chicago: University of Chicago Press.

Lieberman, M. (2005). Principles, processes, and puzzles of social cognition: An introduction for the special issue on social cognitive neuroscience. *NeuroImage, 28*(4), 745–756.

Lieberman, M. (2007). Social cognitive neuroscience: A review of core processes. *Annual Review of Psychology, 58*(1), 259.

Linan, R. (2006). *The effect of music instruction on student success in the age of high-stakes testing and accountability*. Doctoral dissertation, Texas A&M University, College Station, TX. AAT 3250008.

Lind, N., Moustgaard, A., Jelsing, J., Vajta, G., Cumming, P., & Hansen, A. K. (2007). The use of pigs in neuroscience: Modeling brain disorders. *Neuroscience and Biobehavioral Reviews, 31*(5), 728–751.

Lindblom-Ylänne, S., & Lonka, K. (1999). Individual ways of interacting with the learning environment: Are they related to study success? *Learning and Instruction, 9*(1), 1–18.

Linden, D. (2007a). *The accidental mind: How brain evolution has given us love, memory, dreams and God*. Cambridge, MA: Harvard University Press.

Linden, D. (2007b). The working memory networks of the human brain. *The Neuroscientist, 13*(3), 257–267.

Lindsey, G. (1999). Brain research and implications for early childhood education: Research reviews. *Childhood Education, 75*(2), 97–100.

Lipkens, R., & Hayes, S. (2009). Producing and recognizing analogical relations. *Journal of the Experimental Analysis of Behavior, 91*(1), 105–126.

Liston, C., & Kagan, J. (2002). Brain development: Memory enhancement in early childhood. *Nature, 419*, 896.

Little, D., Shin, S. S., Sisco, S. M., & Thulborn, K. R. (2006). Event-related fMRI of category learning: Differences in classification and feedback networks. *Brain and Cognition, 60*(3), 244–252.

Littleton, J. (1998). Learning to laugh and laughing to learn. *Montessori Life, 10*(4), 42–44.

Liu, J. (2004). Malnutrition at age 3 years and externalizing behavior problems at ages 8, 11, and 17 years. *American Journal of Psychiatry, 161*(11), 13.

Lodico, M. G., Spaulding, D. T., & Voegtle, K. H. (2006). *Methods in educational research: From theory to practice.* New York: Wiley.

Loeb, D., Store, C., & Fey, M. E. (2001). Language changes associated with Fast ForWord-language: Evidence form case studies. *American Journal of Speech–Language Pathology, 10*(3), 216–231.

Long, (2006). *The mind of a mnemonist: II.* Retrieved October 25, 2009, from *www.drbilllong. com/CurrentEventsVI/MnemonistII.html.*

Louie, P. (2007). *Acquiring a new musical system.* Doctoral dissertation, University of California, Berkeley, CA. AAT 3275497.

Lucas, B. (2006). *Boost your brain power week by week: 52 techniques to make you smarter.* London: Duncan Baird.

Luhmkuhl, D. (1993). *Organizing for the creative person: Right-brain styles for conquering clutter, mastering time, and reaching your goals.* New York: Three Rivers Press.

Luna, B., Thulbor, K. R., Munoz, D. P., Merriam, E. P., Garver, K. E., & Minshew, N. J. (2001). Maturation of widely distributed brain function subserves cognitive development. *NeuroImage, 13*, 786–793.

Luo, J., & Knoblich, G. (2007). Studying insight problem solving with neuroscientific methods. *Methods, 42*(1), 77–86.

Lupien, S., Maheu, F., Tu, M., Fiocco, A., & Schramek, E. (2007). The effects of stress and stress hormones on human cognition: Implications for the field of brain and cognition. *Brain and Cognition, 65*(3), 209–237.

Luria, A. (1968). *The mind of a mnemonist.* New York: Basic Books.

Luria, A., & Bruner, J. (2006). *The mind of a mnemonist: A little book about a vast memory* (L. Solotaroff, Trans.). Cambridge, MA: Harvard University Press. (Original work published 1968)

Luzzati, F., De Marchis, S., Fasolo, A., & Peretto, P. (2006). Neurogenesis in the caudate nucleus of the adult rabbit. *Journal of Neuroscience, 26*(2), 609–621.

Lynch, G., & Granger, R. (2008). *Big brain: The origins and future of human intelligence.* New York: Palgrave MacMillan.

Lyon, G., & Rumsey, J. M. (Eds.). (1996). *Neuroimaging: A window to the neurological foundations of learning and behavior in children.* Baltimore: Brookes.

Madigan, K. (2001). *Buyer beware: Too early to use brain-based strategies.* CBE Education online Edition. Retrieved September 10, 2007, from *www.c-b-e.org/be/iss0104/a2madigan.htm.*

Maguire, E., Gadian, D. G., Johnsrude, I. S., Good, C. D., Ashburner, J., Frackowiak, R. S. J. et al. (2000). Navigation-related structural change in the hippocampi of taxi drivers. *Proceedings of the National Academy of Sciences of the United States of America, 97*(8), 4398–4403.

Males, M. (2009). Does the adolescent brain make risk taking inevitable? A skeptical appraisal. *Journal of Adolescent Research, 24*(1), 3–20. doi: 10.1177/0743558408326913

Maloney, K. (2004). *The evolutionary development of the scientific mind: a grounded theory of adventuring.* Doctoral dissertation, Fielding Graduate Institute, Santa Barbara, CA. AAT 3120901.

Mangels, J., Butterfield, B., & Lamb, J. (2006). Why do beliefs about intelligence influence learning success? A social cognitive neuroscience model. *Social Cognitive and Affective Neuroscience* (2), 75–86. Retrieved September 12, 2007, from *http://scan.oxfordjournals.org/cgi/content/abstract/1/2/75.*

Manning, J. (2006). *Modeling human spatial navigation using a degraded ideal navigator.* Senior honors thesis, Brandeis University, Waltham, MA.

Maquet, P. (Ed.). (2003). *Sleep and brain plasticity.* South Melbourne, Victoria, Australia: Oxford University Press.

Maquet, P., Laurey, S., Peigneux, P., Fuchs, S., Petiau, C., Phillips, C., et al. (2000). Experience-dependent changes in cerebral activation during human REM sleep. *Nature Neuroscience, 3*(8), 831–836.

Marantz, A., Miyashita, Y., & O'Neil, W. (2000). *Image, language, brain.* Cambridge, MA: MIT Press.

Maren, S. & Quirk, G. J. (2004). Neuronal signalling of fear memory. *Nature Reviews Neuroscience, 5*(11), 844–852,

Marcason, W. (2005). Can dietary intervention play a part in the treatment of attention deficit and hyperactivity disorder? *Journal of the American Dietetic Association, 105*(7), 1161–1162

Marcus, S. (2004), *Neuroethics: Mapping the field.* New York: Dana Press.

Maren, S., Quirk, G. J. (2004). Neuronal signalling of fear memory. *National Review of Neuroscience, 5,* 844–852.

Mareschal, D., Johnson, M. H., Sirios, S., Spratline, M., Thomas, M., & Westermann, G. (2007). *Neuroconstructivism: How the brain constructs cognition.* Oxford, UK: Blackwell.

Margulies, N. (1997). *Inside Brian's brain.* Tucson, AZ: Zephyr Press.

Marian, V., Spivey, M., & Hirsch, J. (2003). Shared and separate systems in bilingual language processing: Converging evidence from eyetracking and brain imaging. *Brain and Language, 86*(1), 70–82.

Markham, A., & Gentner, D. (2001). Thinking. *Annual Review of Psychology, 52*(1), 223–247.

Marsh, R., Landau, J. D., & Hicks, J. L. (1997). Contributions of inadequate source monitoring to unconscious plagiarism during idea generation. *Journal of Experimental Psychology: Learning, Memory, and Cognition, 23*, 886–907.

Martens, S., Munneke, J., Smid, H., & Johnson, A. (2006). Quick minds don't blink: Electrophysiological correlates of individual differences in attentional selection. *Journal of Cognitive Neuroscience, 18*(9), 1423–1438.

Martin, A., & Caramazza, A. (2003). Neuropsychological and neuroimaging perspectives on conceptual knowledge: An introduction. *Cognitive Neuropsychology, 20*(3–6), 195–213.

Martin, J. (2003). *Neuroanatomy: Text and atlas* (3rd ed.). New York: McGraw-Hill Medical.

Martin, K. (2006). *Perceptions of brain-based learning from principals in the Bulloch County School System, Georgia.* Doctoral dissertation, Union Institute and University, Cincinnati, OH. AAT 3244187.

Martin, A., & Caramazza, A. (2003). Neuropsychological and neuroimaging perspectives on conceptual knowledge: An introduction. *Cognitive Neuropsychology, 20*(3–6), 195–213.

Martin, S., & Morris, R. G. M. (2002). New life in an old idea: The synaptic plasticity and memory hypothesis revisited. *Hippocampus, 12*, 609–636.

Martinez, M. (2006). What is metacognition? *Phi Delta Kappan, 87*(9), 696–699.

Marzano, R. (2003). *What works in schools: Translating research into action.* Alexandria, VA: Association for Supervision and Curriculum Development.

Marzano, R. (2007). *The art and science of teaching: A comprehensive framework for effective instruction.* Arlington, VA: Association For Supervision and Curriculum Development.

Marzano, R., Pickering, D. J., & Pollock., J. E. (2004). *Classroom instruction that works: Research-based strategies for increasing student achievement.* New York: Prentice-Hall.

Mascolo, M., & Fischer, K. W. (2003). Beyond the nature–nurture divide in development and evolution. Review of Gilbert Gottlieb's "Individual development and evolution." *Contemporary Psychology, 48*, 842–847.

Mascolo, M., & Fischer, K. W. (2007). The co-development of self and socio-moral emotions during the toddler years. In C. A. Brownell & C. B. Kopp (Eds.), *Transitions in early socioemotional development: The toddler years.* New York: Guilford Press. Retrieved January 28, 2008, from *gseweb.harvard.edu/ddl /publication.htm.*

Mascolo, M., Pollack, R., & Fischer, K. W. (1997). Keeping the constructor in development: An epigenetic systems approach. *Journal of Constructivist Psychology, 10*, 25–49.

Mash, E. J., & Barkley, R. A. (2006). *Treatment of childhood disorders.* New York: Guilford Press.

Mashal, N., & Faust, M. (2008). Right hemisphere sensitivity to novel metaphoric relations: Application of the signal detection theory. *Brain and Language, 102*(8), 103–112.

Maslow, A. H. (1998). *Toward a psychology of being* (3rd ed.). New York: Wiley. (Original published in 1943)

Matsumoto, K., & Tanaka, K. (2004). Neuroscience: Conflict and cognitive control. *Science, 303*(5660), 969.

Maturana, H., Varela, F. J., & Paolucci, R. (1998). *The tree of knowledge: The biological roots of human understanding.* Boston: Shambhala.

Maus, S., & Johnson, K. J. (2004). *What are some brain-based movement activities that contribute to learning in a kindergarten classroom?* Master's thesis, Hamline University, St. Paul, MN.

Max Planck Institute (2010). *Research for the future.* Retrieved from *www.mpg.de/english/portal/index.html.*

Mayer, E. (2007). *Extraordinary knowing: Science, skepticism, and the inexplicable powers of the human mind.* New York: Bantam.

Mayer, R. (1998). Does the brain have a place in educational psychology? *Educational Psychology Review, 10*(4), 389–396.

McBrien, J., & Brandt, R. S. (1997). *The language of learning: A guide to education terms.* Alexandria, VA: Association for Supervision and Curriculum Development.

McBurney, D., Gaulin, S. J. C., Devineni, T., & Adams, C. (1997). Superior spatial memory of memory: Stronger evidence for the gathering hypothesis. *Evolution and Human Behavior, 18*(3), 165–174.

McCandliss, B. (2003). *Brain-based education.* Retrieved March 19, 2007, from *www.sacklerinstitute.org/cornell/people/bruce.mccandliss/publications/publications/McCandliss.2003.encyofed.pdf.*

McCandliss, B., & Noble, K. G. (2003). The development of reading impairment: A cognitive neuroscience model. *Mental Retardation and Developmental Disabilities Research Reviews, 8,* 196–205.

McCann, E., & Garcia, T. (1999). Maintaining motivation and regulating emotion: Measuring individual differences in academic volitional strategies. *Learning and Individual Differences, 11*(3), 259–270.

McClelland, J., Feldman, J., Adelson, B., Bower, G., & McDermott, D. (1986). *Connectionist models and cognitive science: Goals, directions, and implications.* Washington, DC: Report to the National Science Foundation.

McClure, S., Yoir, M., & Montague, P. (2004). The neural substrates of reward processing in humans: The model role of fMRI. *Neuroscientists, 10*(3), 260–268.

McCutcheon, L. E. (2000). Another failure to generalize the Mozart effect. *Psychological Reports, 87,* 325–330.

McDonnell (James S.) Foundation. (2005a). *John T. Bruer, president's biography.* Retrieved January 21, 2008, from *www.jsmf.org/about/jbio.htm.*

McDonnell (James S.) Foundation. (2005b). *The neuro-journalism mill: Separating the wheat from the chaff of media reporting on brain sciences.* Retrieved September 13, 2007, from *www.jsmf.org/about/jpubs.htm.*

McDonnold, L. (1981). *Implications of selective brain research for the philosophy of education.* Doctoral dissertation, University of Oklahoma, Norman, OK. AAT 8129402.

McGaugh, J. (2004). The amygdala modulates the consolidation of memories of emotionally arousing experiences. *Annual Review of Neuroscience, 27*(1), 1–28.

McIntosh, A. (1999). Mapping cognition to the brain through neural interactions. *Memory, 7*(5–6), 523–548.

McKelvie, P., & Low, J. (2002). Listening to Mozart does not improve children's spatial ability: Final curtains for the Mozart effect. *British Journal of Developmental Psychology, 20*(2), 241–259.

McKinsey & Company. (2007). *How the world's best performing school systems come out on top.* Retrieved December 19, 2007, from *www.mckinsey.com/clientservice/socialsector/resources/pdf/Worlds_School_Systems_Final.pdf.*

McManus, C. (2002). *Right hand, left hand: The origins of asymmetry in brains, bodies, atoms, and cultures.* Cambridge, MA: Harvard University Press.

McNamara, D. S. (2006). Bringing cognitive science into education and back again: The value of interdisciplinary research. *Cognitive Science, 30*, 605–608.

McNeil, L., & Valenzuela, V. (2000). The harmful impact of the TAAS system of testing in Texas: Beneath the accountability rhetoric. In G. Orfield & M. Kornhaber (Eds.), *Raising standards or raising barriers? Inequality and high stakes testing in public education* (pp. 127–150). Cambridge, MA: Harvard Civil Rights Project.

Medline Plus. (2009). *Dictionary.* Retrieved August 23, 2009, from *www.nlm.nih.gov/medlineplus/mplusdictionary.html.*

Mednick, S., Nakayama, K., & Stickgold, R. (2003). Sleep-dependent learning: A nap is as good as a night. *Nature Neuroscience, 6*(7), 697–698.

Meegan, D., Purc-Stephenson, R., Honsberger, M. J., & Topan, M. (2004). Task analysis complements neuroimaging: An example from working memory research. *NeuroImage, 21*(3), 1026–1036.

Mehler, J., Nespor, M., Shukla, M., & Pena, M. (2006). Why is language unique to humans? *Novartis Foundation symposium, 270*, 251–291.

Meier, D. (2000). *Will standards save public education?* Boston: Beacon Press.

Meissner, W. (2006). The mind–brain relation and neuroscientific foundations: II. Neurobehavioral integrations. *Bulletin of the Menninger Clinic, 70*(2), 102–124.

Meister, I., Krings, T., Foltys, H., Boroojerdi, B., Miller, M., & Topper, R. (2004). Playing piano in the mind: An fMRI study on music imagery and performance in pianists. *Cognitive Brain Research, 19*(3), 219–228.

Meltzer, L. (2007). *Executive function in education: From theory to practice.* New York: Guilford Press.

Meltzoff, A. (2007). "Like Me": A foundation for social cognition. *Developmental Science, 10*(1), 126–134.

Meltzoff, A., & Decety, J. (2003). What imitation tells us about social cognition: A rapprochement between developmental psychology and cognitive neuroscience. *Philosophical Transactions of the Royal Society of London B Biological Science, 358*(1431), 491–500. Retrieved September 14, 2007, from *home.uchicago.edu/decety/publications/Meltzoff_Decety_PTRS03.pdf.*

Mendaglio, S. (2002). Dabrowski's theory of positive disintegration: Some implications for teachers of gifted students. *AGATE, 1*(2), 14–22. Retrieved July 20, 2009, from *www.sengifted.org/articles_social/Mendaglio_DabrowskisTheoryOfPositiveDisintegration.shtml*.

Menon, V., & Levitin, D. J. (2005). The rewards of music listening: Response and physiological connectivity of the mesolimbic system. *NeuroImage, 28*(1), 175–184.

Mercer, C. D., & Mercer, A. R. (2004). *Teaching students with learning problems* (7th ed.). New York: Prentice-Hall.

Merriam-Webster Online Dictionary. (2009). Retrieved August 23, 2009, from *www.merriam-webster.com/dictionary*.

Merton, R. (1968). *Social theory and social structure.* New York: Free Press. (Original work published 1949)

Merzenich, M. (2008, April). About brain plasticity. *On the Brain.* Retrieved May 22, 2009, from *http://merzenich.positscience.com/?page_id=143*.

Mesulam, M. M. (2000). *Principles of behavioral and cognitive neurology.* New York: Oxford University Press.

Metzinger, T. (Ed.). (2002). *Neural correlates of consciousness: Empirical and conceptual questions.* Cambridge, MA: MIT Press.

Meyerer-Ortiz, S. (2003). *Brain-compatible and culturally relevant education in literacy learning: A comparative inquiry project blending theory, research, and practice.* Master's thesis, University of New Mexico, Albuquerque, NM.

Mignot, E. (2008). Why we sleep: The temporal organization of recovery. *PLoS Biology, 6*(4): e106. doi:10.1371/journal.pbio.0060106

Mikels, J. (2004). *Hold on to that feeling: Working memory and emotion from a cognitive neuroscience perspective.* Doctoral dissertation, University of Michigan, Ann Arbor, MI. PowerPoint version retrieved September 14, 2007, from *www.ntpu.edu.tw/library/lib/PQDD/ Psychology.xls*.

Milivojevic, B. (2003). *Turn that frown upside-down: An ERP study of the effects of "thatcherisation" on neural processing of faces.* Master's thesis, University of Auckland, New Zealand.

Miller, A. (2003). *A descriptive case study of the implementation of brain-based learning with technological support in a rural high school.* Doctoral dissertation, Northern Illinois University, DeKalb, IL. AAT 3102762.

Miller, C. L., Miller, S. R., Newcorn, J. H., & Halperin, J. M. (2008). Personality characteristics associated with persistent ADHD in late adolescence. *Journal of Abnormal Child Psychology, 36*(2), 165–173.

Miller, E. (2007). *Getting from psy-phy (psychophysiology) to medical policy via music and neurofeedback for ADHD children.* Doctoral dissertation, Bryn Mawr College, Bryn Mawr, PA. AAT 3258205.

Miller, E., & Cohen, J. D. (2001). An integrative theory of prefrontal cortex function. *Annual Review of Neuroscience, 24*(1), 167–202.

Miller, G. (2003). The cognitive revolution: A historical perspective. *Trends in Cognitive Sciences, 7*(3), 141–144.

Miller, G. (2004). Society for neuroscience meeting: Brain cells may pay the price for a bad night's sleep. *Science, 306*(5699), 1126.

Miller, J. (2002). *A case study of Price Farm School, an independent, integrated day school: Straw into gold.* Doctoral dissertation, University of Massachusetts, Amherst, MA. AAT 3039378.

Miller, M., Van Horn, J. D., Wolford, G L., Handy, T. C., Valsangkar-Smyth, M., Inati, S., et al. (2002). Extensive individual differences in brain activations associated with episodic retrieval are reliable over time. *Journal of Cognitive Neuroscience, 14*(8), 1200–1214.

Mills, D., Plunkett, K., Prat, C., & Schafer, G. (2005). Watching the infant brains learning words: Effects of language and experience. *Cognitive Development, 20*(1), 19–31.

Mind, Brain, and Education Journal. (2008). Wiley Interscience library online. *Mind, Brain and Education, 2*(1), pp. 29–47. Retrieved July 10, 2010, from *www3.interscience.wiley.com/journal/117982931/home.*

Mitchell, N. (2007). *Brain compatible learning: Neuroscience in the classroom.* Retrieved August 13, 2007, from *www.abc.net.au/rn/science/mind/s988614.htm.*

Mitchell, M. L. & Jolley, J. M. (2009). *Research design explained.* Florence, KY: Cengage Learning.

Mobbs, D., Greicius, M.D., Abdel-Azim, E., Menon, V., & Reiss, A. (2003). Humor modulates the mesolimbic reward centers. *Neuron, 5*(40), 1041–1048.

Mohammed, A. (2002). Environmental enrichment and the brain. *Progress in Brain Research, 138,* 109–133.

Molfese, D. (2000). Predicting dyslexia at 8 years of age using neonatal brain responses. *Brain and Language, 72,* 238–245.

Möller, J., Streblow, L. & Pohlmann, B. (2009). Achievement and self-concept of students with learning disabilities. *Social Psychology of Education, 12,* 113–122.

Mollison, M. (2005). *Event-related potentials in humans during spatial navigation.* Senior honors thesis, Brandeis University, Waltham, MA.

Molteni, R. (2002). A high-fat, refined sugar diet reduces hippocampal brain-derived neurotrophic factor, neuronal plasticity, and learning. *Neuroscience, 112*(14), 803–814.

Monfils, M., Cowansage, K. K., & LeDoux, J. E. (2007). Brain-derived neurotrophic factor: Linking fear learning to memory consolidation. *Molecular Pharmacology, 72*(2), 235–237.

Montgomery, T. (2005). *The effects of brain-based learning on student engagement.* Master's thesis, Gratz College, Melrose Park, PA.

Moore, K. (2003). *The experiences of first graders in a brain compatible classroom: A scholarly study.* Ed.S. thesis, Georgia State University, Atlanta, GA.

Morasch, K. (2007). *Explicit memory and brain-electrical activity in 10-month-old infants.* Doctoral dissertation, Virginia Polytechnic University, Blacksburg, VA. Retrieved September 14, 2007, from *scholar.lib.vt.edu/theses/available/etd-04202007-152907/.*

Moscovitch, M., Nadel, L., Winocur, G., Gilboa, A., & Rosenbaum, R. S. (2006). The cognitive neuroscience of remote episodic, semantic, and spatial memory. *Current Opinion in Neurobiology, 16*(2), 179–190.

Mosher, C. (2003). *Effects of Brain Gym movements on fourth-grade mathematical computation performance.* Master's thesis, Mercer University, Atlanta, GA.

Moss, M., & Scholey, A. B. (1995). Oxygen administration enhances memory formation in healthy young adults. *Psychopharmacology, 124*(3), 255–260.

Moy, V. (2005). *Building written expression skills with fifth grade learning support students using right- and left-brain strategies.* Master's thesis, Gratz College, Melrose Park, PA.

Muetz, K. (2002). *The brain revisited: Implications for learning in higher education.* Master's thesis, Regis University, Denver, CO.

Munte, T., & Matzke, M. (1997). Brain activity associated with syntactic incongruencies in words and pseudo-words. *Journal of Cognitive Neuroscience, 9*(3), 318–330.

Muris, P., Merckelbach, H. & Damsma, E. (2000). Threat perception bias in nonreferreed, socially anxious children. *Journal of Clinical Child Psychology, 29*(3), 348–359.

Murray, B. (2000a). From brain scan to lesson plan. *Monitor on Psychology, 31*(3). Retrieved September 5, 2007, from *www.apa.org/monitor/mar00/brainscan.html.*

Murray, B. (2000b). To John Bruer, cognitive psychology is the critical bridge between brain science and education. *Monitor on Psychology, 31*(3). Retrieved June 3, 2008, from *www.apa.org/monitor/mar00/cognitive.htmlon3.*

Murray, S. (2002). *Neural mechanisms of human shape perception.* Doctoral dissertation, University of California, Davis, CA. AAT 3065281.

Musik, O., Janisse, J., Ager, J., Shen, C., Chugani, C. T., & Chugani, H. T. (1999). A mathematical model of the analysis of cross sectional brain glucose metabolism data in children. *Progress in Neuro-Psychopharmacology and Biological Psychiatry, 23*(4), 589–600.

Muthukumaraswamy, S. (2005). *Neurophysiological representations of the actions of others.* Doctoral dissertation, University of Auckland, New Zealand.

Nation, K. (2006). Reading and genetics: An introduction. *Journal of Research in Reading, 29*(1), 1–10.

National Child Care Information Center. (2002). *Brain development in infants and toddlers: Information for parents and caregivers.* National Child Care Information Center. Retrieved September 12, 2007, from *nccic.org/cctopics/brain.html.*

National Education Association. (1978). *Brain research and learning.* Washington, DC: Author.

National Institute of Child Health and Human Development. (2006). *The NICHD study of early child care and youth development: Findings for children up to age 4½ years* (NIH Pub. No 05-4318). Washington, DC: U.S. Government Printing Office.

National Joint Committee on Learning Disabilities. (2008). Glossary. Retrieved August 22, 2009, from *www.ldonline.org/glossary.*

National Science Foundation. (2010). Science of Learning Centers (SLC). Retrieved from *www.nsf.gov/funding/pgm_summ.jsp?pims_id=5567 &WT.mc_id=USNSF_39.*

Nature Editorial. (2006). Neuroethics needed. *Nature, 441*(7096), 907.

Nature Neuroscience Editorial. (2004). Better reading through brain research. *Nature Neuroscience, 7*(1), 1.

Nelson, C. A. (Ed.). (2000a). *The effects of early adversity on neurobehavioral development.* Mahwah, NJ: Erlbaum.

Nelson, C. A. (2000b). Neural plasticity and human development: The role of early experience in sculpting memory teams. *Developmental Science, 3*(2), 115–136.

Nelson, C. A., & Luciana, M. (2001). *Handbook of developmental cognitive neuroscience.* Cambridge, MA: MIT Press.

Nessler, D. (2002). *Is it memory or illusion? Electrophysiological characteristics of true and false recognition.* Doctoral dissertation, Saarbrücken University, Leipzig.

Neuman, L. (2005). *Music plays a "reading" role.* Master's thesis, Georgian Court University, Lakewood, NJ.

Neuman, W. (2005). *Social research methods: Quantitative and qualitative approaches* (6th ed.). Boston: Allyn & Bacon.

Neumärker, K. J. (2000 Jun). Mathematics and the brain: Uncharted territory? *European Child and Adolescent Psychiatry, 9*(2) [Electronic version]. Available online at *www.springerlink.com/content/jw7blmtg0f3l6258/*.

Nevills, P. A., & Wolfe, P. (2004). *Building the reading brain, Pre-K–3.* Thousand Oaks, CA: Corwin Press.

Newberg, A. B. & Iversen, J. (2003). The neural basis of the complex mental task of meditation: Neurotransmitter and neurochemical considerations. *Medical Hypotheses, 61*(2), 282–291, doi:10.1016/S0306-9877(03)00175-0.

Newberger, J. (1997). New brain development research: A wonderful window of opportunity to build public support for early childhood education! *Young Children, 52*(4), 4–9.

Nieder, A. (2005). Counting on neurons: The neurobiology of numerical competence. *Nature Reviews Neuroscience, 6*(3), 177–190.

Nigg, J. (2005). Neuropsychologic theory and findings in attention-deficit/hyperactivity disorder: The state of the field and salient challenges for the coming decade. *Biological Psychiatry, 57*(11), 1424–1435.

Nigg, J., & Casey, B. J. (2005). An integrative theory of attention-deficit/ hyperactivity disorder based on the cognitive and affective neurosciences. *Development and Psychopathology, 17*(3), 785–806. [Electronic version] doi:10.1017/S0954579405050376

Nithiananthararajah, J., & Hannan, A. (2006, Sep). Enriched environments, experience dependent plasticity and disorders of the nervous system. *Nature Reviews Neuroscience, 7*(9), 697–709.

Njeri, S. (2002). *Brain research and literacy instruction: Using neuroscience to assist the adult new reader.* Doctoral dissertation, Pepperdine University, Malibu, CA. AAT 3071363.

Noble, K., Norman, M. F., & Farah, M. J. (2005). Neurocognitive correlates of socioeconomic status in kindergarten children. *Developmental Science, 8*(1), 74–87.

Noble, K., Tottenham, N., & Casey, B. J. (2007). *Neuroscience perspectives on disparities in school readiness and cognitive achievement.* The Future of children/Center for the Future of Children, the David and Lucile Packard Foundation, Los Altos, CA.

Noesselt, T., Shah, N. J., & Jancke, L. (2003). Top-down and bottom-up modulation of language related areas: An fMRI study. *BMC Neuroscience, 4,* 13.

Nolan, C. (2002). *Using the arts and emotions to implement brain-friendly learning in the elementary classroom.* Master's thesis, California State University, Chico, CA.

Norman, K., Polyn, S. M., Detre, G. J., & Haxby, J. V. (2006). Beyond mind-reading: Multi-voxel pattern analysis of fMRI data. *Trends in Cognitive Sciences, 10*(9), 424–430.

North Central Regional Educational Laboratory. (2002). *Glossary of education terms and acronyms.* Retrieved August 22, 2009, from *www.ncrel.org/sdrs/areas/misc/glossary.htm.*

Norton, E. S., Kovelman, I., & Petitto, L. A. (2007). Are there separate neural systems for spelling? New insights into the role of rules and memory in spelling from fMRI. *International Journal of Mind, Brain, and Education, 1*(1), 48–59.

Novitt-Moreno, A. (1995). *How your brain works.* Emeryville, CA: Ziff-Davis.

Nummela-Caine, R., & Caine, G. (1994). *Making connections: Teaching and the human brain* (rev ed.). Palo Alto, CA: Dale Seymour Publications.

Nummela-Caine, R., & Caine, G. (1998). *Building a bridge between the neurosciences and education: Cautions and possibilities: Brain-based education.* Retrieved September 10, 2007, from *edc.gov.ab.ca/k_12/special/ aisi/pdfs/bbased_learning.pdf.*

Nummela-Caine, R., & Caine, G. (1999). *MindShifts: A brain-compatible process for professional development and the renewal of education* (2nd ed.). Tucson, AZ: Zephyr Press.

Nummela-Caine, R., Caine, G., McClintic, C., & Klimek, K. J. (2008). *12 brain/mind learning principles in action.* Thousand Oaks, CA: Corwin Press.

Nuñez, P. L. (2005). *Electric fields of the brain: The neurophysics of EEG.* Oxford, UK: Oxford University Press.

Nunley, K. (2002a). Active research leads to active classrooms. *Principal Leadership, 2*(7), 53–56.

Nunley, K. (2002b). *Layered Curriculum™: Dr. Kathie Nunley's web site for educators.* Retrieved September 8, 2007, from *help4teachers.com/.*

Oates, J. (2004). FOCUS: *A distinctive pedagogic approach for maximising the teaching and learning value of analysing digital video.* Centre for Childhood Development and Learning, The Open University, Milton Keynes, UK. Retrieved July 20, 2009, from *www.open.ac.uk/observation skills/pics/d77980.pdf.*

O'Boyle, M. (2008). Mathematically gifted children: Developmental brain characteristics and their prognosis for well-being. *Roeper Review, 30*(3), 181–186.

O'Boyle, M., & Gill, H. S. (1998). On the relevance of research findings in cognitive neuroscience to educational practice. *Educational Psychology Review, 10*(4), 397–409.

O'Dell, J. (1981). *Neuroeducation: Brain compatible learning strategies.* Doctoral dissertation, University of Kansas, Lawrence, KS. AAT 8218826.

O'Doherty, J., Hampton, A., & Kim, H. (2007). Model-based fMRI and its application to reward learning and decision making. *Annals of the New York Academy of Sciences, 1104,* 35–53.

O'Donnell, N. (1999). Using early childhood brain development research. *Child Care Information Exchange, 126*, 58–62.

Odorfer-Butterfield, M. (2004). *Students' conceptions of the brain and learning.* Master's thesis, University of Calgary, Alberta, Canada. AAT MQ93390.

Oestrich, J. (2004). *From neural mechanisms to ecology: A neuroethological approach to a novel form of memory.* Doctoral dissertation, University of Texas, Austin, TX. AAT 3150703.

O'Herron, P., & Siebenaler, D. (2005). The intersection between vocal music and language arts instruction. *A Review of the Literature Applications of Research in Music Education, 25*(2), 16–26.

Oishi, S., Diener, E. F., Lucas, R. E., & Suh, E. M. (1999). Cross-cultural variations in predictors of life satisfaction: Perspectives from needs and values. *Personality and Social Psychology Bulletin, 25*(8), 980–991.

O'Keefe, J., & Nadel, L. (1978). *The hippocampus as a cognitive map.* New York: Oxford University Press.

Oldham, J. M. (2007). Psychodynamic psychotherapy for personality disorders. *The American Journal of Psychiatry, 164*(10), 1465.

Olsson, A. (2006). Learning from and about others: The cognitive neuroscience of social fear learning. Doctoral dissertation, New York University, New York City. AAT 3221985.

Opris, I., & Bruce, C. J. (2005). Neural circuitry of judgment and decision mechanisms. *Brain Research Reviews, 48*(3), 509–526.

Organisation for Economic Co-Operation and Development. (2002). *Understanding the brain: Towards a new learning science.* Paris: OECD. Available online at *www.oecd.org*.

Organisation for Economic Co-operation and Development. (2007). *The brain and learning.* Retrieved March 10, 2007, from *www.oecd.org/department/0,2688,en_2649_14935397_1_1_1_1_1,00.html*.

Ormrod, J. E. (2000). *Educational psychology: Developing learners* (3rd ed.). Columbus, OH: Merrill Prentice-Hall.

Ornstein, R. (1992). *The evolution of consciousness: The origins of the way we think.* New York: Simon & Schuster.

Ornstein, R. (1995). *The roots of the self: Unraveling the mystery of who we are.* London: Octagon Press.

Ornstein, R., & Thompson, R. (1984). *The amazing brain.* Boston: Houghton Mifflin.

Ortega-Perez, I., Murray, K., & Lledo, P. M. (2007). The how and why of adult neurogenesis. *Journal of Molecular Histology, 38*(6), 555–562.

O'Shea, M. (2005). *From standards to success: A guide for school leaders.* Alexandria, VA: Association for Supervision and Curriculum Development.

Ou, L., & Gean, P. W. (2007). Transcriptional regulation of brain-derived neurotrophic factor in the amygdala during consolidation of fear memory. *Molecular Pharmacology, 72*(2), 350–358.

Ozmon, H., & Craver, S. M. (2002). *Philosophical foundations of education* (7th ed.). NJ: Prentice-Hall.

Pace-Schott, E., & Hobson, J. A. (2002). The neurobiology of sleep: Genetics, cellular physiology, and subcortical networks. *Nature Reviews Neuroscience, 3*(8), 591–605.

Palmer, P. (1997). *The courage to teach: Exploring the inner landscape of a teacher's life.* San Francisco: Jossey-Bass.

Paniagua, C. (2004). Convergencias actuales entre la neurociencia y el psicoanálisis [Current convergences between neuroscience and psychoanalysis]. *Ars Medica, Revista de Humanidades, 2,* 194–211.

Panksepp, J. (2003). At the interface of the affective, behavioral, and cognitive neurosciences: Decoding the emotional feelings of the brain. *Brain and Cognition, 52*(1), 4–14.

Pantev, C., Oostenvel, R., Engelien, A., Ross, B., Roberts, L. E., & Hoke, M. (1998). Increased auditory cortical representation in musicians. *Nature, 392,* 811–814.

Paradis, M. (2006). More belles infidèles—or why do so many bilingual studies speak with a forked tongue? *Journal of Neurolinguistics, 19*(3), 195–208.

Paré-Blagoev, J. (2006). *Connecting neuroscience and education: The neural correlates of phonemic awareness in normal reading children.* Doctoral dissertation, Harvard University, Cambridge, MA. AAT 3221615.

Parent, A. (1996). *Carpenter's human neuroanatomy* (9th ed.). Baltimore: Williams & Wilkins.

Parry, T., & Gregory, G. (1998). *Designing brain-compatible learning.* Andover, MA: Skylight.

Pashler, H., McDaniel, M., Rohrer, D., & Bjork, R. (2008). Learning styles: Concepts and evidence. *Psychological Science in the Public Interest, 9*(3), 103–199.

Pashler, H., Johnsyon, J. C., & Ruthruff, E. (2001). Attention and performance. *Annual Review of Psychology, 52*(1), 629–651.

Passarotti, A., Paul, B. M., Bussiere, J. R., Buxton, R. B., Wong, E. C., & Stiles, J. (2003). The development of face and location processing: An fMRI study. *Developmental Science, 6*(1), 100–117.

Paterson, S., Heim, S., Friedman, J. T., Choudhury, N., & Benasich, A. A. (2006). Development of structure and function in the infant brain: Implications for cognition, language and social behaviour. *Neuroscience and Biobehavioral Reviews, 30*(8), 1087–1105.

Patton, M.Q. (2008). *Utilization-focused evaluation.* Thousand Oaks, CA: Sage.

Paul, R. & Elder, L. (2005). *The miniature guide to critical thinking: Concepts and tools.* Dillon Beach, CA: Foundation for Critical Thinking. Retrieved from *www.criticalthinking.org.*

Payne, J. (2005). *Stress and episodic memory: The fate of neutral versus emotional information.* Doctoral dissertation, University of Arizona, Tucson, AZ. AAT 3167250.

Pears, S., & Jackson, S. R. (2004). Cognitive neuroscience: Vision and touch are constant companions. *Current Biology, 14*(9), R349–350.

Pediatric Services. (2002). *Doomed before kindergarten? On growing brains: Infant years, teen aged years.* Retrieved September 9, 2007, from *www.pediatric services.com/prof/prof-25.htm.*

Pelegrina, S., Bajo, M. T., & Justicia, F. (1999). Allocation of time in self-paced memory tasks: The role of practice, instructions, and individual differences in optimizing performance. *Learning and Individual Differences, 11*(4), 401–410.

Peretta, L. (2004). *Nutrición para un cerebro en forma: La guía máxima para estimular las funciones cerebrales* [Nutrition for growing brains: The maximum guide for brain function stimulation]. Mexico: Octopus Publishing.

Peretz, I., & Zatorre, R. J. (2005). Brain organization for music processing. *Annual Review of Psychology, 56*(1), 89–114.

Pérez-Chada, D., Pérez Lloret, S., Videla, A. J., Cardinali, D. P., Bergna, M. A., Fernández-Acquier, M. (2007). Sleep disordered breathing and daytime sleepiness are associated with poor academic performance in teenagers: A study using the Pediatric Saytime Sleepiness Scale (PDSS). *Sleep, 30*(12), 1698–1703.

Perkins, D. (1995). *Outsmarting IQ: The emerging science of learnable intelligence*. Washington, DC: Free Press.

Perry, B. (2000). How the brain learns best. *Instructor, 110*(4), 34–35.

Pert, C. (1997). *Molecules of emotion: Why you feel the way you feel*. New York: Scribner.

Petursdottir, A. L., Farr, S. A., Moreley, J. E., Banks, W. A., & Skuladorrtir, G. V. (2008). Effect of dietary n-3 polyunsaturated fatty acids on brain lipid fatty acid composition, learning ability, and memory of senescence-accelerated mouse. *Journals of Gerontology: Series A: Biological Sciences and Medical Sciences, 63A*(11), 1153–1161.

Phelps, E. (2006). Emotion and cognition: Insights from studies of the human amygdala. *Annual Review of Psychology, 57*(1), 27.

Phelps, E., Labar, K. A., Anderson, A. K., Phelps, E. A., O'Connor, K. J., Fulbright, R. K., et al. (1998). Specifying the contributions of the human amygdala to emotional memory: A case study. *Neurocase, 4*, 527–540.

Phelps, M. E., & Mazziotta, J. C. (1985). Positron emission tomography: Human brain function and biochemistry. *Science, 228*, 799–809.

Phillips, J. (2002). *The influence of perceived object function on action: Time-course and specificity of response activation*. Doctoral dissertation, University of Wales, Bangor, UK.

Phillips, M., Williams, L. M., Heining, M., Herba, C. M., Russell, T., Andrew, C., et al. (2004). Differential neural responses to overt and covert presentations of facial expressions of fear and disgust. *NeuroImage, 21*(4), 1484–1496.

Phipps, P. (1999). Is your program brain compatible? *Child Care Information Exchange, 126*, 53–57.

Phuong Phan, H. (2010). Students' academic performance and various cognitive processes of learning: An integrative framework and empirical analysis. *Educational Psychology, 30*(3), 297.

Piaget, J. (1928). *The child's conception of the world*. London: Routledge & Kegan Paul.

Piaget, J. (1953). *The origins of intelligence in children*. London: Routledge & Kegan Paul.

Piaget, J. (1955). *The child's construction of reality*. London: Routledge & Kegan Paul.

Piaget, J. (1971). *Biology and knowledge*. Chicago: University of Chicago Press.

Piaget, J. (1976). *To understand is to invent: The future of education*. New York: Penguin.

Piaget, J., & Ihhelder, B. (2000). *The psychology of the child*. New York: Basic Books. (Original work published 1969)

Piaget, J., & Szeminska, A. (1941). The child's conception of number. Selected pages reprinted in H. E. Gruber & J. J. Voneche (1977), *The essential Piaget* (pp. 298–311). Northvale, NJ: Jason Aronson.

Piazza, M., Pinel, P., Le Bihan, D., & Dehaene, S. (2007). A magnitude code common to numerosities and number symbols in human intraparietal cortex. *Neuron, 53*(2), 293–305.

Pickering, S., & Howard-Jones, P. (2007). Educator's views on the role of neuroscience in education: Findings from a study of UK and international perspectives. *Mind, Brain, and Education, 1*(3), 109–113.

Pickering, S., & Phye, G. D. (2006). *Working memory and education*. Burlington, MA: Academic Press.

Pietsch, P. (2001). *How does a brain store a mind?* Retrieved September 7, 2007, from *www.indiana.edu/%7Epietsch/home.html*.

Pineda, J. A. (2008). *Mirror neuron systems: The role of mirroring processes in social cognition*. New York: Humana Press.

Pinel, P., Dehaene, S., Riviere, D., & LeBihan, D. (2001). Modulation of parietal activation by semantic distance in a number comparison task. *NeuroImage, 14*, 1013–1026.

Pinker, S. (1994). *The language instinct*. New York: Morrow.

Pinker, S. (2002). *The blank slate: The modern denial of human nature*. New York: Penguin Books.

Pinker, S. (2003). Language as an adaptation to the cognitive niche. In M. Christiansen & S. Kirby (Eds.), *Language evolution: States of the Art*. New York: Oxford University Press.

Pinker, S. (2009). *How the mind works*. New York: Penguin Books.

PISA (2007). *Executive summary of the definition of key competencies*. Paris: Organization for Economic Cooperation and Development.

Plomin, R. (1994). The genetic basis of complex human behaviors. *Science, 264*(5166), 1733–1740.

Plomin, R., & Kosslyn, S. M. (2001). Genes, brain and cognition. *Nature Neuroscience, 4*(12), 1153–1155.

Pokorni, J. L., Worthington, C. K., & Jamison, P. J. (2004, November). *Phonological awareness intervention: Comparison of Fast ForWord, Earobics, and LiPS: A comparison of three phonological awareness programs*. Paper presented at a technical session, American Speech–Language–Hearing Association, Philadelphia.

Poldrack, R., & Sandak, R. (2004). Introduction to this special issue: The cognitive neuroscience of reading. *Scientific Studies of Reading, 8*(3), 199–202.

Poldrack, R., & Wagner, A. D. (2004). What can neuroimaging tell us about the mind? Insights from prefrontal cortex. *Current Directions in Psychological Science, 13*(5), 177–181.

Poppel, E. (2004). Lost in time: A historical frame, elementary processing units, and the 3-second window. *Acta Neurobiologiae Experimentalis, 64*(3), 295–301.

Posner, M. (1976, April). *Applying theories and theorizing about applications*. Paper presented at the Conference on Theory and Practice of Beginning Reading Instruction, University of Pittsburgh, Learning Research and Development Center.

Posner, M. (1981). *Cognition and neural systems. Cognition*, 10, 261–266.

Posner, M. (1984). Mechanisms of attention. In H. Stevenson & C. C. Ching (Eds.), *Studies of cognition: Proceedings of a joint meeting of the Chinese and U.S. Academy of Sciences* (pp. 373–380). Washington, DC: American Psychological Association.

Posner, M. (1988). What is it to be an expert? In M. T. H. Chi, R. Glaser, & M. J. Farr (Eds.), *The nature of expertise* (pp. xxix–xxxvi). Hillsdale, NJ: Erlbaum.

Posner, M. (1989). *Foundations of cognitive science*. Cambridge, MA: MIT Press.

Posner, M. (2001). Cognitive neuroscience: The synthesis of mind and brain. In E. Dupoux (Ed.), *Language, brain and cognitive development: Essays in honor of Jacques Mehler* (pp. 403-416). Cambridge, MA: MIT Press.

Posner, M. (Ed.). (2004a). *Cognitive neuroscience of attention*. New York: Guilford Press.

Posner, M. (2004b). Is the combination of psychology and neuroscience important to you? *Impuls: Tidsskrift for Psyckhologi*, 3, 6–8.

Posner, M. (2004c). Neural systems and individual differences. *Teachers College Record, 106*(1), 24–30.

Posner, M. (2008). *Posner, narrative bio 2007*. Sent by e-mail to the author on January 25, 2008.

Posner, M., Nissen, M. J., & Ogden, W. C. (1978). Attended and unattended processing modes: The role of set from spatial location. In H. J. Pick (Ed.), *Modes of perception* (pp. 99–126). Hillsdale, NJ: Erlbaum.

Posner, M., & Rothbart, M. K. (1990). The evolution and development of the brain's attention system [Abstract]. *Quarterly Journal of Experimental Psychology, 42A*, 189–190.

Posner, M., & Rothbart, M. K. (1998a). Attention, self-regulation and consciousness. *Philosophical Transactions of the Royal Society of London, 353*(1377), 1915–1927.

Posner, M., & Rothbart, M. K. (1998b). Developing attention skills. In J. Richards (Ed.), *Cognitive neuroscience of attention: A developmental perspective* (pp. 317–323). Hillsdale, NJ: Erlbaum.

Posner, M., & Rothbart, M. K. (2007a). *Educating the human brain*. Washington, DC: American Psychological Association.

Posner, M., & Rothbart, M. K. (2007b). Research on attention networks as a model for the integration of psychological science. *Annual Review of Psychology 58*(1), 1–23.

Posner, M. I., Rothbart, M. K., & Rueda, M. R. (2008). "Brain Mechanisms and Learning of High Level Skills" In Battro, A. M., Fischer, K. W. & Lena, P. J. (Eds.), *The Educated Brain* (pp. 151–165). Cambridge UK: Cambridge University Press.

Posner, M., Rothbart, M. K., Farah, M., & Bruer, J. (2001). Human brain development. *Developmental Science, 4*(3), 253–384.

Posner, M., Rothbart, M. K., & Harman, C. (1994). Cognitive science contributions to culture and emotion. In S. Ktayma & H. Marcus (Eds.), *Culture and emotion* (pp. 197–216). Washington, DC: American Psychological Association.

Pressley, M., & McCormick, C. B. (1995). *Advanced educational psychology for educators, researchers, and policymakers.* New York: HarperCollins.

Preuschoff, K., Bossaerts, P., & Quartz, S. R. (2006). Neural differentiation of expected reward and risk in human subcortical structures. *Neuron, 51*(3), 381–390.

Prince, S. (2007). *Functional neuroimaging investigations of human memory: Comparisons of successful encoding and retrieval for relational and item information.* Doctoral dissertation, Duke University, Durham, NC. AAT 3255598.

Puckett, M., Marshall, C. S., & Davis, R. (1999). Examining the emergence of brain development research: The promise and the perils. *Childhood Education, 76*(1), 8–12.

Pugh, K., Shaywitz, B. A., Shaywitz, S. E., Shankweiler, D. P., Katz, L., & Fletcher, J. M. (1997). Predicting reading performance from neuroimaging profiles: The cerebral basis of phonological effects in printed word identification. *Journal of Experimental Psychology: Human Perception and Performance, 23*(2), 299–318.

Purhonen, M., Kilpelainen-Lees, R., Valkonen-Korhonen, M., Karhu, J., & Lehtonen, J. (2004). Cerebral processing of mother's voice compared to unfamiliar voice in 4-month-old infants. *International Journal of Psychophysiology, 52*(3), 257–266.

Putnam, J., Spiegel, A. N., & Bruininks, R. H. (1995). Future directions in education and inclusion of students with disabilities: A Delphi investigation. *Exceptional Children, 61*(6), 553–577. Retrieved from ERIC database.

Qiu, A., Crocetti, D., Adler, M., Mahone, E. M. (2009, Jan). Basal ganglia volume and shape in children with attention deficit hyperactivity disorder. *American Journal of Psychiatry, 166*(1), 74–82.

Quartz, S. & Sejnowski, T. J. (1997, Dec). The neural basis of cognitive development: A constructivist manifesto. *Behavioral & Brain Science, 20*, 537–596.

Radin, J. (2005). *Brain research and classroom practice: Bridging the gap between theorists and practitioners.* Doctoral dissertation, Colorado State University, Fort Collins, CO. AAT 3173083.

RadiologyInfo. (2008). *Functional magnetic imaging description.* Retrieved May 7, 2008, from *www.radiologyinfo.org/en/info.cfm?pg=fmribrain&bhcp=1.*

Ramachandran, V. (2002). *The encyclopedia of the human brain.* San Diego: Academic Press.

Ramachandran, V., & Blakeslee, S. (1999). *Phantoms in the brain: Probing the mysteries of the human mind.* New York: HarperCollins.

Ramón y Cajal, S. (1911). *Histologie du système nerveux de l'hommes et des vertébrés.* Paris: Maloine.

Ramos-Voigt, L. (2007). *Examining the relationship of instructional time to student achievement.* Doctoral dissertation, Capella University, Minneapolis, MN. AAT 3251337.

Ramscar, M., & Gitcho, N. (2007). Developmental change and the nature of learning in childhood. *Trends in Cognitive Sciences, 11*(7), 274–279.

Ramsperger, E. (2006). *Brain Gym.* Master's thesis, State University of New York, Brockport, NY.

Ramus, F. (2006). Genes, brain, and cognition: A roadmap for the cognitive scientist. *Cognition, 101*, 247–269. [Electronic version] doi: 10.1016/j.cognition.2006.04.003

Ratey, J. (2002). *A user's guide to the brain: Perception, attention, and the four theaters of the brain.* New York: Vintage Books.

Rattazzi, D. (2002). *Implementing brain-based learning theory in the classroom.* Master's thesis, California Pacific University, San Diego, CA.

Rauch, S., Shin, L. M., & Wright, C. I. (2003). Neuroimaging studies of amygdala function in anxiety disorders. *Annals of the New York Academy of Sciences, 985,* 389–410.

Rauscher, F. H., Shaw, G. L, & Ky, K. N. (1993). Music and spatial task performance. *Nature, 365,* 611.

Rauscher, F. H., Shaw, G. L., Levine, L., Wright, E., Dennis, W., & Newcomb, R. (1997). Music training causes long-term enhancement of preschool children's spatial–temporal reasoning. *Neurological Research, 19*(1), 1–8.

Raz, A., & Buhle, J. (2006). Typologies of attentional networks. *Nature Reviews Neuroscience, 7*(5), 367–379.

Reeve, J. (2004). *Understanding motivation and emotion* (4th ed.). New York: Wiley.

Reid, L., & Baylis, F. (2005). Brains, genes, and the making of the self. *American Journal of Bioethics, 5*(2), 21–23.

Reid, V., Csibra, G., Belsky, J., & Johnson, H. M. (2007). Neural correlates of the perception of goal-directed action in infants. *Acta Psychologica, 124*(1), 129–138.

Restak, R. (1984). *The brain—The last frontier.* New York: Warner Books, Inc.

Restak, R. (1991a). *The brain has a mind of its own: Insights from a practicing neurologist.* New York: Crown.

Restak, R. (1991b). *The evolution of consciousness: The origins of the way we think.* New York: Simon & Schuster.

Restak, R. (2006). *The naked brain: How the emerging neurosociety is changing how we live, work, and love.* New York: Harmony Books.

Restak, R. (2008). How our brain constructs our mental world. In *The Jossey-Bass reader on the brain and learning* (pp. 3–11). San Francisco: Wiley.

Restak, R. (2009). *Think smart: A neuroscientist's prescription for improving your brain's performance.* New York: Riverhead Books.

Reynolds, D., Nicolson, R. I., & Hambly, H. (2003). Evaluation of an exercise-based treatment for children with reading difficulties. *Dyslexia, 9*(2), 124–126.

Reynolds, S. (2000). *Learning is a verb: The psychology of teaching and learning.* Scottsdale, AZ: Holcomb Hathaway.

Riccardelli, L. (1992). Creativity and bilingualism. *Journal of Creative Behaviour, 26*(4), 242–254.

Richard, G. J. (2000). *The source for treatment methodologies in autism.* East Moline, IL: LinguiSystems.

Rickard, T., Romero, S. G., Basso, G., Wharton, C., Flinton, S., & Grafman, J. (2000). The calculating brain: An fMRI study. *Neuropsychologia, 38,* 325–335.

Ridley, M. (2003). *Nature via nurture: Genes, experience and what makes us human.* New York: HarperCollins.

Rivera, A. (2003). *The effectiveness of a brain based learning and multiple intelligence theory teaching approach on reading comprehension of third grade English as a second language students of Aibonito School District.* Doctoral dissertation, Inter American University, San Germán, Puerto Rico.

Rivera, J., Estrada, M., & Estrada, L. (2007). Posibilidades de la rehabilitación neuropsicológica en población geriátrica con deterioro cognoscitivo [The possibility of neuropsychological rehabilitation in aging populations with mental decline]. *Medicina Interna de México, 23*(2). 133–137.

Rizzolatti, G., & Craighero, L. (2004). The mirror-neuron system. *Annual Review of Neuroscience, 27*(1), 169–192.

Rizzolatti, G., Fogassi, L., & Gallese, V. (2008). Mirrors in the mind. In *The Jossey-Bass reader on the brain and learning* (pp. 12–19). San Francisco: Wiley.

Roberts, R., & Stankov, L. (1999). Individual differences in speed of mental processing human and cognitive abilities: Toward a taxonomic model. *Learning and Individual Differences, 11*(1), 120.

Robson, D., Fort Brenneman, J., & Kiesa, K. (2007). *High IQ kids: Collected insights, information, and personal stories from the experts.* Minneapolis, MN: Free Spirit.

Rodriguez, E. (2003). *Asymmetric interference in directing attention during math processing.* Master's thesis, University of Oregon, Eugene, OR.

Roe, K. (2005). *Cognitive neuro-psychology and the psychological explanation of delusional belief.* Master's thesis, University of Waikato, Hamilton, New Zealand.

Ronis, D. (2007). *Brain-compatible assessments* (2nd ed.). Thousand Oaks, CA: Corwin Press.

Ropper, A., & Brown, R. H. (2005). *Adams and Victor's principles of neurology* (8th ed.). New York: McGraw-Hill.

Rose, D. & Dalton, B. (2008). *Thinking reader.* Retrieved from *www.tomsnyder.com/products/product.asp?sku=THITHI.*

Rose, D. H., Meyer, A., & Strangman, N. (2002). *Teaching every student in the digital age: Universal design for learning.* Alexandria, VA: Association for Supervision and Curriculum Development.

Rose, R. (2005). *The connection of brain compatible learning theory and leadership.* Doctoral dissertation, Indiana University, Bloomington, IN. AAT 3175993.

Rose, S. (2005). *The future of the brain: The promises and perils of tomorrow's neuroscience.* New York: Oxford University Press.

Rosenberg, N.T. (2006). *Sullivan's evidence.* Waterville, ME: Thorndike.

Rosenweig, M., Breedlove, M. S., & Watson, N. V. (2005). *Biological psychology: An introduction to behavioral and cognitive neuroscience* (4th ed.). Sunderland, MA: Sinauer.

Rosenzweig, M., Krech, D., & Bennett, E. L. (1958). *Neurological basis of behaviour.* London: Ciba Foundation Symposium.

Rosiek, J. (2003). Emotional scaffolding: An exploration of the teacher knowledge at the intersection of student emotion and the subject matter. *Journal of Teacher Education, 54*(5), 399–412.

Rourke, B., & Conway, J. A. (1997). Disabilities of arithmetic and mathematical reasoning: Perspectives from neurology and neuropsychology. *Journal of Learning Disabilities, 30*(1), 34–46.

Rouse, C. E., & Krueger, A. B. (2004). Putting computerized instruction to the test: A randomized evaluation of a "scientifically based" reading program. *Economics of Education Review, 23*(4), 323–338.

Rubin, I., & Herbert, C. (1998). Models for active learning: Collaborative peer teaching. *College Teaching, 46*(1), 26–30.

Rueda, M., Fan, J., McCandliss, B. D., Halparin, J., Gruber, D., Lercari, L. P., et al. (2004). Development of attention during childhood. *Neuropsychologia, 42*, 1029–1040.

Runco, M. A., & Pritzker, S. R. (1999). *Encyclopedia of creativity*. London: Elsevier.

Ruppert, S. (2006). *How the arts benefit the student achievement*. Washington, DC: National Assembly of State Arts Agencies. Retrieved May 6, 2010, from *www.keepartsinschools.org /Research/.../Critical Evidence.pdf*.

Rupprecht, P. (2003). *A study of the effects of a neurocognitive-based reading instruction program*. Doctoral dissertation, Arizona State University, Tempe, AZ.

Russell, R. (1994). *Using the whole brain: Integrating the right and left brain with hemi-sync sound patterns*. Charlottesville, VA: Hampton Roads.

Sabatella, M. (1999). Intelligence and giftedness: Changes in the structure of the brain. *Gifted Educational International, 13*, 226–237.

Sabbatini, R. (1997). *The PET scan: A new window into the brain*. Retrieved September 8, 2007, from *www.epub.org.br/cm/n01/pet/pet.htm*.

Sacks, O. (1990). *The man who mistook his wife for a hat and other clinical tales*. New York: Perennial Library.

Sacks, O. (2008). *Musicophilia: Tales of music and the brain*. New York: Picador.

Sadato, N., Pascual-Leone, A., Rafman, J., Ibanez, V., Deiber, M. P., Dold, G., et al. (1996). Activation of the primary visual cortex by Braille reading in blind subjects. *Nature, 380*, 526–528.

Sagvolden, T. (2005). *Behavioral and brain functions: A new journal. Behavioral and Brain Functions*. Retrieved June 6, 2008, from *www.pubmedcentral.nih.gov/tocrender. fcgi?iid=119271*.

Sakai, K. (2005). Language acquisition and brain development. *Science, 310*(5749), 815–819.

Samoilov, A. (2000). Role of emotion in cognitive–behavior therapy. *Clinical Psychology: Science and Practice, 7*(4), 373.

Samuels, B. M. (2009). Can differences between education and neuroscience be overcome by Mind, Brain, and Education? *Mind, Brain, and Education, 3*(1), 45–53.

Sander, D., Grafman, J., & Zalla, T. (2003). The human amygdala: An evolved system for relevance detection. *Reviews in the Neurosciences, 14*(4), 303–316.

Sander, D., Grandjean, D., Pourtois, G., Schwartz, S., Seghier, M., Scherer, K. R., et al. (2005). Emotion and attention interactions in social cognition: Brain regions involved in processing anger prosody. *NeuroImage, 28*, 848–858.

Santamaria, A. (2006). *Testing and modeling a two-component hypothesis of timing*. Doctoral dissertation, University of Colorado, Boulder, CO. AAT 3212111.

Santarelli, L., Saxe, M., Gross, A., Surget, A., Battaglia, F., Dulawa, S., et al. (2003). Requirement of hippocampal neurogenesis for the behavioral effects of antidepressants. *Science, 301*(5634), 805–809.

Santrock, J. W. (1998). *Children*. New York: McGraw-Hill.

Sapolsky, R. (2001). Depression, antidepressants, and the shrinking hippocampus. *Proceedings of the National Academy of Sciences, 98*(22), 12320–12322.

Sapolsky, R. (2003). Taming stress. *Scientific American, 289*(3), 86–95.

Sarter, M., Gehring, W. J., & Kozak, R. (2006). More attention must be paid: The neurobiology of attentional effort. *Brain Research Reviews, 51*(2), 145–160.

Sass, E. J. (1989). Motivation in the college classroom: What students tell us. *Teaching of Psychology, 16*(2), 86–88.

Saunders, J. (2003, February 14). Take your kids to the Brain Gym. *Times Educational Supplement Scotland*, (1891), 23.

Saxe R. (2006, Feb). Why and how to study: Theory of mind with fMRI. *Brain Research, 1079*(1), 57–65.

Schacter, D. (2001). *The seven sins of memory: How the mind forgets and remembers*. New York: Houghton Mifflin.

Schacter, D., & Addis, D. R. (2007). The cognitive neuroscience of constructive memory: Remembering the past and imagining the future. *Philosophical Transactions of the Royal Society of London Series B, Biological Sciences, 362*(1481), 773–786.

Schacter, D., & Buckner, R. I. (1998). Priming and the brain. *Neuron, 20*, 185–195.

Schacter, D., & Wagner, A. D. (1999). Medial temporal lobe activation in fMRI and PET studies of episodic encoding and retrieval. *Hippocampus, 9*, 7–24.

Schall, J. (2004). On building a bridge between brain and behavior. *Annual Review of Psychology, 55*(1), 23.

Schall, J. (2005). Decision making. *Current Biology, 15*(1), R9–11.

Schatz, K. (2002). *The mindful reader: Using brain compatible techniques to improve reading comprehension in learning disabled high school students*. Master's thesis, Gratz College, Melrose Park, PA.

Scherer, M. (2001). The brain and learning. *Educational Leadership, 59*(3), 5.

Scherer, M. (2006). *Celebrate strengths, nurture affinities: A conversation with Mel Levine*. Retrieved August 31, 2007, from *www.ascd.org/authors/ed_lead/el200609_scherer2.html*.

Schirmer, A. (2003). *Emotional speech perception: Electrophysiological insights into the processing of emotional prosody and word valence in men and women*. Doctoral dissertation, Max Planck Institute of Cognitive Neuroscience, Leipzig Universitat, Leipzig, Germany.

Schlaggar, B., & McCandliss, B. D. (2007). Development of neural systems for reading. *Annual Review of Neuroscience, 30*(1), 475.

Schmidt, A. (2002). *Theoretical background on brain-based learning and resources for teachers and parents.* Master's thesis, Bethel Collage, Mishawaka, IN.

Schmidt, D. (2005). *Building pathways: Connecting brain research to the classroom.* Master's thesis, Hamline University, St. Paul, MN.

Schmidt, L. (2007). Social cognitive and affective neuroscience: Developmental and clinical perspectives. *Brain and Cognition, 65*(1), 1–2.

Schmidt, M. (2003). *The relationship between the Wechsler Intelligence Scale for Children—Third Edition and the Test of Memory and Learning in a pediatric traumatic brain injury population.* Doctoral dissertation, Texas Woman's University, Denton, TX. AAT 3084186.

Schmithorst, V. J., & Douglas Brown, R. (2004). Empirical validation of the triple-code model of numerical processing for complex math operations using functional MRI and group independent component analysis of the mental addition and subtraction of fractions. *NeuroImage, 2*(3), 1414–1420.

Scholes, K. E., Harrison, B. J., O'Neill, B. V., & Leung, S. (2007). Acute serotonin and dopamine depletion improves attentional control: Findings from the Stroop task. *Neuropsychopharmacology, 32*(7), 1600–1610.

School Wise Press. (2008). *Glossary of educational terms.* Retrieved August 22, 2009, from *www.schoolwisepress.com/smart/dict/dict6.html.*

Schreiber, M., & Schneider, R. (2007). Cognitive plasticity in people at risk for dementia: Optimising the testing-the-limits-approach. *Aging and Mental Health, 11*(1), 75–81.

Schultz, D., Izard, C. E., & Bear, G. (2004). Children's emotion processing: Relations to emotionality and aggression. *Developmental Psychopathology, 16*, 371–387.

Schultz, R. (2001). *Human intelligence: Theories and developmental origins.* Yale University, New Haven Teachers Institute. Retrieved August 28, 2007, from *www.yale.edu/ynhti/curriculum/units/2001/6/01.06.intro.x.html.*

Schumann, J. (1997). *The neurobiology of affect in language.* Michigan: Blackwell.

Schunk, D. (1998). An educational psychologist's perspective on cognitive neuroscience. *Educational Psychology Review, 10*(4), 411–417.

Schwartz, C., Wright, C. T., Shin, L. M., Kagan, J., & Rauch, S.L. (2003). Inhibited and uninhibited infants "grown up": Adult amygdalar response to novelty. *Science, 300*, 1952–1953.

Schwartz, J. (2003). *The mind and the brain: Neuroplasticity and the power of mental force.* New York: HarperCollins.

Schwartz, J., & Begley, S. (2002). *The mind and the brain: Neuroplasticity and the power of mental force.* New York: HarperCollins.

Schwartz, M., & Fischer, K. W. (2003). Building vs. borrowing: The challenge of actively constructing ideas in post-secondary education. *Liberal Education, 89*(3), 22–29.

Schwartz, M., & Fischer, K. W. (2006). Useful metaphors for tackling problems in teaching and learning. *About Campus, 11*(1), 2–9.

Schwartz, M., & Sadler, P. (2007). Empowerment in science curriculum development: A microdevelopmental approach. *International Journal of Science Education, 29*(8), 987–1017.

ScienceCentral Archives. (2007). *Humor and brains*. Retrieved July 23, 2009, from *www.sciencentral.com/articles/view.php3?type=article& article_id=218392154*.

Scientific American. (1993). *Mind and brain: Readings from* Scientific American Magazine. New York: Freeman.

Scientific Learning Corporation. (2009). *Scientific learning: FastForWord*. Retrieved August 4, 2009, *from www.scilearn.com/*.

Scientific Learning Corporation. (n.d.). *Founder's story*. Retrieved February 29, 2007, from *www.scilearn.com/our-approach/ourfounder s-story/index.php*.

Sears, D. (2006). *Effects of innovation versus efficiency tasks on collaboration and learning*. Doctoral dissertation, Stanford University, Stanford, CA. AAT 3219375.

SEDL. (2009). *Curriculum details for RAVE-O (retrieval, automaticity, vocabulary, engagement with language, orthography)*. Retrieved May 30, 2009, from *www.sedl.org/cgi-bin/mysql/afterschool/curriculum-choice.cgi?subj=l&resource=23*.

Seely, J., & Collins, A. (1989). Situated cognition and the culture of learning. *Educational Researcher, 18*(1), 32–42.

Selye, H. (1974). *Stress without distress*. Philadelphia: Lippincott.

Serendip Bryn Mawr. (2009). *Glossary of terms*. Retrieved August 22, 2009, from *serendip.bryn-mawr.edu/bb/kinser/Glossary.html*.

Sergerie, K., Lepage, M., & Armony, J. L. (2006). A process-specific functional dissociation of the amygdala in emotional memory. *Journal of Cognitive Neuroscience, 18*(8), 1359–1367.

Sethi, A., & Mischel, W. (2000). The role of strategic attention deployment in development of self-regulation: Predicting preschoolers' delay of gratification from mother–toddler interactions. *Developmental Psychology, 36*(6), 767–777.

Shapiro, E. S. (2004). *Academic skills problems: Direct assessment and intervention*. New York: Guilford Press.

Shavelson, R. J., & Towne, L. (Eds.). (2002). *Scientific research in education*. National Research Council. Washington, DC: National Academy Press.

Shaw, D., Grillion, M., Ingoldsby, E. M., & Nagano, P. S. (2003). Trajectories leading to school-age conduct problems. *Developmental Psychology, 39*(2), 189–200.

Shaywitz, B., & Shaywitz S. E. (2005, April). *The brain science of overcoming dyslexia*. Paper presented at the Learning and the Brain Conference, Cambridge, MA.

Shaywitz, B., & Shaywitz S. E. (2007). What neuroscience really tells us about reading: A response to Judy Willis. *Educational Leadership*, 74–76.

Shaywitz, B., Shaywitz S. E., Blachman, B. A., Pugh, K. R., Fulbright, R. K., Skudlarski, P., et al. (2004). Development of left occipitotemporal systems for skilled reading in children after a phonologically-based intervention. *Biological Psychiatry, 55*, 926–933.

Shaywitz, S., Shaywitz, B. A., Fulbright, R. K., Skudlarski, P., Mencl, W. E., Constable, R. T., et al. (2003). Neural systems for compensation and persistence: Young adult outcome of childhood reading disability. *Biological Psychiatry, 54*(1), 25–33.

Shaywitz, B., Shaywitz, S. E., Pugh, K. R., Mencl, W. E., Fulbright, R. K., Skudlarski, P., et al. (2002). Disruption of posterior brain systems for reading in children with developmental dyslexia. *Biological Psychiatry, 52*(2), 101–110.

Sheridan, K., Zinchenko, E., & Gardner, H. (2005). Neuroethics in education. In J. Illes (Ed.), *Neuroethics* (pp. 281–308). Oxford, UK: Oxford University Press. Retrieved September 10, 2007, from *www.tc.umn.edu/athe0007/BNEsig/papers/NeuroethicsEducation.pdf.*

Sheridan, K., Zinchenko, E., & Gardner, H. (2006). Neuroethics in education. *The.MBE.PONS, 1*(2), 4–5.

Sheridan, S. (1997). *Excerpts from "Hitchhiker's guide to brain science." Drawing/writing and the new literacy.* Retrieved September 11, 2007, from *drawingwriting.com/HichHike.html.*

Sherman, J., & Bisanz, J. (2007). Evidence for use of mathematical inversion by three-year-old children. *Journal of Cognition and Development, 8,* 333–344.

Shing, L. K. (2003, December 15). *Knowledge as our core value.* Inauguration ceremony of Science Building, Peking University of Technology, Beijing, China.

Shintani, E. (2003). *Teaching film to enhance brain-compatible learning in English-as-a-foreign language instruction.* Master's thesis, California State University, San Bernardino, CA.

Shore, R. (1997). *Rethinking the brain: New insights into early development.* New York: Families and Work Institute.

Shors, T. J., Townsend, D. A., Zhao, M., Kozorovitskiy, Y., & Gould, E. (2002). Neurogenesis may relate to some but not all types of hippocampal-dependent learning. *Hippocampus, 12*(5), 578.

Sibley, B., & Etnier, J. L. (2003). The relationship between physical activity and cognition in children: A meta-analysis. *Pediatric Exercise Science, 15*(30), 243–256.

Siegel, D. (1999). *The developing mind: How relationships and the brain interact to shape who we are.* New York: Guilford Press.

Siegel, D. (2007). *The mindful brain: Reflection and attunement in the cultivation of well-being.* New York: Norton.

Sigman, M. (2004). Bridging psychology and mathematics: Can the brain understand the brain? *PLoS Biology, 2*(9), E297.

Simos, P., Fletcher, J. M., Foorman, B. R., Francis, D. J., Castillo, E. M., Davis, R. N., et al. (2002). Brain activation profiles during the early stages of reading acquisition. *Journal of Child Neurology, 17*(3), 159–163.

Simpson, R. L., Smith Myles, B., Griswold, D. E., Adams, L. G., de Boer-Ott, S. R., & Kline, S. A. (2004). *Autism spectrum disorders: Interventions and treatments for children and youth.* Thousand Oaks, CA: Corwin Press.

Singer, T. (2007). The neuronal basis of empathy and fairness. *Novartis Foundation Symposium, 278,* 20–30.

Siok, W., Perfetti, C. A., Jin, Z., & Tan, L. H. (2004). Biological abnormality of impaired reading is constrained by culture. *Nature, 431*, 71–76.

Skilbeck, M., & Connell, H. (1994). *The vocational question: New directions in education and training*. New York: Routledge.

Skinner, B. (1974). *About behaviorism*. New York: Knopf.

Slavkin, M. (2002a). Brain science in the classroom. *Principal Leadership, 2*(8), 21–23.

Slavkin, M. (2002b). The importance of brain functioning on cognition and teacher practice. *Journal of Teaching and Learning, 2*(1), 21–34.

Small, G.W., Moody, T D., Siddarth, P., & Bookheimer, S. Y. (2009). Your brain on Google: Patterns of cerebral activation during Internet searching. *American Journal of Geriatric Psychiatry, 17*(2), 116.

Smallwood, J., Fishman, D. J., & Schooler, J. W. (2007). Counting the cost of an absent mind: Mind wandering as an under recognized influence on educational performance. *Psychonomic Bulletin and Review, 14*(2), 230.

Smilkstein, R. (2002). *We're born to learn: Using the brain's natural learning process to create today's curriculum*. Thousand Oaks, CA: Corwin Press.

Smith, A. (2004). *Accelerated learning in practice: Brain-based methods for accelerating motivation and achievement*. London: Network Education Press.

Smith, G. (2002). *Multiple intelligences, Bloom, and brain research*. Retrieved September 11, 2007, from *www.gp.k12.mi.us/ci/ce/computer/brainbased.htm*.

Smith, K. (2002). Typologies, taxonomies, and the benefits of policy classification. *Policy Studies Journal, 30*(3), 379–391.

Smith, M., Gosselin, F., & Schyns, P. G. (2007). From a face to its category via a few information processing states in the brain. *NeuroImage, 37*(3), 974–984.

Smith, W. (2002). *Authenticity, an unprejudiced heart: Establishing equality, emotional intelligence, and empowerment within an educational system*. Doctoral dissertation, Fielding Graduate Institute, Santa Barbara, CA. AAT 3090836.

Snow, C. E., Burns, M. S., & Griffin, P. (1998) (Eds.). *Prevention of reading difficulties in young children*. Washington, DC: National Research Council.

Society for Neuroscience. (2007a). *Adult neurogenesis*. Retrieved September 11, 2007, from *www.sfn.org/index.cfm?pagename=brainbriefings_adult_neurogenesis*.

Society for Neuroscience. (2007b). *Biological clocks*. Retrieved September 11, 2007, from *www.sfn.org/index.cfm?pagename=brainBriefings_biologicalClocks*.

Society for Neuroscience. (2007c). *Brain plasticity, language processing and reading*. Retrieved September 11, 2007, from *www.sfn.org/index.cfm?pagename=brainBriefings_brainPlasticityLanguageProcessingAndReading*.

Society for Neuroscience. (2007d). *Child abuse and the brain*. Retrieved September 11, 2007, from *www.sfn.org/index.cfm?pagename=brainBriefings_childAbuseAndTheBrain*.

Society for Neuroscience. (2007e). *Depression and stress hormones*. Retrieved September 11, 2007, from *www.sfn.org/search.aspx?keyword=depression%20and%20stress%20hormones*.

Society for Neuroscience. (2007f). *Humor and laughter in the brain*. Retrieved September 11, 2007, from *www.sfn.org/index.cfm?pagename=brainBriefings_humor LaughterAndTheBrain*.

Society for Neuroscience. (2007g). *Memory enhancers*. Retrieved September 11, 2007, from *www.sfn.org/index.cfm?pagename=brainBriefings_memoryEnhancers*.

Society for Neuroscience. (2007h). *The mind–body link*. Retrieved September 11, 2007, from *www.sfn.org/index.cfm?pagename=brainBriefings_theMindBodyLink*.

Society for Neuroscience. (2007i). *Reading failure*. Retrieved September 11, 2007, from *www.sfn.org/index.cfm?pagename=brainBriefings_reading_failure*.

Society for Neuroscience. (2007j). *Standards*. Retrieved July 10, 2007, from *www.sfn.org/index.cfm*.

Society for Neuroscience. (2007k). *Stress and the brain*. Retrieved September 11, 2007, from *www.sfn.org/index.cfm?pagename=brainBriefings_stressAndTheBrain*.

Soehner, C. (2005). *Using brain based techniques for secondary science curriculum*. Master's thesis, Regis University, Denver, CO.

Sohn, Y., Doane, S. M., & Garrison, T. (2006). The impact of individual differences and learning context on strategic skill acquisition and transfer. *Learning and Individual Differences, 16*(1), 13–30.

Solomon, M., & Hendren, R. L. (2003). A critical look at brain-based education. *Middle Matters, 12*(1), 1–3.

Sousa, D. (1998a). Brain research can help principals reform secondary schools. *NASSP Bulletin, 82*(598), 21–28.

Sousa, D. (1998b). Is the fuss about brain research justified? *Education Week, 18*(16), 52–53.

Sousa, D. (1998c). *The ramifications of brain research*. School Administrator Web Edition. Retrieved September 8, 2007, from *www.aasa.org/publications/sa/1998_01/sousa.htm*.

Sousa, D. (2000). *How the brain learns*. Thousand Oaks, CA: Corwin Press.

Sousa, D. (2006). How the arts develop the young brain: Neuroscience research is revealing the impressive impact of arts instruction on students' cognitive, social and emotional. *School Administrator, 11*(63), 26–31.

Sousa, D. (2008). The brain and the arts. In *The Jossey-Bass reader on the brain and learning* (pp. 331–358). San Francisco: Wiley.

Southwest Educational Development Laboratory (SEDL). (1997). How can research on the brain inform education? *Classroom Compass, 3*(2), Retrieved September 9, 2007, from *www.sedl.org/scimath/compass/v03n02/brain.html*.

Sowell, E., Peterson, B. S., Thompson, P. M., Welcome, S. E., Henkenius, A. L., & Toga, A. W. (2003). Mapping cortical change across the human life span. *Nature Neuroscience, 6*(3), 309–315.

Sowell, E., Thompson, P. M., Colmes, C. J., Jeringan, T. L., & Toga, A. W. (1999, Jan). In vivo evidence for post-adolescent brain maturation in frontal and striatal regions. *Nature Neuroscience, 2*(10), 859–861.

Sowell, E., Thompson, P. M., Leonard, C. M., Welcome, S. E., Kan, E., & Toga, A. W. (2004). Longitudinal mapping of cortical thickness and brain growth in normal children. *Journal of Neuroscience, 24*(38), 8223–8231.

Speer, N., Zacks, J. M., & Reynolds, J. R. (2007). Human brain activity time-locked to narrative event boundaries. *Psychological Science, 18*(5), 449–455.

Sprengelmeyer, R. (2007). The neurology of disgust. *Brain: A Journal of Neurology, 130*(7), 1715–1717.

Sprenger, M. (1999). *Learning and memory: The brain in action.* Alexandria, VA: Association for Supervision and Curriculum Development.

Sprenger, M. (2002). *Becoming a "wiz" at brain-based teaching.* Thousand Oaks, CA: Corwin Press.

Sprenger, M. (2003). *Differentiation through learning styles and memory.* Thousand Oaks, CA: Corwin Press.

Springer, S., & Deutsch, G. (1997). *Left brain, right brain: Perspectives from cognitive neuroscience.* New York: Worth Publishers.

Squire, L. (2007). Neuroscience: Rapid consolidation. *Science, 316*(5821), 57.

Squire, L., & Bayley, P. J. (2007). The neuroscience of remote memory. *Current Opinion in Neurobiology, 17*(2), 185–196.

Squire, L. & Kandel, E. (1999). *Memory: from mind to molecules.* New York: Scientific American Library.

Squire, L., & Schacter, D. L. (Eds.). (2002). *Neuropsychology of memory* (3rd ed.). New York: Guilford Press.

Srinivasan, N. (2007). Cognitive neuroscience of creativity: EEG-based approaches. *Methods, 42*(1), 109–116.

Stafford, T., & Webb, M. (2005). *Mind hacks: Tips and tools for using your brain.* Sebastapol, CA: O'Reilly.

Stahl, M. (2005). *Brain Gym and its effect on reading abilities.* Doctoral dissertation, Barry University, Mami Shores, FL.

Stahl, R. (1990). *Using "think-time" behaviors to promote students' information processing, learning, and on-task participation: An instructional module.* Tempe, AZ: Arizona State University.

Stander, M. (2005). *Curriculum integration and brain research: Implications for student learning.* Master's thesis, Regis University, Denver, CO.

Stanek-Rattiner, L. (2005). *The role of brain derived neurotrophic factor in amygdala dependent learning and memory.* Doctoral dissertation, Emory University, Atlanta, GA. AAT 3176059.

Stanovich, K. (1998). Cognitive neuroscience and educational psychology: What season is it? *Educational Psychology Review, 10*(4), 419–426.

Staumwasser, F. (2003). Imaging a science of mind. *Trends in Cognitive Science, 7*(10), 450–445.

Steen, R. (2007). *The evolving brain: The known and the unknown.* New York: Prometheus Books.

Steffens, B. (2006). *Ibn al-Haytham: First scientist.* Dallas, RX: Morgan Reynolds.

Stein, D., Collins, M., Daniels, W., Noakes T. D., & Zigmond, M. (2007). Mind and muscle: The cognitive–affective neuroscience of exercise. *CNS Spectrums, 12*(1), 19–22.

Stenberg, G., Johansson, M., & Rosen, I. (2006). Conceptual and perceptual memory: Retrieval orientations reflected in event-related potentials. *Acta Psychologica, 122*(2), 174–205.

Stephens, K. (1999). Primed for learning: The young child's mind. *Child Care Information Exchange, 126,* 44–48.

Sternberg, R. J. (1985). *Beyond IQ: A triarchic theory of human intelligence.* New York: Cambridge University Press.

Sternberg, R. J. (1998). *Handbook of creativity.* Cambridge, UK: Cambridge University Press.

Sternberg, R. J. (2006). *Cognitive psychology* (4th ed.). Belmont, CA: Thomson Wadsworth.

Sternberg, R. J., & Davidson, J. (2005). *Conceptions of giftedness* (2nd ed.). Cambridge, UK: Cambridge University Press.

Sternberg, R. J., & Lubart, T. I. (1999). The concept of creativity: Prospects and paradigms. In R. J. Sternberg (Ed.), *Handbook of creativity* (pp. 3–15). Cambridge, UK: Cambridge University Press.

Sternberg, R. J., & Subotnik, R. F. (2006). *Optimizing student success in school with the other three Rs: Reasoning, resilience, and responsibility.* Charlotte, NC: Information Age Publishing.

Stewart, L., Henson, R., Kampe, K., Walsh, V., Turner, R., & Frith, U. (2003). Brain changes after learning to read and play music. *NeuroImage, 20*(1), 71–83.

Stewart, L., von Kriegstein, K., Warren, J. D., & Griffiths, T. D. (2006). Music and the brain: Disorders of musical listening. *Brain, 129*(10), 2533–2553.

Stickgold, R. (2005). Sleep-dependent memory consolidation. *Nature, 437*(7063), 1272–1279.

Stickgold, R. (2006). Neuroscience: A memory boost while you sleep. *Nature, 444*(7119), 559–560.

Stoops, T. (2005). *Understanding mindfulness: Implications for instruction and learning.* Doctoral dissertation, West Virginia University, Morgantown, WV. AAT 3201748.

Stover, D. (2001). Applying brain research in the classroom is NOT a no-brainer. *Education Digest, 66*(8), 26.

Strauch, B. (2003). *The primal teen: What the new discoveries about the teenage brain tell us about our kids.* New York: Doubleday.

Strauss, M. (2003). *A cognitive neuroscience study of stress and motivation.* Doctoral dissertation, Boston University, Boston. AAT 3077480.

Strauss, V. (2001). Brain research oversold, experts say. *Teachers.net Gazette, 2*(4). Retrieved September 10, 2007, from *teachers.net/gazette/ APR01/strauss.html.*

Strong, C. (2005). Brain-imaging technology moves beyond medicine and into unchartered territory. *Neurology Reviews.com.* Retrieved September 11, 2007, from *www.neurologyreviews.com/ apr05/brainimaging.html.*

Strong, J. (2005). *Kinesthetics and brain power: Exploring the benefits of integrating movement into class instruction.* Master's thesis, Colorado College, Colorado Springs, CO.

Sullivan, E. (1990). *Critical psychology and pedagogy: Interpretation of the personal world.* Westport, CT: Bergin & Garvey.

Sullivan, T. (2006). *Computational models of feedforward and feedback pathways in the visual cortex.* Doctoral dissertation, University of California, San Diego. AAT 3236624.

Suslow, T., Ohrmann, P., Bauer, J., Rauch, A.V., Schwindt, W., Arolt, V., et al. (2006). Amygdala activation during masked presentation of emotional faces predicts conscious detection of threat-related faces. *Brain and Cognition, 61*(3), 243–248.

Sylwester, R. (1985). Research on memory: Major discoveries, major educational challenges. *Educational Leadership, 42*(7), 69–75.

Sylwester, R. (1994). How emotions affect learning. *Educational Leadership, 52*(2), 60–65.

Sylwester, R. (1995). *A celebration of neurons: An educator's guide to the human brain.* Alexandria, VA: Association for Supervision and Curriculum Development. Retrieved September 10, 2007, from *www.ascd.org/readingroom/books/sylwester95book.html.*

Sylwester, R. (1997a). A brainstorm is brewing. *Learning, 26*(1), 58–60.

Sylwester, R. (1997b). The neurobiology of self-esteem and aggression. *Educational Leadership, 54*(5), 75–79.

Sylwester, R. (1997c). Unconscious emotions, conscious feelings, and curricular challenges. Originally printed in *MindShift Connection, 1*(1), Zephyr Press. Retrieved August 20, 2007, from *www.newhorizons.org/neuro/sywester3.htm.*

Sylwester, R. (1997d). *Windows to the mind: Social interaction and brain development.* Tucson, AZ: Zephyr Press.

Sylwester, R. (1998). Art for the brain's sake. *Educational Leadership, 56*(3), 36–40.

Sylwester, R. (1998b). The brain revolution. *School Administrator Web Edition, January 1998.* Retrieved September 10, 2007, from *www.aasa.org/publications/sa/1998_01/sylwester.htm.*

Sylwester, R. (2003). *A biological brain in a cultural classroom: Enhancing cognitive and social development through collaborative classroom management.* Thousand Oaks, CA: Corwin Press.

Sylwester, R. (2006). Cognitive neuroscience discoveries and educational practices: Seven areas of brain research that will shift the current behavioral orientation of teaching and learning. *School Administrator, 63*(11), 32–37.

Szabados, C. (2003). *Utilizing the principles and strategies of brain based learning in educating the deaf.* Master's thesis, California State University, San Bernardino, CA.

Taher, B. (1996). *Bridging the gap between neuroscience and education.* Denver, CO: Education Commission of the States.

Tainturier, M., Schiemenz, S., & Leek, E. (2006). Separate orthographic representations for reading and spelling? Evidence from a case of preserved lexical reading and impaired lexical spelling. *Brain and Language, 99*(1–2), 31–32.

Tamraz, J., & Comair, Y. (2005). *Atlas of regional anatomy of the brain using MRI: With functional correlations.* New York: Springer.

Tanaka, J., & Pierce, L. (2009). The neural plasticity of other-race face recognition. *Cognitive, Affective, and Behavioral Neuroscience, 9*(1), 122–131.

Tanner, H., & Jones, S. (2000). *Becoming a successful teacher of mathematics.* New York: Routledge.

Tashiro, A., Makino, H., & Gage, F. H. (2007). Experience-specific functional modification of the dentate gyrus through adult neurogenesis: A critical period during an immature stage. *Journal of Neuroscience, 27*(13), 3252–3259.

Taylor, D., Jenni, O. G., Acebo, C., & Carskadon, M. A. (2005). Sleep tendency during extended wakefulness: Insights into adolescent sleep regulation and behavior. *Journal of Sleep Research, 14*(3), 239–244.

Tervaniemi, M., & Huotilainen, M. (2003). The promises of change-related brain potentials in cognitive neuroscience of music. *Annals of the New York Academy of Sciences, 999,* 29–39.

Thomas, G. (2003). *Effects of cross lateral brain exercises on freshmen social studies test scores.* Master's thesis, Urbana University, Urbana, IL.

Thomas, J. (1972). The variation of memory with time for information appearing during a lecture. *Studies in Adult Education, 4,* 57–62.

Thomas, K., Hunt, R. H., Vizueta, N., Sommer, T., Durston, S., Yang, Y., et al. (2004). Evidence of developmental differences in implicit sequence learning: An fMRI study of children and adults. *Journal of Cognitive Neuroscience, 16*(8), 1339–1351.

Thomas, R. M., Hotsenpiller, G., & Peterson, D. A. (2007). Acute psychosocial stress reduces cell survival in adult hippocampal neurogenesis without altering proliferation. *Journal of Neuroscience, 27*(11), 2734–2743.

Thompson, P., Giedd, J. N., Woods, R. P., MacDonald, D., Evans, A. C., & Toga, A. W. (2000). Growth patterns in the developing brain detected by using continuum mechanical tensor maps. *Nature, 404,* 190–193.

Thompson, P., Vidal, C., Giedd, J. N., Gochman, P., Blumenthal, J., Nicolson, R., et al. (2001). Mapping adolescent brain change reveals dynamic wave of accelerated gray matter loss in very early-onset schizophrenia. *Proceedings of the National Academy of Sciences, 98*(20), 11650–11655.

Thompson, W. (1999). Individual differences in memory-monitoring accuracy. *Learning and Individual Differences, 11*(4), 365–377.

Thorndike, E. L., & Bruce, D. (2000). *Animal intelligence: Experimental studies.* Piscataway, NJ: Transaction Publishers.

Ticker, P. (2007). The rise of brain-focused teaching: Teachers look to neuroscience for help in the classroom. *The Futurist, 41*(3).

Tokuhama-Espinosa, T. (2008a). *Living languages: Multilingualism across the lifespan.* Westport, CT: Greenwood.

Tokuhama-Espinosa, T. (2008b). *Summary of the international Delphi expert survey on the emerging field of neuroeducation (Mind, rain, and Education/educational neuroscience)*. Unpublished manuscript.

Tokuhama-Espinosa, T., & Schwartz, M. (2008c). *Defining academic disciplines*. Unpublished manuscript.

Tokuhama-Espinosa, T. (2010). *The new science of teaching and learning: Using the best of mind, brain, and education science in the classroom*. New York: Columbia University Teachers College Press.

Tolstoy, L., & Akar, N. Z. (2001). *Brain based learning. Another passing fad?* Retrieved September 24, 2007, from *www.angelfire.com/ok2/metu/brainbased.html*.

Tomasello, M. (1999). *The cultural origins of human cognition*. Cambridge, MA: Harvard University Press.

Tomasello, M. (2001). Perceiving intentions and learning words in the second year of life. In M. Tomasello & E. Bates (Eds.), *Language development: The essential readings* (pp. 111–128). Malden, MA: Blackwell.

Tomlinson, C. (1999). *The differentiated classroom: Responding to the needs of all learners*. Alexandria, VA: Association for Supervision and Curriculum Development.

Tomlinson, C., & Kalbfleisch, M. L. (1998). Teach me, teach my brain: A call for differentiated classrooms. *Educational Leadership, 56*(3), 52–56.

Tomlinson, C., & McTighe, J. (2006). *Integrating differentiated instruction and understanding by design: Connecting content and kids*. Alexandria, VA: Association for Supervision and Curriculum Development.

Tompkins, A. (2007) *Brain-based learning theory: An online course design model*. Doctoral dissertation, Liberty University, Lynchburg, VA. AAT 3254325.

Tootell, R., & Hadjikhani, N. (2000). Attention? Brains at work! *Nature Neuroscience, 3*(3), 206–209.

Torrance, E. (1974). *Torrance tests of creative thinking*. New York: Scholastic Testing Service.

Torriero, S., Oliveri, M., Koch, G., Caltagirone, C., & Petrosini, L. (2004). Interference of left and right cerebellar rTMS with procedural learning. *Journal of Cognitive Neuroscience, 16*(9), 1605–1611.

Touyarot, K., Venero, C., & Sandi, C. (2004). Spatial learning impairment induced by chronic stress is related to individual differences in novelty reactivity: Search for neurobiological correlates. *Psychoneuroendocrinology, 29*(2), 290–305.

Townsend, E. (2005). *Declarative learning and memory in childhood: A brain-based approach to studying the development of hippocampal functions*. Doctoral dissertation, University of Minnesota, Minneapolis, MN. AAT 3180032.

Tracy, A., Jarrad, L. E., & Davidson, T. L. (2001). The hippocampus and motivation revisited: Appetite and activity. *Behavioral Brain Research, 127*(1–2), 13–23.

Traill, R. R. (1978). *Molecular explanation for intelligence, including its growth, maintenance, and failings.* Master's thesis, Brunel University, Uxbridge, Middlesex, UK. Available online at *hdl.handle.net/2438/729.*

Trautwein, A. (2006). *A neurophilosophical study of the taxonomy and epistemology of memory.* Doctoral dissertation, University of Iowa, Iowa City, IA. AAT 3225678.

Treffert, D. A. (2009). The savant syndrome: An extraordinary condition—a synopsis: past, present, future. *Philosophical Transactions of the Royal Society of London B: Biological Sciences, 364*(1522), 1351–1357.

Trimble, M. R. (2007). *The soul in the brain: The cerebral basis of language, art, and belief.* Baltimore: Johns Hopkins University Press.

Tucker, P., & Stronge, J. H. (2005). *Linking teacher evaluation and student learning.* Alexandria, VA: Association for Supervision and Curriculum Development.

Tufts University. (2009). *The Center for Reading and Language Research.* Retrieved May 30, 2009 from *ase.tufts.edu/crlr/RAVE%2DO/Home.html.*

Turkeltaub, P. (2003). *Functional imaging studies of the development of neural mechanisms for reading.* Doctoral dissertation, Georgetown University, Washington, DC. AAT 3180272.

Turner, D., & Sahakian, B. J. (2006). Neuroethics of cognitive enhancement. *BioScience, 1*(1), 113–123.

Tzeng, J. T. (2009). The impact of general and specific performance and self efficancy on learning with computer-based concept mapping. *Computers in Human Behavior, 25*(4), 989–996.

Underwood, J., Cavendish, S., Dowling, S., & Lawson, T. (1996). *Integrated Learning Systems: A study of sustainable gains in UK schools.* Coventry, UK: NCET.

United Nations. (2001). *Millennium development goals.* Retrieved April 15, 2010, from *www.un.org/millenniumgoals/.*

UNESCO (United Nations Educational, Scientific, and Cultural Organization). (2008). *Educational Strategies.* Retrieved January 28, 2008, from *portal.unesco.org/education/en/ev.php-URL_ID=48792&URL_DO=DO_TOPIC&URL_SECTION=201.html.*

United States National Library of Medicine. (2010). *Stress versus anxiety.* Retrieved from *www.nlm.nih.gov/medlineplus/ency/article/002140.htm.*

University of Washington's Institute for Learning and Brain Sciences Program. (2007). *Recommended books.* Retrieved October 20, 2007, from *ilabs.washington.edu/news/faqsmore.html#recommend%20books.*

Vallar, G. (2006). Memory systems: The case of phonological short-term memory: A festschrift for cognitive neuropsychology. *Cognitive Neuropsychology, 23*(1), 135–155.

Vance, A., Silk, T. J., Casey, M., Rinehart, J. L., Bradshaw, J. L., Bellgrove, M. A., et al. (2007). Right parietal dysfunction in children with attention deficit hyperactivity disorder, combined type: A functional MRI study. *Molecular Psychiatry, 12*(9), 826–832.

Van Der Jagt, J., Ramasamy, R., Jacobs, R. L., Ghose, C., & Lindsey, J. D. (2003). Hemisphericity modes, learning styles, and environmental preferences of students in an introduction to special education course. *International Journal of Special Education, 18*(1), 24–35.

Van Horn, J., Grafton, S. T., Rockmore, D., & Gazzaniga, M. S. (2004). Sharing neuroimaging studies of human cognition. *Nature Neuroscience, 7*(5), 473–481.

van Praag, H., Christie, B. R., Sejnowski, T. J., & Gage, F. H. (1999). Running enhances neurogenesis, learning, and long-term potentiation in mice. *Proceedings of the National Academy of Sciences, USA, 96*(23), 13427–13431.

van Praag, H., Kempermann, G., & Gage, F. H. (2000). Neural consequences of environmental enrichment. *Nature Reviews Neuroscience, 1*(3), 191–198.

van Roekel, B. (2002). *Brain-based learning: Implications for the elementary classroom.* Doctoral dissertation, Dordt College, Sioux City, IA.

van Wyhe, J. (2006). *Phrenology: An overview.* Retrieved December 12, 2007, from *www.victorianweb.org/science/phrenology/ phrenologyov.html.*

Varma, S., McCandliss, B., & Schwartz, D. (2008). Scientific and pragmatic challenges for bridging education and neuroscience. *Educational Researcher, 37*(3), 140–152.

Vázquez Recio, R. & Ojeda Díaz, J. (2010). Social Guarantee Programme: Principles for classroom procedure with students who have suffered failure at school—the Spanish educational system case. *Educational Studies, 36*(2), 175.

Vasquez-Cropper, M. (2005). *Engaging cognitive neurosciences in the classroom.* Master's thesis, University of Toledo, OH.

Vellutino, F., Scanlon, D. M., & Tanzmanm, M. S. (1991). Bridging the gap between cognitive and neuropsychological conceptualizations of reading disabilities. *Learning Individual Differences, 6,* 191–203.

Vera, C., Félez, J., Cobos, J. A., Sánchez-Naranjo, M. J., & Pinto, G. (2005). Experiences in education innovation: Developing tools in support of active learning. *European Journal of Engineering Education, 31*(2), 227–236.

Vesely, L. (2006). *Cerebral asymmetry and detection of affective prosody.* Senior honors thesis, Brandeis University, Waltham, MA.

Vibell, J., Klinge, C., Zampini, M., Spence, C., & Nobre, A. C. (2007). Temporal order is coded temporally in the brain: Early event-related potential latency shifts underlying prior entry in a cross-modal temporal order judgment task. *Journal of Cognitive Neuroscience, 19*(1), 109–120.

Victor, T. (2003). *Executive function, processing speed, and working memory as mediators of age-related decline in verbal memory encoding and retrieval processes.* Doctoral dissertation, Michigan State University, East Lansing, MI. AAT 3146123.

Voelkle, M., Wittmann, W. W., & Ackerman, P. L. (2006). Abilities and skill acquisition: A latent growth curve approach. *Learning and Individual Differences, 16*(4), 303–319.

Vogeley, K., & Kupke, C. (2007). Disturbances of time consciousness from a phenomenological and a neuroscientific perspective. *Schizophrenia Bulletin, 33*(1), 157.

Voges, A. (2005). *An evaluative analysis of a whole brain learning programme for adults.* Doctoral dissertation, University of Pretoria, South Africa. Available online at *upetd.up.ac.za/thesis/available/etd-08112005-153748/.*

Volpe, J. (2000). Overview: Normal and abnormal human brain development. *Mental Retardation and Developmental Disabilities Research Reviews, 6*(1), 1–5.

Volpe, R. L., DuPaul, G. J., Jitendra, A. K., & Tresco, K. E. (2009). Consultation-based academic interventions for children with attention deficit hyperactivity disorder: Effects on reading and mathematics outcomes at 1-year follow-up. *School Psychology Review, 38*(1), 5–13.

Volz, K., & von Cramon, D. Y. (2006). What neuroscience can tell about intuitive processes in the context of perceptual discovery. *Journal of Cognitive Neuroscience, 18*(12), 2077–2087.

Von, A. (2003). *Brain compatible learning in the radiation sciences.* Master's thesis, Peninsula Technikon, Capetown, South Africa.

Voyer, D., Voyer, S., & Bryden, M. P. (1995, March). Magnitude of sex differences in spatial abilities: A meta-analysis and consideration of critical variables. *Psychological Bulletin, 117*(2), 250–270.

Vuilleumier, P. (2002). Facial expression and selective attention. *Current Opinion in Psychiatry, 15,* 291–300.

Vuilleumier, P., & Driver, J. (2007). Modulation of visual processing by attention and emotion: Windows on causal interactions between human brain regions. *Philosophical Transactions of the Royal Society of London Series B, Biological Sciences, 362*(1481), 837–855.

Vuilleumier, P., Armony, J., & Dolan, R. (2003). Reciprocal links between emotion and attention. In R. S. J. Frackowiak (Ed.), *Human brain function* (pp. 419–444). San Diego: Academic Press.

Vygotsky, L. (1987). *Thought and age* (rev. ed., A. Kozulin, Transl.). Cambridge, MA: MIT Press. (Original work published 1934)

Wager, K. (2009). Biological psychology: An illustrated survival guide. *Journal of Mental Health, 18*(3), 274.

Wagmeister, J., & Schifrin, B. (2000). Thinking differently, learning differently. *Educational Leadership, 58*(3), 45–48.

Wagner-Heaston, M. (2006). *Brain compatible teaching and learning in the foreign language classroom: Teachers' voices.* Doctoral dissertation, Colorado State University, Fort Collins, CO. AAT 3233380.

Walker, D., Toufexis, D. J., & Davis, M. (2003). Role of the bed nucleus of the stria terminalis vs. the amygdala in fear, stress, and anxiety. *European Journal of Pharmacology, 463,* 199–216.

Walker Tileston, D. E. (2003). *What every teacher should know about learning, memory, and the brain.* Thousand Oaks, CA: Corwin Press.

Waller, G. (2007). *The impact of music education on academic achievement, attendance rate, and student conduct on the 2006 senior class in one Southeast Virginia Public School Division.* Doctoral dissertation, Virginia Polytechnic Institute and State University, Blacksburg, VA. Retrieved September 14, 2007, from *scholar.lib.vt.edu/theses/available/etd-05012007-153415.*

Walsh, P. (2000). A hands-on approach to understanding the brain. *Educational Leadership, 58*(3), 76–78.

Walsh, V., & Cowey, A. (2000, Oct). Transcranial magnetic stimulation and cognitive neuroscience. *Nature Reviews Neuroscience, 1*(1), 73–79.

Wamsley, E. J. (2007). *The cognitive neuroscience of cognition in sleep: Chronological features and hippocampal memory sources.* Doctoral dissertation, City University of New York, New York City.

Wamsley, E. J., & Antrobus, J. (2006). A new beginning for empirical dream research. *American Journal of Psychology, 119*(1), 129–135. Retrieved August 1, 2009, from *proquest.umi.com/pqdweb?index=3&did=1008602851&SrchMode=2&sid=2&Fmt=2&VInst=PROD &VType=PQD&RQT=309&VName=PQD&TS=1249165755&clientId=86884.*

Wang, A., Peterson, G.W., & Morphey, L. K. (2007). Who is more important for early adolescents' developmental choices? Peers or parents? *Marriage and Family Review, 42*(2), 95.

Ward, E. E. (2008). *An examination of the effects of mathematics anxiety, modality, and learner-control on teacher candidates in multimedia learning environments.* Doctoral dissertation, Queensland University, Kingston, Ontario, Canada. AAT MR42743.

Waxler, D. (2007). *The modulation of learning by stress: Identification of critical circuitry.* Doctoral dissertation, Rutgers State University of New Jersey, New Brunswick, NJ. AAT 3253025.

Weber, E. (1998). Marks of brain-based assessment: A practical checklist. *NASSP Bulletin, 82*(598), 63–72.

Webster, G. D., & Weir, C. G. (2005). Emotional responses to music: Interactive effects of mode, texture, and tempo. *Motivation and Emotion, 29*(1).

Wegerif, R. (1998). The social dimension of asynchronous learning networks. *Journal of Asynchronous Learning Networks, 2*(1), 34–49.

Weinberg, J. (2003). *Cognitive load on the brain as children learn to read: Toward a theory of maximizing limited processing capacity.* Doctoral dissertation, University of Nevada, Reno, NV. AAT 3090912.

Weinberger, N. (1998). The music in our minds. *Educational Leadership, 56*(3), 3–40.

Weisberg, R.W. (1993). *Creativity: Beyond the myth of genius.* New York: Freeman.

Weiskopf, N., Scharnowski, F., Veit, R., Goebel, R., Birbaumer, N., & Mathiak, K. (2004). Self-regulation of local brain activity using real-time functional magnetic resonance imaging (fMRI). *Journal of Physiology—Paris 98*(4–6), 357–373.

Weiss, R. (2000a). Brain-based learning. *Training and Development, 54*(7), 20.

Weiss, R. (2000b). Emotion and learning. *Training and Development, 54*(11), 44.

Weiss, R. (2003). Designing problems to promote higher-order thinking. *New Directions for Teaching and Learning, 95*(3), 25–33.

Werner, S. (2003). *"Because my brain knows the picture of it": An investigation into the nature of comprehending after one year at school.* Master's thesis, University of Auckland, New Zealand.

Wernicke, K. (1874). *Der aphasische Symptomencomplex Eine psychologische Studie auf anatomischer Basis*. Breslau, Germany: Cohn und Weigert.

Westermann, G., Sirois, S., Schultz, T. R., & Mareschal, D. (2006). Modeling developmental cognitive neuroscience. *Trends in Cognitive Sciences, 10*(5), 227–232.

Westwater, A., & Wolfe, P. (2000). The brain-compatible curriculum. *Educational Leadership, 58*(3), 49–52.

Whalley, K. (2008). Neuronal circuits: Dissecting learning. *Nature Reviews Neuroscience, 9*(3), 161.

Wheatley, M., & Kellner-Rogers, M. (1998). *A simpler way*. San Francisco: Berrett-Koehler.

Wheeler, M. (2002). *Stimulating brain function through physical activity*. Master's thesis, University of Wisconsin, Green Bay, WI.

Whitebread, D. (2002). *The implications for early years education of current research in cognitive neuroscience*. Retrieved September 26, 2007, from *www.leeds.ac.uk/educol/documents/00002545.doc*.

Whitlow, J. W. (2010). Effect of outcome valence on positive and negative patterning in human causal reasoning. *Learning & Behavior, 38*(2), 145–159.

Whitney, C. (2004). *Investigations into the neural basis of structured representations*. Doctoral dissertation, University of Maryland, College Park, MD.

Wiedenfeld, (1990). Impact of perceived self-efficacy in coping with stress on components of the immune system. *Journal of Personality and Social Psychology, 59*(5), 1082–1094.

Wiersema, J., & Roeyers, H. (2009). ERP correlates of effortful control in children with varying levels of ADHD symptoms. *Journal of Abnormal Child Psychology, 37*(3), 327–336.

Wiggins, G., & McTighe, J. (1998/2005). *Understanding by design*. Alexandria, VA: Association for Supervision and Curriculum Development.

Wilfond, B., & Ravitsky, V. (2005). On the proliferation of bioethics sub-disciplines: Do we really need "genethics" and "neuroethics"? *American Journal of Bioethics, 5*(2), 20–21; discussion, W3–4.

Wiley. (2008). *The Jossey-Bass Reader on the brain and learning*. San Francisco: Wiley.

Willey, S. (2003). *Developing differentiated lessons using brain-based strategies in middle school social studies*. Doctoral dissertation, Mount St. Mary's College, Emmitsburg, MD.

Williams, J. H. G., Whiten, A., Suddendorf, T., & Perrett, D. I. (2001). Imitation, mirror neurons, and autism. *Neuroscience and Biobehavioral Reviews, 25*(4), 287–295.

Williams, M. (1998). *The effects of a brain-based learning strategy, mind mapping, on achievement of adults in a training environment with consideration to learning styles and brain hemisphericity*. Doctoral dissertation, University of North Texas, Denton, TX. AAT 9934688.

Willingham, D. (2007a). Critical thinking. *American Educator, 31*(2), 9–19.

Willingham, D. (2007b). How can brain imaging help education research? *Mind, Brain, and Education, 1*(3), 140–149.

Willingham, D., & Dunn, E. W. (2003). What neuroimaging and brain localization can do, cannot do, and should not do for social psychology. *Journal of Personality and Social Psychology, 85*(4), 662–671.

Willingham, D., & Llyod, J. W. (2007). How educational theories can use neuroscientific data. *Mind, Brain, and Education, 1*(3), 140–149.

Willis, J. (2006). *Research-based strategies to ignite student learning: Insights from a neurologist and classroom teacher.* Alexandria, VA: Association for Supervision and Curriculum Development.

Willis, J. (2007a). *Brain-friendly strategies for the inclusion classroom.* Alexandria, VA: Association for Supervision and Curriculum Development.

Willis, J. (2007b). Cooperative learning is a brain turn-on. *Middle School Journal, March,* 4–13.

Willis, J. (2007c). The gully in the "brain-glitch" theory. *Educational Leadership, 64*(5), 68–73.

Willis, J. (2007d). Which brain research can educators trust? *Phi Delta Kappan, 88*(9), 697–699.

Willis, T. (2004). Anatomy of the brain and nerves. In C. Zimmer (Ed.), *Soul made flesh: The discovery of the brain—and how it changed the world.* New York: Free Press. (Original work published 1664)

Willoughby, A. (2005). *Medial frontal brain potentials following feedback during probabilistic learning.* Doctoral dissertation, University of Michigan, Ann Arbor, MI. AAT 3163969.

Wilson, A. J., & Dehaene, S. (2007). Number sense and developmental dyscalculia. In D. Coch, K. Fischer, & G. Dawson (Eds.), *Human behavior and the developing brain* (2nd ed., pp. 212–238). New York: Guilford Press.

Wilson, A. J., Dehaene, S., Pinel, P., Revkin, S. K., Cohen, L., & Cohen, D. (2006). Principles underlying the design of "The Number Race," an adaptive computer game for remediation of dyscalculia. *Behavioral and Brain Functions, 2,* 19. doi:10.1186/1744-9081-2-19.

Wilson, A. J., Revkin, S. K., Cohen, D., Cohen, L. & Dehaene, S. (2006). An open trial assessment of "The Number Race," an adaptive computer game for remediation of dyscalculia. *Behavioral and Brain Functions, 2*(20). Retrieved June 1, 2010, from *www.ncbi.nlm.nih.gov/pubmed /16734906.*

Wilson, L., & Spears, A. (2003). *Overview of brain-based learning.* Retrieved August 20, 2007, from *www.uwsp.edu/education/1wilson.*

Winter, B., Breitenstein, C., Mooren, F. C., Voelker, K., Fobker, M., Lechtermann, A., et al. (2007). High impact running improves learning. *Neurobiology of Learning and Memory, 87*(4), 597–609.

Winter, M. (2003). Brain science and language acquisition. *Human Ecology, 31*(1), 8.

Wismer Fries, A., & Pollack, S. D. (2007). Emotion processing and the developing brain. In D. Coch, K. W. Fischer, & G. Dawson (Eds.), *Human behavior, learning, and the developing brain: Typical development* (pp. 329–361). New York: Guilford Press.

Wittman, M., Carter, O., Hasler, F., Rael Cahn, B., Grimberg, U., Spring, P., et al., (2007). Effects of psilocybin on time perception and temporal control iof behaviour in humans. *Journal of Psychopharmacology, 21,* 50–64.

Wittrock, M. (1998). Comment on "The educational relevance of research in cognitive neuroscience." *Educational Psychology Review, 10*(4), 427–429.

Wojtczak, A. (2006). *Glossary of medical education terms.* Institute for International Medical Education. Retrieved August 22, 2009, from *www.iime.org/glossary.htm.*

Wolf, M. (1999). What time may tell: Towards a new conceptualization of developmental dyslexia. *Annals of Dyslexia, 49*(1), 3–28.

Wolf, M. (2007). *Proust and the squid: The story and science of the reading brain.* New York: Harper.

Wolf, M. (2008). A triptych of the reading brain: Evolution, development, pathology, and its interventions. In A. Battro, K. W. Fischer, & P. J. Léna (Eds.), *The educated brain* (pp. 183–197). Cambridge, UK: Cambridge University Press.

Wolf, M., Barzillai, M., Gottwald, S., Miller, L., Spencer, K. Norton, E., et al. (2009). The RAVE-O intervention: Connecting neuroscience to the classroom. *Mind, Brain, and Education, 3*(2), 8–93.

Wolf, M., & Bowers, P. G. (2000). Naming-speed processes and developmental reading disabilities: An introduction to the special issue on the double-deficit hypothesis. *Journal of Learning Disabilities, 33*(4), 322–324.

Wolf, M., Goldberg O'Rourke, A., Gidney, A., Lovett, M., Cirino, P., et al. (2002). The second deficit: An investigation of phonological and naming-speed deficits in developmental dyslexia. *Reading and Writing, 15*, 43–72.

Wolf, M., & Goodman, G. (1996). *Speed wizards: Computerized games for the teaching of reading fluency.* Boston: Tufts University, and Rochester, NY: Rochester Institute of Technology.

Wolf, M., Greig Bowers, P., & Biddle, K. (2000). Naming-speed processes, timing and reading: A conceptual review. *Journal of Learning Disabilities, 33*(4), 387–407.

Wolf, M., & Katzir-Cohen. (2001). Reading fluency and its intervention. *Scientific Studies of Reading, 5*(3), 211–239.

Wolf, M., Miller, L., & Donnelly, K. (2000). Retrieval, automaticity, vocabulary, elaboration, orthography (RAVE-O): A comprehensive, fluency-based reading intervention program. *Journal of Learning Disabilities, 33*(4), 375–386.

Wolfe, P. (1996). *Mind, memory, and learning: Translating brain research into classroom practice—a staff developer's guide to the brain.* Napa, CA: Author.

Wolfe, P. (2001a). *Brain matters: Translating research into classroom practice.* Alexandria, VA: Association for Supervision and Curriculum Development.

Wolfe, P. (2001b). *Brain research and education: Fad or foundation?* Retrieved July 17, 2007, from *www.brainconnection.com/content/160.*

Wolfe, P. (2006). Brain-compatible learning: Fad or fashion? *School Administrator, 63*(11), 10–15.

Wolfe, P., & Brandt, R. (1998). What do we know? *Educational Leadership, 56*(3), 8–13.

Wolfe, P. & Nevills, P. (2004). *Building the reading brain synopsis.* Thousand Oaks, CA: Corwin Press.

Wolfson, A. R., & Carskadon, M. A. (1998). Sleep schedules and daytime functioning in adolescents. *Child Development 69*(4), 875–887.

World Bank. (2008). *Economics of education.* Retrieved January 28, 2008, from *web.worldbank. org/WBSITE/EXTERNAL/TOPICS/EXTEDUCATION/0,,contentMDK:20264769menuPK:613701p agePK:148956piPK:216618theSitePK:282386,00.html.*

Worsley, L. (2004). *Brain research and its implications for average and gifted students.* Master's thesis, Bethel College, Mishawaka, IN.

Wright, S. (2003a). *The arts, young children and learning.* Boston: Allyn & Bacon.

Wright, S. (2003b). *Cognitive neuroscience of episodic memory: Behavior, genetic, electrophysiological, and computational approaches to sequence memory.* Senior thesis, Boston University, MA.

Wunderlich, K., Bell, A., & Ford, A. (2005). Improving learning through understanding of brain science research. *Learning Abstracts, 8*(1), 41–43.

Wundt, W. (1882). Logische Streitfragen [Logical questioning and argumentation]. Vierteljahrschrift für wissenschaftliche *Philosophie, 6,* 340–355.

Wyoming Clearinghouse for Mathematics and Science (WCMS). (2000). *Brain research and learning.* Retrieved September 14, 2007, from *nasc.uwyo.edu/wcms/Math/Resources/mathBrainResLinks.htm.*

Yamauchi, T., & Yakugaku, Z. (2007). Molecular mechanism of learning and memory based on the research for Ca(2+)/calmodulin-dependent protein kinase II. *Journal of the Pharmaceutical Society of Japan, 127*(8), 1173–1197.

Yan, Z., & Fischer, K. W. (2002). Always under construction: Dynamic variations in adult cognitive development. *Human Development, 45*(3), 141–160.

Yan, Z., & Fischer, K. W. (2007). Pattern emergence and pattern transition in microdevelopmental variation: Evidence of complex dynamics of developmental processes. *Journal of Developmental Processes, 2*(2), 39–62.

Yehuda, R. (2001). Biology of post-traumatic stress disorders. *Journal of Clinical Psychiatry, 62*(17), 41–46.

Yoo, S., Hu, P. T., Gujar, N., Jolesz, F. A., & Walker, M. P. (2007). A deficit in the ability to form new human memories without sleep. *Nature Neuroscience, 10*(3), 385–392.

Yordanova, J., Falkenstein, M., Hohnsbein, J., & Kolev, V. (2004). Parallel systems of error processing in the brain. *NeuroImage, 22*(2), 590–602.

Zanker, J. (2005). *Conceptual issues in psychology: Neuroscience.* Retrieved March 23, 2007, from *www.pc.rhul.ac.uk/staff/J.Zanker/teach/PS2080/L4/ PS2080_4.htm.*

Zatorre, R. J. (2003 Nov). Music and the brain. *Annals of the New York Academy of Sciences, 999,* 4–14.

Zatorre, R., Chen, J. L., & Penhune, V. B. (2007). When the brain plays music: Auditory–motor interactions in music perception and production. *Nature Reviews Neuroscience, 8*(7), 547–558.

Zeman, A. (2009). *The portrait of the brain.* New Haven, CT: Yale University Press.

Zemelman, S., Daniels, H. & Hyde, A. (2005). *Best practice: New standards for teaching and learning in America's schools,* (3rd ed.). New Hampshire: Heinemann.

Zero to Three®, Erikson Institute, and Boston University School of Medicine. (2001). *BrainWonders: Helping babies and toddlers grow and develop.* Retrieved September 26, 2007, from *www.zerotothree.org/brainwonders/index.html.*

Ziegler, J., & Goswami, U. (2005). Reading acquisition, developmental dyslexia, and skilled reading across languages: A psycholinguistic grain size theory. *Psychological Bulletin, 131*(1), 3–29.

Zohar, A. (2004). *Higher-order thinking in science classrooms: Students' learning and teachers' professional development.* New York: Springer.

Zohar, A., & Dori, Y. J. (2003). Higher-order thinking skills and low-achieving students: Are they mutually exclusive? *Journal of the Learning Sciences, 12*(2), 145–181.

Zull, J. (2002). *The art of changing the brain.* Herdon, VA: Stylus.

INDEX

Numbers in bold correspond to references in the Glossary or Appendices.